THE LIFE AND GOOD TIMES OF

# William Randolph Hearst

BY JOHN TEBBEL

*Biography*
    The Life and Good Times of William Randolph Hearst
    An American Dynasty
    The Marshall Fields
    George Horace Lorimer and The Saturday Evening Post

*Novels*
    Touched with Fire
    The Conqueror

*History*
    The Battle for North America (editor)

*Medical*
    Your Body: How to Keep It Healthy

*Textbook*
    Makers of Modern Journalism
      (with Kenneth N. Stewart)

E·P·DUTTON & CO.INC.
1852 1952
CELEBRATING 100 YEARS OF PUBLISHING

# THE LIFE AND GOOD TIMES OF

# William Randolph Hearst

BY

## JOHN TEBBEL

NEW YORK

E. P. DUTTON & CO., INC.

1952

Library of Congress Catalog Card Number: 52-8258

# CONTENTS

# FOR BOB AND ETHEL

# CHAPTER ONE

## DOWN FROM THE MOUNTAIN

Four years before his death on August 14, 1951, William Randolph Hearst came down from the seclusion of his mountain paradise, Wyntoon, and settled at last in the cream-tinted Beverly Hills palace of Marion Davies, the woman who had shared his life for more than thirty years.

Hearst took leave of Wyntoon with sorrow and reluctance. It had been his mother's summer place, and there were a thousand memories of her gracious presence to remind him of happier days, though she never saw the incredible Bavarian village he built on the remains of their original retreat, most of which had burned in 1930.

Other memories clung to Wyntoon. His five sons had learned to swim and ride there, deep in the shadow of Mount Shasta, with the liquid music of the McCloud River in their ears. On the velvety lawns he had often played deliberate, amiable croquet games with Marion and the courtiers who always surrounded him.

At Wyntoon, probably more than elsewhere, Hearst had been himself—that is to say, his youthful, carefree, less complicated self. It was natural he should have sought peace there in his old age, after the financial alarums of the thirties and the patriotic excursions of that decade and the next. In those turbulent years he had no opportunity to visit Wyntoon until sometime during the war, when it was suggested that San Simeon would be in easy range of a Japanese warship standing off the California coast.

Whether it was this consideration or others which prompted

9

the action, Hearst left the Enchanted Hill and spent a good part of his time at Wyntoon for the duration and a few months after. Then, in the spring of 1947, he suffered a heart attack. The diagnosis was auricular fibrillation, which signals an advanced and serious condition.

His doctors urged him to leave Wyntoon. They feared the thin air of the nearly mile-high Sierra plateau would overtax that stubborn heart which had already outlasted friends and enemies alike, persisting at least a decade beyond the time he had been left for dead by his most articulate journalistic foes.

Those who knew Hearst only by reason of the power he exerted on their lives would have been astounded to see him when he left Wyntoon for the last time. He was not the calmly ruthless potentate in that moment, but a sentimental old man whose pale, cold eyes were misty with honest tears.

No tears lingered in the warm blue orbs of Miss Davies. In these later times, when Wyntoon had lost most of its earlier gaiety, she had found its pleasures intermittent and dull. Never one who adored cuddling up to nature, however magnificent, she had sometimes become so lonely that she felt herself compelled to call her hairdresser and a few intimate friends in Hollywood to come up and console her.

Marion had a disrespectful word for Hearst's retreat. The word was "Spittoon."

Now, however, it was time to go, for both Marion and W. R. One must suppose that Hearst knew he had an appointment with Death. He was no fool about it, in spite of the sensitivity which had led to exaggerated reports that he feared even the mention of its name. While he could, he forestalled thoughts of the inevitable moment by pretending it did not exist. But now the time was beyond pretense. One line of retreat remained open and Hearst took it.

The house where he came to die was like all of the fabulous places he had lived: ornate, overdone and full of memories. Its exterior resembled the neighboring pleasure domes that sprawled atop the hills called Beverly. Number 1007 Beverly Drive was all stucco and palms, huge and rambling, three stories, set in luxuriant foliage and surrounded by formal gardens, sunny patios and the omnipresent swimming pool. Two special police-men, former Los Angeles *Examiner* employees, stood guard at the gate. That was the sign of majesty dwelling within.

Not that Hearst was afraid some disgruntled Democrat or "New Deal Communist" might steal into his chamber and exact a bloody vengeance for attacks by Hearst newspapers. It was simply that he needed privacy and quiet more than ever before; the days of high living and endless activity were over.

Years ago Marion had bought the house for herself, but when Wyntoon was no longer possible and the doctors wanted Hearst nearer than isolated San Simeon, it was logical that he should buy it from Miss Davies. Soon after, however, his tax experts told him he should deed the house to Marion and not bequeath it to her in his will, as he intended. This was done, with the stipulation in the deed that he should have "life tenure," meaning he was entitled to live in the place until he died. Legally he became Marion's house guest, a renter for life.

Number 1007 held a fortune valuable enough to be guarded by a regiment. The paintings, furniture, silver and art objects in every room made it different from the homes of other rich men, because they reflected Hearst's taste and temperament in a way most such collections do not. Critics of Hearst's collecting were apt to confuse his prodigality with a lack of discrimination, but it was not so: he bought what he liked, and his likes were inclined to be definite.

The paintings in the Beverly Hills mansion, for example, were typical of his love for brilliant coloring, his aversion to subjects not at least moderately cheerful, or religious, and his distaste for any artistic creation executed after the eighteenth century. Nicholas Maes's "Portrait of Two Girls" smiled from one wall space, along with Jan Steen's "Grace Before Meals," and similar examples of the luminous Dutch school. And there were Bou-guereaus, Vernets and Bonheurs, all of them bright with color, none of them morbid in any respect.

Much of the furniture reflected Hearst's preoccupation with medieval and Renaissance art, but there were also some fine English eighteenth-century pieces. Oriental rugs covered the floors, and such valuable bric-a-brac as Venetian glass, antique gold snuffboxes and English and continental silver were scattered about.

The single concession to modern art was in the center hall connecting the two wings of the H-shaped mansion, where hung four life-size portraits depicting Marion in various cinematic ventures. Once she had posed, with justifiable pride, between two of these portraits showing her as she appeared in the greatest successes of her silent-picture career, *Little Old New York* and *The Red Mill*. The pictures had been removed from her beach house at Santa Monica when it was sold, and taken to 1007 because there was no other place to hang them.

Thus the house was, in a special way, an amalgam of its two occupants, and that was as it should have been. When Lord Beaverbrook called from London after Hearst's death to settle the delicate point of who actually owned the place, he could have been told that it belonged to Miss Davies legally, to Hearst artistically, and to them both from a practical standpoint.

In any case, it was the last stronghold. Mentally, Hearst was as active as ever, but he was constantly reminded that his body was failing by reason of the palsy which had followed his attack. It irritated him, embarrassed him sometimes, and compelled him to withdraw to a second-floor nerve center, where a bedroom, an office and a sitting-room, in which he had his meals, marked the limits of his world. He rarely went down to the first floor, except to walk briefly in the sunny garden, or to be taken for a drive.

On his good days, he liked to stroll about the gardens, wandering aimlessly in the bright sunshine, touching the earthy stability of the trees, examining the profusion of flowers about the place. He loved trees and flowers.

During these excursions he was often accompanied by the gardener, who followed respectfully at his heels, attentive to criticism or praise. One day Hearst regarded a bank of dormant rosebushes and observed, "Too bad they're not in bloom. I do love roses."

The gardener made a perfunctory reply, but next day, when Hearst took his walk, he saw the same row of bushes in full bloom. The zealous gardener had repaired to a greenhouse the night before and transplanted the blooming shrubs so that the master would not be disappointed.

History does not record that Hearst expressed any astonishment over this miracle. He was a man thoroughly accustomed to such transformations, and undoubtedly thought it no more than he deserved.

One miracle, however, was not to be expected, and the man who could command nearly anything the world had to offer understood as the months slipped by that the appointment he had postponed for so long was near at hand. The strolls in the garden had to be abandoned. People who had known him for years were shocked when they were admitted to his presence. There seemed no connection between the big man with the broad, sloping shoulders who had moved quietly and with driving purpose about the business of empire and this bent, almost pitiful figure in the chair.

"He seemed all shrunken up, as though some witch doctor had been working on him," one visitor murmured, abashed by the sight.

The man chiefly responsible for keeping Hearst alive long after most men would have succumbed was Dr. Myron Prinzmetal, one of the nation's leading heart specialists, who took the case about January 1948 and brought his patient safely through a severe crisis in March of that year.

It was the choicest piece of irony in an ironic career that Hearst, the most ardent anti-vivisectionist in the country, should have been permitted a few more years of life by the skill of a man known in medical circles as one of the foremost champions in Southern California of this research method. Moreover, Dr. Prinzmetal was enabled by virtue of the high retaining fee Hearst paid him to invest the time and money necessary to his research, and from the vivisection involved in it he acquired some of the knowledge that helped him treat Hearst's condition.

W. R. never learned this fact, of course. If he had, the results would have been disastrous, a contingency the doctor was always fearful would occur. He was not afraid for himself, but for the harm that might come to the old man's subordinates, because W. R. would certainly have felt that he had been betrayed by them.

Nevertheless, Hearst benefited by the conspiracy to keep him in ignorance. Dr. Prinzmetal once showed to a distinguished gathering of heart specialists a color film he had prepared depicting the heart actions of vivisected dogs. About a half hour of the film was devoted to a study of auricular fibrillation. The doctor told one of his eminent guests that he had used twenty-seven dogs to make the film.

With the aid of a science he had attacked violently all his life, Hearst was able for some time to continue functioning as ringmaster of the largest journalistic show on earth—as much a one-man show as it had ever been at its peak performance. Out of the bedroom in Beverly Hills flowed the familiar messages beginning, "The Chief says," or "The Chief suggests," or simply the "Please" which carried all the force of "You must." The messages traveled out along the sensitive network binding the Hearst newspapers, magazines and radio stations to their vital center, and as always, they were obeyed instantly and without question. The Chief might be dying, but a Hearst man could not tell it by any change or interruption in the word delivered to him from on high.

In these last days, however, Hearst appeared to concentrate on his favorite paper, the Los Angeles *Examiner*. As soon as it came from the presses, each edition was delivered to him, and he was in daily telephone communication with its editors. Usually it was Marion who put in the call, and as soon as a familiar voice was heard at the other end, the Chief came on.

Occasionally Marion called on her own account, as she did

during the Robert Mitchum case, to complain that she thought the actor, involved in a dope charge, was getting "a raw deal" in the *Examiner* and elsewhere.

"Of course it's only my own opinion," she concluded, "but I'm going to speak to Mr. Hearst about it tomorrow. I don't think we should persecute this boy."

Next day an instruction from the Chief ordered, "Play the Mitchum case straight." The order caused the *Examiner's* city editor considerable pain, since he was at the moment in possession of a series of signed stories by Lila Leeds, the beautiful blonde actress in the case, and had no choice but to scrap them.

No one at the *Examiner* could ever be sure what the next request from number 1007 would be. One night it was a box of Kleenex, which a reporter rushed out to the mansion, passing en route several drugstores within walking distance of the house. At the other extreme, on an early autumn night in 1948, Hearst called to order a Constellation chartered, and prepared for him by taking out the first four seats so a bed could be installed. He wanted to fly up to Seattle and talk with his old friend Anna Boettiger, President Roosevelt's daughter.

The *Examiner's* night editor must have been momentarily stunned by this request, but after a few hectic, ulcer-producing hours he procured aerial transport from Howard Hughes, who had reason to be grateful to Hearst for the support W. R.'s papers had given him in his battles with Congress. The plane was held from one of TWA's regular flights and was nearly ready to receive Hearst, at a total estimated cost of $5186.80, when he called again to say, without any further explanation, that he had given up the idea.

Hearst's minute attention to the *Examiner* sometimes nearly paralyzed its staff. He was forever comparing its final edition with that of the rival *Times*, particularly the picture coverage, and often the city desk would get a *Times* tear sheet with a red-penciled scrawl in the margin, "Why can't we have a picture like this?" As a result, *Examiner* photographers seldom dared to do more than copy *Times* pictures, and if there was too much variation in shots of the same scene in the first editions of the two papers, an editor might order a page replated to eliminate chances of comparison.

But it was not only the *Examiner* that occupied Hearst's attention. As he had done for more than sixty years, he still spread his papers on the floor before him and turned them over with his feet. This process, his most enduring characteristic, had changed little. In the beginning he had walked around his second journalistic child, the New York *Journal*, fondly flipping its pages with one foot and bending down now and then to make penetrating comments and suggestions on the margins with his big black pencil. As time went on he developed such facility that he could sit in a chair and turn the pages with his remarkably agile bare toes. And eventually, when he could spread the entire product of his network on the priceless carpeting of San Simeon, his fabulous castle, he might dance among them like a possessed dervish in a garden of beloved flowers.

Now he eased his fading body carefully into a chair, spread two or three of the products before him, and poked at them with one slippered foot, reaching down to slash the margins with that decisive scrawl, calculated to pierce the heart of an editor at a distance of three thousand miles.

Always his devoted companion was Marion. Her days were adapted to his needs. She kept what she called "the theater routine," meaning a day that began at four in the afternoon and ended near dawn. Arising, she settled the household problems first and then dealt with her own business affairs. Her three large houses were rented at an average of $1500 a month to such well-known tenants as the actor Paul Douglas, and his wife Jan Sterling.

In the afternoon she shopped, usually once a week, in Beverly Hills, and came home late to welcome close friends who might stop in for a cocktail or dinner. Three times a week or more, from two to six guests sat at her table. Infrequently she went out for dinner, to some noted Hollywood emporium like the Mocambo.

Her amusements were few, particularly as the circle of Hearst's life drew ever closer. No longer was the customary motion picture shown every night. Now the schedule was one or two a month. "My eyes get tired of it every night," Marion said.

Occasionally she went to a party given by one of her friends —Cobina Wright, Sonja Henie, Clifton Webb, or Mike Romanoff. These people belonged to her "inner circle," along with Eileen Ruby, the wife of Harry Ruby, the songwriter; Kay and Adolph Spreckels, of the sugar fortune; the L. B. Mayers; Louella Parsons, Constance Talmadge, the Huntington Hartfords, the Sam Goldwyns, Harry Crocker, Doris Duke and Gloria Swanson.

To these intimates Marion appeared to have faded surprisingly little from the lovely woman she had once been. As Zsa Zsa Gabor said, "She has still a sort of beauty." It was there in her good figure, in her large, pale blue eyes, in her rippling shoulder-length hair and her husky voice.

She was given to reminiscing of the days that were gone. At night, when she was alone with Hearst, she sat in his room reading and sewing while he read his papers. She recalled to one visitor: "Do you know I got so interested in sewing during the war that I gave up most of my work. I used to make quilts and shirts and hospital stuff. I got to thinking I was the best seamstress in the world, but I don't suppose anyone ever wore what I made. Out at Ocean House [her Santa Monica beach place] we used to have sewing machines near the swimming pool and Norma Shearer and Merle Oberon and lots of others and I used to make shirts and things for the hospitals."

Then, again, she would recall nostalgically the old days at San Simeon: "Oh, it was gay, let me tell you. We were riding and swimming and playing tennis and Mr. Hearst was very active then. I remember the animals at San Simeon and how we used to throw pebbles at the lions and watch the ape shaking the bars on the cage. We were always running, always doing something, always with people all around the place and we had fun.

We even draped the statues. But when we came back here, things settled down. I had said to myself, 'Marion, you better stop before you break down.' Here things are slower. For a long time I didn't do much at all. . . ."

Things were certainly slower. Sewing, and reading fiction —"psychological things, Dickens and Thackeray and those boys are behind me"—the routine of the house, the three nurses making their twenty-four-hour rounds of the second floor, the doctor's daily call, sometimes a visit from one or another of the Hearst boys and their families; often a visit from her niece, Pat Lake, and her actor husband Arthur with their children, or from her nephew, Charles Lederer, one of those closest to her.

To some women it might have been a confining and depressing affair, while the old man upstairs waited to die, but Marion did not feel that way. Her affection for Hearst was sincere— as deep as human relations can be. "I don't care what you say about me," she once told a reporter, "but don't hurt him. . . . He is a wonderful, wonderful man."

One of the nurses on duty recalled how the two of them sat together only four days before Hearst died, "in his room in the easy chairs, as they always did. He was reading the papers and she was reading a book. When he wanted to talk she would talk to him. She told him about the party she had given for the orphans that afternoon. He was very happy about the party and after she left he had his nurse call the paper. He walked over himself and got on the phone and he said, 'Give that party for the orphans a good spread. Make it big.' He was very pleased with what she had done. She is a very fine woman, that Miss Davies. Everybody loves her."

That was on a Friday night. On the following Monday evening, Hearst complained that his leg hurt, and said he felt weak. Near midnight Dr. Prinzmetal and his assistant, Dr. Elliot Corday, decided to give him a transfusion. As Marion described it: "They brought in a special bed and all the equipment and W. R. asked me what they were doing. He said he felt fine, but the doctors said I should keep up a running chatter, so I kept talking to him about the old days in the movies. Then he told me I should get some sleep. Me, I should get some sleep! I stayed there with him all night."

It was the most compelling scene Miss Davies had ever played in her career. While the night time ticked away, she talked to him hour after hour, reliving the high, the low, the remembered, the tender moments of that life which was so extraordinary it could be compared with no other American's. How much or how little of it Hearst heard and understood, no one knows. Probably it set his own mind to rambling along a million hidden byways, poking into corners long since forgotten.

The setting for this last act in the drama of Hearst's life was wholly appropriate. He lay in no ordinary bed, because Hearst owned nothing ordinary. A high-canopied antique, graceful and elegant, it stood in a room of comparative simplicity. Turning his head to the right, he could gaze into the dim Gothic recesses of "The Interior of an Antwerp Cathedral," by B. van Bassen, symbolizing his magnificent collection of religious art of that period. Near it on another wall, but out of sight, was the remembrance of another cherished portion of his collecting, "A Spanish Church Interior," by J. Gallegos. A lovely example of oriental carpeting covered the floor, leaving a margin of bare tiles, California style. In the bathroom adjoining was a reminder of the fabulous luxury to which he was accustomed: a handsome barber chair whose modern foam-rubber cushions had held his aging bones in comfort.

More than these appearances, however, the little touches in the room disclosed Hearst. A metal ash tray sat on a desk, and in it lay a note from General Douglas MacArthur, in whose behalf Hearst had launched the final crusade of a career filled to satiety with crusades. On a bureau stood two framed pictures of his beloved dachshunds, and when he turned his tired eyes to the left, he saw the most cherished item in his death chamber, a picture in a gray-specked jade frame of Marion as she looked at the climax of her blonde beauty. On it was inscribed in her sprawling, careless hand: "To W. R. from Marion," and the vow Juliet breathes to Romeo before the nurse interrupts them in Act II, Scene 1: "My bounty is as boundless as the sea, my love as deep; the more I give to thee, the more I have, for both are infinite."

And through the long night Marion sat by his side, the final proof of the devotion implicit in these words, though no proof was needed. While she talked to him, Helena, one of the sad-eyed dachshunds, padded in and out restlessly; otherwise the household appeared to hold its breath, waiting for that moment which somehow seemed improbable.

When Marion left the room for a few minutes very early in the morning, a nurse recalled, "Mr. Hearst puckered up his lips like he always did to kiss her good night. That was the last thing he did."

A little later, one of the doctors gave Marion a sedative. She had scarcely slept for forty-eight hours. "He came at me with that little old needle and one, two, I was out," she reported later. "They said I needed some rest. He was asleep and they said I ought to be asleep too."

The house was quiet. Two nurses hovered near Hearst's bed, hearing his irregular breath rising and falling. The official version given to the newspapers afterward depicted the traditional scene—family and associates gathered at the bedside when death came. It was not so. The most spectacular career of this century ended on a note of anticlimax, like the world's end once described by T. S. Eliot, "Not with a bang, but a whimper." Two of his sons, Bill Jr. and David, were in the guesthouse. Marion was asleep. Except for the nurses, he was alone.

At 9:45 A.M., Pacific Daylight Time, on Tuesday morning the fourteenth, the signal of expiration appeared—a rising of mucus in the throat. One of the nurses hurried out to call a throat specialist; the other stood by the bed, listening to the flutter of breath that remained. The little square-faced traveler's clock showed nine-fifty. The nurse's trained eye caught it and her mind remembered as the flutter paused . . . resumed . . . paused again . . . and stopped.

The remarkable career of William Randolph Hearst was at an end.

# CHAPTER TWO

## WHERE HE LIVED

WHAT DID William Randolph Hearst think about as he lay dying in his Beverly Hills four-poster, amid the remnants and symbols of his eighty-eight years?

If his crowded life reviewed itself on the screen of his inner consciousness like a jumbled, endless Metrotone Newsreel, he had more remembrances to contemplate than a dozen average men, and it is a reasonable speculation that he thought most of the places he had lived.

Perhaps no man in history was better housed than Hearst. The favorite comparisons in this respect are Genghis Khan and Louis XIV, but the Khan's oriental splendors and the formal magnificences of Louis's Versailles were certainly surpassed by the sheer variety of Hearst's dwelling places.

From their owner's point of view, they were not the huge, impersonal places they appeared to the outsider, but homes in which he took as much pride and in which he enjoyed living as much as the suburban dweller in his ranch-type, three-bedroom, one-and-a-half-bath, large-plot establishment. It is difficult for the ordinary mortal to comprehend how a man could feel homey about a ranch of 275,000 acres, with more bedrooms than a small-town hotel and enough bathrooms to cleanse and purify the entire population of the residence simultaneously. But those were the outsize measurements of Hearst's life. He was accustomed to them.

His sunlit childhood was a succession of home places illuminated by the luxury of quick wealth, and darkened by no more than two relatively unhappy interludes. He could not remember that he was born in a hotel, the Stevenson House, a respectable family hostelry lying athwart the southwest corner of California and Montgomery streets in San Francisco, because his father moved the new family almost at once into better quarters after "Sonny's" advent on April 29, 1863.

George Hearst was no child of poverty, having been raised on his father's Missouri plantation amid the appurtenances of Southern ante-bellum society, but he had spent ten grinding years on the rugged frontier of Nevada before he made his spectacular silver strike in the Comstock Lode and became a millionaire overnight. When he went back home, married his wealthy neighbor's daughter, Phebe Apperson, against the better judgment of her parents, and brought her West, he was determined that this sheltered, cultured girl, twenty-two years younger, should have the best his new wealth could buy.

The immediate best was San Francisco's Lick House, whose genuine mahogany lobby and red plush sofas and chairs were the most recent samples of the city's elegance. Why George took Phebe subsequently to the Stevenson House for the birth of her first child is not recorded, but it may have been because he thought the somewhat gaudy hospitality of the Lick House was out of key with a woman *enceinte*.

In any event, when Sonny was safely in the world, George Hearst lost no time in surrounding him with the luxury to which he would ever after be accustomed. Before George himself went back to the dirty business of grubbing more wealth out of the Nevada hills, he installed Phebe on fashionable Rincon Hill in a large brick house, where she might open her fashionable French windows and stare down, until she lifted her eyes to the bay, upon the unfashionable frame shacks of the Irish laborers who were building the material foundations of San Francisco's wealth.

Phebe, who lived all her life in another world of beauty and innocence, aspired without cupidity or envy to better things. She admired particularly the fine houses of Chestnut Street, which was then in the rural precincts of the bluffs frowning over

the Golden Gate, and on warm afternoons she would take
Sonny and go spanking along behind her two bays for a country
drive to see these spacious residences, which were occupied for
the most part by politicians and railroad builders.

One house especially took her fancy. It was a double chalet,
erected by a nostalgic Frenchman caught up in the New World's
turmoil, and as she later discovered, he had filled it with a splendid collection of seventeenth-century pieces which delighted
Phebe's as yet undeveloped artistic tastes. From the chalet's
garden there was sheer, breathless beauty in every direction.
Eastward lay the sparkling sapphire of the bay, white patches
of sail disclosing the great ships resting from their salty struggles
with the Horn, or heavy with spice-laden Orient trade. West-
ward at sunset the clouds and mists of the Golden Gate threw
patterns of burning gold against the sky. Northward, Mount
Tamalpais lifted serenely.

Of course George bought the house for her when she mentioned it on one of his infrequent trips home. He would have
bought her anything her ardent heart desired. And it was this
house, filled with beauty inside and out, which first impinged
on the memory of Sonny Hearst.

He was still Sonny in those days, a fair-haired, handsome infant, adored by his mother, his nurse, the servants and everyone
else in his immediate periphery. He loved the chalet, particularly the garden, not only for its vistas but for its flowers and
shrubs, a profusion of boxwood, lemon verbena, hollyhocks,
geraniums, lilies of the valley and more exotic blooms. Sonny
was surrounded by trees, flowers, natural beauty and unquestioning love. It was a childhood that would abash a psychiatrist
seeking a key to his later behavior.

Even the two unhappy interludes were mercifully brief. The
first occurred when the family left Chestnut Street temporarily
to spend a few damp winter months in the capital city of Sacramento, where George Hearst was serving a term in the State
Assembly. They lived in a dull hotel, the Brannan House, where

the night-and-day preoccupation was politics. Phebe and her son were spared the smoke-filled rooms and the spittoon-bright lobby, but it was not much fun. They wanted to go home.

By this time young Hearst was out of his "Sonny" phase, as far as his forthright father was concerned, and had assumed a more manly "Billy Buster," in keeping with his sturdy, growing body. His face still had the serene, contemplative charm of Sonny, but his behavior was definitely Billy Buster.

Back on Chestnut Street, George temporarily left the pursuit of silver, then in the doldrums, and took up the classic California occupation, real estate. His son went back to playing in the garden with his young friends, the sons and daughters of George's rich neighbors. None had more advantages than Billy Buster, who proudly exhibited to them the first Punch and Judy show seen in San Francisco, with which he happily demonstrated that lifelong affinity for the theater which was to cost him so much money in later years. Flowers, trees, beauty, acting—they were all elements inextricably bound up in his nature from the first, and to these were added a pair of large black dogs named, with unwitting symbolism, Caesar and Pompey.

Dogs were Hearst's most constant companions as he strode down the years. He was never without them. Even when he left Chestnut Street for visits with his maternal grandparents, whom Phebe had installed in a flower-drenched ranch house in the foothills not far from Santa Clara, he had as playmate a ponderous Newfoundland called Prince who gave him a devotion which could only be described as doglike.

There was a garden at the ranch to play in—a place of chromatic brilliance, with hollyhocks, lilacs, carnations, geraniums, enormous cacti, and roses everywhere. Sun and flowers, adoration and dogs, charm and peace. They may have come flooding back upon the tired old man struggling for breath eight decades later.

When Billy Buster was ten, he and his mother left Chestnut Street and Santa Clara for their famous grand tour of Europe, which appears in these pages in another connection. They returned to the Panic of 1874, and the second unhappy interlude began, in which George had to sell Phebe's beloved chalet, her horses, her carriages and much else besides. Briefly the Hearsts were reduced to boarding with old friends, while Billy Buster was farmed out to his grandparents' ranch.

But again, the pain was short and probably the youngster never comprehended the threat of disaster. It was the only time he ever had to live with financial insecurity until he had the whole world to share the experience with him in the 1930s.

Within a year, George was a millionaire once more, this time a sharer in a veritable eternal fountain of money, the Homestake Mine, which was still faithfully helping to support George's son in his extreme old age, seventy-five years later.

It was this new fortune that enabled George to acquire his vast Mexican acres and proliferating mining properties, and to buy another home for Phebe and Billy Buster. They chose an ornate mansion atop Nob Hill, where society had by this time more or less clustered itself. It stood on a street with a dignified name, Van Ness Avenue, and the final touch of aristocratic chi-chi was the presence of two aloof stone lions guarding its entrance.

Life on the Hill and life below it were vastly different milieus. On the Hill, in the gilded palaces of the railroad empire builders, there were gay parties and extravagant entertainments. Behind the lions at the Hearst residence there was culture. Phebe held salons for the city's intellectuals, and in the art gallery which had been built under her direction, she displayed the sculpture, paintings and tapestries she had begun collecting in earnest on her European trip.

Down below the agitators were busy with the masses, coalescing their resentments over cheap Chinese labor and the unholy alliance between railroad owners and government into an amorphous organization known as the Workingman's Party, which was not so much a political party as a dangerous mob, lean from cruelly long hours and short pay, lashed to black fury by such organizers as Irish Denis Kearney. They had no power except that of mob violence and Nob Hill knew it, but it was enough to still the music of the parties and the genteel hum of Phebe Hearst's salon for a time while the palace owners formed their own vigilante guard corps and prepared to defend themselves to the last capitalist.

One breathless night the sullen mob gathered at the foot of the hill while its leader urged them to ascend and tear down George Hearst's lions as the symbol of predatory wealth. Fortunately, wiser agitators prevailed, and the lions, George, Phebe and Billy Buster remained intact.

It was characteristic of Phebe that she understood these proceedings not at all. As Annie Laurie, the perennial sob sister of the Hearst papers, wrote years later in her privately printed biography of the gentle lady, Phebe was "so hurt and astonished at the strange things that had come over the city that she loved so dearly that she would have been glad to go away and never return."

As for young Will, he was not intimidated by Kearney's mob because he was still preoccupied with the pleasures of his youth. These he pursued even more vigorously when the Hearsts exchanged the Van Ness Avenue house for a vaguely Spanish small palace done in white stucco, on Taylor Street. Will was delighted to find that it had a stable big enough to be converted into a miniature theater, and there he continued chasing Thespis through the mazes of horrendous melodramas and occasional minstrel shows, an art form to which he remained addicted the rest of his life. He had learned to play the banjo and sing the folk songs of the lone prair-ees while he idled away the long hot months at the family summer place on the bay, near Sausalito. How these ballads sounded in blackface, history does not say.

By this time, too, Will had been introduced to the budding enchantment of San Simeon, then a modest 45,000-acre ranch which his father adorned with a simple white, green-shuttered ranch house, sheltered by cypress groves and giant oaks. Nearly seventy-five years later it was still standing, utterly overpowered by the Gothic-Moorish reaches of the fabulous castle on the hills above it. In this castle Hearst the man could do nearly anything in the world he desired. At the ranch, the boy struggled to learn how to throw a lariat, and was supremely happy when he succeeded.

With such plain amusements, Hearst's early West Coast phase of living ended. His housing in the next few years, except for occasional periods at home, was more democratic and incomparably dreary. He hated being lumped in with the mob at prep school, and he was not a great deal happier in his Cambridge lodgings when he went to Harvard, although he used his unlimited allowance to furnish them in a style that impressed even the financiers' sons who were his classmates.

Occasionally he was permitted to observe how he might have been living if growing up and getting an education had not interfered. His father, now a United States senator, had characteristically erected at 1400 New Hampshire in Washington an edifice only slightly less grand than the White House. Grover Cleveland, in fact, appeared to prefer it, judging by his frequent social appearances there, and he was always certain to find livelier company, since George Hearst disdained ambassadors for such companionable Western constituents as Bill Nye, Bret Harte, Mark Twain and any other golden representative of the golden land who was homesick for the hearty handclasp and sun-kissed hospitality of a native.

Whenever he could manage it, Will Hearst forsook Cambridge for Washington and mingled with these personages, and in time he was invited not to return to Harvard Yard, thus freeing him permanently from any confines whatsoever.

There followed a new San Francisco period, in which William Randolph Hearst, no longer Sonny or Billy Buster or even Will, blossomed as the oddest newspaper flower any journalistic gardener ever saw, even in such an exotic bouquet as the San Francisco newspapers of the early nineties. As the proprietor of his father's gift to him and to history, the *Examiner*, he was a publisher in his own right at last.

In this phase, his living was not so much lavish as merely varied. He scarcely saw the apartments and houses that were his official residences during the *Examiner's* hectic early days. He was in them only a small part of the time; the rest he spent in the lurid cubbyholes of his newspaper. In the summer, he managed to spend considerable time in the old Hearst place at Sausalito, and there, his enemies whispered, he gave Roman orgies of a kind to be expected from a boy with more money and power than were good for anybody. The orgies were the envious fancies of his competitors. Hearst was never a man for personal moral excesses, though doubtless he made no effort to save his friends and companions from sin, and endured with indifference the consequent reflections on his own character.

Sometimes he went with his closest *Examiner* friends—such childhood playmates as Eugene Lent, "Cosey" Noble and Petey Bigelow, and newly acquired playmates like the dapper, drunken genius of the *Examiner*, managing editor Sam Chamberlain—to the stock farm George Hearst had begun near Pleasanton, across the bay. This old-fashioned ranch W. R. transformed into an up-to-date country place, with the help of an architect, and there he relaxed while he indulged in his best-loved sports, riding and swimming. The others amused themselves after their own fashions.

El Rancho del Oso, as he called it, was Hearst's only real home on the West Coast until he built San Simeon in the early twenties. After George Hearst died and while his son was busy setting new fires in New York, Phebe retired to the ranch and altered it to suit herself as a pleasant place to spend her remaining years. She changed its name to La Hacienda del Poco de la Verona, after a five-ton wellhead which Hearst spotted in the Italian city in 1892, had dragged down to the sea, and then shipped to Pleasanton, where its fashioned iron lifted graceful traceries in a not so alien climate.

The silver cord of his mother's California real estate made Hearst a transcontinental traveler for a long time, and when he had children of his own, Phebe took pains to bind them in the same way while she could. By 1909 she had finished a humble

fourteen-room shack for their especial benefit, tucked away
in an oak grove hard by the Hacienda. She called it the Boys'
House, and Hearst himself had never been indulged so luxuriously. The second story consisted of thirteen rooms devoted to
sleeping quarters for her three grandchildren, George, William
Randolph, Jr., and John Randolph (the twins came six years
later), and for their assortment of tutors, nurses and governesses.
The entire ground floor was an enormous playroom, filled with
every device money could buy to entertain growing boys. If
they became bored even then, they could go outside and ride
and shoot and swim.

Thus Billy Buster's past was re-created with new and better
fixtures, while Billy himself was moving onward to larger, more
imaginative dwellings.

When he transferred his endeavors from San Francisco to
New York in 1895, he entered upon a different era. Ranches and
sunshine were behind him, and for a while the transplanted Californian did not create an atmosphere appropriate to his personality. He went at first to the Hoffman House, and took a
suite behind its marble façade while he went about astonishing
New York with his new delight, the *Journal*.

The Hoffman House, one of those fine old hostelries clustered
about Madison Square, was not without its attractions. Hearst
chose it because it was the unofficial feeding grounds of the Democratic Party organization in New York. There the most eminent Tammany tigers prowled at dusk in search of food, drink
and deals. The hotel provided all of these in abundance. Its famous bar, a long, narrow room with a mosaic ceiling and a
checkered floor, harbored the largest and most selective free
lunch in town, and inspirational decoration in the form of lush
French nudes by Bouguereau gazing down in innocent simplicity upon the connivers.

Hearst was never profoundly interested in food as such, and
wine and beer in sparse amounts were his only concessions to
alcohol, nor was he avid for nudes, whether French or Broadway types, in spite of the gossip whispered about him. But con-

niving he understood and enjoyed, and when it was the high-level political conniving practiced by the sachems of Fourteenth Street, he was in his glory.

It was in the Hoffman House suite that Hearst planned his early journalistic ventures in New York, conferred with his editors, bought Pulitzer's editors, and involved himself thoroughly with the Democratic machine. He spent very little time in the bar, preferring to sit back in a plush chair and receive in state upstairs.

But Hearst was not a man to be contained in a suite. Through the hotel's owners, he acquired the entire third floor of a smaller establishment, the Worth House, on Twenty-fifth Street, and proceeded to rebuild it in a style somewhat reminiscent of a California ranch, with beamed ceilings and tiled floors. He furnished it with a few choice items from his rapidly growing collection of mantels, furniture and tapestries. Then he skittered off on one of his periodic jaunts to Europe.

While he was gone, the Hoffman Company sold the building out from under him, and the new owners tore it down so rapidly that Hearst's harassed lieutenants had no more than time to rescue his expensive fittings from the ruins.

This rude dispossession led to his first purchase of New York real estate, a four-story brownstone at 123 Lexington Avenue. It was a structure so modest by comparison with what he had been accustomed to in the West that Hearst always referred to it as "the shanty."

As a shanty, 123 Lexington possessed considerable distinction. In its formal living room, stalwart Chester Alan Arthur had been sworn in as President of the United States in the early morning hours of September 20, 1881, while Garfield lay dead in Washington. And in the dim, lofty master bedroom on the second floor, on a November night only five years later, the respected but unloved twenty-first Chief Executive of the White House, whom Pulitzer's *World* had praised with eloquent faintness as "one of the best salmon fishers in the country," laid down his heavy six-foot-two frame and joined Garfield.

Hearst had no affection for the dignified town-house atmosphere of Arthur's shanty. Where the President's simple deathbed
had stood, he put a splendid example of Parisian couch-making.
In the oak-paneled dining room, he hung deer antlers as chan-
deliers, whose lights shimmered down incongruously on collections of Delft and old glass. Elsewhere in the house, Egyptian
mummy cases and German armor stood in astonishing juxtaposi-
tion to French art works, and the rosewood pianola supported
bronze statuettes of other disregarders of tradition, Caesar and
Napoleon.

The people around him at number 123 were as various as the
furnishings. In his early bachelor days there, Arthur Brisbane
and such old California friends as Jack Follansbee were his companions, and the calling cards on the silver tray that stood in the
hallway bore the names of prominent New Yorkers, most of
them politicians. But the house acquired a mistress in 1903, when
Hearst carried his dark-eyed Millicent under the fanlight and
established her among his other treasures. The politicians soon
had to share the tray with names more familiar on Broadway
and Fifth Avenue.

It was a new dispensation, and only one enduring trace of
the bachelor days remained: George Thompson, the perennial
valet, the one man in the world who thought Hearst could do
no wrong. Thompson was much more than a valet. He had
started life as a bellboy in the Hoffman House, worked himself
up to waiter, and in that office had so endeared himself to Hearst
that the young publisher took him along as a souvenir of the
hotel when he moved to Lexington Avenue. In the shanty,
Thompson ruled backstairs as major-domo and butler, and in the
parlor as the buffer between the master and the people he did
not care to see, of whom there were an increasing number.

Thompson was short, rotund and redheaded in his youth.
Later the red shrank to a crimson tonsure around an expanse of
glistening nude skin which somehow gave him added dignity.
For thirty years he followed Hearst from one residence to another, and in every one he made the household wheels mesh

with smooth efficiency, anticipating the master's desires, in the tradition of perfect English servants.

Such familiarity bred, obversely, a sincere hero-worship and a certain frankness which Hearst enjoyed, not only because it was expressed with his own brand of folksy humor, but because it was uncommon for him to hear it. Thompson could be equally eloquent on the subject of Hearst's religious art—he called the saintly Marys "McDonoughs"—and on his boss's taste in neckties, which was inclined to be unrestrained.

One of Hearst's biographers recalls that when George was asked his opinion of some new cravats, he remarked honestly, "Well, Mr. Hearst, I don't know as they are any worse than the others."

Thompson had to be pensioned eventually, but before he died in 1927, he often appeared at dinner parties, like a fond remembrance of things past, to serve the wine, whisper asides in Hearst's ear, and beam upon everyone present.

George supervised the migration of 1907, when Hearst moved his entire entourage uptown into one of the city's finest apartment houses, the Clarendon, at the corner of Riverside Drive and Eighty-sixth Street. The household had been bulging at the seams. George, the first-born, had arrived in 1904, and Millicent was expecting William Randolph, Jr. However, it was not so much in anticipation of human progeny that Hearst made his move. His art collection was months pregnant with tapestries for which there was no wall space on Lexington Avenue, and its various offspring were bred to new dealers in antiques nearly every day. A major operation was clearly indicated.

The Clarendon was only about two years old, a twin of the adjoining Dorchester. The two were filling rapidly with wealthy West Side families, and Hearst was one of the last tenants to move in before the "no vacancy" sign was hung out in both houses, seldom to be removed for a good many years. Hearst leased the three top floors, a hideaway of more than thirty rooms.

It might have been supposed by someone who didn't know

Hearst that thirty rooms would reasonably hold a man, his wife
and three children, but the estimate would not have considered
the frightening growth of the world's largest private art collection. In a half-dozen years it grew to such alarming proportions
that Hearst knew something would have to go, in this case the
walls and ceilings of the Clarendon. The owner of the property,
a realtor named Ronald H. Macdonald, objected to quite so
drastic an alteration, even if his tenant paid for it, and so in
July 1913, in a characteristic fit of financial petulance, Hearst
bought the whole building for a little more than $900,000.

Now the partitions and ceilings flew with the proverbial
will. With five stories and a penthouse to manipulate, Hearst
took out floors to make an echoing, cavernous Gothic hall,
straight from the Middle Ages, on whose stone walls his great
tapestries took on the proper proportions, and on whose spacious
floors his armor collection looked quite at home. In time he added
on one of the floors a splendid Georgian library and a well-
equipped art gallery, in which he hung a small museum full of
valuable pictures.

The purchase of the Clarendon was significant in the Hearst
history of housing for several reasons. Through it he met Martin
Huberth, of Huberth & Huberth, brokers in the deal, who became his friend and counselor. The firm itself thereafter assumed
the role of agent in the numerous real estate transactions with
which Hearst occupied himself in New York for the next three
decades.

Then too the purchase marked the beginning of a long
legal quarrel between Hearst and the New York Central Railroad which tortured the courts for years, while the Squire of
Riverside Drive sought to compel the road to remove its tracks
from his front yard, and its smoky, cinder-spewing locomotives
from his view of the rolling Hudson. Years later, when it was no
longer being pursued, the Central covered its tracks.

Finally, acquisition of the Clarendon signified the putting
down of roots, the only roots Hearst put down anywhere until
he finally came to earth at San Simeon in the twenties. In these

restless early years of his life, the Clarendon was as much a home place as was possible for such a man. It was there he gathered his five children about him and played Santa Claus at Christmas time, pretending to come down the Gothic fireplace, which was one of a pair appraised by experts as the world's most beautiful. There, too, Millicent held some of the most elaborate entertainments ever seen in a city that was no stranger to them. Among the sixty rooms was one which would accommodate easily a party for 250 people.

Out of the Clarendon, Hearst stepped forth to Congress, and it was there he later immured himself against the patriotic wrath of citizens who thought him in league with the Kaiser, while Secret Service operatives poked about among his portraits and armor, searching for agents of the Wilhelmstrasse.

Altogether, it was a tenancy which stretched out to twenty-five years, approximately as long as his San Simeon residence. The two overlapped, because Hearst held onto his New York home until about 1938, when it reverted to the Mutual Life Insurance Company, holders of the $525,000 mortgage Hearst had taken out when he bought it.

In later years Hearst had other less pretentious lodgings in both New York and Los Angeles. Moses Koenigsberg, a long-time executive employee, recalls in his memoirs that he often lunched with Hearst and Miss Davies in a studio apartment of the Beaux Arts Building on Sixth Avenue. It appears that there was also an apartment in the Warwick Hotel, New York, and an entire floor of the Ambassador Hotel in Los Angeles, besides a number of other rendezvous points on both coasts.

But these were transient affairs, designed to give Hearst a small measure of the privacy no public figure can hope to enjoy except in small doses. The Clarendon, like San Simeon, was a symbol. It represented in New York the fact of his presence, and for years it was a constant reminder of the time he was a power in the city.

The day came in 1940 when a passer-by on Eighty-sixth Street could see that a piece of white paper had been pasted neatly on one of the tall glass panels in the doors which guarded the ornate entrance of the Clarendon. Peering at it, he could read the legend, "House closed. Please ring bell." And he knew that an era had closed, along with the house.

II

The final phase of Hearst's housing career might well be called his palace period, or Billy Buster in Cloudland. Its manifestations —they were too grand to be called examples—could be found on Long Island, in Wales, at Santa Monica, in the High Sierras, and of course at San Simeon itself.

The castles on Long Island and in Wales were remarkable in the history of millionaire dwellings if only because their owner seldom lived in them, but nevertheless treated them on occasion as though he intended to spend the rest of his life there.

The castle at Sands Point, Long Island, was where he lived least. It was bought in 1929, presumably as part of a settlement with Mrs. Hearst, who by that time was his wife, as the saying goes, in name only. Nevertheless, it will be shown, this pleasant fiction only added to their mutual esteem, and he was not a stranger to St. Joan, as they named it, either at the formal occasion of its opening in 1930, or in the months preceding.

St. Joan had belonged to Hearst's one-time political friend, August Belmont, whose widow called it Beacon Towers. It spread over thirteen acres on the shore of Long Island Sound, complete with a real lighthouse. The house was a rambling French château with Gothic towers, built of stone and resembling a small barony.

Inside were the familiar characteristics of a Hearst home: a great hall with an enormous fireplace, carloads of art objects, opened and unopened, and furniture of every period from the early Louis to Early American. The separate suites designed for the owners were French: Louis XVI for Millicent, Empire for her husband.

With a strange collector's insight, Hearst furnished the light-house in Early American, making it into a kind of circular Williamsburg. Visitors in 1939 often found him in it, uncrating new pieces, chopping away at the boxes with a hatchet. Anyone who came for breakfast or lunch might discover himself confronted by a servant bearing hatchets for everyone, and a hacking bee would take place while Hearst carried on a lively conversation.

Emile Gauvreau, one of Hearst's editors caught up in this occupation one Sunday morning, was mercifully saved by the intervention of Millicent, who sounded like any wife as she remarked, "A lot of people can uncrate that furniture, and you know very well you'll never look at this lighthouse again. You have visitors waiting."

The visitors were waiting, and so were the banks, which appeared to be lurking around the corner of so many Hearst properties. In 1943 the Dime Savings Bank sold St. Joan, unoccupied by either Hearst for some time, to a new owner.

Four years before he acquired his lighthouse with attached estate, Hearst had enjoyed a dry run in castle-owning with the purchase of that medieval gem in Wales known as St. Donat's. His feeling about this property was far different. St. Joan was just a pile of Long Island architecture, authentic in neither lighthouse nor château, but St. Donat's had nearly nine hundred years of tradition behind it, and most especially, it was steeped in the atmosphere of the Middle Ages. That had always been the period he loved best, as his collecting showed so clearly.

Buying a Welsh castle was really no more effort to Hearst than buying a new suit would be to an ordinary man. What made this purchase a little extraordinary was that he bought it without seeing it. A New York art dealer had shown him the photograph of one room in it—a lovely room, he thought. "Where is it?" he wanted to know, and when he learned its whereabouts, the rest was simply a matter of a memo to his London agent, Jane Head, asking her to let him know when there was an English castle on the market, particularly St. Donat's. He would settle for Leeds Castle, in Kent, or some other stray castle, if he had to, but he had really set his heart on St. Donat's.

By a coincidence unusual even in the castle business, St. Donat's was advertised for sale only four months later in *Country Life*, the British magazine in whose advertising pages are the rich man's equivalents of the ranch-type-bungalow-near-schools. Hearst saw it and cabled Miss Head at once: "Buy St. Donat's castle." She made an offer the same day, although she had never seen the place either, and twenty-four hours later it belonged to Hearst.

After that nothing further happened for three years, except that the castle came to life by remote control through the never-failing magic of cables from San Simeon. Servants appeared from London, a corps of gardeners went to work, and as a final Hearstian touch, the antiquarian who had redecorated Buckingham Palace itself came down to supervise the temporary restoration.

Any restoration of consequence had to wait, however, until the new owner got around to an inspection tour in 1928. Mrs. Fremont Older, Hearst's semi-official biographer, reports that he arrived about ten o'clock of a moonlit night, and while she does not permit herself to indulge the speculation, it is not difficult to picture the American multimillionaire, the golden boy of the Western world, standing triumphantly before a thousand years of English history rising sheer in the moonlight on its cliff high above the Bristol Channel. The invading Roman legions had stormed it when it was but a fortified camp. St. Paul, so the legends said, had prayed there, and William the Conqueror once owned the protection of its moat, drawbridge and battlements. Now it belonged to another William the Conqueror, who could have bought and sold the Bastard King a dozen times over but was somehow less certain of his position in history.

Mrs. Older has told us that he was so excited by the first sight of St. Donat's that he refused to sit down to his overdue supper until he had gone on a tour of inspection, peering about with a lantern through the dismal passages and ancient dungeons until he emerged, cobwebbed from head to foot and utterly happy, ready to dine.

Thereafter he took a more practical view of St. Donat's.

What it lacked was quality, that was obvious. There was quantity in its 135 rooms, but the place was lamentably deficient in plumbing. Hearst ordered this remedied in a tone that implied, "And don't spare the fixtures." They took him literally. In a short time it had as many baths as San Simeon, most of them destined never to know a friendly hand on their faucets.

Another defect was its furnishings, which were medieval but not necessarily rare. Nothing was more easily remedied. By the time Hearst found a few weeks to see the place again—in 1931, after another three-year interval—it was a museum worth coming a distance to see, and not a few collectors made the journey. They were lost in admiration of the Elizabethan silver, most of it bought in London auction rooms.

Naturally the collectors found Hearst's own room most fascinating, and in fact it puzzled as well as fascinated some of his friends who saw it. Hearst had always been fond of vivid colors, but his bedroom at St. Donat's was a mass of red, perhaps inspired by the castle's bloody history—or more likely because red was a color he happened to like at the time. It was a chamber spacious enough not to be crowded by a superb array of lacquer cabinets lining the walls, which themselves were red-paneled, with furniture in red upholstery to match. There were a half dozen of these cabinets, from the time of Charles II, and Hearst, who always loved to lie where royalty had lain, slept in the bed where the unhappy first Charles had slumbered fitfully before the battle of Naseby in 1645. This fact was inscribed on a carved silver panel at the foot.

"W.R. showed poor taste there," an English friend remarked on a tour of inspection. "He would have done better to get a Charles II bed. There was a man who knew what to do with one."

Hearst would not have been amused by such frivolities. If the second Charles had possessed a bed worth collecting, he would have had it. It might even be lying about somewhere in a packing case, unopened, for all he knew.

What proved to be most remarkable about the exceedingly

brief intervals Hearst spent at St. Donat's was the salmagundi
of English and California country life he created behind the
battlements.

The English side was confined largely to mealtimes. At
luncheon, for instance, mutton and hothouse fruits were regular
guests. In the afternoon it was tea in the library, no different
from any English home except that the hot water arrived in a
George II teakettle worth enough to buy a whole tea plantation,
and the guests drank the brew they were permitted to make
themselves from an equally valuable Chamberlain Worcester tea
service. At dinner it was likely to be mutton again, or a joint
of beef in the inimitable English style, but this humbleness was
offset by a quarter million dollars' worth of silver on the table,
with a pair of Cellini cups flanking the centerpiece and other
priceless bric-a-brac strewn about.

Otherwise the entertainment was strictly California, out of
San Simeon: cards and charades in the evening, tennis, swimming
and riding in the afternoon. It hardly needs mentioning that a
large swimming pool was installed almost at once.

But the final touch was one only Hearst would have thought
of. He laid a velvety sward in the moat and played croquet on
it.

By one of those ironies which seemed to dog him, his castle
was among the first victims of the war he opposed so bitterly.
Early in 1940 the British Government requisitioned it for the
duration. He had not seen it for several years, and he never saw
it again.

Much as Hearst enjoyed the evocation of the past which St.
Donat's provided, however, California was always his real home,
as it had been in the New York days. He was possessed of the
true Californian's burning pride of state, and it was natural that
his show places were built there and that he himself spent most
of his time on the West Coast after about 1922.

The second phase of his California career began in these early
years of the twenties, more than a quarter century after he had
departed as a young man to make a name for himself in New

York. He had gone away rich but obscure. He returned still richer, with an international reputation that was good or bad, depending rather largely on who was doing the estimating. His political hopes were buried, his marriage had verged into an understanding, his business affairs were reaching a peak of affluence. He had, in brief, reached the stage where he had little to do but watch the money roll in and out again. The direction of his empire required only part of his time. For the rest he could devote himself wholeheartedly to his favorite diversion —acquisition.

Since he spent money mostly on art and places to put it in, aside from newspapers, it was logical that as his collecting reached a climax of accumulation in the twenties, the houses he erected to house it were proportionately stupefying. They included Miss Davies' Santa Monica "beach house," the fabulous San Simeon, and Wyntoon.

A visiting magazine writer once described the beach house as "a white-pillared manse, huge as a railway terminal." It was San Simeon in miniature, a little white palace beside the sea, devoted to luxury and the finer things.

Like its companion piece to the north, it was constantly saturated with guests, probably even more so because it was handier to Hollywood and the gregarious Marion urged her innumerable friends to come see her any time. They seldom refused. Life at the beach house was endless fun. There was swimming, of course, not in the ocean a few feet away, but in the inevitable swimming pool laid out beside it. There were food and drink enough to stock a large restaurant. Art of every variety abounded, from original Rembrandts and Holbeins to portraits of Marion in various roles, pictures later removed to the Beverly Hills house.

The beach house reflected Marion's personality more than Hearst's. It was not a museum, nor a castle, but a sunny, light, informal place. Her bedroom was enormous, facing the ocean, and it boasted two baths, one at each end. As Ilka Chase remarked, this was "the kind of thing which haunts one when waking up in the middle of the night, and brings hazily to mind the story of the donkey who starved to death between two bales of hay."

At Santa Monica, Hearst lived much as he did anywhere else, running his empire through the traveling corps of secretaries and telegraphers who followed him about, swimming and playing tennis, and watching motion pictures every evening of his life.

Once, during the second World War, the beach house proved more useful when a German submarine was sighted and shelled off Santa Monica. Hearst watched the whole affair eagerly from a balcony and refused to come in.

His last and most spectacular public appearance at the manse beside the sea was in 1938, when he celebrated his seventy-fifth birthday with a huge white birthday cake and two orchestras to wish him "Happy Birthday to You." It was a traditional sort of party. The theme of the costume ball was, appropriately, Early American, and the three hundred guests came disguised as pioneers. Hearst himself appeared as James Madison, another firm believer in the Constitution and gracious living.

That was one of the last gay occasions at Santa Monica. Ten years later, with the circle of Hearst's living drawn tightly into Beverly Hills, the beach house was sold and the new owners converted it into a hotel.

If this is the eventual fate of San Simeon, it will become the finest hotel in the world, as in its first incarnation it was the most splendid roof a man ever put over his head, the ultimate in earthly magnificence, inside and out.

As many words as dollars have been spent on San Simeon, describing this monumental, and in a way monstrous, extravagance of Hearst's. Articulate guests, aware that they had been permitted to live intimately for a space with one of the world's wonders, were at once impelled to talk and write about it.

In the welter of words and impressions, there is little to disclose how the owner felt. To most of the reporters, San Simeon was the act of a man drunk with power and money. Drunk he may have been, but it is also true that Hearst was accustomed to money and power and in his eyes San Simeon was anything but a gigantic, mad gesture of impulsiveness. It was a carefully planned, deliberate attempt, accomplished over a long period of time, to create a shrine to beauty. A psychiatrist would be able to tie the loose ends together, perhaps demonstrating the building of San Simeon as a final devotion to his mother, but it requires no complex analysis to see that, on the Enchanted Hill, Hearst meant to concentrate all the meaning he had been able to find in his personal life.

One observer came close to insight in noting that when guests appeared bowled over by San Simeon, Hearst "smiled a pleased little smile, for he was human enough to want people to like him and be grateful to him." More than that, he was gratified to know that other people thought he had succeeded in his act of creation.

The incongruity lay in the fact that the shrine to beauty housed a court life which, in some respects, approached that of the French monarchs whose personal belongings furnished so much of the place. But Hearst saw nothing incongruous in it. He lived as he liked to live, whether in San Simeon or elsewhere, and in San Simeon only the setting was different.

To Hearst it was always "the ranch," a twenty-million-dollar repository for his memories and his collections. It began with the memories. As early as 1905, Hearst discussed the possibilities of the ranch with Julia Morgan, the young San Francisco architect, first woman graduate of the Beaux Arts in Paris, whom he had called in to help with the plans for altering his mother's hacienda. Miss Morgan was a friend of Phebe's.

Undoubtedly the two discussed the place again in the next dozen years, but it was not until 1919, when Hearst's life turned away from politics, that he decided definitely to build upon the dream his father had begun.

It may be that George Hearst regarded the ranch's beginnings as merely a typically large real estate operation, because what he did at first was to corner those parcels of land lying in

San Luis Obispo and Monterey counties surrounding the Bay of San Simeon. The total, by the time George and his son were through, amounted to 275,000 acres, with the Santa Lucia Mountains making a diagonal hump through the property.

After he had assembled it, however, George became attached to the country and built a family retreat, beginning with a small cabin atop what was then no enchanted but simply Camp Hill. For years it was just that—a camping place where Hearst could bring Millicent and the children in the summer, and for a little while stop playing the exacting game of empire building and "rough it" with his growing sons, as he had done with his own father.

Yet even then it was San Simeon in miniature. There was an enormous portable main tent, roughly the size of a circus sideshow canvas, and around it three smaller guest tents, each one divided into four rooms and a bath. By the time the servants, tutors, nurses, chauffeurs, et al., had pitched their bivouacs, it resembled Virginia City in the days of George Hearst's first strivings there. As in the later days of the Enchanted Hill, there were paper napkins and an assemblage of fruits, jams, marmalade and condiments on the oaken dining table—the Hearst idea of roughing it—and after dinner, even in those remote days, everybody gathered to watch the flickering silver screen.

This was the status of San Simeon in 1919, when Hearst and Julia Morgan went to work in earnest. At first he visualized it as no more than a collection of small concrete buildings to house his Indian rugs and to obviate the nuisance of setting up camp every summer. But before these plans could be carried out, the death of his mother altered them profoundly. Until then Phebe's hacienda had been his California home. Now he could build one to suit himself.

At some early stage in the planning, it appears, the San Simeon obsession began to grow on Hearst and he could not stop. The search for beauty, the scope of his collecting, his insistence on perfection—all these led him on for nearly eighteen years.

Beginning in November 1919, Hearst literally carved his fabulous home out of the rocky mountaintop. A small regiment of workers battled tarantulas, rattlesnakes and weather, not to mention the technical problems of hauling materials from the bay up the mountainside.

In a surprisingly short time, the four Spanish palaces of San Simeon rose where the tent city once had squatted. There were three guesthouses as before, La Casa del Mar, facing the Pacific; La Casa del Sol, lifting toward the sun; and La Casa del Monte, confronting the Santa Lucias. And surmounting them all, the big tent, La Casa Grande. The houses were connected by Italian gardens, redolent with flowers, splashing with fountains, and filled with the statuary treasures of Greece and Rome.

Hearst always refused to call La Casa Grande a castle. To him St. Donat's was a castle, so, possibly, was Wyntoon, but La Casa Grande was the ranch, and in it were the paper napkins, the fruits and jellies and condiments of the tent camps.

In it, too, was the essence of his unrestrained dreams. It was typical of him that when he had climbed to the top level of Casa Grande during its construction and remarked with satisfaction that this was indeed the place for his Imperial Suite, and Miss Morgan informed him he was on the roof, Hearst replied calmly, "Then put on another story. We'll call it the Celestial Suite."

When this suite was finished, it was in the form of two bedchambers looking out to the ocean in front and the mountains behind, with a sitting room connecting them. Stepping from lofty solitude there, Hearst descended in an elegant carved-wood elevator, past his medieval Gothic study, past the cloisters and the library, down, down—and stepped out on the ground floor every evening at seven-thirty into the assembly hall, where his guests waited for him. They wore evening dress only once, when Hearst's favorite President, Calvin Coolidge, came to dinner with his wife.

Hearst moved among these guests in the assembly hall, singling out a few to talk with, while the others watched covertly to see where favor would fall next. It was a royal progress in the old style. No Louis could have done it better, except that Hearst's manner was shy rather than regal, concentrated rather than arrogant. Then everyone went in to dinner in that "long, noble, high" refectory, as Mrs. Older so aptly characterized it, which was the pride of Hearst's collection, and where he lavished his choicest treasures. There have never been any adequate reports of what the guests ate. It would have been like describing a fine steak eaten in St. Patrick's Cathedral.

After dinner Hearst ushered the guests into his 200-seat theater, hung with crimson Italian brocatelle. "If you don't like the picture," Hearst told them, "you can go to sleep." No film ever lulled the master to slumber, but occasionally he would slip out quietly for a glass of milk and a look at next morning's San Francisco or Los Angeles Hearst paper.

The multiple diversions of San Simeon were not meant entirely for the ceaseless flow of guests who came by air to the airport, by private train to the little station, or by car. Hearst enjoyed them all himself. He could be found splashing about like a leisurely porpoise in his white marble swimming pool, playing his steady game on the excellent tennis courts, feeding the animals in his private zoo, floating on the surface of the salt-water pool in his private gymnasium—a pool which cost him almost a million dollars—or poking about amid the art works which filled two acres of cellars beneath La Casa Grande and overflowed into a row of packing cases a block long outside.

Everywhere was the combination of ancient art and California divertissement. In the Great Hall, for example, a ping-pong table and a pool table were grouped serenely with seventeenth-century tapestries, Italian coffers, Persian rugs, oriental vases, Spanish columns and French Renaissance objects.

The tales about life at San Simeon are innumerable. They deal mostly with the incredible luxury available to every guest. Horses and cars, valets and maids, ample suites (usually two bedrooms with a bath each, and a sitting room), clothes for any occasion, movie contracts tucked beneath the plate of someone picked for a part in Hearst Cosmopolitan Pictures, picnics forty miles away but still on the ranch, where servants and a portable kitchen preceded the guests and created elaborate barbecues in the wilderness.

And telephones everywhere, until the legend rose that once, on a camping party a day's ride from the Enchanted Hill, an executive speculating on the outcome of a baseball game was startled out of his wits when Hearst, overhearing, pulled a telephone from behind a rock, called New York, and got the score. The switchboard at San Simeon, known to the telephone company as Hacienda, could be relied upon to get anything anywhere in the world.

As the twenties wore on, Hearst spent more and more time on the Hill, and the switchboard was busy summoning guests and the comforts to please them. There were always at least fifty or sixty visitors about—usually a few Hearst executives (it was a grim joke, though not literally true, that they came to San Simeon twice, to be hired and fired), a smattering of politicians who happened to be in Hearstian favor at the moment, perhaps a celebrity or so (anyone from Father Coughlin or Mayor Hylan of New York, to Winston Churchill or Bernard Shaw), and a gay collection of movie people, usually young ones. Hearst liked to have youth about him, especially pretty girls, which led to a widespread misunderstanding about the kind of goings-on at San Simeon.

There were no wild parties. They were not only obnoxious to Hearst's peculiarly moral nature, but he was shrewd enough to realize what would happen eventually to a fine old American publisher, no matter how powerful his money made him, if he permitted a houseful of celebrities to behave any way they pleased. As one of his biographers points out, Hearst knew that people could be trusted, more or less, to drink in packs, but the trouble came when they forgathered in pairs or small groups behind their doors. Hence the rule: "No drinking in your room."

Not that the atmosphere of San Simeon was indistinguishable from a nunnery. The aura of the court was one of intrigue beneath the surface—but always beneath the surface, whether it was sneaking a drink to the room or plotting an assignation.

No one cared to risk the rise of cold, pale displeasure in the host's eyes.

There is considerable evidence that Hearst was not only aware of the intrigue but even enjoyed some of it. A frequent visitor to San Simeon, who recalls it affectionately as "the corrupt court," believes that Hearst enjoyed Marion's young friends, because he sought to surround himself with youth and beauty, but he was under no illusions about it. He understood that his parties were used as auctions for the buying and selling of starlets.

At dinner one night, this visitor remembers, a young stage hopeful who had just arrived in Hollywood for screen tests (she is now a star) sat at dinner next to one of Hearst's more distant relatives, who began forthrightly to woo her in the direction of moral turpitude. She handled him beautifully, reminding him, "I'm jail bait," and skillfully maneuvering away from his questing hands.

"On the surface," says this source, "everything was orderly and the presumption was that everyone was only kidding. But the raw corruption of these people"—meaning the kind of guest of whom the relative was typical—"was pretty plain underneath."

Looking away, the visitor caught Hearst's eyes. He was laughing at the scene, amused and not offended, though it was something he himself would never have done.

After an evening during which this kind of amorous jousting was enjoyed by all, Hearst was up early the next morning. It was Sunday, and the visitor heard him complaining mildly but firmly to Marion as they went in to breakfast, "Where are all these young girls? Round them up and get them off to church." He had no intention of going to church himself, though he was not irreligious, but he believed everybody else ought to go, especially those who had been in danger of mortal sin the night before.

As for the other rules at San Simeon, the one calling for assemblage of all the guests at 7:30 P.M. in the Great Hall was adhered to rigidly, since no other restrictions were placed on the visitors' time schedules. But the widely publicized third rule, "Never mention death in Hearst's presence," was much exaggerated. Death was not his favorite subject, and he definitely did not want to talk or even think about his own, but he had no pathological aversion to mention of the word and never showed any reluctance to discuss it abstractly or in relation to someone else. Most of the topics about which it was whispered, "Don't ever mention that in front of Mr. Hearst," were in reality not taboo at all. Hearst could and would talk about anything.

The visitor to San Simeon, even if he had been everywhere and seen everything, could not help but be impressed. Ilka Chase, in a gay and irreverent description of her two visits, depicts the full treatment, beginning with the drive up from Hollywood. There was the realization that for the last thirty miles you had been driving along Hearst's property, and then the seven-mile climb up the Enchanted Hill itself, the gatehouse where no man passed without permission from on high, the signs warning of wild animals, and finally the four pleasure domes, where Miss Chase recalls she drifted to sleep in Cardinal Richelieu's bed. This last experience was also the delight of a good many movie stars, some of whom were so exhilarated by the experience that they had their pictures taken in it.

Before the zoo was disposed of, visitors like Miss Chase were likely to be awakened by the coughing of lions and the night sounds of other beasts, but in the daytime all was serene again, with swimming, tennis, lunch, more swimming, dinner, and movies, and the bottle of scotch pirated to the room. Sadie Murray, whom Miss Chase describes as "a vague relation of Mr. Hearst's by marriage," did the pirating in her case, with the apt remark, "He'd be mad as a hornet if he caught the butler bringing it over [ice and soda, that is], but what the hell, it's a free country."

It was difficult to remember sometimes that it *was* a free country at San Simeon, so completely was it dominated by Hearst's powerful personality, by his prejudices and whims. This was accentuated at Wyntoon, a far more isolated spot. It was here that Hearst uttered on his seventy-second birthday the much-quoted lament, "At my time of life, you just sit here and people bring you final decisions to make."

If that was true, and there is every reason to doubt it, a multitude of decisions must have been made at Wyntoon, because the little shingled bungalow which was the modern nerve center of the quaint Bavarian village ran twenty-four hours a day, under the driving lash of Joe Willicombe, Hearst's perennial Man Friday. Willicombe's staff included his own secretary, a telegraph operator and three telephone operators. Among them they made McCloud 30K3 the busiest exchange in Northern California. At seventy-two, Hearst sent dozens of "The Chief says . . ." messages crackling out on the wires every day. He was still doing it at eighty-two and beyond.

The guests at Wyntoon were unconscious of this activity behind the scenes. They were hardly conscious even of each other, because unlike the San Simeon gatherings, which were week-endish in character, Wyntoon was like a perpetual house party, in which thirty to sixty guests enjoyed the hospitality and never knew all their companions. Since it was harder to get there, people stayed longer, anywhere from a week to a month, until the common greeting was, "How long have you been here?" As at San Simeon, nobody was ever urged to leave unless he was falling-down drunk or otherwise disorderly.

And the people were the same: Hearst executives, coming and going; pretty young starlets, eager producers, celebrities, and the ever-present amorphous collection of persons never quite identified.

It was a place of pine and sunshine, the roar of the McCloud River in the ears, the good clean smell of forest in the nostrils, the wonders of nature in Californian abundance, and the wonders of Hearstian good times available in equal plenty. There were tennis, swimming and riding, as usual, and a good deal of croquet, which Hearst loved next to tennis. He played both these games earnestly, moving with deliberate intent upon the wandering croquet balls, and using the free-swinging, open style of the Western game on the tennis court. Swimmers performed in a gemlike heated pool hidden in the majestic pines, cedars and firs.

Life in general was more relaxed at Wyntoon because Hearst was more relaxed there. The guests were a half mile down the river from the Bavarian village where their host lived, sequestered in a huge pine-paneled alpine château large enough to house sixty people comfortably, with room enough left over for the inevitable movie theater.

Hearst's village consisted of three main buildings, Fairy House and Cinderella House, and the main residence, called Bear House, with a sturdy bronze fisherwoman, brought over from Salzburg in 1913, standing guard before it. When Hearst emerged from Bear House, he came to mingle with his guests, often wearing jauntily one of his dozen Tyrolean hats. When he went back in again, it was understood by everyone that no guest was to appear there without invitation, except at lunch and dinner. A possible exception might be a visitor like Hearst's old friend, Eleanor "Cissy" Patterson, publisher of the Washington *Times-Herald* (a onetime Hearst property), who arrived at Wyntoon in her private car, *Ranger*. Cissy usually stayed in what had been Phebe's place, a relatively simple establishment called River House.

Luncheon was always at 2 P.M., served buffet style for the first course, then by butlers. Dinner was nominally at eight, but Hearst was usually later there than at San Simeon, and it was often nine-thirty before he came in to eat. The food was excellent, and as at San Simeon, it was served on collectors' items of silver and plate, along with the ranchlike catsup bottles and jars of jams and condiments. Guests lit their cigarettes from blue-and-gold match packages with "Buy American" stamped on the back, but the wines that preceded them were not produced in the Napa or Livermore valleys. They came from the vineyards of that France in which Hearst was no longer *persona grata*. But he was not one to permit a matter of politics to stand between him and the better life.

Hearst's attitude toward Wyntoon developed in much the same way as it had toward San Simeon. Originally it had been a rustic retreat for his mother. After she died, he made few changes until a destructive fire in 1930 inspired him to build a new Wyntoon on the ruins, once more with the help of Julia Morgan.

Again there was the blending of childhood memories with latter-day luxury, the mushrooming growth beyond his first plans, and finally the creation of what was really a forest museum to house the parts of his collection which belonged there, items like cuckoo clocks and German medieval art. Before the great reversal in his living occurred in 1937, he had already transported three carloads of art objects up the mountainside and was making large plans for more buildings to shelter further acquisitions.

Yes, in summertime the living at Wyntoon was easy, and the pine trees were high, the fish were jumping and it was not hard to believe if you were young and pretty that God had made Hearst for the benefit of pleasure-loving mankind, placing him on earth to erect great castles by the sea and build vast forest retreats for the amusement of the fortunate few.

How harsh it must have been to be reminded that the "He" in Bear House, who was always referred to by this biblical pronoun, also had his commandments, which carried an earthly enforcement more immediate than divine wrath.

The essence of being W. R.'s guest was expressed in the immortal words of that young lady, bilked of a midnight drive by an edict from above, who cried out in epic frustration: "Darn old Mr. Hearst! I wish he wasn't up here!"

# CHAPTER THREE

## THE WOMEN IN HIS LIFE

HEARST WAS a man who liked axioms. He could spot an eternal verity at fifty paces, and one of his favorites was, "A boy's best friend is his mother." The psychiatry Hearst despised would say he had a mother fixation, but it takes no University of Vienna degree to realize that he idealized and idolized his mother beyond the natural degree, and that this fact colored all his relationships with women, individually and collectively.

The reason for it lay in the tragic circumstances of his birth, which until now have been known only to a few intimates.

He was born a twin, and presumably the other infant died at birth or shortly afterwards. Twins run in the Hearst family; he later fathered a pair. Hearst was naturally reticent about this circumstance, but according to a source who can hardly be doubted, it came to light from his own lips in the thirties when he needed a birth certificate for some passport procedure. His own certificate had been burned in the fire of 1906, but California's "hearsay" law permitted him to obtain a new one by testifying that he had heard his mother and/or father say he was born in a particular place at a particular time. It was then, probably because he no longer cared whether anyone knew, that he disclosed his twinship.

What he did not disclose was the far more significant fact that his mother had an exceedingly difficult time at his birth. The doctor told her she must never have any more children, and so the physical side of her marriage came to an end. Such an event would have had a profound effect on a more sensual woman, but Phebe easily turned her energies into the artistic channels toward which she had already diverted them. The love that might ordinarily have been diffused among a large family and whatever passion she now denied her husband were given to her only child.

Those circumstances may have been the most important in Hearst's life. Because of them, he was led in his earliest years to the pleasures of collecting; because of them, he did not marry until he was forty; because of them, he was able to spend his father's fortune with indulgent freedom until he had added his own millions. They made him appear as a far different person to women than to men, and they were responsible for a good many of his crusades as well as some of his social and political attitudes.

Not that Hearst gained nothing from his father. He inherited George's sense of humor, his generous manner of dealing with money, and his satiric outlook on the world. He loved his father, but for years he was the willing prisoner of his mother's enveloping love.

George Hearst also provided his son with a solid Scotch Presbyterian lineage which W.R. deplored in later years when reviewing his ancestry in the light of his antipathy to things British. He once wrote that he attributed the "vivacity, alertness and beauty" of American women to the "Irish blood in the American race," and he followed this curious anthropological observation with the declaration: "I am sorry that I haven't a great deal of Irish blood in my veins but my sons have. I remedied that defect at the earliest possible moment, and in the most satisfactory manner."

The genealogists Hearst employed to excavate in the family's past turned up no Irishmen at all, but only a descent, as their unhappy end product once lamented in the columns of the London *Evening Standard*, "from the British people in uninterrupted blood stream." The Scotch Lowland name was originally Hyrst, meaning "a thicket," was later changed to Hurst, and finally to its present spelling when the original family settlers in Virginia moved up to North Carolina.

This kind of background produced in George Hearst the

temperament he passed on to his son, a blend of noblesse oblige and enjoyment of property inherited from the slave-owning plantation dwellers among the early Hearsts, together with a certain carelessness about money derived from the fact that it was nearly always abundant.

To Hearst the figure of his father was a symbol of rough good humor and affection—a tall, bearded, booted figure who would give his son a twenty-dollar gold piece when the boy asked for ice-cream money, and who was equally generous with his wife and his old mining comrades who lay in wait for him at the corner of Montgomery and Market. A gambler, a rough-and-ready personality who scorned dress suits, books, art and education as too rarefied for his pioneering blood, a man who loved animals, poker and the sporting chance—that was George Hearst.

The times young Hearst spent with his father were enjoyable but infrequent. It was Phebe who held him up on the back of a horse at his grandparents' ranch, when he was little more than a baby, and taught him to ride, and she who taught him to read before he started school, she who supervised his life from the moment he arrived on earth until he was nearly a man.

It is sometimes said that George Hearst did not trust his son, and for this reason he left his fortune of eighteen million dollars entirely to his wife when he died on March 1, 1891. But it was a natural act, not only prescribed by family custom, but because she had managed his money shrewdly while he was alive. When Phebe wrote to her son in later years, informing him that he was to be her sole heir, a hardly surprising development, Hearst replied affectionately, "My father never did a better thing than when he made the will he did. I have admired him for it and have been happy to concur in it, and I have never told you how many times I have been advised by fools and scoundrels otherwise. That is the kind of thing for our own kind of people, and I hope to so live that you will have as much confidence in me as my father had in you. . . ."

This was not the dutiful letter of a dutiful son; it was one more expression of Hearst's devotion and admiration for his mother.

They were wholly merited. Phebe Elizabeth Apperson Hearst was an admirable woman by any standard, petite, with an erect carriage, a modest, gentle manner, and wide gray eyes which regarded the world with a trust it did not always deserve. She had three major interests in life: her son, art and philanthropy. She was the everlasting benefactor of the University of California and dozens of other educational and cultural institutions, and the number of young girls she sent through college was in the hundreds. Her art collection was the nucleus and the inspiration of the one that helped make her son famous. And it was this son who became her chief philanthropy, the principal ornament of her collection.

From her earliest days in San Francisco, Phebe Hearst sought to learn everything she could about art, and this knowledge she passed on to her son. With Billy Buster in tow, she visited the excellent collection of Isadora Duncan's father, which included an Andrea del Sarto; R. B. Woodward's public gallery on Mission Street, filled mostly with reproductions of old masters; and every exhibition, public or private, that opened in the city.

Mrs. Hearst also exposed her son to the cultural effects of opera, without result. His taste in music remained consistently low-brow all his life. It was art he loved. Phebe saw it and joyfully exploited his interest at the first opportunity, which came when he was ten years old and she took him on the grand tour of Europe.

They departed in a haze of farewell parties which went on for ten days, finally sailing on the *Adriatic* from Boston.

The adventures of Little Willie Abroad comprise the first fabulous episode in his fabulous life, and in them can be plainly discerned the prime characteristics of the adult Hearst. Here are a few snapshots from the family album:

Ireland: Willie deplored poverty, which Mrs. Older says he saw for the first time, and begged his mother to let him take off his rich boy's clothes and give them to the children of the poor.

He was restrained from this charitable but undignified act. He was "pained" by the harsh treatment Dublin draymen gave their patient nags.

Edinburgh: Down with whooping cough, but revived to visit art galleries, where Phebe reported he was "picture crazy."

London: Still whooping, and so unable to hear Adelina Patti, a disappointment he bore with equanimity. On a tour of the city, was heard to observe that he would like to live in Windsor Castle. Shared a sack of peanuts with grateful elephants in the Zoological Gardens.

Germany: Studied the language every day in Dresden, and floated down the Rhine immersed in a book of German legends. He consumed five books a month. At Hanover, produced tin soldiers and re-fought the Battle of Waterloo. Asked if he might buy the royal horses at Hanover. Mother said no. Told that no one under seventeen was permitted to enter one of the country's museums, he bribed the guard. Phebe wrote home to her husband: "He has a mania for antiquities."

Switzerland: Pleaded with his mother to let him buy every watch and woodcarving he saw. Mother counseled discretion, but he came away with a substantial haul.

Paris: Outstanding event of the tour—he discovered Charlemagne, from that moment his lifelong hero. Tutor explained that King of the Franks was the first monarch who considered peasants as human beings, was probably father of democracy. Mother unknown. Hearst viewed Charlemagne's tomb at Aix-la-Chapelle, climbed into his chair, saw the spot at St. Denis where his coronation took place. Later, he became an authority on Charlemagne. While in Paris, the Hearsts ran into Eugene Lent, a boyhood friend from home, also on tour with his mother. Boys compared notes and collections. Willie had good start on half-dozen collections: stamps, coins, pictures of theater personalities, beer steins, porcelain, and German comic pictures, converted twenty years later by Rudolph Dirks into the immortal "Katzenjammer Kids" comic strip.

Florence: Took art lessons, learned to play the guitar. He next played Verona, reading *Romeo and Juliet* on the way there.

Rome: Delivered Cicero's orations where the orator stood, walked in the Colosseum by moonlight, began collecting papal medallions, was blessed by the Pope. When his tutor pointed out to him and Eugene a light which had burned in the Eternal City for a thousand years, he regarded it thoughtfully and remarked, "Eugene, I'd like to put out that light. Isn't there some way it can be done?"

A ten-year-old capable of making such a remark was understandably unwilling to exchange his childhood for adolescence. In Hearst's case, the wrench of leaving home was doubly difficult. He loved California, his life there, and the company of his mother. At St. Paul's, a preparatory school in New Hampshire which he entered to prepare for Harvard in 1880, he found the dour New England climate and a regimented, disciplined life completely abhorrent to him—and he was desperately homesick for his mother.

Phebe solaced herself by going to Germany for the baths, and there she got frequent glum reports from Willie, who hated everything about St. Paul's and obviously anticipated an early departure from it.

Whether he was pushed or jumped has never been determined, but whatever the reason, it was necessary for him to spend a summer being tutored before he could enter Harvard, and in those restless months love came to him for the first time.

It was the first, that is, if one discounts the idyllic affair he carried on over the garden fence with little Katherine "Pussy" Soule, daughter of Senator Frank Soule, whose garden adjoined the Hearsts' behind the house on Chestnut Street. Pussy was a blonde, blue-eyed charmer who seemed to belong in the old-fashioned garden where she played all day. She had a penchant for newspapermen. Her father was editor of the *Morning Alta*, and Willie Hearst was her favorite entertainer. He sang to her, a talent the other boys in the neighborhood discouraged him from exercising.

While the grown-up Soules and Hearsts traded plants from their gardens, these two exchanged an innocent affection which was scarcely preparation for the devastating late-adolescent passion that smote young Will in the summer before he went to Harvard.

As his fellow sports of the day would have put it, he was a good picker. The object of his desire was a girl who stood on the threshold of a sensational career and was already considered a great beauty. Sybil Sanderson was the daughter of a justice of the Supreme Court of California. The circle of her family included an adoring older sister, Jennie, and a mother who was convinced that Sybil had a voice sent from heaven. Surprisingly, Mother was right. When the Sanderson girl stood up in the parlor to sing for company, no one had to pretend approval.

Hearst met this paragon at the Hotel del Monte, in Monterey, soon after he came home from St. Paul's. He surveyed her entrancing figure, gazed into her dark eyes, and listened to the soprano music of her voice. He was lost. At this period of his life, Will Hearst was a tall, slim, but well-built lad, with a kind of recklessness in his manner that Sybil must have found appealing to her own ardent, romantic nature. Under the celebrated Monterey moon, they strolled hand in hand, and when the sun came out again, they rode and swam together, and before things got altogether out of hand, they became engaged.

Hearst was in earnest. Sybil presumably agreed with a mental reservation, because it was no secret that in the autumn she intended to leave for Paris to study at the Conservatoire.

Mrs. Sanderson and Phebe Hearst heard the news of betrothal with indulgence and even stronger reservations. The former refused to take it seriously, since she would permit nothing to stand in the way of dear Sybil's career. As for Phebe, she had no objection to Sybil as a prospective daughter-in-law, but the liaison was out of the question in her opinion. Willie was much too young. He was hardly more than Billy Buster to her.

After a summer of sighs, protestations and denials, the love of the century came to an abrupt end. Sybil and her mother

departed for Paris, and a lovelorn Hearst entrained for Harvard
Yard.

Was it only a youthful summer romance? At least one of the
people who knew Hearst well doubts it. He believes, and there
is some confirmation, that W.R. never really got over Sybil, and
that if they had married, the course of Hearst's life and the
history of American journalism might very well have been
different.

It would also have robbed nineteenth-century opera of a
singer who is still fondly remembered in music-loving circles.
Sybil fell in love with Paris, and Paris was enchanted with La
Belle Sanderson. The composer Massenet joined the love feast,
and while all Paris whispered about their enjoyment of each
other's company, he wrote his operas *Thaïs* and *Manon* for her.
At least Hearst was succeeded by a genius.

As a young publisher, Hearst was often in Paris and always
he saw Sybil. When she arrived in New York for her debut at
the Metropolitan, the San Francisco *Examiner* devoted considerably more space to the event than it warranted—an entire page.

An interesting but erroneous story about Sybil's last days is
in circulation even now. The limpid-eyed toast of Monterey
became a prematurely aging beauty in her late thirties, pursued
by disease, slipping from her high eminence, dogged by gossip,
and while she lay dying in Paris, she was visited frequently by
a mysterious man who wore a black cloak and a discreet air. It
was William Randolph Hearst, the more wishful thinkers among
the scandalmongers whispered.

At the time, however, Hearst was busy wooing his imminent
wife, and in fact they arrived in Paris on their honeymoon the
week Sybil died.

After Sybil, there was no further assault on the Hearst libido
for nearly two years, but when love came again, the pattern was
curiously similar. The girl was Eleanor Calhoun, one of the bouquet of young beauties who always decorated Phebe's drawing
room in Washington, where her husband was busy being a Senator. On one of his frequent excursions there from the confines

of Harvard, Will Hearst sighted Eleanor. They fell in love at first sight.

It seemed like a match: they were both Californians; their ancestors came from the same county in South Carolina (Eleanor was a direct descendant of the famous John); there was the same strong physical attraction between them—Eleanor was remarkably like Sybil in height, subtly rounded figure, compelling eyes, and presence.

That was the rub. The presence was stage presence, and she had it in such abundance that it was plain she was on the brink of a theatrical career. Her ambition, she told Will, was to be the finest Shakespearean actress in the world.

At first this appeared as only a delightful attribute, because Hearst himself loved the theater and theater people, and along with it went a love of music and books which Eleanor shared. The Harvard boy wooed her with even more zeal than he had shown for Sybil, and Miss Calhoun declared herself overcome by it all and consented to become engaged.

Here some familiar and ominous signs appeared on the horizon. Eleanor told him she was leaving shortly for London to study for the stage. Undoubtedly Hearst looked hastily over his shoulder to see if her mother was in the wings, but as he soon learned, it was no matter of maternal prodding. Eleanor meant to achieve what she wanted to achieve. Walter Pater would have said she burned with a hard, gemlike flame. Nevertheless, she was in love and apparently willing to try mixing marriage and a career.

Phebe interposed at this point. It was odd that the gracious lady who had eagerly absorbed the culture of her time was, in the most obtuse Victorian way, blind to the theater as a part of that culture. She knew perfectly well that Eleanor Calhoun was a respectable girl of impeccable family connections, and a distinct asset to her salon, but if she persisted in being an actress, then Phebe could only conclude that she would rapidly become no better than she should be. The idea that such a female should be married to Willie appalled her. If he must marry, she desired his wife to be a nice, quiet girl with no other ambition than to take her proper place in society.

Phebe acted with a mother's shrewdness. She did not propose that they become disengaged immediately. Instead she suggested a compromise: they should wait until Will had finished at Harvard, and meanwhile Eleanor could study drama in London. They agreed, confident that nothing could change their devotion.

Mother knew best. Within little more than a year, the engagement ended with the forlorn society-page phrase, "by mutual consent." In London, Eleanor had found forgetfulness easy in the same kind of whirl that had swept Sybil away. As a new bright star on the London stage, taken up by the Princess of Wales herself, in the constant company of Robert Browning, Bernard Shaw, Oscar Wilde, Henry James, Whistler and other brilliant figures of London society, she was transported almost instantly to the dream world she had burned to inhabit. Her subsequent notable career on the London and Paris stage was a foregone thing, and eventually she attained the ultimate by becoming a princess, as the bride of a Serbian prince without portfolio, princes having gone somewhat out of fashion in the Balkans.

Again, it was not easy for Hearst to forget, but apparently he forgave. During the first World War, he dispatched a troubleshooter all the way from London to see if he could extricate the Princess from the Balkans.

Thus far Hearst's love life had been in a psychological rut. He had aspired to girls who were beauties, talented enough to be outstanding in their own right, and older than he was. They had been alike physically and mentally, neither had been wholly approved of by his mother, and they had gone on to other fields —except the long-forgotten Pussy Soule, who was by that time well on the way to being a little old maiden lady in a big house, surrounded by cats and dogs.

Hearst's enemies later declared that he consoled himself at Harvard, and for the next few years until his marriage in 1903, with a series of chorus girls and other women of uncertain character. There is no proof of this, and it seems wholly inconsistent with Hearst's character. He liked to be seen in public with girls, and take them wining and dining and to the theater, more or less because it was expected of him. But the idea that he was using his bank account to buy flesh in the most elegant manner is denied first of all by the fact that he almost invariably appeared with two girls, and by the shy, romantic attitude he exhibited toward women during his lifetime.

In any event, the one woman who remained constant to him, who never failed him, was his mother, and he found no one to replace her until he was forty. Even then his correspondence shows that he regarded her with the same childhood feelings he had always displayed, and in this respect he did not change until Phebe died in 1919. As much as possible, he wanted her to share his marriage, and while she was realistic enough about this to stay most of the time in California, he grieved when she did not come East to visit.

On one such occasion he wrote: "I feel blue that you didn't come. I am getting kind of aged, and so are you. We ought to stop working and worrying and have some fun together before we die. . . ." Another time, shortly after he had been defeated by Charles Evans Hughes for the governorship of New York, he wrote to her: "I think California is the best country in the world, and always will be, no matter who comes into it or what is done to it. Vive le ranch! I am going to save up and build a cabin down at the ranch just big enough for you and Millie and the baby and me."

Whether this arrangement would have suited either Millie or his mother is open to question. While nothing was said on either side, it was clear that the two women were not soul mates, though Millicent Willson was strangely like her mother-in-law in several ways. They were both essentially "good" women, idealistic, philanthropic and gentle. The trouble was that they both loved Willie.

Phebe must have been a little chagrined by the marriage.

After having saved her son from the clutches of two women of the theater, Willie was ungrateful enough to marry a hoofer in a Broadway musical comedy. In retrospect, Sybil and Eleanor undoubtedly appeared as catches by comparison.

Yet Millicent Willson, billed with her sister Anita as the dancing Willson sisters in *The Girl from Paris*, possessed attributes of her own. Although she came from a rather distinguished line of performers—her father, whose stage name was George Leslie, had been one of the best-known clog dancers on the vaudeville stage of the nineties—Millicent had only modest theatrical ambitions of her own. Like her predecessors in Hearst's affections, she was tall and beautiful and she was not frivolous or rattlebrained. She had Phebe's innate good taste and love of beauty, and her rather lofty set of principles.

One must also suppose that, being human, she was not altogether unconscious that young Hearst was a millionaire and a triumphant conquest for a chorus girl. Cynics sneered that it was simply a case of another rich man caught in a familiar trap, and Hearst's political opponents circulated the story that he was getting married to improve his position as a potential candidate for public office, since marriage would serve to quiet the rumors assiduously spread by the numerous enemies he had made, both in journalism and in politics. He was pictured in these rumors as a wealthy voluptuary, a myth that pursued him most of his life. He never bothered to deny it, largely because he never took it seriously. The stories of wild parties on his yacht, orgies on Lexington Avenue and high life in Europe amused rather than annoyed him.

In the case of Millicent, it was love again, as it had been twice before, and the difference was that by this time he had severed the more practical restraints of the silver cord. He was nearly forty, a successful publisher, and he was in New York while Phebe was in California.

Love caught him during a lull in his life. He had been elected to Congress, but his term had not yet begun, and he was whiling away the evenings in the early spring of 1903 at a favorite occupation, going to musicals and vaudeville, which he had loved since childhood. His companion was usually George Pancoast, the genius of printing machinery, and the two were soon taking the Willson sisters out. They watched the girls from the front row of the Herald Square Theatre, where their show was playing, and afterward the foursome went out on the town, or retired to the intimacy of a midnight supper.

The whole town gossiped, but Hearst's behavior during the affair was hardly that of a man conducting a worldly seduction. He sent her notes and flowers from the *Journal* office, walked hand in hand with her about the chaste precincts of Gramercy Park, and shamelessly stuffed the ballot box so that she would win the *Morning Telegraph's* popularity contest.

They were married the day before his fortieth birthday, on April 28, 1903. George Willson, resplendent in frock coat and gardenia, gave the bride away. Orrin Peck, the portrait painter, who had been Hearst's childhood friend in San Francisco, was best man, and Bishop Henry Codman Potter, a friend of Phebe's, performed the ceremony at Grace Church.

Phebe herself sent word that she was not well and would be unable to attend. She did not recover her health until the happy couple returned from their honeymoon and she could face the inevitable with dignity. As a gesture of good will, she sent Millicent a splendid brooch as a wedding present.

Both the wedding and the honeymoon were completely successful. As Hearst put it in his report to Phebe: "It was cheerful, and not to be taken for a funeral." After the ceremony, Oscar had laid out a magnificent wedding breakfast in the old Astoria's dining room, but the free-loaders got most of it. The bride and groom were too busy opening presents, messages of congratulation, and getting their pictures taken to do much more than consume a little soup and ice cream before it was time for their midafternoon sailing on the *Kaiser Wilhelm II.*

The honeymoon was a reprise of Hearst's European excursion at ten with his mother, except that this time he was the guide. Back home again, they went immediately to Phebe's ranch at

Pleasanton. There the Senator's widow issued invitations to the best names in San Francisco society and the new Mrs. Hearst was presented formally as a *fait accompli*. If the best names had their doubts about Millicent's social qualification, they dared not refuse to accept her. In any case, she carried the introduction off with charm and assurance, as though she had been born to the drawing room.

This beachhead she reinforced steadily as time went on, and shortly there was no further question that she "belonged." Society has always been the better for her presence in it; she improved its moral tone.

For the fifteen years or so following her marriage, Millicent was a devoted wife and mother, giving birth to her five sons, managing the splendid parties and salons which Hearst's position commanded, and helping him whenever and wherever she could.

Then she fell victim of her own generous nature, and there began one of the most remarkable domestic dramas of our time.

Among Millicent's numerous philanthropies was the helping of young girls trying to get a start in the theater. As a theatrical Lady Bountiful, she never forgot her own humble beginnings and she often used her money and Hearst's numerous connections to help some struggling young actress who seemed deserving.

A girl who appeared particularly deserving to her in 1918, according to a source close to the family for many years, was Marion Davies, who was then appearing in the Ziegfeld *Follies*. Marion's brother-in-law is popularly credited with introducing her to Hearst, but it was Millicent herself who brought Marion home and displayed her proudly to her husband, with the idea that he would give her a part in one of the movie epics he was financing that year.

It must be said that there are other versions of this story and no way of telling which is absolutely correct. Marion's friend, Hedda Hopper, who believes that Marion is "the kindest woman who ever put foot in this town," says the meeting occurred when Hearst happened to drop in at the *Follies* one night, saw her, and came back every night for the next eight weeks, though it was supposed at the time that it was her sister Rose who so fascinated him. But one night, so this version goes, Hearst asked Marion to come to supper after the show. She consented and would have gone with some friends, but the friends gave her good advice: They told her to go alone, and the result was a lifelong attachment.

Marion's own story of the meeting, told in a reminiscent mood after Hearst died, is as follows: "It was in 1918. I was in the chorus before that. I used to hold up the backdrop. Do you realize that I was studying ballet when I was four years old? Sure, at the same school Marilyn Miller went to. She was a much better dancer, much better. In one show at the *Follies* I had seventeen dance numbers, all on my toes. It was hard work but I loved it. Then I made a movie which my brother-in-law George Lederer directed. It was called *Runaway Romany*, and it was a flop, but Mr. Hearst saw it and he told his film company to sign me up. They gave me $500 a week. Oh, I was living!

"I was just there for a little while when one day I was in the projection room looking at my rushes and a man came in and told me about a new studio that he was going to rent to Mr. Hearst for many, many years at something like $500 a week. A little while later I bumped into Mr. Hearst and told him about it. I said, 'Sir'—I called him Sir then—'if I may be presumptuous, I would like to tell you that the man I talked to inside said he's going to rent you a studio for $500.' Well, W.R. went to his head man and found that the guy had made a deal for a week and was going to keep $500 for himself. W.R. fired him, and he thanked me for letting him know. We became friends after that."

Whatever version is correct, it can be said that this "lovely blonde kitten of a girl," as an old family friend describes her, had just turned twenty-one, and the turn left her on the threshold of a career more amazing than any she had dreamed.

As a Brooklyn girl, the daughter of a local judge, Marion Douras had been educated at a Catholic convent in Hastings, New York, and at an early date aspired to a job on the stage—

like Sybil and Eleanor and Millicent before her. The details of her early life are lacking, but in 1916 she was dancing as Marion Davies in the chorus of *Chu Chin Chow*, where she attracted Florenz Ziegfeld's attention. Two years later she was in the *Follies*.

At this time, it must be remembered, Hearst was fifty-five. He was the proprietor of a chain of newspapers, a prominent if unsuccessful figure in the nation's political life, and already considered a remote and fairly improbable personality by the general public. He was accustomed to having people treat him with respect and deference, if not fear, and consequently he was totally unprepared for the reception he got from Marion.

"She crawled up into his lap, ruffled his hair, and called him daddy," the old family friend reports.

This may or may not be true in a literal sense, but the effect was the same. Marion would be grateful for any help in her career he could give her, but at the same time she refused to be awed by him. She treated him like a member of the family—her family. And he loved it.

The first result was Miss Davies' emergence as a motion-picture star virtually overnight. She appeared that same year in a pair of productions which were mercifully silent. These events were celebrated with fireworks and editorial huzzahs in all the Hearst papers, which seemed to have discovered her simultaneously.

The second result of Marion's entry into Hearst's life was a gradual "estrangement" from his wife. It was a separation that has been widely misunderstood.

When Millicent observed what had resulted from her effort to help the pretty Brooklyn dancer, she was neither indignant nor distraught. She acted on those high principles so like Phebe's. If bringing another woman into her husband's life had been her own fault, her responsibility, she would take the consequences and not attempt to hold him within the confines of their marriage. On the other hand, she absolutely refused to divorce him.

She arrived at these conclusions during a confused four-year

period in which at first she could not understand Hearst's behavior, and sometimes appeared even to doubt his sanity. On his
part, Hearst seemed to be torn by indecision. He had nothing but
respect and affection for his wife, yet the freely given, spontane-
ous love of a beautiful girl nearly thirty-five years younger must
have been both flattering and stimulating. She urged him to get
a divorce, if Millicent would not grant him one, and Hearst made
the attempt.

For nearly a year, according to a reliable source, he had
detectives trailing Mrs. Hearst, in the expectation of finding
some indiscretion upon which to base a suit. He might as well
have tried to find a moral flaw in one of the innumerable
Madonnas in his collection. Millicent's private life was as spotless
as his own mother's.

At last, about 1922, Hearst seems to have come to a decision.
He would do anything in the world for Marion, he told her,
except divorce his wife. There ensued a long series of stormy
scenes in which Marion, not acting now, gave some emotional
performances which might have earned her an Oscar if they
could have been filmed. But Hearst was adamant.

What influenced his decision was not only Millicent's impeccable reputation, but numerous other considerations, financial and
legal, and the effect on his growing sons of what would undoubtedly have been a messy divorce.

Thus in 1922 the odd triangle entered upon its final and most
unusual phase. The fiction of the marriage was maintained, Mrs.
Hearst assumed her position whenever it was advisable on occasions of state, the boys were able to spend some time with their
parents during the summer, and Hearst could do whatever else
he wished with his private life.

It was a satisfactory arrangement after a few years, when
emotions had cooled a bit and all hands had time to get used
to it. During the infrequent periods when Millicent was at San
Simeon, Marion was elsewhere. Those few guests who found
themselves entertained by both hostesses at different times were
expected to exhibit no surprise. If Marion ever felt a victim of

very strange circumstances, she could always remind herself that Hearst was really paying her the highest compliment a man could extend to a woman in such a situation, by making the great and near-great of the world who came to San Simeon accept her unofficial status.

There were no open conflicts between the two women, and only minor ones behind the scenes. Emile Gauvreau, one of Hearst's editors, notes that in the early days of the New York *Mirror*, when he was editor and A. J. Kobler was publisher, Miss Davies and Mrs. Hearst both contributed suggestions from time to time on how to run the paper. Kobler listened to Marion; Gauvreau was in charge of Millicent. "Comparing notes," says Mr. Gauvreau, "we found that the recommendations we absorbed never seemed to agree."

Mrs. Hearst, for example, thought the *Mirror* would look more newsy if it had a quantity of small ten-line informational items. She also thought Hearst was making a mistake in his current effort to do away with American ambassadorships.

"Willie feels very strongly about it," Gauvreau reports her as saying, "but it would certainly be an awful blow to social life."

Marion's suggestions were often more practical. She arranged for the *Mirror* to get an exclusive on the confessions of Alma Rubens, the silent-picture star, which resulted in a 65,000 circulation rise for the paper.

The Hearst press in general continued to publicize both the women. Marion's abilities were extolled and her friends and enemies rewarded in equal measure. Millicent's charities were well advertised, and the chronicling of her social life was more than adequate.

By special cable from Paris, for example, came the shattering news on June 26, 1922: "All Paris traditions were broken today by Mrs. William Randolph Hearst, who defied the time-honored custom in the French social world of leaving Paris immediately after the Grand Prix."

This coup d'état was accomplished, it turned out, by means

of an exclusive luncheon at the Hotel Crillon, "thus prolonging the social season by one day." With a fine disregard for her husband's political feelings, the luncheon was given in the League of Nations Room, which had once been President Wilson's sitting room. Yet there was an ironic compensation in the fact that this place which had once sheltered the one man in American political life who was consistently against Hearst had now become a part of Mrs. Hearst's Crillon suite. The walls which had once observed the idealistic struggle of one man to save the world, in a later redecorated era now looked upon a Hearst-financed luncheon which was "notable for the brilliance of the toilettes," as the Universal Service staff correspondent put it before he was overcome by emotion.

A little later, upon returning from a two-month stay in Europe, Mrs. Hearst found herself met on the *Leviathan* at quarantine by a delegation consisting of her husband, Commissioner Grover Whalen, and Mayor John F. Hylan's secretary, John Sinnott. The emissaries from City Hall, where Honest John sat enthroned largely by virtue of Hearst's efforts in his behalf, had come to announce formally to Mrs. Hearst that she had been appointed Honorary Deputy Commissioner of Correction. Mrs. Hearst replied that she was eager to take up her new duties, and implied indiscreetly that there seemed to be quite a bit of correcting to do.

In later years, the Hearst papers in New York devoted themselves mostly to publicizing Millicent's favorite charity, the New York Free Milk Fund for Babies. The other papers, however, never hesitated to join in, because the real worth of this philanthropy was well recognized and appreciated, and everybody knew it had been initially organized and kept alive by Millicent and no one else.

Other papers solemnly recognized her official position as Hearst's wife. As late as October 8, 1930, the New York *Times* reported that the Hearsts had entertained at a formal dinner marking the opening of their Sands Point house. The formidable guest list, headed by President and Mrs. Coolidge, included such

New York society names as Young, Swope, Astor and Stewart, along with the Brisbanes and Cissy Patterson.

While the marriage had become no more than a social pretense, the remarkable thing about it was the survival of a real affection between the two principals. It was remarkable, that is, under the circumstances. From the standpoint of the individuals themselves, they enjoyed each other's company, as they always had, and invariably found a good deal to talk about. Until he died, Mrs. Hearst spoke of him affectionately as "Willie," or "the old scoundrel," and although only those closest to them knew it, he called her by telephone nearly every day of his life for years, and frequently thereafter until his lips could no longer form the high-pitched, querulous "Millie?"

What was it that flared between Hearst and Marion Davies, so strong it made them faithful and devoted to each other for more than three decades? Presumably we shall never know, because Miss Davies' lips are legally sealed and Hearst would never have discussed it if he had lived to be twice as old.

Nevertheless, it was Hearst himself who provided the most apt summary of the great romance, in the late twenties, when one of his closest advisers urged him for reasons of morality and policy to forsake Marion and go back to his wife.

"I'm not saying it's right," he replied, the cold light coming into his eyes. "I'm saying that it *is*."

There could hardly be a better explanation. In spite of the difference in their ages, the unbroken marriage, a frequent clash of temperaments, and all the other things that stood in the way, their relationship *was*, and from the beginning there was never more than a suggestion that anything save death would end it.

Marion idolized him, but she was capable of temperamental outbursts of anger. A friend who was present at a Christmas party remembers that when the gift of a diamond brooch from Hearst proved to be something less than she had expected, a few choice words passed between them, after which Marion calmly tossed the offending gems out an open window.

They quarreled now and then over who should pay for the

orchids in the Santa Monica beach house, as Ilka Chase recalls, and one who was present in the early days of Marion's moviemaking remembers that she sometimes flared at Hearst in furious bursts of temper, giving him several thousand words on one subject or another, with her face only a few inches from his own, while he mopped himself with a crisp white handkerchief and tried in vain embarrassment to calm her.

Some who knew them both well think they might have ended their relationship if it had not been for the stubborn, dominant side of Hearst's character. He had pledged himself to the arrangement, it was said, and would never back down, particularly if he were opposed by others.

This may be doubted, however, because in the immortal words of the old cliché, to know Marion was to love her. She was a completely frank and uninhibited girl, addicted to fourletter words, irreverent and unimpressed, warm and lovable, inordinately fond of fun and luxury, the very model of a model extrovert. She was wonderful company, a woman liked by everyone from her hairdresser to such a professional curmudgeon as Bernard Shaw.

Blanche Patch, Shaw's secretary for thirty years, reports in her memoirs that a Hearst emissary once invited G.B.S. to "a small and entirely private dinner to Marion Davies in one of the private rooms at the Savoy," an occasion Mr. Hearst himself would attend if he could get to England in time. According to Miss Patch, Shaw scribbled on the invitation: "I never heard of Marion Davies, and would not go to a little dinner at the Savoy if she were all the 11,000 virgins of St. Ursula rolled into one. I am no good for games of that sort." A little later he added: "I have now ascertained that Miss D. is a film star. Do you seriously believe that these young and beautiful ladies want to meet old gentlemen at 65 and 72, or to be made an excuse for their meeting one another? If so, you must be more innocent than the wooliest lamb in Hamley's toy shop. I just won't go. Mr. Hearst and I, old as we are, have still gumption enough to be able to

meet without making Miss Davies yawn and spoiling your fes-
tivities."

In vain the Hearst intermediary argued that his employer
had "expressed more interest" in Shaw's work than that of any
living writer, but apparently someone took G.B.S. aside at a later
time and explained, because five years after the London snub
the Shaws visited America and San Simeon was their only overnight stop on this country's soil. Hearst sent one of his own
planes to pick them up and fly them to the Enchanted Hill.

Miss Patch says that G.B.S. "enjoyed Mr. Hearst as a social
phenomenon and liked him as a man," an enthusiasm shared by
his wife. As for Marion, the visitors came away bearing pictures
of her, and Shaw remarked to Miss Patch: "Marion is by far
the most attractive of the stars who are not really eighteen."

Everyone who came to San Simeon liked Marion, including
Hearst's own sons, who must have found the situation a little
awkward sometimes, when they grew old enough to understand. One of Hearst's advisers once asked the oldest son,
George, why he called his father's friend "Aunty Marion."

George appeared honestly surprised. "What would *you* call
her if you were in my place?" he inquired.

If the lady had a fault, it was her fondness for liquid con-
viviality. As Miss Chase put it, Marion was "quite a girl for the
golden wine; it matched her hair. . . ." Marion herself is said
to have remarked facetiously, "I'd like to drown in a barrel full
of gin."

Hearst sometimes detailed a visiting executive to keep a fa-
therly eye on Marion so that she would not overdo this indulgence, but it was usually her custom to take a bottle and a few
friends after dinner and retire to the ladies' room, where they
would sit and exchange reminiscences and gossip.

Miss Chase, who was present at one or two of these gin
klatches, remembers that Marion told them a story designed to
illustrate the beauty of having friends. She told it with the charming stutter that crept into her voice when she was animated.

"One night there was nobody here but W.R. and old sourpuss C-C-Coolidge and Brisbane," she began, her eyes dim with the memory of it. "They didn't pay any attention to me all through dinner, wouldn't even join me in a little champagne, so I c-c-c-came in here all b-b-by myself and looked in the mirror, and I remember saying, 'Marion, you p-p-poor kid, it's a shame, they're a bunch of d-d-dull old bastards!' "

"What were they talking about?" Miss Chase inquired.

"Their g-g-g-goddamn circulation," Marion replied bitterly.

Miss Davies was not inclined to be impressed by names and titles, and she treated Hearst like another human being instead of an awesome public figure, which may have been one source of his fascination for her. Miss Chase recalls that at luncheon one day in Marion's small palace of a dressing room on the Metro lot, Hearst was late and the star called him, finding him in conference with Louis B. Mayer. They debated briefly over the wire as to whether he could come, until Marion cried in mild irritation, "Oh, c-c-come on over, W.R., and I'll give you a b-b-b-ig k-k-kiss." And she added affectionately, hanging up, "The old b-b-bum."

The master of San Simeon arrived a few minutes later.

Their life together was more or less open, but it was nevertheless subject to rumors so persistent that they are accepted as fact in some quarters today. One was the story that they had several children, the number depending on the imagination of the narrator, but always put forth as something everyone "on the inside" knew about.

Hearst took notice of these rumors in his will by denying specifically and truthfully that he had fathered any other children than his five sons. He foresaw that even with this denial there was a strong possibility that imaginary progeny might turn up in court to take a small slice, at least, from his estate. If anyone could prove himself an offspring of his, said Hearst in the will, with typical Hearstian humor, he would be entitled to an award of one dollar. No claimants appeared when the will was probated.

A friend of Marion's, denying this story for the hundredth time, said with justifiable frankness, "Why, if Marion had had any kids, everyone in the world would have known about it, she'd have been so proud and happy."

The rumor had its roots in Marion's generosity. One of her housekeepers had two small children to bring up, and Marion informally adopted what remained of this family. She sent the children to school and gave them clothes, toys and trinkets until they grew up. Hearst often added to these gifts; he was very fond of children. Sometimes when they were asked at school or in a playmate's house where they had acquired some particularly expensive item, one of the children would reply innocently, "Oh, Mr. Hearst gave it to me." Thus it was easy for the gossips to multiply Hearst's already substantial family into something only a sultan could have produced.

Another rumor which grew out of Marion's generosity was the unjustified reputation for extreme virility which attended Hearst even in his old age. This came about because Miss Davies, not at all inhibited by the memory of her own experience with Millicent, took pleasure in helping young ladies break into the movies. Often she would tell these discoveries of hers, "Now l-l-look, k-k-kid, what you n-n-need for this screen t-t-test is a new d-d-dress and the things to g-g-g-go with it." Then she would send the hopeful to one of the stores where she had charge accounts, with instructions on what to buy and the admonition to "j-j-just charge it t-t-to W.R. He w-w-won't mind."

Usually W.R. never knew of these incidents, but the natural conclusion drawn by the salesgirls and credit managers who dealt with Marion's protégées was that Hearst kept a veritable stable of delectable young houris whom he bent to his sybaritic will.

Marion's engaging stutter, accompanied by an ingratiating blinking of her eyes, was absent when she played a scene for the cameras. What was present, however, was the dead hand of Hearst, who killed her career, in the opinion of a good many people, with the best of intentions. His intention, of course, was to make her an idol of the screen, and to this end he made her study French, diction and whatever else she needed, compelling her to work hard. He trained her himself in many scenes, and at times devoted the intent concentration to her that he gave to his papers.

The trouble came about because Marion, with a sure instinct of her own, wanted to play tough blondes, which she did perfectly. She yearned for roles like Sadie Thompson in *Rain* and the *Diamond Lil* character which Mae West immortalized. She considered, in fact, that Mae had pirated this idea from her, resulting in the famous boycott of Miss West by the Hearst papers.

Hearst wouldn't let Marion play tough blondes. He wanted her to play sweet young things, like the heroines of her early successes, *Little Old New York* and *Peg o' My Heart*. These were appropriate at the time, but even ingenues grow up, and in later years Marion was ready for something with more meat in it. She never got it. Hearst refused to let her grow up, and when the days of her picture-making were past, she could only sit entranced at San Simeon while the celluloid glories of the early days were unreeled over and over.

The girl who could have been a versatile light comedienne was still playing fluffy young things in the new era of sound, and Hearst could not be kept off the set even by the red light which shines over a sound-stage door, meaning that words are being caught for posterity and even a sheriff with a foreclosure notice cannot enter. Hearst slipped in at the first opportunity, a symbol of devotion that stifled while it flattered.

Hearst gave Marion all the material things any woman could desire in this world, including a supreme gesture of patriotism in the form of an American flag made of diamonds, sapphires and rubies, but what really counted was his devotion. It had nothing to do with wealth or power or conventional morality or anything but real emotion. It was probably the most honest emotion Hearst ever had.

In return, Marion gave him an affectionate loyalty and devotion of her own not to be found in a good many marriages, let alone in such an arrangement as she lived. And though she enjoyed Hearst's wealth to the fullest, her motives were far from mercenary, as she demonstrated when she gave him a million dollars to tide him over a financial rough spot, an act which profoundly touched him, probably more than anything anyone else ever did for him.

If Hearst did much for Marion, it can be said with equal justice that Marion did a great deal for him. She made him grow up, gave him the few really human contacts a man in his position could hope to enjoy, and proved to be the one woman in a million who could have shared that position without avarice, vanity or inordinate ambition.

Marion may not have been an angel among women, and her Elizabethan vocabulary may not have endeared her to the servants or to some proper guests, and it may even be said that she was the apotheosis of lilies of the field, but she was a human being, and she brought a quality into Hearst's life it might not otherwise have had. She was (and is, one presumes) what a woman who is not her friend reluctantly describes as "a thoroughly sympathetic character."

On this the defender of Hearst's love life may well rest his case.

# CHAPTER FOUR

## HOW HE RAN HIS BUSINESS

THE BUSINESS of William Randolph Hearst was selling printed paper in various formats. As a paper salesman, he was one of the best in the field, but as a salesman of the ideas the papers contained, he was only moderately successful. He was not the powerful force in American journalism he imagined himself to be, nor was he the abject failure his enemies hopefully described him as being.

It was Hearst's own idea to be a paper salesman instead of a publisher like most of his contemporaries. He made numerous ringing pronouncements on the importance of news, but in reality circulation was his god and he put it before everything else, consequently "news" became only the commodity that made circulation. And since the Hearst circulation depended on sin, crime and corruption, the scope of the news in his papers was for the most part limited to these subjects.

There was nothing very novel in this formula; it had been extant in American journalism for nearly a hundred years before Hearst came on the scene. He merely perfected the art and kept on practicing it in the twentieth century long after most of the press had become institutional in character.

It must be remembered that Hearst was strikingly different in one respect from every other editor of importance who preceded him. Without exception his predecessors were men who had begun at the bottom, most of them in direst poverty, and created their newspapers out of the sheer force of their own personalities. Hearst applied his personality to an already existing method, and he made the combination stick with his

inherited wealth. In brief, he showed the publishing business
what could be done with a formula if millions of dollars were
applied to it.

"There is no substitute for circulation," Hearst proclaimed
when his first newspaper was leaping ahead at the rate of a thousand new buyers every week. In other words, quality is no substitute for quantity, a pragmatic viewpoint not unknown to
some present-day publishers with better reputations than
Hearst's.

It is true he added a few things to the original formula. We
are indebted to him for the modern comic strip, for the elevation
of gossip and gossipers to equal status with news and its reporters, and for the ascendancy of the political-opinion column
over both.

In general, however, the net result has not inspired enthusiasm
anywhere outside the most partisan circles. It has always been
easy to find politicians who were willing to cite Hearst as one
with Washington and Lincoln, and many of his fellow publishers
have been reluctant to criticize so prominent a member of the
club, but aside from these, there have been few admirers of the
Hearst method of making newspapers.

It was a method which Ambrose Bierce sourly observed had
"all the reality of masturbation," and Stephen Crane remarked:
"I see no difference between the [New York] *Journal* and Ham-
merstein's roof garden. You get the blonde with the tin can in
her gullet and the comic speaker and the song about mother's
wayward boy in both shows." Crane thought Oscar Hammer-
stein was the only entrepreneur who understood the popular
mind as well as Hearst.

Always Hearst conducted his business in the grand manner
of the very wealthy. Where other publishers might lie awake
nights, tormented by rising costs and the inroads of competitors,
Hearst even in his later days could tell someone like Cornelius
Vanderbilt, Jr., who came to ask him about starting a newspaper in Los Angeles: "[This] is not the place for you. Here's
what I want you to do. I am about to start a tabloid in New

York. I will hire you as an editor. You know nothing about editing a newspaper but your name is worth thirty thousand dollars a year to me. You will leave tonight for New York and report to Arthur Brisbane. My secretary will attend to your transportation. Good-by and good luck."

He could not understand why Vanderbilt turned down such a magnificent offer.

The newspapers themselves changed little along the way, nor did Hearst's method, except as he broadened the stage of his operations and could no longer deal with his properties at first hand.

In the early days of the New York *Journal*, Hearst functioned like any other editor, presiding at daily conferences with the staff and listening to opinions about policies and handling of the news. He was polite but he usually did what he pleased regardless of what the other editors thought. At first he was a little self-conscious about asserting himself before a large group and asked whether five or six at a time wouldn't do as well. "Too many give me stage fright," he added.

But those were the early, *early* days. Before long he could not only oppose a newspaper staff of any size with equanimity, but came in time to consider his will a mightier instrument than the governments of nations.

As his empire grew, his conferences narrowed down to those with executives, and in the end he was running his newspapers, radio stations and 31,000 employees from San Simeon. There he carried on day-to-day business by means of his supersecretary, Joe Willicombe, the reporter who found himself in one of the country's toughest jobs because he knew shorthand. Willicombe's system was admirably simple. He screened everything, reducing mail, telephone messages, telegrams and memos to short paragraphs, typed and numbered on a clipsheet.

Then it was his job to find Hearst. He seemed to know by instinct where the old master might be—in bed, playing croquet, on the tennis court, or floating lazily about the pool. Whatever occupied him, he would stop doing it long enough to go over

Willicombe's list with his soft black pencil, writing in his careless hand in the space under each paragraph the decisions affecting salaries of men he had never seen, deciding quarrels, making policy, hiring and firing, and directing make-up and news treatment on papers three thousand miles away.

Old pictures show him happily engaged in this occupation, using a croquet mallet as a desk, curled up comfortably in a lawn chair, or sitting on the arm of an antique sofa.

It was also his custom to lay out a week's editions of one paper on the carpet at San Simeon and critically tear them apart in the margins with his soft scrawl. They were then bound up and shipped to the editor of the paper, who was expected to carry out the suggestions explicitly, or leave town. If he were obtuse enough to do otherwise, a second batch of marked copies would arrive in six weeks or so, accompanied by a note: "When I remark about the condition of this masthead six times more, perhaps something will be done about it."

No one ignored the tone of such a communiqué unless he was prepared to sit out his contract in idleness or had another job in mind.

There was a world of difference between the broad pronouncements of policy, often written as editorials but addressed as letters, and the terse orders which went out over the teletypes or the regular wires. In the former, Hearst appeared to be portraying himself as he wished to be seen; in the latter, he was the strong, ruthless man of power accustomed to being obeyed, though he never raised his voice and prefaced his commands with "Please . . ."

Anyone who examines the voluminous selection of Hearst's writings which the San Francisco *Examiner* published privately in 1948 cannot help being impressed by the monotony of his opinions as well as their variety—the reiteration of already well-iterated ideas, and the wide, sometimes almost ludicrous difference between what was proclaimed and what was done in the Hearst newspapers.

Hearst wrote like Brisbane, or maybe it was Brisbane who

wrote like Hearst. In either case their writing styles were indistinguishable, consisting of short, punchy sentences and employing only the simplest of vocabularies. Both men insisted this was the only way to write if ideas were to be transmitted clearly and accurately to the reader. Neither gave the reader much intellectual credit, whether he was a regular member in good standing of the "masses" who supposedly constituted Hearst-paper readership, or one of the high-priced, presumably educated executives who ran the papers.

One of the last general letters of editorial instruction Hearst sent to his managing editors before he retired to Beverly Hills in 1947 was a short treatise on the short sentence. It was written in the abbreviated paragraph style characteristic of the Brisbane and Hearst columns and of the editorials in their papers. W.R. wrote:

"I have asked a number of times to have the reporters and correspondents on our papers use short sentences.

"The fault in most newspaper writing is that the reporter tries to tell everything he knows in one sentence.

"The result is hard reading and often hard understanding of what is written.

"It is easy to break up the articles into short sentences and to paragraph more, and so make the article more easily read and more easily understood.

"Please ask the reporters and copyreaders to write in short sentences, and please insist that they do so, and please employ reporters and copyreaders who will do so."

In such succinct terms, Hearst asserted himself for more than sixty years in what must certainly have been the most voluminous tide of instruction to emanate from any publisher in journalistic history. He had opinions about everything. Considering only the ideas which had to do with editorial policy, their content was remarkable. These were samples:

"Let me say a brief word of the intent and character of my publications. You have probably sometimes heard them described as extremely radical. I do not think that they are. I do not think that I am very radical. Indeed, I sometimes think that as I have grown older and slowed down a bit, I am really not radical enough. . . ." (This in a speech at a banquet given in his honor at Baltimore; the date, April 15, 1923.)

"Absolute independence of all political, financial or other influences which might use any news service or newspaper for their own advantage has been one of the greatest assets of the Hearst Papers and News Service. The object of our institution is to serve the public only and to present the news without bias or prejudice of any kind."

"I think the public demands in a newspaper both information and entertainment. That entertainment is not entirely supplied by features. It should largely be found in the news."

"A good many people who object to the attention that newspapers give to their private affairs forget that their affairs have become a public interest and public importance through their own fault entirely, and through no fault of the newspapers. A newspaper's right and duty are to print public facts in which the public is interested, whether the individuals concerned are public or private."

". . . The mass of pictures in a newspaper should have definite news value or else they should not be in the newspaper."

"It is the lack of judgment in the use of big type which is chiefly responsible for the protest against it."

"Try to be conspicuously accurate in everything, pictures as well as text. Truth is not only stranger than fiction, it is much more interesting."

"Newspapers make countless unnecessary enemies by unnecessary attacks in the news columns as well as the editorial columns. . . . Anyone can say that a thing is wrong, but to say how it can be made right is more difficult. But to propose right courses and to offer helpful and kindly suggestions and to extend praise for good work are much more beneficial both to the public and the paper than haphazard criticism."

"News and editorial character are built on reliability of statement. We cannot hope to build advertising on any other basis.

No man who misrepresents facts must be allowed on our newspapers. Honesty is a form of common sense."

"Make a paper for the NICEST KIND OF PEOPLE—for the great middle class. . . . Omit things that will offend nice people. Avoid coarseness and slang and a low tone. The more sensational news can be told if it is written properly. Make the paper helpful and kindly. Don't scold and forever complain and attack in your news columns. Leave that to the editorial page. Be fair and impartial. Don't make a paper for Democrats or Republicans, or Independent Leaguers. Make a paper for all the people and give unbiased news of ALL CREEDS AND PARTIES. . . . Don't allow exaggeration. It is a cheap and ineffective substitute for real interest. Reward reporters who can make THE TRUTH interesting, and weed out those who cannot. Make your headlines clear and concise statements of interesting facts. . . ."

"I cannot emphasize enough the importance of an impressively illustrated and brilliantly printed paper."

"My great difficulty, as an editor, with columnists is not that these columnists do not know enough but that they know too much. . . ."

"Please try, when interviewing or photographing reputable people, to make the interview or photograph as pleasing as possible. We want our representative to be welcome. . . . People are often afraid of the newspaper reporter and photographer primarily because something unpleasant which develops in the interview or in the photograph will be seized upon as the 'best news' by the reporter—or the editor."

A multitude of other gems could be gathered from this dream stuff, all of it polite and high-minded and redolent of virtue. And only the capital letters, characteristic of Hearst editorial and column writing, would suggest anything of the jungle atmosphere of Hearst newspaper shops or the unreality of Hearst newspaper method.

For a man who had written so much, Hearst was surprisingly

humble, at least in public, when in 1940 he took over the column "Today" which Brisbane had turned out seven days a week for thirty-nine years. It had lapsed for a while after his death, while Hearst tried to find a successor, but on March 7 it resumed again as the publisher's own, unsigned and with a new title, "In The News," in the left-hand column of page one, its customary position.

Responding to an inquiry from *Editor and Publisher*, the trade journal, Hearst wired his general manager, J. D. Gortatowsky: "Tell *Editor and Publisher* that I am writing the column to inaugurate it. I am not particularly anxious to take on the extra work, but if the column proves by good fortune to be a success, I will continue it. In the meanwhile, as the story goes, 'Please do not shoot the organist. He is doing the best he can.'"

This last was typical Hearstian humor.

Answering another query, from *Time* magazine, asking whether Hearst really wrote it, the old man answered: "Yes, I write the column, it is nothing to be proud of. I am not a columnist exactly. I have always written my stuff as editorials. But a column gives one a freer style. . . . I do not think my column compares with Brisbane, nor do I expect it to. I do not use a byline as I do not know how long I will continue to do the column. . . . I have never written a column before. This is my first offense. I urge that in extenuation."

For all his modesty, however, Hearst had an author's sensitivity, as he showed five years before in an "editorial letter" addressed to Paul Mallon, the Washington correspondent, who had nettled Hearst by asking him whether he wrote all the articles he signed. "That, sir, is not a very complimentary question," Hearst replied tartly.

"I am a professional newspaperman, Mr. Mallon, and I have been working at the newspaper business—not playing with it, but working at it—day and night for over fifty years. Would I not be a 'dumb cluck,' as the saying goes, if I did not know the rudiments of my trade by this time? Of course I write my signed articles, and many more that I do not sign. . . . Furthermore, Mr. Mallon, I do not think it is such a trick to write. Anybody who can think can write. It does not take much practice to put thoughts into words. All you have got to do is to have some thoughts which are worth putting into words."

There was scarcely a time in his life when Hearst did not consider that he had an abundance of such thoughts. Young as he was when his mother took him on his first tour of Europe, he listened to Phebe's urgings and worked on the letters to his father until they sounded like a travelogue at one of the better lyceums.

For the first decade of his career as a publisher, however, he was shy about his writing, and never signed his name to anything until he became a self-made war correspondent in his self-made war amid the beaches and jungles of Cuba.

Once the spigot was turned on, there was no turning it off. Hearst wrote prolifically all the rest of his life, a steady flow of editorials, memos, "editorial letters," letters of instruction, articles, and finally columns. His notes for this output were made wherever he happened to be and on whatever came to hand—old envelopes, pieces of paper, margins of books and magazines and newspapers, or even in shorthand on the convenient cuff of Joe Willicombe, who took them down while he walked. He wrote everywhere except at a desk, which he loathed, and at all hours of the day and night. An unconsciously boring dinner guest relating a story might find himself chilled to see Hearst fish around in his pocket until he found a stray scrap of paper on which he would begin to compose an editorial.

Hearst believed his night thoughts were often his best. "A stray thought is likely to come swirling out of the darkness like a bat and light on you," he once remarked poetically.

He credited Brisbane with giving him the courage to write. It was Brisbane who coined that ringing message of hope, "Anybody can write," which Hearst hurled peevishly back at Mallon so many years later. "People forget to write simply enough," the master of the banal phrase added to his original dictum, and he urged Hearst to write his own editorials.

W.R. never got out from under Brisbane's hypnotic influence on his style. He might deride "Artie" about other things, and even turn on him if the occasion justified, but when he wrote he could not help writing like the Great Thinker, and the two of them thus set the editorial style of the Hearst papers. It was the reign of the pithy platitude.

In spite of the fact that he treated them with an impersonal ruthlessness, Hearst respected the professional abilities of the reporters who gathered the news for his papers, and he got a kind of perverse pleasure in 1936 when he scored a clean news beat on them, and on every reporter in the world, with an exclusive cable from London carrying the first unqualified statement that Edward VIII had determined to abdicate the throne and marry Mrs. Simpson. He did not sign his story, but the style was unmistakable.

He had the grace to acknowledge, in admitting his authorship, that he had a distinct advantage over the common garden variety of reporter. "I am not any better reporter than my colleagues —in fact, generally not as good," he said, "but sometimes I have contacts and opportunities which enable me to get news that other correspondents cannot secure. . . . Most of our correspondents, had they been in possession of the facts, could have constructed as good a dispatch or a better one."

Nevertheless it was no secret in the Hearst organization that the Chief was enormously pleased with himself. Some of those who worked with him believe nothing he ever did on the editorial side pleased him as much.

Like that other "greatest American of them all," Colonel Robert R. McCormick, Hearst had a definite flair for the mechanical side of newspaper production. Their talents were slightly different. McCormick's ran to invention, a talent he came by honestly from his forebear Cyrus. Hearst was an idea man. He had an encyclopedic understanding of printing machinery and he was often smitten with ideas on how to improve it. These he entrusted to his old friend George Pancoast, superintendent of the mechanical department of all Hearst newspapers. Pancoast, an inventive genius in his own right, then worked out the Chief's ideas and added a few of his own.

One of their first collaborations occurred in 1897, after Hearst had come home from London impressed by the use of hand-set type to make a "fudge," or insertion of late bulletins on a front page already on the press. He saw that this would be a decided asset to a highly competitive paper like his New York *Journal* if a linotype could be used for the job. He gave the problem to Pancoast, who solved it in time to beat every other newspaper by fifteen minutes on the outcome of the Corbett-Fitzsimmons fight in Carson City.

The stories of Hearst-Pancoast collaboration are plentiful but fall mostly into the category of shop talk except for the astounding and somewhat theatrical feat they perpetrated upon their competitors at the Panama-Pacific Exposition of 1915 in San Francisco.

A few months before the Exposition opened, Hearst and Pancoast were mousing about the grounds, according to their faithful biographer, Mrs. Older, when the master voiced a complaint that could have come from no one else.

"George," he said, "we are asking the world to come here. What can the *Examiner* show?"

George confessed that the world would probably have to continue living in benighted ignorance of the Monarch of the Dailies. It was too late to set up an exhibit.

Even now it is possible to imagine Hearst's soft, high, silky voice saying to his old friend, gently suggesting the impossible, "Won't you build one of your presses to exhibit?"

Pancoast knew better than to say no. Probably it never occurred to him. As he put it, obliquely but accurately, "The Chief will forgive a lie, anything except not trying."

By "your presses" Hearst had meant the big twelve-cylinder Universal Unit presses which Pancoast had invented and patented. This giant of the day was what Pancoast suggested that the Hoe Company in New York should build and ship out to

San Francisco—in four and a half months. He added that this was Mr. Hearst's wish, and apparently the Hoe executives knew what side their best account was buttered on, because they did the job and thereby set a record. Pancoast then added to the miracle by setting up the six carloads of machinery in fourteen days.

When the Exposition opened, Hearst had his heart's desire. The *Examiner's* huge press, set up in the Palace of Machinery, turned out a 66-page special issue of 250,000 copies, and for days thereafter printed daily editions of 300,000 copies. This, naturally, was the largest production of any newspaper in the world.

It might have been supposed that Hearst would stand about admiring his handiwork. But it was like him that he had already passed on to other surpassing endeavors. Exposition visitors saw his tall, big-shouldered figure stooping, squatting and bending about the fountains and buildings of San Francisco's gift to the neo-Grecian revival in fairs and carnivals. He was infatuated with beauty, and, like his mother before him, he was trying to capture some of it for himself. Not a single rare picture to exhibit and cherish, however. Phebe had ended with the largest and best private collection of paintings in San Francisco. Her son's photographs were the best anyone ever took of that elegant salute to the nineteenth century in Baghdad-by-the-Bay.

II

To study Hearst's way with newspapers and magazines is an excursion into another world, a kind of journalistic interplanetary travel, in which old rules of gravity and cause and effect are suspended.

The limitations and standards imposed on other publishers were largely inoperative in Hearst's case, and so were the conventional ethical codes. Consequently it is idle to attempt to judge and compare Hearst papers with others. They were so much the product of their owner's mind and personality that they became like daily letters from Hearst to the American people. Some of those people couldn't wait to get to the post office. Others returned the gaudy missives unopened to the dead-letter office.

But it would be equally frivolous to dismiss these papers because they failed to attain the distinction of the New York Times. Like Hearst's affection for Miss Davies, it wasn't a question of whether they were right; they *were*. They lived and breathed and exuded sheer personality, and if in the end they were not the potent influence Hearst hoped and imagined they were, it was not for any lack of effort.

Although they thrive and flourish today in another incarnation, it is proper to speak of them in the past tense, because as long as Hearst lived, they were his personal voice. The image he created may remain in shadow, but the substance is no longer there. Thus by understanding his newspapers, a better understanding of Hearst may be possible.

The striking fact which at once emerges is the fanatical consistency of those papers in some respects, and their absurd inconsistency in others. Nothing could better express their one-man character. Hearst himself managed to stand foursquare on both sides of every great public issue during his lifetime, a feat made easier by the truism that politics has many faces, and yesterday's friends are today's enemies.

The question has always been this: Did Hearst mean anything he said in his papers, or did he use them only in a cynical, calculating way for personal aggrandizement, money and political advantage? Was it true conviction or only hypocrisy?

The question will never be settled to the satisfaction of either side, but what follows is an attempt at a more balanced answer by means of a fresh examination of old evidence in the light of new facts and the perspective provided by Hearst's death.

The whole fantastic episode of the San Francisco *Examiner*, for example, becomes more reasonable when it is placed in the context of the times, of journalistic history, and of Hearst's own stage of growth.

It was not the starveling little sheet that some have supposed it, given by an indulgent father to his playboy son as an elaborate toy. It was the foremost Democratic newspaper in California, and a valuable propaganda weapon in the hands of George Hearst, one of the state's leading Democratic politicians.

The *Examiner* had a background of violence, like many of the newspapers of the day. At the time George Hearst acquired it, its editor was a firebrand named George Penn Johnson, who had once shot and killed a state senator in a duel on Angel Island. William Moss, its first publisher when it began in 1865, had so offended the sachems of Sacramento with a previous venture that they contrived to suppress it.

When George Hearst bought the *Examiner* in 1880 he hoped to use it as a lever to get him the nomination for governor. It failed to do the job—George's friend, General William Stoneman, got the call—but at the same time, with Hearst money behind it, the paper attained a stature it had never enjoyed before. The new owner had no ambitions to be a publisher; he was content to let others run his property. They were doing so at a substantial loss, simply because no one required them to show a profit.

George was astute enough to see that the paper enhanced his own prestige and that it could be his personal voice in the endless California argument between the monopoly of the railroad builders and the monopoly of those not fortunate enough to have a piece of the railroads.

That was where the *Examiner* stood in 1885 when William, a Harvard junior of twenty-two, wrote the now famous letter to his father, urging that he be allowed to take over the *Examiner* and run it. The inducement he offered could hardly have excited George. His son proposed ways and means to make the paper show a good profit. George was not particularly concerned as to whether or not it made money.

Hearst was aware that his proposal was a brash one. He did not release this now much-quoted letter from his files until nearly a half century later, first in Mrs. Older's biography, and four years afterward—with some curious discrepancies between these two texts—in an anthology, *A Treasury of the World's Great Letters*, edited by M. Lincoln Schuster.

The latter was accompanied by a historical note from Hearst, presumably contained in a letter to Mr. Schuster, which said in part: "At that time my father was the only person in the world who, in my modest opinion, knew more than I did, although I have learned since, to my consternation, that quite a number of other people in this surprising world are gifted with thought reservoirs of a more spectacular order than my own."

There was very little of this modesty in the letter. It was written from Washington, during one of those periods when Hearst fled from Harvard to spend a few days in the house on New Hampshire Avenue, gloomily and contemptuously contemplating the antics of Congress, and bursting with ambition to express himself.

The letter discloses that the owner's son had already been attempting to run the paper by remote control. He had written a letter to the editor, he notes, recommending his friend Eugene Lent for a job, and at the same time taking the management to task for the unimaginative character of its illustrations. He had not mentioned a recent "crowning absurdity," he told his father, for fear of offending the editor, but in the next breath he reports that he *did* mention his opinion that "the cuts that have recently appeared in the paper bore an unquestionable resemblance to the Cuticura Soap advertisements. . . ."

Through the next few paragraphs runs the fear which was apparently on Hearst's mind: that his father was beginning to tire of writing off the *Examiner's* losses, was indeed becoming bored with the venture and might let it die. "In fact," he says, coming to the point in haste, "to tell the truth, I am possessed of the weakness which at some time or other of their lives pervades most men; I am convinced that I could run a newspaper successfully. Now if you should make over to me the *Examiner* —with enough money to carry out my schemes . . ."

And he goes on to outline what he would do. Mostly it was to imitate his idol of the moment, Pulitzer's New York *World*, which depended for its success, he noted with masterful understatement, on "a certain startling originality." He even argued for some kind of "arrangement" with the *World*, by which the *Examiner* would get the resulting publicity and a few exclusive telegrams, and in which the advantages to the *World* are nowhere apparent.

"Your affectionate son" sent out the letter in anxious hope. The answer was a flat no. It was characteristic of Hearst that he took this refusal in stride and went right on planning the *Examiner's* future.

The letter was not the turning point it has been pictured. It was merely the opening gun of a campaign that went on for nearly two years. As a diversionary move, Hearst advised his father to hire the brilliant Ballard Smith as editor. Smith was then an executive of the New York *Herald*, earning $7000 a year, which George Hearst thought was unheard of for a newspaper editor. His energetic son, however, moved to get Smith in exactly the manner he employed when he became a publisher himself. But here he was, still an undergraduate, cabling his mother in Paris: "Please see Ballard Smith in London and ask him if he will be editor of the San Francisco *Examiner*."

To his father he wrote again, offering to "give you the benefit of my large head and great experience on this subject—and not charge you a cent. . . . You must reconcile yourself to paying the salary or giving up the *Examiner*. It has been conclusively proven that poor wages and mediocre talent will not do, and the only thing that remains to be tried is first-class talent and corresponding wages. You could not even sell the paper at present, so I think this is the only thing to be done. Mr. Ballard Smith will state his terms and I would say, 'Mr. Smith, I guarantee you this amount and I promise you a certain interest in the paper in case you make a glittering success. You are to have entire control of the paper, Mr. Smith, with the privilege of employing whomever you please.' "

There was Hearst the publisher, speaking in his early twenties the same ideas he would employ later: go out and buy talent at whatever price it costs to get it, turn your man loose with instructions to produce, and watch for results.

The effect of this advice was to alarm the Senator rather than to convince him. He looked on newspapers as the tools of politicians and the occupation of radical idlers. When Billy Buster came home for summer vacation between his junior and senior years, his father undertook to dissuade him from his ambition with a method time-honored in politics—offering him something else.

The first bribe was magnificent, nothing less than the great Babicora ranch in Mexico. That summer George took Willie and his son's two closest friends, Eugene Lent and Jack Follansbee, on a royal tour of Mexico and the ranch. Like the devil tempting Christ, if the comparison is not irreverent, he spread the riches of Babicora before his son, and for good measure offered Follansbee a neighboring 100,000 acres, just to keep Willie company.

Willie refused, but Follansbee was no fool. He accepted and went to live on his Mexican acres at once. The Senator took his son home, aware that he would have to make a better offer. He tried next, therefore, the ranch at San Simeon, his favorite spot in California. Willie refused. The Senator, with increasing desperation, offered him the incredibly rich Anaconda copper mine in Montana, and then laid on the line his pride and joy, the notable Homestake Mine in South Dakota. Willie admired these properties but he insisted on the *Examiner*. In disgust, the Senator sent him back to Harvard.

Sometime during the next academic year Hearst ended his halfhearted affair with the university by request and went down to New York, where he got a job on the exciting, sensational paper he considered the best in the universe, the *World*.

When he heard of this development, George Hearst gave in. It was obvious that his son intended to devote himself to the newspaper business, and if he could not do it on the *Examiner*, he would do it wherever he could. The Senator accepted defeat gracefully and wired his son that he could have the paper. Hearst resigned immediately and prepared to leave for San Francisco. He made an effort to take Ballard Smith with him, but Smith turned down his offer and gave him some advice instead: "Don't employ any of these expensive New York editors. You understand the work pretty well. Be your own editor."

It was good advice, but Hearst was not in need of it. He intended to be his own editor in the most complete sense of the word, as shown by an amazingly frank letter he wrote his father just before he took the train for the West Coast.

"I have all my pipes laid, and it only remains to turn on the gas," he wrote confidently. "One year from the day I take hold of the thing, our circulation will have increased ten thousand.

"It is necessary that the *Examiner* destroy every possibility of being considered an organ. I know it is not an organ exclusively devoted to your interests, but there are many people who do not know this, and so, the influence and accordingly the sale of the paper is thus largely affected. . . .

"We must be alarmingly enterprising and we must be startlingly original. We must be honest and fearless. We must have greater variety than we have ever had. We must print more matter than we have printed. We must increase our force, and enlarge our editorial building. . . . There are some things that I intend to do new and striking which will constitute a revolution in the sleepy journalism of the Pacific slope and will focus the eyes of all that section on the *Examiner*. I am not going to write you what these are, for the letter might get lost, or you might leak. You would be telling people about the big things that Billy Buster was proposing to bring out in the paper, and the first thing I knew somebody else would have it. No, I will tell you when we meet, but cut this out and paste it on Pickering [the owner of the San Francisco *Call*]. In a year we will have increased at least ten thousand in circulation. In two years we will be paying. And in five years we will be the biggest paper on the Pacific slope. We won't be paying for two years because up to that time I propose turning back into the improvement of the paper every cent that comes in."

Armed thus with such a refreshingly realistic approach to the job, and aided in an even more realistic way by the $100,000 additional capital his father gave him, "Your affectionate son" took over the *Examiner* in February 1887, on the same day his father took the oath of office as a United States senator and began to serve his first full term.

It was quite a day in San Francisco, as well as in Washington. Hearst said later it was the best day of his life. Now he stood figuratively in the shoes of his idol, Ballard Smith, and with the production of a newspaper on his hands for the first time, he tried to do what Smith would have done. He was everywhere in the *Examiner's* shabby little office on Sacramento Street, facing the blank frame front of the What Cheer House. Every line of copy that went in the first edition passed through his hands, and every head had to be shaped in the image of the *World*. He stayed in the plant all night, until the creaking press rolled out the first edition, then he slumped down wearily and began to plan next day's paper. In the foggy dawn he walked home, too tired to think any more, and sank into sleep in a house where he had once lived, the Spanish-style mansion on Taylor Street.

In the next few months he worked as hard as though he were a poor boy pulling himself up by the proverbial bootstraps, as hard as his predecessors in the business, who had often burned themselves out at an early age in the hard struggle to establish themselves. Whatever it was that drove Hearst—egocentricity, the need for recognition, or simply the love of what he was doing—he did not spare himself. He wrote to his mother in Washington: "I don't suppose that I shall live more than three or four years if this strain keeps up. I don't get to bed until two o'clock and I wake up about seven in the morning and can't get to sleep again, for I must see the paper and compare it with the *Chronicle*. If we are the best, I can turn over and go to sleep with quiet satisfaction, but if the *Chronicle* happens to scoop us, that lets me out of all sleep for the day. . . ."

This hardly squares with the popular picture of Willie Hearst, the carefree youth, tossed out of Harvard and spending his father's money like a drunken printer on wild and extravagant schemes. The *Examiner* may have been the most sensational paper in a city whose life matched it, but it was not the spree of an intellectual drunk. It was the sober effort of a man who knew what he was doing.

At once he began to assemble the men who could best help him do it. He had begun with a nucleus of Harvard friends—Eugene Lent, Phineas Thayer and Fred Briggs. Lent covered the financial and social news, Thayer wrote a humorous column and Briggs drew cartoons. It was Thayer, of course, who wrote in his weekly Sunday-morning column, which he continued after he returned East, the classic of baseball literature, "Casey at the Bat," thereby providing De Wolf Hopper with a vehicle from which he extracted every last sweet drop of mock agony on every stage of consequence in the country for the next forty-seven years.

With this nucleus, and a few able men who came with the paper, Hearst was able to begin, but it was not long before he instituted the primary policy of hiring the best talent at whatever cost.

His first catch was the formidable Ambrose Bierce, already a literary arbiter on the Coast, although his work had appeared only in such weeklies as the *Wasp* and the *Argonaut*. In some liberal circles of our time, Bierce's various accounts of his relations with Hearst are used to prove that W.R., then as later, was a man without conscience or purpose, unloving and unloved.

In the "Thumbnail Sketch" of Hearst most often quoted, Bierce remarks in his cutting way, "Never just, Mr. Hearst is always generous," and ". . . the man has not a friend in the world. Nor does he merit one," and of his public writings, "I fancy there are none; he could not write an advertisement for a lost dog." And more in a similar vein.

Not so often quoted is Bierce's frank declaration in the same piece: "If ever two men were born to be enemies, he and I are they. Each stands for everything that is most disagreeable to the other, yet we never clashed. He did not once direct nor request me to write an opinion that I did not hold, and only two or three times suggested that I refrain for a season from expressing opinions that I did hold, when they were antagonistic to the policy of the paper, as they commonly were."

This is all the more remarkable when it is considered what Hearst was for and Bierce was against. Hearst's sincerity in his beliefs may be a debatable point, but ostensibly he was making in San Francisco a paper which presented itself as the friend and ally of the workers, the voice of the Democratic Party, and the upholder of the people against exploitation and corruption in high places. On this platform he placed his present and future hopes of circulation.

Yet here was Bierce in his column, writing as "The Prattler," attacking these principles, by and large, along with sniping at an astounding variety of trivial things, and doing it as though it were H. L. Mencken advancing the political and social ideas of Westbrook Pegler. Bierce was chronically "agin." The combination of Mencken and Pegler is plain in his phrases, "thinkerless unspeakables," "Improved Order of Red Baboons," "the embullioned and behorred spectacularians," "a splayfooted mongeress of raucous rhyme," "the glorified *cuspidorarii.*" His biographer, Paul Fatout, noting these, adds that he called feminists (whom Hearst supported) "Them loud," and the ignorant masses (to whom the Hearst papers were supposedly addressed) "Hoopole County, Indiany." A pure Peglerian trick was his habit of beginning a column, "Unlearned in the law," "I am indifferently versed in theology," "I am no architect," followed by a thorough denunciation of the subject at hand, with a belaboring of anybody who happened to disagree with him reserved for a later column.

He was bitterly against organized labor and had little belief in democracy, with a large or small *d*. Concluding his acid portrait of Hearst, he remarks: ". . . I think that he would be about the kind of President that the country—daft with democracy and sick with sin—is beginning to deserve."

Yet his was the only dissenting voice on the *Examiner*, and one supposes Hearst estimated correctly that the masses would not be reading Bierce's intellectual prose. The people who were most irritated by The Prattler were other intellectuals whose beliefs had been trod upon.

Hearst was apparently a little afraid of Bierce, if it could be said that he was ever really afraid of anyone. He treated his cantankerous columnist with what amounted to deference, probably because of Bierce's unique combination of shock and circulation values. Once he sent Ambrose, whom he seldom saw in the office, two cases of wine as a Christmas present. Informed that Bierce was against Christmas too (as Pegler pronounced himself sixty years later), he tried to stop the gift until someone relieved his anxiety with the report that his columnist would not be offended by good cheer if it came in bottles.

That was fortunate for Bierce, who might otherwise have found himself a lonely dry island in the great damp sea of Hearst reporters and editors who gathered in the Frenchman's, on Merchant Street, and daily sopped up enormous quantities of food and drink with painters from the Latin Quarter. It was a flamboyant crowd in a flamboyant city in a flamboyant time.

There was Petey Bigelow who, declared Arthur McEwen, was so "frail and pale" that once, when he was walking down Market Street just after he had shaved off his beard, a drunk sighting him cried in awe, "Good God, the Holy Grail!"

Petey, whose legal name was Henry D., was the *Examiner's* star reporter. He was the man who pursued the Southern Pacific train robbers, Sontag and Evans, to their mountain hideout and calmly interviewed them there.

McEwen was a tall, blond Scotsman from an exceedingly religious family. As the *Examiner's* chief editorial writer, he applied an intense idealism to his job which matched the tone of Hearst's Democratic crusading.

It is ironic that McEwen is best remembered today for a chance remark about the "gee-whiz emotion" which he said the *Examiner* tried to get into its news handling. This subsequently became a convenient label for Hearst journalism, but even then McEwen was cheated of full credit. In reality, his "gee whiz" was uttered only when he saw the *Examiner's* first page. Thereafter, he said, the second page brought forth an astonished "Holy Moses!" and the third page an entirely reverent "God Almighty!"

That was a fuller explanation of the Hearst editorial method as it was introduced via the San Francisco *Examiner*. The application of it has been discussed pro and con and at length, but present-day hindsight makes it possible to arrive at what may be a clearer view of his actual accomplishments.

The *Examiner* was Hearst's proving ground. There he had to demonstrate, first of all, that his ideas of running a newspaper were justified from a circulation standpoint. They were not original ideas. In terms of make-up and mass appeal, of emphasis on the sensational and the human-interest story, they were only extensions and elaborations of the elder Bennett's *Herald* and Pulitzer's *World*, to cite the more illustrious examples. But in fact, except for the New York *Times* and the New York *Evening Post* under Godkin, few American newspapers of any consequence had a sober, responsible tone. Hearst simply improved on the prevailing method in a number of ways, and because his bank account permitted him to hire an aggregation of superior people, he was successful where others had either failed or been compelled to moderation.

The method, which dates from the early part of the nineteenth century, consisted of two parts. One was to employ writers who could ferret out every exploitable piece of sin and crime and corruption in the daily grist of news and extract the last ounce of sensation from it. Hearst improved this by getting better writers and reporters, adding the photographic side, and going just a little farther than the others had gone in enterprise, frankness and disregard of nobler motives.

The second part was political. Until Hearst came, publishers had been partisan according to party, and their excesses had been notorious since the administration of George Washington.

Hearst was partial enough in behalf of the Democrats, and no excess was too excessive for him, but he projected the appeal of his papers beyond party to represent them as so many St. Georges in search of those dragons intent on devouring good honest citizens and middle-class taxpayers. There were more than enough dragons in that era of predatory, unregulated wealth, but if the supply failed, Hearst could always produce one from under the bed.

His weapon in the search was a time-honored one, the crusade, and in the California of the *Examiner's* early days, there was only one crusade worth embarking upon: an attempt to break the strangle hold of the Southern Pacific Railroad, and of the ex-Sacramento hardware dealer, Collis Potter Huntington, who owned the railroad, the state and a splendid assortment of United States senators and representatives.

Huntington, at a later date, would have been the kind of man capable of driving a Kefauver crime committee insane. He was very nearly bigger than the United States Government, and in fact believed he was. A huge man, with a heavy, lined face and a beard that became beautifully white, he appeared on the Coast only spasmodically to keep the machinery running. The rest of the time he spent in New York and Washington.

People called California "Huntington's plantation" and it was almost literally true. Politics was completely under his domination, the press mostly so, either by subsidy or intimidation; banks, stores, the law, universities, even the clergy, were virtually helpless against his power.

For young Willie Hearst to oppose such a man was sheer audacity on the face of it. Whatever the subsequent rights or wrongs, it is an eloquent testimonial to Hearst's extraordinary confidence in himself that he should attack Huntington and his Southern Pacific cartel with no stronger weapon than a struggling newspaper. Here his money did him no good: Huntington was rich too.

In a way it was a grudge fight on Hearst's part. He was no stranger to the evil ways of practical politics, and he understood why his father had failed to be nominated for governor in 1882. George had been the candidate of the Republican machine in San Francisco operated by Chris (Blind Boss) Buckley from his saloon on Bush Street. This singular and powerful man, whose blindness had given him the politician's most useful asset, a lengthy memory for voices and names, was the kingmaker in San Francisco. He was a Democrat but he was in the same bed with Bill Higgins, the Republican boss, and both took their orders from an elusive gentleman named Bill Stow, who in turn was the apostolic representative in California of Huntington himself.

George Hearst had wanted office badly enough to make a deal with Buckley, which of course meant a deal with Higgins, Stow, Huntington and the Southern Pacific. At the convention it was not convenient for these dignitaries to keep their part of the bargain, and they threw poor George to the wolves. Later Buckley amended this action by getting him the senatorial post left vacant in 1885 by the death of John T. Miller. Hearst's partner in the Senate was Leland Stanford, an associate of Huntington's in the Southern Pacific.

Willie Hearst had met all these men socially at the home of his parents in the days when it would never have occurred to such personages that an upstart boy would dare to assault their empire. So in attacking Southern Pacific, he was not only opposing some of the most potent men in America, he was also mortally offending old friends and colleagues of his father.

Why did Willie do it? There may have been minor considerations, but the main one was the simple fact that there was no quicker, surer route to circulation success for a California newspaper than to fight the Southern Pacific, no better way to endear a publication to the innumerable small people who were victims of the railroad's economic and political domination. Still, only a man sure of himself and insensitive to everything except success would have dared try it.

The charge that this particular crusade came to an abrupt end because Hearst sold out to the railroad for $30,000 rests entirely on evidence presented by the San Francisco *Call*, a bitter rival of the *Examiner*. This evidence purported to show that in return for $30,000 worth of Southern Pacific advertising in the *Examiner's* special World's Fair edition, the paper, through its business manager, agreed to cease and desist. The deal came to light when the company stopped payment, charging the *Examiner* with bad faith in carrying out its end of the bargain.

A man who was close to Hearst's financial operations for some time at a later period believes this evidence was either fabricated or represented a side deal made by some Hearst associate. He believes it not because he thinks Hearst was above selling out, but because $30,000 was a ridiculously low figure for a crusade that was the most profitable operation the paper ever carried out.

It is difficult to find any heroes or villains in the entire story of the *Examiner* vs. the Southern Pacific. Huntington "admitted" the bribery, which was a cheap enough way to attack the *Examiner*. The other papers took a high moral position on the matter. They were nearly all on the railroad's payroll too. The *Call*, which engineered the exposé, was owned by the sugar king, John Spreckels, who aspired to control the city's political machinery. An attack on Hearst in Congress was led by Grove L. Johnson, Hiram's father, who had long been a political enemy of George Hearst's. Hiram, who carried on the fight against Hearst, later joined forces with W.R.

In the end, bribe or not, Hearst got what he wanted. Congress passed a bill—not the one he wanted, but one just as good— curbing the Southern Pacific's arrogant refusal to pay its debts to the government. The *Examiner* took the credit, much as some pretentious crusading papers do today. Boss Buckley had to leave town.

It was hardly a triumph of virtue over evil, but the practical result was high esteem for the *Examiner* and the transfer of considerable political power to Hearst. What he did with it was a further lesson in practical politics to the voters, who were the real victims of the whole business. His new power was so complete that, though he had gone to New York by that time, he succeeded in electing a mayor of San Francisco in 1901. Ostensibly it was a triumph for Democratic reform. Eugene E. Schmitz, the successful candidate, ran on a Union-Labor Party ticket. He was backed not only by labor but by the people who were sick of the old, corrupt Huntington Republican machine. Reelected in 1903 and 1905, again with Hearst backing, Schmitz and his able colleague Abraham Ruef, once an honor student at the University of California, created a new machine fully as corrupt as the old one.

During their trial on extortion charges, the same mob which had cheered Hearst on against the Southern Pacific milled outside the *Examiner* office and yelled that they would burn it down and lynch the owner if he showed his face. But justice prevailed. Schmitz and Ruef were put behind bars and the Hearst organization was defeated, mostly on the evidence collected by William J. Burns—who later became one of Hearst's close associates.

The other crusades Hearst initiated on the *Examiner* were less spectacular but more enduring. He came out against prize fighting and eventually got a law passed against it. He came out strongly against liquor and narcotics, two of his most sincere crusades. He came out ardently for better schools and free textbooks and higher salaries for teachers, reforms which cost him nothing whatever to advocate and were universally acclaimed. He urged the fortification of San Francisco Harbor, first of a lifelong series of campaigns for preparedness. And in 1888, at twenty-five, he proclaimed himself an isolationist, an advocate of Washington and the avoidance of foreign entanglements.

An unsuccessful crusade to prevent Postmaster General John Wanamaker from building the San Francisco Post Office on a piece of insubstantial swampland which had cost the government more than a million dollars ended in a historic colloquy. Wanamaker, refusing to talk about the matter, issued a statement: "I never give interviews on Sunday." The *Examiner* replied in a caustic McEwen editorial: "He is a truly good man."

Hearst had the last word on this one. Wanamaker's folly disappeared from public view in the earthquake of 1906.

In practice, the formula Hearst tried out in San Francisco worked better on its non-political side because of his imagination and the ability of the men who surrounded him. Who but Hearst would have thought to make a news beat out of the census, which he did in 1890 when, happening to be in Washington at the time of its release, he telegraphed the *Examiner* the name and population of every city and hamlet on the Coast. It filled an entire page of 6-point Eyestrain, but it was one of the most thoroughly read pages he ever printed.

He also printed, without shame or apology, the kind of classified advertising for young masseuses and practitioners of mysterious health treatments which led to an irreverent staff member's designation of the *Examiner* as "The Whore's Daily Guide and Handy Compendium." To have neglected this advertising, which no other newspaper in town did, would have been handsomely moral but impractical from a business standpoint in a city whose immorality in that day has never since been equaled in America.

Hearst not only printed the news first if it could possibly be done, he was first in everything else he could think of. Ouida, Anna Katharine Green and Gertrude Atherton appeared in newspaper pages for the first time. The first music ever printed by a daily paper in the West appeared in the *Examiner*.

Willie's carnival was complete even to a balloon ascension. Accompanied by a flight of homing pigeons and a photographer, the daring young publisher floated majestically over San Francisco, and while he stared down the sunburned gullets of his fellow natives, sent the birds fluttering back to the *Examiner* office with truly exclusive descriptive stories and pictures.

The *Examiner's* early ascendancy in pictures stemmed from George Pancoast, who taught Hearst his own amateur enthusiasm for the art. The two men had met as early as 1888 and their relationship began forthwith. Pancoast was already at work in the composing room, where his best talents lay, but while his boss's new enthusiasm for photography was in its first and most intense phase, he did little else but encourage him. They toured Europe and parts of Africa together in 1891 and 1892, accompanied by trunkfuls of plates.

On this trip Hearst created his first international incident by busily snapping his flashlights at the Tombs of the Kings in Egypt. The natives were superstitiously aghast and the British Government ordered Hearst to stop annoying them at once. He desisted, but in the end proved once more that all things come to Hearst. It was Phebe who backed the ill-fated Carter Expedition which dug out Tutankhamen's remains, thereby starting a King Tut craze in America which immortalized the Pharaoh in a popular song.

The European photographic junket was the whim of a rich kid with a fascinating new toy, but most of Willie's whimseys had more serious purposes. They were designed to further either his circulation or his political prestige. For example, on Washington's Birthday in 1888 he sent half his staff to Washington, where they published a special edition of the *Examiner*. This was not simply a sensational stunt. It was intended to persuade the Democratic National Committee, then meeting in the capital, to hold the next party convention in San Francisco. The persuasion was an expensive failure, but at least Willie enjoyed the publicity and personal satisfaction of having the *Examiner* laid at his father's doorstep on New Hampshire Avenue. Its circulation was already 47,526.

A few weeks later Hearst gave the *Examiner* a birthday party. His present to the staff was a new press.

Less than a week after that the press turned out another stunt, an edition printed in both German and English to mark the death of Kaiser Wilhelm I. The demand was so great that Hearst had to follow it up with a second edition.

In these and the other furious activities which made the *Examiner* city room a free-wheeling madhouse, the motivating force was Hearst's, but the machinery which moved it from startling edition to edition was lubricated by the ability of the people he had shrewdly gathered around him. McEwen, Bierce, Petey Bigelow were important, but transcending them were a quartet of strangely assorted talents: George Pancoast, Charles M. Palmer, S. S. Chamberlain and Annie Laurie.

Pancoast made possible the extraordinary display of pictures and headlines Hearst demanded every day. Charley Palmer, a Minneapolis boy who had published newspapers there, later dabbling in Missouri journalism and the trade field, came to the *Examiner* in 1889 as business manager. His mind in that department operated as Hearst's did in the editorial, and that was how the business side came to have at an early date something of the editorial side's fragrant reputation.

As managing editor, Sam Chamberlain was the one man Hearst could have chosen who understood his approach to the news as well as or better than he did himself. Chamberlain's background qualified him uniquely for the job. He had worked in Paris first as editor of *Le Matin*, whose columns in that era were hardly above the level of bedroom farce, and then as editor of Bennett's Paris *Herald*, where the farce technique was translated into its ultimate form. Bennett training would have been enough, but Chamberlain had also worked for Pulitzer, and it was the practices of these two publishers upon which the Hearst method was based—if that is the word for it.

Sam's weaknesses were liquor and clothes. He was undoubtedly the best-dressed drunk the newspaper business ever possessed. Yet those who sneered at him for one or both of these faults were confronted with the hard fact that he was a prime circulation-getter, drunk or sober. There was good reason for Hearst's cable from Europe in response to a plea from the business office that he fire Chamberlain: "If he is sober one day in thirty that is all I require."

Hearst was a temperance man by conviction and personal taste, but he knew a good man when he had one and he refused to let alcohol influence his business judgment, even if the good man were saturated in it. As Bierce sardonically reported:

"At one time on the *Examiner* it was customary, when a reporter had a disagreeable assignment, for him to go away for a few days, then return and plead intoxication. That excused him. They used to tell one of a clever fellow in whose behalf this plea was entered while he was still absent from duty. An hour afterward Mr. Hearst met him and, seeing that he was cold sober, reproved him for deceit. On the scamp's assurance that he had honestly intended to be drunk, but lacked the price, Mr. Hearst gave him enough money to re-establish his character for veracity and passed on."

Another favorite Bierce anecdote had to do with the managing editor (not Chamberlain) who was fired, then reappeared a few months later. In response to Bierce's surprised query, Hearst said reassuringly: "Oh, that's all right. I have a new understanding with him. He is to steal only small sums hereafter; the large ones are to come to me."

With Chamberlain these leniencies were unnecessary as far as Hearst was concerned. Sam the elegant, Sam the drunken— it was all the same to Hearst, who would have forgiven him anything except the loss of his golden circulation touch.

Only one other person so won his confidence, and that was the red-haired Army colonel's daughter named Winifred Sweet, who in time made herself known to millions of readers as Annie Laurie. Like Chamberlain, this bouncing, pink-and-white, energetic dynamo of a woman had an instinctive knowledge of people in the mass. She particularly understood children, and it was during a picnic in Golden Gate Park with a covey of them that she met Hearst for the first time—as Mrs. Older idyllically describes him, "a tall, slender, fair youth with arms full of toys, a stranger to her, but he was not long a stranger to the children. He sat on the ground and joined in their games. . . ."

Hearst put her in charge of the women-and-children department; in brief, she became the first of the sob sisters. As such she inaugurated activities which are now standard promotion procedure on many large dailies: the Christmas tree for children, the gathering of presents and money for needy youngsters, parties and trips for the older ones.

Annie Laurie applied the Hearst method from "the woman's angle," then a novelty in the business. She exposed the inadequacies of San Francisco's ambulance service and the crude nature of the young interns in its receiving hospital by pretending to faint on the street. This was a superb illustration of the mixture of civic reform and sex which Hearst fed to his readers. It was assumed they would be simultaneously stirred to indignation by the spectacle of poor Annie lying in the street until the laggard ambulance came, and at the same time titillated by her description of the brash passes made at her person by the examining doctors.

(Students of civic reform will note that in 1952 citizens were still lying in the streets of some of America's largest cities, victims of civic maladministration after more than a half century of supposed progress, and newspapers were still indignant about the situation. The morals of interns, however, seem to have improved considerably.)

Annie laid about her with a fine, free hand. She compared the women who watched the pigeon-shooting matches at Del Monte with the Roman society girls who enjoyed the blood-and-guts of the arena. Yet, smothering her finer sensibilities, she became the first woman to report a prize fight. She invaded President Harrison's train in Nevada and got the first presidential interview given to a woman since Ann Royall discovered John Quincy Adams floating peacefully naked in the Potomac and sat on his clothes during the compulsory press conference which followed.

Sometimes it seemed to *Examiner* readers that wherever they looked about the world there was the ubiquitous Annie, hot on the trail of sin, corruption and old-fashioned human interest. She turned up in such unlikely places as the leper colony of Molokai, and for a time shared the lot (journalistically, that is) of the Mormon wives in Utah. One day she would be in Hawaii interviewing King Kalakaua. The next time one heard of her, she was cuddled up cozily with William Jennings Bryan on his silver campaign caravan.

Whether she wrote as Annie Laurie or as Winifred Black, her married name, this lady who spent her long life in Hearst's service somehow came to typify his way with newspapers. In her perfervid prose could be found the basic appeals to basic emotions, the constant search for novelty and excitement, the whole attempt to place newspaper enterprise at the lowest common denominator. She was one of that little band of loyal souls who believed in Hearst as much as in his methods.

With the *Examiner*, and the help of Annie and the others, Hearst established those methods in the waning years of the nineteenth century, building a strong bridge that would extend them far into the next century, far past the time when those who had originated his ideas disappeared into the history books and their newspapers were translated into more modern terms.

In San Francisco, Hearst accomplished what he had intended. He tried out both himself and his ideas and found them satisfactory. He attracted the public notice he had hoped for, emerging in the role of young-man-to-be-watched in both politics and journalism. He made a few friends and a good many powerful enemies. If all this was gained at the expense of an unenviable notoriety, Hearst did not care. He had the experience, the money and the general background he needed to make the grand invasion, the assault on New York.

### III

Several interesting theories have been advanced as to why Hearst deserted San Francisco for New York. At the time it was said he had been compelled to it by the general distaste for his presence on the Coast, but this distaste was confined mostly to Republicans, businessmen and believers in the kind of newspaper that lowered its voice when it spoke. Others attributed the removal to scandalous reasons. In some quarters it is still believed that he had no motive, that it was only another impulsive move by a power-mad boy with a fortune to spend.

The theories are interesting but untrue. It was, from all the available evidence, the plan he had in mind from the beginning. San Francisco was to be the testing ground, as noted, and when a New York opportunity presented itself that was as good as the *Examiner* had been, he would make his move.

Three years before the move was actually made, Hearst began to look for the opportunity, using as his searchlight the *Examiner's* business manager, Charley Palmer, who later demonstrated his skill in such matters by leaving Hearst to become a successful newspaper broker in New York.

Palmer made a trip to New York in 1892. He stopped off in Chicago, because Hearst had indicated he might be willing to settle temporarily for something in that city, in case there should be nothing for sale in New York. As it turned out, the time was not propitious in either place. The only proposition offered to Palmer in Chicago was made by the astute Victor Lawson, who intimated he would be willing to part with his *Morning Record*, the unsuccessful half of his morning-evening team, for two million dollars.

As Palmer well knew, this figure was what it had cost Lawson to try to make the paper go. He said no politely and went on to New York. There much the same situation prevailed. The *Times*, then in the worst straits of its post-Raymond and pre-Ochs days, could be had for a million and a quarter, but again this was a great deal of money to ask for a paper whose profit was infinitesimal. James B. Duke, the tobacco king, and his partner, Joseph B. Knapp, head of the American Lithographing Company, were anxious to dispose of their ill and dying *Recorder*, but they too, like Lawson, were mainly anxious to get back the money they had put into a bad investment. Palmer said no again and went home.

Hearst was not disappointed when he heard what had happened. He was prepared to wait, and wait he did for three years while the *Examiner* circus went on as before. Then the whole idea was revived in 1895, almost by chance, when Palmer and Hearst met in Paris. Palmer was on his way home to go into business for himself, but Hearst persuaded his friend to make another attempt in New York.

This time Palmer found any number of papers for sale. The *Times* and the *Recorder* were still on the block, and so were the *Advertiser* and the *Morning Journal*. None of these ventures was making any money, but the *Journal* had the virtue of being cheap. It also had a reputation not only worse than the others, but more odious than any other organ for miles around. Ironically, it had acquired that reputation by doing unsuccessfully what Hearst had been perpetrating on the citizens of San Francisco.

John R. McLean, its rich owner, had been adding to his already substantial fortune with the income from his Cincinnati *Enquirer*, an outspokenly sex-and-sensation sheet. Transferring this formula to New York, he found himself unable to compete with the superior talents of the *Herald* and the *World* in that field. Yet he was reluctant to give up the paper because he had intended to use it as a stalking horse for himself in New York politics. His ambitions were dampened a little more each week, however, when he had to write another check to cover the *Journal's* losses. Meanwhile he ran his ailing rag from the drawing room of August Belmont's mansion on Fifth Avenue, which he had leased upon his invasion of New York. His office in the deserted grandeur left by the departing Belmonts was a decrepit kitchen table, a telephone and some chairs.

There Palmer found him, shouting orders into the phone and suffering from gout, his swollen, bandaged extremity propped on a chair. When McLean found out who his visitor represented and what he had come for, his first impulse was doubtless to kiss Charley Palmer, but he restrained himself, and in fact retreated into a coy reluctance about his property. No, he wouldn't sell outright but he would relinquish a half interest for $180,000, representing half of what the paper had cost him.

It was easy to see that he hoped by this arrangement to split his losses and save the paper for himself.

Palmer shrugged and said doubtfully that he would be glad to convey the offer to Mr. Hearst. Mr. Hearst, when he heard it, snorted like a bull confronted with a timid toreador. "Go back and tell him," he said grandly, "that I'll give him $180,000 for the whole property."

Back up Fifth Avenue went Palmer, where he found the gouty prospect in conference with his lawyer, who happened to be Senator David B. Hill. Palmer repeated Hearst's offer, and McLean winced as though his ailment had stabbed him viciously. He retired to another room to consult with Hill, who apparently told him not to be a fool.

"Is that absolutely the best Mr. Hearst can do?" he asked, hobbling back.

"It is," Palmer replied quietly. He knew he had his man.

"I'll accept then," McLean sighed, his face screwed up in physical and financial anguish.

The deal was closed in that month of August 1895, and Hearst wrote out his check and signed the final papers on October 7. The transaction was a deep secret. Hearst intended to burst suddenly upon New York as he had in San Francisco, and he needed a few weeks to organize.

His first move was to call Sam Chamberlain, Arthur McEwen, Homer Davenport and Winifred Black to New York. Here was the dependable nucleus he had carefully assembled. They knew what to do. He instructed Chamberlain, as managing editor, to hand-pick a staff and organize it like the *Examiner's*. Sam found this not so easy as anticipated. New York newspapermen were highly skeptical of Hearst. They thought he was a playboy who would play with the *Journal* awhile and then leave it in a corner. Chamberlain applied the persuasion he knew best—fat salaries and contracts. He got his staff.

The news circulated in the profession and seeped upward into the rarer levels of Fifth Avenue society, where Hearst's advent was greeted with well-mannered huzzahs by those innocents who imagined that because he was rich and of excellent family he would naturally produce a socially acceptable paper. Obviously they had never seen the *Examiner*.

One of Hearst's biographers describes him as entering the New York arena "with his check suits, tan shoes, brown derbies, chromatic ascot scarves—and about half his inheritance of seventeen million." These gaudy appurtenances may have been appreciated at the Hoffman House, but when he put his inheritance and social position on display in the mansions strung like a necklace up and down the Avenue, no one thought of him as a dude from the Coast, nor did he look the part. He was correct and elegant in his evening clothes—he did not share his father's abhorrence of them—and the ladies fairly quivered at his presence, particularly the mothers, who saw in him a highly eligible bachelor.

How must these good souls have shuddered into their aspic on November 8, 1895. A tremor ran from Twenty-third Street, where the world began, and rippled up to Forty-second Street, where it ended, save for the bastions of the millionaires in bucolic seclusion in the Sixties. They saw the *Journal* in all the glory of its new incarnation—and it looked exactly like the despised *World*, which society considered a low scandal sheet.

One of society's currently celebrated events occupied the entire front page, the wedding of Consuelo Vanderbilt and the Duke of Marlborough. But where the event was treated with dignity by the *Times* and the *Sun*, Hearst had spread a drawing of the wedding procession over two thirds of the page, and the rest was occupied with Julian Ralph's story of the affair, which ran over three inside pages as well. It was a story so intimate in its details that it might have been written in the bride's diary.

This was the kind of thing McLean had lacked the imagination to do, and Pulitzer's brother Alfred, who had established the *Journal* in 1881, had not the courage to do, inasmuch as he was a member in good standing of this same society. Hearst, who had as much standing, said in effect with this first issue, "To hell with the upper classes. The *Journal* is for the people."

The people loved it. They got everything the *World* carried and more, and the ailing Pulitzer, blind and agonizingly sensitive to the slightest noise, realized that he would have to compete not only with Hearst's penny price but with his own techniques in the hands of a man who obviously knew what to do with them.

Within a year Hearst was giving a celebration party at Delmonico's to mark the passing of the *World's* circulation mark by the surging *Journal*, and Chauncey M. Depew was proclaiming in an effulgent after-dinner speech that he had never seen anything like the *Journal* in his four decades in New York.

This was a masterpiece of understatement. When Hearst coined the slogan, "While Others Talk, the *Journal* Acts," he provided a hardly adequate description of what went on in the shabby little building at the corner of Spruce Street and Park Row, squatting in the gilt-domed shadow of the proud World Building. The *Journal's* home was the second and third floors of the Tribune Building, but all the two papers had in common was joint tenancy.

On the second floor, in the extreme northwest corner, surrounded by period furniture and various other collector's items, illumined by daylight filtered through windows overlaid with photographic transparencies, worked the new publisher, often in his shirt sleeves, with the same driving energy he had displayed in the early days of the *Examiner*.

One of his early employees, Harry J. Coleman, who later became a top Hearst picture executive, describes his young boss at work.

"One day," Coleman writes in his memoirs, "I delivered tremulously some of George Palmer's cut proofs across an elaborately inlaid ebony desk straight to the hands of the 34-year-old publisher. I stood aside enthralled, with a strange boyish reaction of amused bewilderment. My eyes strained wide and I tried vainly to keep from swallowing my bubble gum when Hearst suddenly spread the proofs in precise order upon the floor and began a sort of tap dance around and between them. It was a mild, uncostumed combination of Carmen Miranda, a rumba, a Russian dagger dance and the Notre Dame shift, with lively castanet accompaniments produced by his snapping fingers. After I had observed W.R.'s strange dance, I learned that it was his customary method of absorbing pictures and reproductions on newspaper pages. The cadence of it speeded up in tempo with his reactions of disturbance, and slowed down to a strolling rhythm when he approved. Between dances, he scribbled illegible scrawls in longhand on the margins and gave the proofs back to me."

At night when he went home to the Hoffman House, Hearst continued the process by spreading out the town's other newspapers on the floor and dancing among them, comparing, analyzing, seeking always to broaden the basis of the *Journal's* appeal.

For all its seemingly careless sensationalism, the *Journal* was put together painstakingly to get the effect the publisher wanted. At the office he was given dummy drafts of every page—"Let's see the little papers," he would ask—and on these he arranged type, headlines and pictures exactly as he wanted them. It was a one-man show. Hearst selected the pictures, decided what would be played up and what could safely be reduced to an inside page, even picked the type sizes for headlines. When the proof sheets came up from the composing room, he hacked away at them with a blue pencil and thought nothing of holding an edition until some shift of pictures or text had been made, though it meant missing mail schedules. "The paper must be right. Nothing else matters," Hearst told the astounded printers, who probably thought he was insane.

Nobody else could have afforded it, but Hearst was right. He realized he was up against big-time competition, and if the method he had developed in San Francisco was to succeed in New York, he knew that he had to give it unceasing work. Everything was at stake with the *Journal*. His journalistic future would end with its demise, if that incredible event occurred. Hearst had his low moments, but apparently he never admitted the possibility of failure. Besides, he loved what he was doing.

Unlike other men, he did not have to work for a living, and so hours meant nothing to him. His work was his life.

Sometimes this was difficult for an outsider to understand. Moses Koenigsberg, who later headed Hearst's International News Service, recalls his second meeting with his employer in the house on Lexington Avenue. Hearst was sitting on the floor, surrounded by colored proof sheets of the *Journal's* new comics. After greeting his visitor, he returned to his shuffling of the pages, talking while he worked, chuckling at the pictures, sliding around them on his haunches like a kid at a picnic.

"As the moments dragged," Koenigsberg relates, "an overtone of unreality settled on the scene. It smothered a fear that I was witnessing something not intended for my eyes. That big husky, rolling on the carpet and fussing with 'funnies,' with an abandon a nursery scamp might envy—was that actually my . . . employer? Was that sprawling person really the noted journalist . . . ? There was nothing about that slack figure to suggest the epic tableaux through which I was yet to see him pass. There was no indication of what I was to learn months later,—that instead of being relaxed in amusement, Hearst was really at work. He studied comics from the planes and angles of the juvenile enthusiast."

That was one answer to the *Journal's* ultimate success and the subsequent expansion of the Hearst organization: the unwavering enthusiasm and energy Hearst gave to the job.

A second answer was money. No other publisher entering the New York field could have afforded to take the financial punishment necessary to establish a paper against such powerful and entrenched opposition. The purchase price had been absurdly cheap, but in the end it cost Hearst nearly ten million dollars to make himself a New York publisher. He poured close to a half million into coverage of the Spanish-American War alone.

Every newspaper in the city felt the impact of Hearst's wealth on its own circulation and stability. The *World*, his chief com-

petitor, spent all that Pulitzer could scrape together in the epic
dogfight that went on between the two publishers, and in the end
Pulitzer had to retreat. He should never have been fighting in
the gutter. As soon as the *World* lifted itself to a higher level of
news presentation and editorial integrity it became as respected
as it was respectable.

Before that occurred, however, Hearst had removed from its
employ the key men who had made it successful in the sensational phase of its career. Through them he prepared the mixture
as before, men and method, and treated New York to the same
three-ring performance he had given San Francisco. But these
men were not required to improvise, as had been the case on the
Coast. They were already masters of the method, having practiced it under the wizard in the field who had preceded Hearst.
Now they worked for a man who went a few steps farther with
it, had some ideas of his own, and stood at their shoulders as they
carried out their shattering assault on the sensibilities of New
York.

"Mr. Hearst would be pleased to have you call."

That was the discreet little note delivered to the harassed
Pulitzer's executives one by one, indicating to them with incom-
parable delicacy that, if they could be had, Hearst was prepared
to have them.

One of the first to respond was the morbid young genius of
the *World's* Sunday edition, Morrill Goddard, who had traveled
an unlikely path from Maine to Dartmouth to Pulitzer, where as
one of the *World's* ever-busy reporters he had attracted Ballard
Smith's editorial attention by pursuing the honeymooning President Cleveland virtually into the nuptial bed, thereby scooping
more reticent reporters. Naturally this feat made him an ideal
candidate for editorship of the Sunday *World*.

In that position he justified Smith's faith by inventing the
banner headline and making a Museum of Horrors out of the
*World's* Sunday pages. Goddard's taste ran to the shocking—
nudity, surgery, monsters, ape-men, criminals of various exotic
kinds, and cross sections of everything. He disdained long stories

to accompany these illustrations, estimating correctly that not many of his audience were excessively literate.

Goddard once expressed in the most candid terms his successful formula for a Sunday supplement page: "Suppose it's Halley's comet. Well, first you have a half-page of decoration showing the comet, with historical pictures of previous appearances thrown in. If you can work a pretty girl into the decoration, so much the better. If not, get some good nightmare idea like the inhabitants of Mars watching it pass. Then you want a quarter of a page of big-type heads—snappy. Then four inches of story, written off the bat. Then a picture of Professor Halley down here and another of Professor Lowell up there, and a two-column boxed freak containing a scientific opinion, which nobody will understand, just to give it class."

The particular layout which endeared Goddard to Hearst and brought him the "pleased to have you call" invitation was one which depicted the climax of a dinner given by Stanford White, the architect who contributed so much to the skyline and scandal of New York, for the delectation of a stag guest list that included some of the most prominent names in the city. The climax was dessert, an enormous pie borne to the table by four sturdy waiters. When the pie was opened, the guests began to sing—the low, growling song of the wolf pack. Its delectable filling was a nude model who stepped from the crust, the ultimate triumph of Gay Nineties gastronomy.

This early-day combination of Ziegfeld and Minsky was depicted seven columns wide in the Sunday *World*, and while the guests were still trying out new explanations on their wives, Goddard was sitting down with Hearst in the Hoffman House. He had not been overwhelmed by the invitation. In fact, he remarked bluntly that people were saying about town that Hearst would go back to San Francisco when he was tired of playing with the *Journal*. Where would that leave Morrill Goddard? the genius wanted to know.

"Is this enough of a guarantee?" Hearst is said to have replied, tossing a Wells-Fargo draft for $36,000 across the desk.

It was. Goddard brought his entire staff over to the *Journal*, except for a lone and unexplained stenographer. Pulitzer fought back, and there was a brief tussle during which it was sometimes hard to tell just whom Goddard was working for. But Hearst won in the end, as he always did in these battles, and Goddard became the creator of Hearst's *American Weekly* and eventually pushed its circulation past the 30,000,000 mark.

In the late nineties, Hearst and Pulitzer—who was deprived of Goddard but far from retreat—engaged in a battle of the Sunday colored supplements which amused New Yorkers as much as it increased circulation, although both papers continued to shock the sober element.

Hearst was first in the field, having been stimulated to it by the success of *Puck* and *Judge*, two weeklies printing color comics. He instructed Pancoast to invent a color press—it was actually as simple as that—and one day while the two men were watching the elephants cavort at the circus in Madison Square Garden, meanwhile discussing the problems of color printing, the missing pieces came together and the first color press was on its way.

This invention led to another: the creation of the Yellow Kid. Dick Outcault's yellow-shirted boy, the hero of "Hogan's Alley," had been one of Pulitzer's chief attractions in the Sunday *World* until the artist got one of Hearst's famous invitations and accepted a large check. Pulitzer bought him back, Hearst had to raise the ante, and by that time Outcault was making so much money he could hardly stand it. Under a new title, "McFadden's Row of Flats," since the *World* owned the old title, the Yellow Kid prospered in his new environment against the competition of "Hogan's Alley" and a new Yellow Kid drawn by George Luks.

While the battle of the Yellow Kids went on, to the increasing profit of both Hearst and Pulitzer, the other New York papers, whose motives were certainly far from unselfish, sneered loftily at the struggle. Ervin Wardman, editor of the New York *Press*, a paper subsidized by a group of high-tariff Republicans, and naturally a bitter opponent of the Democratic low-tariff *Jour-*

*nal*, characterized the contest as "yellow journalism," thereby contributing a phrase to the language which far outlasted its inventor. The name stuck to Hearst papers, though it came in time to be applied to any sensational, exposé type of journalism. Hearst's political opponents later applied the ready-made term "Yellow Kid" to Hearst himself, and that name stuck too.

Hearst backed up Goddard's Sunday sensations with a comic-strip line-up which included Rudolph Dirks's "Katzenjammer Kids," inspired by the publisher's old German comic books, and such other names as "Tad," Briggs, McManus, Swinnerton and Opper.

With the combination in the Sunday supplement, the poesy of the *Journal's* self-advertising knew no bounds. Some unsung laureate contributed this pure gem:

*Oh, be sure and call me early, call me early, mother dear—*
*I would buy a Sunday Journal ere the last one disappear.*
*I didn't order it today, and I must early rise*
*To get one from the dealer ere the last one from him flies.*
*So be sure to call me early; call me early, mother dear—*
*Tomorrow'll be the gladdest day of all the glad New Year. . . .*

And much more of the same, verging into prose which went on for two columns, promising the delights to come:

"Therefore, dearly beloved, the Colored Supplement will open tomorrow with a luminous handful of football fancies, in which the Yellow Kid will be a prominent figure. It will also show the beauties of the game, as played by impressionable young women, at the supreme moment when a flying wedge and a grand tumble combine to reveal all the latest conceits and symphonies in lingerie to the enraptured vision of him who only regrets that nature did not endow him with a pair of X-ray eyes.

"The Brash Baboon, the Gay Giraffe and the Subtle Snake is an African romance, told in pictures. This set of pictures also deals with the cocoanut in its natural state, with milk punch attachment, and not in the form it assumes when converted into the barefaced pie which should be seen, but not eaten. It is a most thrilling combination, and to know how it ends, and whether the cocoanut charmed the baboon, until the milk punches revealed to him the snake, don't fail to purchase the *Journal* tomorrow, of all newsdealers, price five cents."

Such were the flights of rhetoric which followed Morrill Goddard's passage down Park Row.

The consequences of that move were at least equaled by Hearst's second big catch, Arthur Brisbane. It seems odd to recall it today, but Brisbane was first attracted to Hearst by what he thought was the young publisher's sympathy for Socialism. The *Journal* had declared itself boldly for the masses and, for reasons not wholly connected with ideology, had begun at once to attack the evils of predatory capitalism. Brisbane read these attacks with approval. He was a man who dwelt in the shadow of his father, Albert, himself a capitalist who had embraced the mild Socialism of Fourier, the French thinker who had been embraced and publicized by Horace Greeley. Albert had been a member of Greeley's Utopian experiment, North American Phalanx, and bought space for Fourier's writings in Dana's *Sun*, where the Frenchman's economic ideas would never have been printed otherwise.

Arthur Brisbane had seen the poverty of France as a boy and the misery of New York's East Side as a young settlement worker, and his mission in life was to bring education to the masses in the most easily digested editorial form. While Goddard catered to the same people with sex and sensation, Brisbane devoted himself to transmitting the culture of the Western world in a diluted Socialist form to Pulitzer's readers.

As time went on, Pulitzer viewed these editorials of Brisbane's with increasing distaste. As an ardent champion of the masses he had created a newspaper with a liberal reputation, but as a practicing capitalist in the years of his success he became increasingly skeptical of efforts to improve the world. He made the mistake of insulting Brisbane, not so much by drastically cutting his $15,000-a-year salary, as by reason of the acid remark he appended: "It ought not to cost very much to get Socialist editorials written." Whereupon Brisbane answered with his oft-quoted: "It will cost a good deal to get them well written by a man who believes them." And went over to Hearst.

Brisbane told Hearst he would work for him for $150 a week, indicating the depth of his belief in Hearst's politics, but he was not so carried away by idealism that he was unable to make a potentially highly profitable agreement by which he was guaranteed a percentage of any money derived from the circulation he promised to bring to the *Journal*. The end result was the salary of which Brisbane boasted so often: $275,000 a year at its peak, the highest ever paid to a newspaperman.

To justify it, Brisbane brought to Hearst the ideas which Pulitzer had steadfastly rejected for the *World*, and which were at the root of Brisbane's disaffection. He wrote the editorials Pulitzer would not let him write, applied Goddard's Sunday treatments to the everyday news and, against Hearst's resistance, increased the size of the *Journal's* headlines.

Hearst had no objection to the large headline, but he thought Brisbane carried the idea too far when he had made for the *Journal* type that was seven inches high, asserting that he had found nothing remotely adequate in the paper's cases. If Hearst had not restrained him, he would have raised the type face of his editorials so that they could be read without difficulty across the street.

Brisbane and Goddard were the most valuable of the men Hearst took from Pulitzer, but there were others. Of the same stature, but in a different way, was Solomon Sells Carvalho, who had been taught by a master, Charles A. Dana. As business manager and publisher of the *World*, he had done a great deal to hold the paper together while the ill Pulitzer directed its operation from his soundproof apartment, his yacht, or a hotel somewhere on the Continent. When Hearst hired him away in 1896, it was a damaging blow to the *World* and a real acquisition for the *Journal*, especially when, a few years later, Hearst gave up the direct management of his papers.

Among the *World* men who succumbed to Hearst's bait were Richard Farrelly, the city editor who departed the day before a banquet was to be given in his honor by Pulitzer to celebrate his promotion to the managing editorship; Rudolph Block, a brilliant art director; and Charles Edward Russell, a scholarly gentleman who also happened to be an excellent city editor.

These men became long-time Hearst employees, but as he had in San Francisco, Hearst also added to his staff men whose names and reputations were calculated to sell papers but who seldom found the climate pleasing enough for more than a short stay. Thus the renowned Richard Harding Davis got $500 to cover one Yale-Harvard football game, and thereafter disappeared from the *Journal's* pages. Ring Lardner worked for Hearst and then went on to better things.

A *Journal* man might find himself almost anywhere in the world. Stephen Crane exposed the doubtful joys of prostitution in the Tenderloin, and thereafter shivered in Alaska, sweltered in Venezuela and traveled with troops in the Balkans. "Willie Hearst has made a bad bargain," Crane wrote from the last of these junkets. Julian Ralph, an expert local reporter, pursued news in London with equal facility. Charlie Michelson, who had come a long way from his cub days in San Francisco but was still a good Democrat, was among the first of the Hearst armada to land in Cuba when the war was no more than a good idea.

"A man must be a drunk, a lunatic or Sam Chamberlain to run the *Journal*," Crane observed, shuddering over a drink.

Who but a lunatic or Sam Chamberlain would yell at his reporters, "Get excited, damn it!" in a moment when the city room was quiet? Who but Hearst himself, whose idea it was to send wagons loaded with coffee and sandwiches about the city, giving of the *Journal's* bounty to the unemployed and hungry, who also got sweaters on cold days.

It was a dizzy, dazzling moment in New York. A bold Hearst reporter extracted a blushing quote from Lillian Russell by asking her why she didn't wear tights. Without benefit of press agent, she replied: "Nature has been too generous," and lowered her shadowy eyelashes. Another *Journal* man talked to Sarah Bernhardt but failed to ask her opinions of the stage and drama. He wanted to know about the dogs she possessed, and the lions and tigers she was said to possess. Hearst liked animals. Charlie Michelson broke onto the front page with an exclusive interview in which the insurgent General Gomez revealed his emotions when he heard that the Senate had recognized Cuba.

If a reader could look up from these enchantments, he might have observed Willie Hearst floating serenely over Staten Island in a flying machine in the soft spring air of 1896.

It was difficult to look up. The bemused reader might miss what did not happen but could have when the *Journal's* drama critic, Alan Dale, went to interview Anna Held and found her clad only in a quotation-bracketed nightie. Winifred Black, now assisted by Dorothy Dix, Ella Wheeler Wilcox and Beatrice Fairfax, was exploring the iniquities of New York and finding them little different from those in San Francisco. "Why Young Girls Kill Themselves," she confided sociably to the *Journal's* eager readers. To his acute embarrassment, Henry James found himself in the same company, having exchanged the reprint rights to *The Other House* for gold and the doubtful pleasure of seeing it in print as his "New Novel of Immorality and Crime," a fit companion for F. Marion Crawford's "New Italian Society Novel of Love, Revenge, Suicide and Poison."

By hansom, carriage and bicycle, the Hearst staff, known to other papers as "the wrecking crew," descended on the scene of spot news. A Hearst kind of story could be assured of the most thorough coverage in the history of journalism. "Accuracy, accuracy, accuracy," Pulitzer thundered at his reporters. "Get there first," said "Cosey" Noble from the city desk to his hypertensive crew. It was quantity and speed the *Journal* desired. But on no other paper did the publisher himself travel with the reporters, murmuring in their ears, "We must have this before any other paper in town," and then come back to the office, staying night after night until three o'clock in the morning.

The Hearst influence spread beneficently everywhere. James

L. Ford, in his "Forty-Odd Years In The Literary Shop," recalls how one of the *Journal's* sob sisters, returning from a colliery disaster, began her story approximately in this fashion: "I sobbed my way through the line, the stern-faced sentinels standing aside to let me pass with a muttered, 'the lady is from the *Journal;* let her by.' I was the first to reach the wounded and dying. 'God bless Mr. Hearst,' cried a little child as I stooped to lave her brow; and then she smiled and died. I spread one of our comic supplements over the pale, still face and went on to distribute Mr. Hearst's generous bounty."

On another occasion, Mr. Ford recalls, one of the *Journal's* female angels of mercy undertook on behalf of her boss to bring an afternoon of Coney Island into the lives of some tenement children.

"Of course the business office kicked at everything like expense," she reported, "so the transportation and the grub were paid for in puffs and advertising. The ice-cream man agreed to furnish an unlimited supply in return for a picture of his daughter, then about to be married, and a puff of her high social station. But the cut went wrong in stereotyping and the girl came out looking like a chimpanzee, in consequence of which the old man gave us only a single can of ice-cream. It was with the greatest difficulty that I induced about twenty children to go down to Coney Island as Mr. Hearst's guests, for previous experiences had rendered them suspicious, but at last we started and all the way down I was trembling to think what would happen when I dealt out that one miserable can of cream. When at last I placed a dab on each saucer, a little fellow in ragged knickerbockers got up and declared that the Journal was a fake and I thought there was going to be a riot. . . .

"I took away the ice-cream from a deaf and dumb kid who couldn't holler and gave it to the malcontent. Then I had to write my story beginning, 'Thousands of children, pale-faced but happy, danced merrily down Coney Island's beach yesterday and were soon sporting in the sun-lit waves shouting, "God bless Mr. Hearst!" ' "

Hearst was the *Journal*. He lived it and breathed it, and his touch was everywhere apparent, notwithstanding the expensive talent he had hired from Pulitzer. It was his idea to print a three-color special section on Grant's Tomb. He was the first man in history to portray the Sistine Madonna in the same three colors. He was sentimental about Christmas, and in the glad season of 1897, he gave his readers a touching picture to remember, "The Pickaninny's Christmas Dream," and along with it, so that no one could be neglected under the *Journal's* tree, a series of sketches from Cuba by Frederic Remington, showing dead rebels being picked apart by buzzards.

Those who said the Hearst press was colorful were as literally accurate in those days as in the comparatively mild modern era of red headlines and Technicolor American flags. Hearst in the nineties was a veritable Picasso of the color printing press, which George Pancoast had dutifully invented and perfected. All manner of attractions rolled from it: "The North Atlantic Squadron on Her Way," steaming out of two solid-color pages, first in history; a colored cookbook; a three-color comic section, another first; green shamrocks and harps around the margin on St. Patrick's Day, in honor of Hearst's favorite citizens and voters.

With all these specialties it is no wonder the regular news of the day ran a slow second. The *Journal* and the *World* copied each other in the manner which is still common practice today, except that they did not bother to rewrite and so make the habit respectable. The *Journal* went further and copied from other papers and news services until the courts put a stop to it.

But the kind of news the courts and most other newspapers talked about was not what Hearst had in mind. And in those days of the *Examiner* and the *Journal*, he placed the imprint of what he did have in mind, personally and with startling force, directly upon the business of newspaper-making. Whether he was "the blackguard boy" that a thinker like Edwin L. Godkin called him in the editorial columns of the *Evening Post*, or, as Brisbane thought of him, one with Washington, Lincoln, Edison and

Henry Ford—the five greatest Americans—he was Hearst, and he had succeeded, at immense cost, in making a place for himself in the business.

Thus he stood at the turn of the century, and soon thereafter rose to the larger ambitions of politics. Like Greeley, he could smell the White House, clear in the November air, and he wanted it more than anything in the world. After 1902 it was apparent that he considered newspaper-making important but more useful in President-making. He exchanged enemies like Pulitzer for more substantial foes like Teddy Roosevelt.

One could measure the transition by Hearst's own writing. In 1897 he called Pulitzer "a journalist who made his money by pandering to the worst tastes of the prurient and horror-loving, by dealing in bogus news, such as forged cablegrams from eminent personages, and by affecting a devotion to the interests of the people while never really hurting the interests of their enemies, and sedulously looking out for his own."

That was Hearst the editor speaking, and with a perfectly straight face.

Fourteen years later, when Pulitzer came to the end of his tortured but distinguished life, Hearst began his obituary editorial: "A towering figure in national and international journalism has passed away; a mighty democratic force in the life of this Nation and in the activity of the world has ceased; a great power uniformly exerted in behalf of popular rights and human progress is ended. Joseph Pulitzer is dead." And he closed it: "The cause of the people Joseph Pulitzer and his newspaper ever espoused ably and intelligently, sympathetically and powerfully. In his death journalism has lost a leader, the people a champion, the Nation a valuable citizen. . . ."

That was Hearst the politician. There were some who could believe in one no more than the other.

# CHAPTER FIVE

## HOW HE RAN HIS BUSINESS: SECOND PHASE

DID WILLIAM RANDOLPH HEARST lower the whole tone of American journalism, as Oswald Garrison Villard charged, "by the example and competition of one whose newspapers were not only unprincipled, but frequently dishonest"?

The easy answer is yes, but the facts contradict it. Until the turn of the century, the Hearst method was no more than an exaggeration of the tone that had dominated American journalism for the whole of that century. Pulitzer was the one publisher to challenge and attempt to out-Hearst Hearst. He had emerged from the struggle a wiser man, and the *World* attained its lasting reputation as a great liberal paper only when it gave up the competition.

Hearst built his empire in the first thirty years of the present century. During that period there was a steady growth of responsibility and stature in the non-Hearst press, and at the time of W.R.'s death there were unquestionably many more papers of integrity than there had been in 1900; the whole level of American journalism had been considerably elevated, with a few conspicuous exceptions.

Villard lived to see the day when some of those who had been most violent in their attacks on Hearst discovered themselves in the same political bed with him. Charles A. Beard was cheered vociferously in 1935 by the liberal press for an attack which the *Nation*, in an article written by Villard, asserted "no future biographer of the world's worst newspaper owner can possibly overlook." Yet Dr. Beard himself overlooked it when he and

Hearst later appeared *flagrante delicto* on the capacious bed reserved for isolationist Roosevelt-haters.

It was not an uncommon experience for Hearst. If circumstance did not bring his enemies around, he believed they could be bought. The anonymous ex-employee quoted by one of Hearst's biographers was correct when he wrote: "Hearst believes that all men are rascals, more or less, and that the secret of all loyalties is money. Pay a man enough money and you can spit in his face as a part of your daily exercise."

A good many of the attackers Hearst converted were not rascals, only human. A conspicuous example was Norman Hapgood, the able, crusading editor of *Collier's* in the early years of the century who was responsible for Will Irwin's series on "The American Newspaper." Hearst was so irritated, apparently, by the rough treatment he got in these articles that he threatened both criminal and civil libel suits.

The suits were never brought, as Robert J. Collier predicted, and a few years later Hapgood became editor of Hearst's *International* magazine.

Hapgood was in excellent company, listed with Fremont Older and David Lloyd George among the distinguished names of those who had come to scoff at Hearst and remained to work for him.

These events and Hearst's activities as an editor are better understood when they are viewed in the framework of the world he lived in after the Spanish-American War was over, the *Journal* was on a firm footing, and a new phase of his life began. This phase, roughly from 1902 to 1922, was an era in which his primary interest was politics, when his own political star rose tentatively and set abruptly, and when the course of his career thrust him inevitably toward the lonely mountaintop of San Simeon.

During this period he lessened gradually and by necessity the single-minded attention he had given the *Examiner* and the *Journal*. His newspapers multiplied like guinea pigs, with several magazines tossed into the litter, and although he worked hard and continuously, his efforts had to be divided among his ventures, his editors took the direct responsibility for individual papers, and Hearst himself more and more came to look upon the whole complex from a lofty altitude.

The metamorphosis was gradual, but the pressures were irresistible. He was no longer Willie Hearst, no longer the boy wonder of the *Examiner*, or the brash youngster of the *Journal*, but a man whose money, properties and politics made him a power to be reckoned with in public life. Increasingly he used his papers as political weapons, and even sin and crime were converted to these ends wherever it was possible.

He was quite shameless about it. When in 1907 he felt the need of public purification to offset the mud thrown at him by the enemies he had made in both major parties, he contrived to set himself up in the public eye as a guardian of morals by "exposing" the *Herald's* famous "Personals" column, which was no different from the *Examiner's* slightly disguised inducements to moral turpitude. These highly classified advertisements were read with amusement by some, and with real or pretended horror by others. The following are fair samples:

YOUNG lady, good figure, wants to pose for artist; references exchanged; positively no triflers.

A CATHOLIC maiden (28) worth nearly $5,000, musical, refined, good appearance, would wed.—Rosalie.

A GENTLEMAN would like to make the acquaintance of a young lady bicyclist matrimonially inclined.

ATTENTION!—Is there a man of honor and sterling worth who can appreciate the cruelty that compels a gentlewoman, superior mental and personal attractions, age 34, to adopt this means of release from hated bondage? No Shylocks nor triflers; object, matrimony.

Then there were the usual advertisements for massage parlors and health treatments, and others of a non-sexual character:

CRAFTSMAN!—Oh, Lord! My God! Is there none to help the widow's son to some employment to prevent starving?

ANY person knowing of impending business failures or having

any other valuable information can make big money by communicating with smart lawyer.

Against these evil enticements, which netted Bennett about $200,000 a year, Hearst moved in his mysterious way. It could hardly have been more mysterious, inasmuch as the man he assigned to the job was Victor Watson, who was later to be the tough managing editor of his Chicago paper, and whose personality and tactics were so formidable, to use the politest word for them, that Hearst admitted wryly there was room for no more than one Watson in any organization.

Watson joined the Reverend Charles H. Parkhurst's Society for the Prevention of Vice, and for a solid year he did espionage work among the fleshpots, visiting lonely ladies, submitting himself to the massages, manicures and Turkish baths offered in the *Herald*. History does not record what difficulties Watson encountered in obtaining evidence without compromising himself, but in a short time he had enough to convince a Federal grand jury that it should indict Bennett for sending obscene matter through the mails.

Bennett was incensed but cautious. As long as he remained on his yacht, or in Europe, where he spent most of his time, he was reasonably safe. But it was galling to be hounded as a fugitive from justice, and he appeared suddenly in court, heard himself pronounced guilty, and paid fines totaling $25,000.

"I'll never forgive you," he wired to Hearst.

"I hope you never will," Hearst returned.

It was a low blow, an uncalled-for slap at an old man whose newspaper was steadily declining and no longer a threat to Hearst or anyone else.

This kind of action contributed materially to the uneasiness about Hearst which was growing in the newspaper business. The uneasiness was economic rather than moral. Rival publishers were afraid that the success of the one-cent *Journal* would be duplicated in other cities, competition would be slowly stifled, and Hearst would emerge as a one-man monopoly. They pointed to the sad history of Chicago as an example.

When Hearst came into Chicago with his *American* there were eight other newspapers. When the smoke cleared away a few years later, some were dying, others dead, and only the imperturbable *Tribune* and the *Daily News* emerged relatively unscathed and unchanged.

The episode of the *American* was a violent, flamboyant example of Hearst in his second phase. Its very reason for existence was purely political, to begin with, the pooh-bahs of the Democratic National Committee having informed Hearst early in June 1900 that if he desired to have his friend William Jennings Bryan in the White House, it would be essential to establish a Midwestern Democratic paper to support him. Then, as now, the number of Democratic newspapers in that part of the country was hardly sufficient to wrap up the fish.

No one but Hearst could have attempted what the Bryan managers asked, and no one else but a man as politically ambitious as Hearst would have desired to try it.

The problem was to establish a newspaper in Chicago within thirty days, before the Democratic Convention in St. Louis. To do the job, Hearst dispatched Carvalho, and after him he sent the necessary equipment, all of which had to be shipped from New York. Freight cars were hard to get, so Hearst sent the linotypes by Pullman at full fare.

Carvalho looked over the available real estate, and with a remarkable lack of tact, considering Hearst's antipathy to alcohol—he later turned Carrie Nation loose upon defenseless Chicago—established offices over the Steuben County Wine Company, an aging building in the decaying precincts of West Madison Street, between Fifth Avenue and Franklin Street. The neighborhood was not fashionable but the rent was cheap. Carvalho brought some life into the run-down district: in no time, he had more than eight hundred men working around the clock in three shifts.

Unbelievably, the *American* appeared as promised on the Fourth of July, 1900, its machinery set in motion by the Boy Orator himself from St. Louis, with the pregnant message flashing over the wires, "Start the presses!" Brisbane was editor of the initial edition, and he stayed for a while to oversee operations. He sent a bundle of the first papers down to the convention in St. Louis, and delirious Bryan supporters waved them about the hall in triumph. Bryan got the nomination next day.

The subsequent history of the *American* did not let down from that high point. At times it outdid Hearst's previous ventures in sheer insanity, and in fact came to be known with awful affection as "the Madison Street madhouse." Only the toughest, most confident newspapermen dared to accept a job on it, consequently the staff was often superlative and never at any time inhibited or intimidated by anything.

An old San Francisco boyhood friend of Hearst's, Andrew M. Lawrence, soon succeeded Brisbane as editor and, after Carvalho returned to New York, took over the business and circulation sides as well. "Long Green Andy," as he was called, was an apt man for the job. His managing editors were in the same vein. They included the redoubtable Victor Watson and Moses Koenigsberg, the large and capable man who took over the general managership of International News Service in 1919.

Koenigsberg has provided the best picture of life on the *American* in his autobiography, *King News*. He describes the surprisingly simple method by which Hearst got the news first in Chicago, not only ahead of the other papers, but often before the police knew about it. The method was to sign up as confidential *American* reporters nine out of the eleven coroner's deputies in the city, and as many supervisors and chief telephone operators in the town's hotels, hospitals and other institutions as could be persuaded to accept Andy's long green.

Life on the *American* even astonished its staff members. Koenigsberg recalls that one James O'Shaughnessy became managing editor overnight, rising gloriously if temporarily to that position from reporter on the *Examiner*, the morning edition of the *American* which Hearst established in 1902.

The transformation came on the direct order of Hearst, who was taking the baths in Mount Clemens, Michigan, and had been flushed from their fragrant waters by a hasty telephone call from Chicago, placed by Andy's brother Fred, who was publisher of the morning edition. Fred called Hearst's attention to a red banner line on page one of the *American* the day before, reporting the sudden elopement of a Roman Catholic priest with the wife of an eminent underworld gambling character. The story was unfortunately accurate and could not have been ignored, but Fred recalled how in the old days the San Francisco *Examiner* had been given a hard time by the local Catholic clergy, and he feared that in Chicago, a strong Catholic town, the *American* might not be able to survive. What should he do?

Hearst had the answer instantly. "Pick out someone on the staff who is a Roman Catholic of good repute and who has a distinctively Irish name. Make him managing editor for as long as necessary."

Next morning O'Shaughnessy found himself, to his painful embarrassment, a managing editor. He had only a scant idea of what a managing editor did, and he never found out. In a day or two, when it appeared there would be no repercussions from the Church, he was relegated to the beats again.

On Hearst's visits to the paper, he occupied a sanctum singularly inappropriate to his position. It was an oversized closet of an office, equipped with a battered roll-top desk, a pine table and some chairs. It was shut off from the ten thousand square feet outside where, without benefit of partitions, reporters, editors, copy-desk men, telegraphers, engravers and sundry other workers labored together in hopeless cacophony.

Koenigsberg recalls that he first met Hearst there in 1904, when the publisher was a candidate for the Democratic presidential nomination. He had been summoned particularly, but by the time he got to the office, Hearst was leaving. He shook Koenigsberg's hand and said, "Never mind, thank you; I must hurry to catch my train."

His secretary called after him: "But, Mr. Hearst, what shall I do with this correspondence? It has been accumulating for several days."

"I'll show you," Hearst answered, and grinned as he shoved the whole batch off the table into a wastebasket. "Every letter answers itself in a couple of weeks," he added, departing.

On the *American* the murderous art of court intrigue, characteristic of Hearst papers in this later phase, was developed to a high point. It was, as Koenigsberg points out, the result of "that inexplicable mixture of ruthlessness and delicacy that was Hearst himself."

As a man who had known Hearst for a long time, Andy Lawrence was well able to keep his head above the muddy waters, but he gave some advice to Koenigsberg (too honest to be a good intriguer himself) that was an apt commentary on Hearst's character.

"The quickest way to get ahead with W.R.," he said, "is to have the other fellows knock you to him. He'll figure that you must have something your colleagues are trying to kill off."

The quickest way to lose ground was to refuse an assignment, Koenigsberg discovered when he declined to leave his managing editor's post for an important position on the business side. Three days later an old friend diffidently appeared at his desk and handed him a note signed by S. S. Carvalho. The friend was Arthur L. Clarke, who had preceded Koenigsberg as city editor of the *American* and then had been transferred to the *Journal*. (Later he became the first managing editor of the New York *Daily News*.) The note said merely that Clarke had been made managing editor of the *American*; there was no mention of what Koenigsberg was to do.

This was a favorite Hearst device, to get what he wanted or to remove a man in such a way that he would not have to fire anyone directly and thus be compelled to hear appeals.

Koenigsberg and Clarke spent an awkward ten days together at the same desk, during which the whole staff carefully avoided mixing in the affair, and then the deposed editor broke down and wired Carvalho, who ordered him to New York and subsequently gave him another assignment, as business manager of the Boston *American*, which was losing money rapidly. Koenigsberg pulled it out of the red and wired the glad news to Hearst, who wired in return: "Fine! Now please add a Metropolitan and an Outing section in colors." Thus, with one stroke, the savings were wiped out and the paper was back where it had been before, a state in which, as its business manager complained, "the evasion of bill collectors required more of my time and ingenuity than anything else in Boston."

It was characteristic of Hearst that he would not tolerate what he considered mediocrity in a newspaper or an employee merely for the sake of saving money or keeping a newspaper solvent. The papers that made money supported the papers that didn't; the executives who failed to produce were fired.

If Hearst was compelled to hear an appeal from a man who had been fired, he reacted customarily as he did in the case of B. P. Guild, publisher of the Los Angeles *Mirror* in the late thirties. Guild was the kind of publisher the movies have celebrated. Of the many legends about him, the most beloved concerns his order to remove the toilet doors in the *Examiner's* washroom, so that employees would not be impelled to enjoy the pleasures of solitude on the company's time.

When it became necessary to fire Guild, so the story goes, Hearst sent E. D. Coblentz to do the job. Informed that W.R.'s right-hand man was without and wished to see him, Guild is said to have muttered in irritation, "Well, tell him I can give him ten minutes. I'm busy."

The message was relayed to Coblentz, who walked into Guild's office and reportedly told him, "I don't need ten minutes, Mr. Guild. I just came to say you're fired."

Guild couldn't believe it. He was able to get through to Hearst by telephone, an accomplishment in itself, but after listening patiently to Guild's side of the story, the Chief only remarked in gentle remonstrance, "Well, Mr. Guild, you know Mr. Coblentz *is* in charge down there now."

Sam Chamberlain once sat down with Charley Palmer, Hearst and the city editor of the New York *Journal* in an effort to make retrenchments in the city room at a time when the paper's losses

had reached an alarming point. Palmer read the news department's payroll, and each man was discussed individually. The
name of Oscar Barnes came up.

"What does he do?" Hearst inquired.

"Why, he sits in this room," the city editor told him. "Barnes
has been with us ever since you bought the paper. I must say
about Barnes that he's always on the job. I've never known him
to show up late or to complain about staying on in an emergency.
And he never falls down on anything he's given to do."

Hearst's thin lips curled and his pale eyes became remote.

"That's like recommending a whore for being good to her
mother," he remarked softly.

Not long after Koenigsberg went to Boston, when he was as
doubtful of the *American's* fate as he was disgusted with his
own, he got a command from Hearst to appear in New York.
The unwilling business manager found the great man, perspiring
and in his shirt sleeves, directing the make-up of one of the
*Journal's* pages. When he was through, they retired to the cubby-
hole of an office he used at the time, and Hearst inquired, "What's
wrong in Boston? What is it that seems to give so many of our
people the tummyache there?"

Koenigsberg explained that this tummyache required, among
other things, another managing editor and a new general manager of advertising. These changes were made, but still the Bos-
tonian indigestion persisted and Koenigsberg, terribly unhappy
in his job, asked persistently for a transfer. But Hearst was always
a man of unrelenting determination when it came to his newspapers. He called Koenigsberg to New York again and they
talked until dawn poked through the windows, after which
Hearst excused himself and went into the next room.

An hour went by, while Koenigsberg fidgeted and became
convinced that he had been forgotten. Then a secretary came
out with an envelope and reported, "Mr. Hearst instructs that
you read this and deliver it to Mr. Carvalho." The note read:
"Koenigsberg can and will handle the business department in
Boston; Coates can and will handle the editorial department;

Whitman can and will handle the advertising. Please arrange accordingly."

Later, Koenigsberg observed Hearst's method with his executives directed against one he had supposed untouchable, Arthur Brisbane. Hearst said to him privately one day, "Brisbane's contract is about to expire. He's acting up. He may become unreasonable. Whom can we get—somebody that Artie will consider a possible successor?" Koenigsberg suggested Herbert Kaufman, who was already contributing a Sunday page. Hearst added to this chore by instructing Kaufman to turn out a daily column much like Brisbane's, at least in its coverage, and he ordered it run conspicuously on Brisbane's own editorial page. Then he used it as a lever to negotiate a fresh contract.

Hearst did not hesitate to treat his fellow publishers in the same manner he treated his own men. In 1926 he took on the ruling clique in the Associated Press, which was attempting to expel him from the organization. The astute Roy Howard, observing this division of sentiment in the royal house, seized the opportunity to suggest to Hearst that he combine the International News Service with Howard's United Press, a combination which would have been powerful enough to challenge and perhaps surpass the AP's supremacy.

The deal fell through because of an unwittingly tactless remark made by Howard, who meant to express doubt as to whether W.R. could subordinate his interest in his newspapers to the creation of a news service. Hearst thought Howard implied that he was not fit to run a news service. The negotiations ended on a cold note, whereupon Hearst determined to face down the AP on its own grounds.

He called in John Francis Neylan, who became his general counsel and chief adviser. Neylan, a San Francisco attorney, was also publisher of that city's *Call-Post*, which held an AP franchise. Using this as an entering wedge, he found a weak spot in the AP's regulations governing the election of directors, and got them revised so that the half-dozen men who virtually controlled the association lost their power. That ended the only organized effort ever made by his fellow publishers to discipline Hearst for the excesses of his papers and the bad repute they sometimes gave to the business.

One says "sometimes," remembering that in 1926 it was the conservative element in the AP which thought Hearst was a menace to the ethics of the profession, and ten years later, when Roosevelt-hating made brothers of them all, discovered virtues in him that they had never suspected.

When it came to the rank and file on his papers, Hearst soon lost touch with them in this second phase of his career, and at the same time, he lost his reputation for high wages and lavish treatment of the men who gathered and wrote the news. The executives still got high salaries, probably higher than those on any other newspaper, which was necessary to insure their service—the money "absorbed some of the strain," as one of them put it. But increasingly the pay of the ordinary reporter was shaved down to the minimum.

Still, it is only fair to say that the salaries Hearst paid when he started a paper usually resulted in a general raise among the others in a given town. For example, the Chicago *American* gave reporters fifty dollars a week at a time when the scale in the city ran as low as fifteen and no higher than thirty-five. That resulted in a general upgrading on the competing papers.

On the other hand, during the depression years of 1929–35, when every newspaper was in the same financial boat, the level of pay in the Hearst organization was lower than in any chain of newspapers. The reason, of course, was Hearst's inability to let a paper build up large capital reserves. He took as freely as he gave, with the result that the early years of the depression, when reserves were needed, found him depleted and the whole organization in a precarious way, a situation which led to Miss Davies' million-dollar gift and the subsequent Great Reorganization of 1937, discussed in a later chapter.

Hearst's own pronouncements on the relationship between employer and employee follow a fairly well-worn path. They show quite clearly why he was denounced with equal fervor by two entirely different political camps.

At the beginning he was rather far to the left. Bierce recalls an early instance in San Francisco which seems well-nigh incredible today.

"During several weeks of a great labor strike in California," says Bierce, "when mobs of ruffians stopped all railway trains, held the state capital and burned, plundered and murdered at will, he 'laid me off,' continuing, of course, my salary; and some years later, when striking employees of street railways were devastating St. Louis, pursuing women through the street and stripping them naked, he suggested that I 'let up on that labor crowd.' No other instances of 'capitalistic arrogance' occur to memory. I do not know that any of his other writers enjoyed a similar liberty, or would have enjoyed it if they had it. . . ."

Bierce also remarks that in "matters of 'industrial discontent' it has always been a standing order in the editorial offices of the Hearst newspapers to 'take the side of the strikers' without inquiry or delay. . . . A typical instance of the falsification of news to serve a foul purpose may be cited here. In Pennsylvania, a ferocious mob of foreign miners armed with bludgeons marched upon the property of their employers, to destroy it, incidentally chasing out of their houses all the English-speaking residents along the way and clubbing all that they could catch. Arriving at the 'works' they were confronted by a squad of deputy marshals, and while engaged in murdering the sheriff, who had stepped forward to read the riot act, were fired on and a couple of dozen of them killed. Naturally, the deputy marshals were put on trial for their lives.

"Mr. Hearst sent my good friend Julius Chambers to report the court proceedings. Day after day he reported at great length the testimony (translated) for the saints and angels who had suffered the mischance 'while peacefully parading on a public road.' Then Mr. Chambers was ordered away and not a word of testimony for the defense (all in English) ever appeared in the paper. . . ."

In 1919, when the Boston police strike generated a wave of anti-union feeling everywhere in the country, and particularly enraged conservatives, Hearst published a signed editorial which deplored the shambles in Boston but asserted forthrightly: "The question involved is not the right of organized labor to strike. Every thinking human being admits the right of ordinary employes to organize and to quit work when conditions are unsatisfactory and to be taken back when conditions are amended."

The pendulum had swung completely to the other side by 1941, when he urged a national court of arbitration for labor disputes and declared: "Strikes should be outlawed and the complete machinery to enforce their suppression should be fully established and fearlessly OPERATED."

On the question of newspaper editorial unions, Hearst declared himself against them as early as 1919. "The efforts to unionize the editorial departments of newspapers," he wrote in one of his "editorial letters" published in all his newspapers, "have largely prejudiced the press of the country against the whole trade union movement, for the absurdity, if not the sinister purpose, of such activity is self-evident. It is only a step further to organizing the doctors of the country so that they will not attend any one unless he has a union card, and to organizing the clergy so that they will not give any one absolution except during union hours."

The press of the country had already been "largely prejudiced" against trade unionism for the past forty years, but it had never been popular for a newspaper to say so. In fact, it may be doubted whether Hearst, the scourge of the "interests" and the trusts, supported unionism and the right to strike because he really believed in them or because it was so plainly illogical to attack the evils of big business and not support labor in the attack on the greatest evil of all, industry's attitude toward wages and hours.

On this question, Hearst consistently plugged away for shorter hours. In the bitter controversy over the eight-hour day, he sided with the workers against the steel trust, and as late as 1931, he astonished at least some of his readers with a vigorous declaration for the six-hour day.

He took the position, however, that "prosperity is based on the good wages which create purchasing power among the mass of the community," and the interference of union rules with productivity and the consequent price of goods seemed to him an upsetting of the balance. "Sweating" employers, he said, was as unwise as "sweating" labor.

From these and other statements it appears that Hearst was really a middle-of-the-roader in his labor views, though he did not appear so to either side. The industrialists denounced him in the twenties and before because he supported shorter hours and higher wages. Union men and most of the working press denounced him from the mid-thirties onward because of his fight against the Newspaper Guild and the extreme statements of some of his columnists.

Hard-pressed newsmen in the difficult years of the depression, just before the Guild was formed, were infuriated by Hearst's statement in June 1934, on the eve of sailing for Europe: "I do not believe in the Guild. I like to think of a man doing his work for the romance of it."

This was not the "airy remark" that one news magazine called it, but an honest and entirely logical declaration—logical, that is, in the light of his attitudes, which were consistent in this respect at least. In the strange, suspended world in which he lived, he considered the gathering and writing of news a romantic business, entirely apart from the business side. And even in the business department, he condoned and initiated practices which he roundly condemned in big business—because it was *his* business that was involved.

He could, therefore, defend the right to strike as a principle, but denounce it as a threat to private property if it involved one of his papers. He could insist on the rights of labor and the rights of capital with equal fervor, but he fought his own organized labor as ruthlessly as he had fought organized capital in the early days. The difference was that the fight against capital was conducted in the editorial columns and on the political platform; he fought his own workers in the realistic terms of the payroll. Yet he never thought of himself as inconsistent.

Hearst had to accept the Guild, as he was compelled to accept a good many other things which he had opposed, and until his death he insisted that he had always been a friend of labor. Certainly the American Federation of Labor and the trade union movement owed him much in the way of support before the vertical unionism of the CIO stirred him to general opposition against any labor movement.

On his own papers, it must be said, he contributed nothing whatever to the welfare of the men who worked for him. The highly paid executives were never more than a breath away from the ax. The working newspapermen, after the early years, were never paid more than was necessary, and their working conditions at any time left a staggering amount to be desired.

Those, however, who believed that the loyalty of a few top executives could never be duplicated in the lower echelons were astonished in 1939 when a Twenty-Year Club was formed among Hearst employees—twenty years that covered the period of highest turnover in the organization. There were 2100 eligible to join.

Hearst's "inconsistent consistency" in the matter of industrial relations was simply another facet of his contradictory nature. It is strange to recall that the man whose name was a byword for sex and sensationalism in journalism at one time banished such words as "rape," "abortion" and "seduction" from his newspapers, along with such stock phrases as "criminal assault," "betrayal under promise of marriage" and "born out of wedlock."

Koenigsberg recalls that before he took over the management of INS in 1919 it was known as "reliably unreliable" among Hearst editors, who used it only because they had to. In reorganizing the service, Koenigsberg changed its Hearstian motto, "Get it first," by adding, "But first get it right." Hearst agreed that this was a sensible change. "How can we expect the editors of our papers to comment intelligently on the actual news, if the news we supply to them is false?" he asked rhetorically. The remark, says Koenigsberg, was primarily, "a disclaimer of direct responsibility for the past. Secondarily, it was a sanction of the altered course."

Perhaps the inconsistencies of Hearst the editor and newspaper owner could be traced at last to the fact that he believed what he wanted to believe, and that whatever he believed at the moment was right. There were those who saw unconscious significance in the code signature he appended to his code telegrams.

The word was "Doctor."

## II

From 1904 onward, Hearst's empire grew like some magic kind of mushroom. A whimsical competitor might well have concluded that there were fairies at the bottom of his garden.

Few of his competitors were given to whimsey. In slug-happy Chicago, they were compelled to undergo nearly three decades of intermittent gang warfare, contained within the framework of the larger struggle for power between the underworld's strong men. Hearst has taken, unjustly, a major share of the blame for the long and bloody circulation wars which followed the establishment of his newspapers there. The conflict was precipitated by the other papers, who employed the customary rude tactics to keep Hearst papers off the newsstands by intimidation, violence and any loose paving stone that came to hand.

Hearst countered by hiring Max and Moses Annenberg to run his circulation department. These practical men recruited a frightening crew of persuaders who quickly equalized the situation so effectively that the *Tribune*, Hearst's chief competitor, hired the Annenbergs and their capable staff entire. Andy Lawrence, in turn, assembled a new and equally efficient, if less well-publicized, organization and the war was on. In 1918 the morning *Examiner* took over the *Record-Herald*, a Chicago paper which had gone through so many ownerships and mergers its original identity was forgotten, and the new

*Herald-Examiner* proceeded to establish itself with the aid of Dion O'Bannion, who directed its circulation activities until 1922. His other activities in behalf of illegal booze put him in the way of a well-aimed bullet in 1925.

The editorial side was involved with the underworld too, but then so were the *Tribune* and the *Daily News*. It was difficult, in fact, for a newspaper not to be involved in those days, unless it relied on its religious page for circulation.

In Boston, the conservative citizens of Beacon Hill were affronted by Hearst as early as 1904, and in the same year he extended his West Coast operations to Los Angeles with another *Examiner*. Meanwhile the *Journal* in New York and its morning edition, called the *American*, had moved from the original cramped quarters into the Rhinelander Building at 238 William Street.

There in the early morning hours of April 18, 1906, the wire ticked off the first flash of an earthquake in San Francisco. Hearst was home asleep, having worked very late the night before, but the agitated desk man who took the flash called him up immediately to relay the news.

"Don't overplay it," the boss's high, sleepy voice came over the wire. "They have earthquakes often in California." He hung up and went back to bed.

When he understood a few hours later that a major disaster had befallen his home town, he took it almost as a personal affront. Not only did he raise money in every direction for the city, but he felt compelled to defend California in his newspapers. The weather, he said, had been only a little unusual.

"The plain facts are that earthquakes in California, which occur at intervals of about twenty-year periods, kill far fewer people than the cyclones in the Middle West, the flood tornadoes in the South Coast states, and the lightning storms and heat waves along the Atlantic States kill every year. . . . Californians don't wholly approve of earthquakes, but they prefer them to cyclones or tornadoes or floods or protracted heat or lightning storms. . . . All of the earthquakes which have occurred

in California since it was discovered nearly four hundred years
ago have not killed so many people as one or two great cyclones of the Middle West."

There were no further assaults on California's honor.

For a man who regarded his home state as the cradle of
civilization, Hearst was paying little attention to it. For a few
years his empire remained relatively static while he pursued his
political ephemera, and when expansion began once more in
1912, it was in Georgia, the home of floods and tornadoes, that
he made his first move by purchasing the Atlanta *Daily Georgian*. Next year, however, he had bought the conservative San
Francisco *Morning Call* and made it into an evening paper.

During the war years, when most publishers disdained expansion for the high circulations of battle extras, Hearst bought
three more papers, the Washington *Times* and the Boston *Daily
Advertiser* in 1917, and the Wisconsin *News*, of Milwaukee,
in 1918. In the depression that followed the war, he acquired
three more, all in the same year, 1921: the Boston *Record*, the
Detroit *Times* and the Seattle *Post-Intelligencer*. To settle the
troublesome Boston situation that year, he merged the *Record*
with the *Advertiser*, which had plodded along its conservative
way since 1813. He took the *Advertiser's* Sunday rights and
features, combined them with his Sunday *American*, and issued
them as the *Sunday Advertiser*, which became a tabloid and in
1929 was changed to the *Record*.

A year after these events, Hearst reached his fifty-ninth birthday, and in his usual philosophic statement to the press—in each
one of which, from about this time on, he portrayed himself as
ready to retire—he declared: "I never plan any extensions, but
newspapers seem just naturally to keep coming to me to be
taken over. I am not as young as I was once, and the older we
get the less likely we are to set out to conquer the world."

Whereupon he bought himself five more newspapers in the
same year, 1922. They were the Washington *Herald*, the Rochester *Journal*, the Oakland *Post-Enquirer*, the Los Angeles *Herald*, and the Syracuse *Telegram*, which lost its identity three

years later in a merger with Hearst's Syracuse *Journal*. For good measure, he established the *Daily Mirror* in New York.

A year after this wholesale purchase, he acquired the Baltimore *News*, and the Albany *Times-Union* the year after that, along with the San Antonio *Light* and the Milwaukee *Sentinel*.

When he rested on his oars, he had an audience of more than three million people for his Sunday morning papers, and perhaps twice that on weekdays. His California papers alone earned him five million dollars a year.

For a man who had lost his inclination to conquer the world and confronted a barren old age, this had been an impressive three years of work. Nor was that the end of it. He bought the Pittsburgh *Sun-Telegraph* in 1927 and the Omaha *News-Bee* a year later. In 1929 he acquired the San Francisco *Bulletin* and combined it with the *Call*, to corner the evening field. A year before he had moved the venerable New York *Journal* from the Rhinelander Building into a whole block of buildings at 220 South Street. At last, in 1931, he took over the Los Angeles *Express* and merged it with the *Herald* to make the *Herald-Express* what the *Call-Bulletin* was in San Francisco.

That was the end of expansion. Henceforth the history of the Hearst empire was one of decline, and then consolidation on a restricted beachhead.

During these nearly three decades of unrestricted growth in the newspaper business, he had simultaneously built a magazine dominion, a field he wandered into almost by accident. It was while he and Millicent were touring Europe in his new car on their 1903 honeymoon that he fell in love with the automobile. He had just learned to drive, and he put his red scorcher over the road at a speed that thrilled him and terrified his bride.

When they got to London, he picked up a copy of a new magazine, *The Car*. It fitted his mood exactly, and he mailed several copies to Carvalho with the suggestion that he would like to establish a similar one in America.

The Chief's word was law and Carvalho brought the magazine *Motor* into almost immediate existence, against the advice of every other executive in the organization. Hearst paid no attention to the opposition. He called in George d'Utassy, circulation manager of the Chicago *American,* gave him a check for $10,000, and told him to consider himself a personal representative of Hearst in charge of *Motor.* The difference between magazines and newspapers was one of details, he said, not essentials, and d'Utassy was instructed to prove that the Hearst executives were wrong when they said he had made a mistake to get into the magazine field.

The executives were partly right. Hearst had his failures, four flat ones and a near miss, but before he was through he had thirteen operating magazines to his credit, and the failures were somewhat offset by one that was so successful it was considered by some experts to be the second most valuable magazine property in the world.

This accomplishment was all the more remarkable when it is considered that Hearst did not pour into his magazines the steady flow of gold which kept the newspapers alive at the beginning. Indeed, if d'Utassy is not exaggerating, the $10,000 check he got along with *Motor* was the only cash that went into the magazines during the years he worked with them. The system was built up, he told Mrs. Older later, "by using credit with printers and paper makers, and by giving bonds and redeeming them out of the profits when other magazines were bought. . . ."

*Motor* turned into the black after less than a year, and in 1905 Hearst was emboldened to form the International Magazine Company and take a real flyer with the purchase of *Cosmopolitan* for $400,000 worth of bonds. Three years later he had redeemed the bonds and taken a nice profit from the magazine's million circulation.

Hearst's editorial way with magazines was much like his practice with newspapers. On *Cosmopolitan,* his particular pet, he scribbled his marginal comments every month, watching its progress carefully. He was still doing this in his last days. Only a year or so before he died the editors of the magazine were getting comments from Beverly Hills, suggesting changes in cover and content.

He wanted *Cosmopolitan* to be the finest magazine in America, printing "not only that which is best, but that which is universally recognized as best." The editors interpreted this to mean big names, and for decades *Cosmopolitan* was a "name" magazine into which no writer without a gold-plated reputation could crash. Whether the prose that the "name" wrote deserved to be printed in *Cosmopolitan* or anywhere else was not a consideration, so the magazine carried such oddly assorted talents as Winston Churchill and Raymond Moley, Einstein and the Grand Duchess Marie, Bernard Shaw and Kathleen Norris, H. G. Wells and Mussolini.

Nor was the appearance of a name any guarantee that his best would be forthcoming, even for the fabulous prices which lured the literary celebrities away from other magazines and their more serious writing. Consequently, the pages of *Cosmopolitan* were sometimes decorated with prose that was something far less than the best efforts of André Maurois, John Galsworthy, Ernest Hemingway and Rudyard Kipling.

D'Utassy has provided posterity with two anecdotes which show Hearst at work on *Cosmopolitan*, and in a particularly revealing light. When David Graham Phillips was preparing his series of shocking articles, "The Treason of the Senate," depicting the crushing grip of the Payne-Aldrich bloc on the legislative process, Hearst happened to be in Washington, where d'Utassy sent him proofs of the first article. This elicited a long telegram which arrived at two o'clock in the morning, while the presses were being prepared to roll with the issue. The telegram began: "Violence is not force. Windy vituperation is not convincing. I had intended an exposé. We have merely an attack. The facts, the proofs, the documentary evidence are an important thing, and the article is deficient in them. . . ."

He went on with a specific example and concluded, "We want more definite facts throughout. Supply them where you can.

Then run the article if you want, and we will try to get the others later."

A few hours after, Hearst called d'Utassy by telephone and asked if the first press run could be stopped. D'Utassy replied that it could, well knowing that it would be in any event. "Fine," Hearst said, and three hours later his rewrite of Phillips' article began to come over the wire. How Hearst managed to round up enough "definite facts" for a rewrite in that time, d'Utassy did not say, although he does remark that Phillips thought the rewrite was "100 per cent better," which seems unlikely.

On another occasion, when d'Utassy remarked to Hearst that he thought *Cosmopolitan's* readers were tiring of a short-story series (George Randolph Chester's "Get-Rich-Quick Walling-ford" stories, which George Horace Lorimer had pioneered in the *Saturday Evening Post*), Hearst replied with an instructive reminiscence.

When he had been trying to acquire the successful "Buster Brown" comic, he said, his own Sunday editor had told him that the "Buster Brown" strip had been running three years, had three more years to go, and people were already tired of it. Nevertheless, said Hearst, unperturbed, sign him when the three years are up.

"We finally got 'Buster Brown,'" Hearst concluded, "and it added a hundred thousand circulation to my Sunday paper. My opinion is that when editors begin to get tired of a feature, the public is just beginning to like it."

D'Utassy observes that the "successful formula" Hearst established in his magazines was, "Find out what your readers want, and give it to them. And give it to them regularly."

That was his newspaper formula, and while it may be questionable whether it was consistent with responsibility in that field, there is no question that it echoed the most earnest sentiments of every other magazine publisher.

Hearst expanded his periodical list slowly but steadily. In 1907 he bought *Motor Boating*, a specialized publication that was about to expire, and hired an expert named Charles F. Chapman to edit it, which he did profitably for several decades.

He formed an English organization, the National Magazine Company, Ltd., in December 1910, and began to publish *Nash's Magazine* as his own. This was a hybrid Anglo-American periodical, a sort of British *Saturday Evening Post*, but under the editorship of J. Y. McPeake, an astute Irishman, it made money, with a good many of the names that appeared in *Cosmopolitan*.

His most profitable purchase came in 1911 with the acquisition of *Good Housekeeping*, an amiable but decaying magazine published in Springfield, Massachusetts. D'Utassy concluded this deal one morning for $300,000 in bonds, had lunch, signed the papers, and caught the 1:02 train back home. *Good Housekeeping* became the best and most successful of all Hearst's magazine properties, and remains so today.

Shortly after this speed record was established, Hearst bolstered *Cosmopolitan* by acquiring *The World Today* for $25,000, jacking up its minuscule circulation to 400,000 and combining it with *Cosmo*.

He got a far better bargain in 1912 when he obtained *Harper's Bazaar*, which had been virtually put out of business by *Vogue*, for only $10,000. He succeeded in resuscitating the *Bazaar* and making a place for it in the high-fashion field, but he never quite caught *Vogue*, though he tried to wreck it as he had the old *World* by hiring away its editors. He hooked some large fish but never the chief editor who maintained the magazine's superiority, Edna Woolman Chase, Ilka's beloved mother. She had little use for Hearst, and even less for the Hearst method.

Hearst had better luck with his other magazines in the women's field. From the new home of his English company, 1 Amen Corner, in the lee of St. Paul's Cathedral, he issued in March 1922 the first copy of the English edition of *Good Housekeeping*, which earned so much money in three years that Hearst bought St. Donat's Castle with the proceeds. He followed this in 1929 with an English edition of *Harper's Bazaar*, two years after he had bought a magazine that really delighted him, an art publication called the *Connoisseur*, read mostly by antique dealers and collectors.

He purchased America's society Bible, *Town and Country*, in 1925, and in 1929 the more plebeian *Home and Field*, which had to be merged four years later with *House Beautiful*, bought in that year.

Two specialized magazines completed his stable: the *American Architect*, added in 1929, and the *American Druggist*, in 1927.

With all these buyings and mergings, both magazines and newspapers, Hearst drifted from his second phase into the late twenties, which constituted a rather ill-defined Third Phase— capital letters, because at this stage he stood at the peak of his fortunes and from there surveyed his empire and the world with the detachment becoming a Lord of San Simeon. His viewpoint was cosmic. As Brisbane put it with sour insight:

"If Mr. Hearst decides that Russia is no good, those who work for him must write that way. That's his prerogative, for which he pays those well who obey him. . . . Treat him as a modern Louis XIV and you can rationalize his actions. He is the last of his kind in the newspaper business. The days of palaces in democracy are over. I've tried to tell him that, but he's going to die like a king. . . ."

The cosmic attitude was sometimes carried to absurd lengths. After Hearst was invited to leave France in 1930, he was unable to report any virtues occurring in that part of the world, not only subsequent to the event, but for several centuries before. Brisbane's editorials began to take a dim view of Napoleon's genius, and several times he pointed out that the Emperor was defeated by a second-rate commander, Wellington, thus slipping a sly knife into England at the same time.

Brisbane's chastisements fell upon just and unjust nations alike, and no man, Brisbane least of all, knew where they would descend next. The geographical point was determined by what country had happened to offend Hearst. In any event, Brisbane was able to prove, no matter what the case in point might be, that the trouble was really caused by the American Government's naïveté in the face of cunning, masterful, self-seeking British diplomacy. Hearst had hit upon this theme in the early pro-Irish, anti-British days in New York, long before Colonel McCormick played infinite variations upon it and it was taken up generally by the isolationist press.

The cosmic touch was applied without difficulty to the less historic society page, where, as Emile Gauvreau recalls from his days as editor of the *Mirror*, "a dowager might be recognized as omnipotent by the *Times*, treated as a Hindu deity by the *Sun*, and land in our wastebasket because she had snubbed Mrs. Hearst." Gauvreau was given a list of those who were inside the pale, but it had to be consulted daily because its composition was subject to change without notice.

Gauvreau, whose autobiography, *My Last Million Readers*, provides as graphic an editorial picture as exists of Hearst in this Third Phase, recalls that Walter Howey took the first copy of the *Mirror* to Hearst in his apartment at the Clarendon. By that time the master was so adept at handling papers with his feet that he flipped the tabloid pages with his bare toes as he sat on a large pile of cushions.

Seven years passed before he appeared in the *Mirror's* office. In anticipation of his coming, the publisher, Albert J. Kobler, had ordered the city-room floor swept and requested the staff to pull up its ties and put on jackets. Hearst appeared and talked first with Gauvreau, tossing off such aphorisms as, "It's what you leave out of a newspaper that keeps the dullness from it. The more you leave out, the brighter the paper becomes."

Then he moved on to the city room and surveyed its spotless expanse with something like apprehension. "This place looks too damned clean for a newspaper office," he said suspiciously.

Gauvreau was under no illusions as to what kind of office it was, nor had he been since the Sunday morning in the summer of 1929 when he met Hearst for the first time. He had just come from directing the mass insanity of Bernarr Macfadden's *Graphic*, after which even Hearst would have appeared sane and reasonable.

Kobler had taken him for a ride that morning. It ended at Sands Point, where unexpectedly he found himself introduced to Hearst, who was sitting at the breakfast table with Millicent. Gauvreau's impression was one of "a big man" who "rolled about restlessly in a massive chair, his head thrust out on a thick neck. His frame seemed to be made of loose, clumsy bones and as he looked at me his heavy hands reached out, here and there, for opened tins of imported delicacies from which he speared choice bits and ate them in a nibbling fashion. . . . The eyes I looked into may have been cold for a fleeting moment but were filled immediately with merriment.

" 'So *you're* the *Graphic*,' Hearst laughed. 'You have created an awful nuisance. It may not be an indictable nuisance, but it is irritating to the *Journal*. . . . Sit down,' he said, pushing some of the tins toward me. 'Try some of these things. They have come a long way and I find them delicious.' "

They discussed the mad career of the *Graphic* at length. Hearst thought Macfadden had made a mistake in not selling it. He went on to praise his morning rival, Captain Patterson's *Daily News*, and appeared not to be intimidated by its commanding lead. He believed it could be caught.

"It will have to be a battle of brains," he said. "Papers are no longer put over by rough and tumble fighting. When I think of what we had to go through in Chicago, I'm glad those days are over."

Gauvreau remembers that their breakfast-table conversation went on, covering an astonishing range of topics—comic strips, motion-picture stars (not Miss Davies, one presumes), the League of Nations. Gauvreau thought him "quick in comprehension, positive in conclusions, strong in his likes and dislikes, emphatic in his utterances. Once or twice he disagreed with me rather harshly but I felt that his manner covered an affectionate nature for those to whom he became attached. Up to that time I had never met a man of more diversified interests. He was endowed with a fascinating charm."

To demonstrate his charm, Hearst told a little story, apropos of bores he had met. A friend of his bought a parrot, he said, with the laudable purpose of insulting a banker friend who was given to excessive bragging, and whom he couldn't insult himself for business reasons. "When the banker visited my friend and began to brag," Hearst related, "the parrot preened in its cage and in a skeptical voice said: 'Aw, Chr-i-i-i-st! Aw, Chri-i-i-st!' The banker finally caught on."

This was all very pleasant, but a little later that day, when Hearst and Kobler and Gauvreau were riding back to town in Hearst's limousine, the *Mirror's* future editor got a chilling preview of what it was like to work for the master of Sands Point and San Simeon. Hearst had been in a very good humor, humming under his breath a melody from the new motion picture, *Broadway*, and keeping time with his fingernails on the window of the car. But when the talk turned to the *Mirror's* current losses, Hearst turned his cold steady eyes on Kobler and remarked: "Remember, Albert, that you are in the position of a man who has moved into a house after buying it under a mortgage. And I'm the man who holds the mortgage. You're running the house and paying off on the mortgage."

When Gauvreau was hired as editor shortly afterward, at a salary of $25,000 a year, he was indoctrinated immediately in the Hearst method by walking into a situation typical of it. Walter Howey, the veteran Hearst editor, who was the inspiration for Hildy Johnson's city-room nemesis in *The Front Page*, was sitting serenely at the helm. He had not been told Gauvreau was to replace him.

Both men were embarrassed, but true to practice, they occupied the same office for a time, smiling at each other, each one undoing the other's work, although it was Gauvreau's orders that were obeyed in the end, since everyone knew who was really boss.

When Gauvreau complained to Kobler about the anomalous situation, the publisher told him, "This matter requires the tactics of a Talleyrand. It is part of the office routine of all Hearst enterprises, which you will understand as you become a part of the family. It will work itself into an explosion and when the fireworks are over, Mr. Howey will no longer be around."

And so it came to pass, but not until a crisis was precipitated in which Howey threw the type of a disputed story on the floor, Gauvreau had appealed to Kobler, and Kobler in turn had taken the matter directly to Colonel Frank Knox, who was then general manager of all Hearst publications. Knox settled things by sending around a notice that Gauvreau was the only official editor.

In the fullness of time Gauvreau, too, was fired summarily for writing a book about Russia which irritated Hearst. He took it philosophically. Like some other Hearst editors, he thought one experience was enough.

### III

If there was a dominant note in the way Hearst ran his newspapers, it was the crusade. From the beginning that was his forte, his métier, the bridge he built between himself and the rest of humanity.

There has been considerable scoffing about these crusades. It is said that they were, without exception, conducted for circulation purposes and nothing else. It is said they were a cynical mockery of reform, that they obscured the efforts of real reformers by leading the yelping pack off on false scents.

Naturally there is some truth in these charges. Unquestionably Hearst ordered crusades which were designed to get circulation, publicity, and to put himself in the best possible light. But he did not invent this practice in the newspaper business, nor was he by any means the only one to practice it. The journalistic underbrush still harbors some strident practitioners of the art.

When the Hearst career is viewed in perspective, it can be seen that there were certain fundamental ideas for which he fought consistently all his life. Everyone who reached an elevated position in the Hearst hierarchy, where he worked directly under W.R., appears to have been aware of this. For these ideas he believed in he would sacrifice circulation if necessary, or men, or institutions, or anything else that opposed him. And because he "believed what he wanted to believe" in such matters, frequently the truth itself was a victim.

That was the difficulty with his crusading. It was fanatical, unyielding, ruthless, as nothing else in his editorial method ever approached being, and it was bound to add to the reputation for which he cared so little. The unremitting attack he made in his newspapers year after year on the most eminent captains of industry baffled and profoundly irritated these fellow capitalists. He used them and their banks and services when he needed them, but he had little in common with them and he let them know it. They had spent their lives in the acquisition of money through the hard discipline of business; Hearst had spent his having fun, working as hard as they, but always at what he liked best and with no particular regard for profit or loss, except at the beginning and end of his career.

One of his former associates, contemplating this odd fact, looked out of his office window recently at the trim, correct apertures in the blank Wall Street faces of the buildings across the street and observed: "The bankers fought him for years, then he turned around and kissed them. They couldn't figure it out."

Hearst had it figured out, down to the last comma. He knew what he believed, though it might appear contradictory, hypocritical or purely cynical to others. The word "crusade" itself had its peculiar meaning to him. It must not be "necessarily considered as an attack," he told a convention of Hearst executives at San Antonio in 1929. "Attack is the easiest form of crusade, but it is the least advantageous to the community, and the least beneficial to the newspapers. It is easy to pull down and difficult to build up. It takes more thought and more knowledge, more conscientious sense of public duty, to outline and develop a constructive campaign than it does to be merely critical of conditions which may be unsatisfactory.

"I feel that it is desirable for the papers not to make enemies by violent attacks: but it is essential for the papers to conduct constructive campaigns for the benefit of the community with which they are associated. . . . Make crusades, but take enough interest in the affairs of your community and give enough thought to the situation existing to be able to make constructive crusades and accomplish results of actual, acknowledged value."

This is an excellent case in point. To the countercharge that the Hearst papers never made attacks except of the most violent kind, Hearst would undoubtedly have replied, "They fight hard"—and believed it. Were the campaigns constructive and in the best interests of the community? The mighty chorus of "nos" in reply would certainly have to be separated as to time and place, and then it would be clearly evident that they were constructive or not depending on whose ox was being gored.

Here is Hearst in March 1917 on universal military service, as hot and controversial an issue then as it is in 1952, when these words are written. Hearst was in favor of it. "I believe it is the only effective system, the only democratic system," he said. "I believe that a small army is of small value in these times of great wars and that a large and standing army would be a menace to our democratic institutions." That was the stand of the Democrats in 1917, as it is now, and the opposition to universal service came from right-wing Republicans. The Republicans thought Hearst was a menace.

Here he is in September 1925, on the question of a unified air force. "Our Government should recognize the special technical knowledge required for the competent conduct of the aircraft service, and create a department like the Navy department or the Army department with a secretary of aviation to manage it. This is deeply and doubly necessary, not only because of the technical knowledge required, but because aviation is becoming even more important than the Army or the Navy, both as an instrument of war and an agency of peace."

Shades of Billy Mitchell! And let us invoke the living presence of Major Alexander P. DeSeversky and the other fighters for air power and a unified air force more than fifteen years later. Both Republicans and Democrats, and a good part of the Chiefs of Staff and the brass of both Army and Navy, thought he was a menace on this one, but he kept at the crusade year after year. He wrote on March 27, 1938: "The next war will be fought in the air and won in the air."

Here is Hearst in October 1930 on the subject of organized charity: "I do not approve of the Community Chest and its method of raising money, particularly the methods of various companies and large employers of labor of assessing employes for the benefit of the Chest, or intimating to employes that it is the desire of the company or employer that they contribute to the Chest, which amounts to a threat and compels for the most part unwilling contributions."

This brought down upon him the condemnation of right-thinking people everywhere, both employers and employees, liberals and conservatives—all, that is, except those large charities which refused to join the Chest. They agreed with him, although they did not consider it expedient to say so.

"I admit that I never did believe that Prohibition would be effective as a temperance measure," Hearst remarked to his millions of readers on January 4, 1925, "for the reason that from the first it seemed inevitable, considering the character of our people, that a campaign of force would not be as effective as a campaign of education. . . . This opinion seems to have been borne out by the facts; and I think it can be truthfully said today that any man who wants a drink can get one; and about the only difference between the present condition and the condition preceding Prohibition is that a man who wants a mild drink is compelled to take a strong one; and a man who wants a good drink is compelled to take a bad one. . . ."

As a result of these words, the Hearst newspapers were received with even less favor than they had been heretofore in Evanston, Illinois, and they angered a large body of conservatives who still believed in Prohibition. Hearst was against drinking for himself, before, during and after Prohibition, but a man could always get a drink from him, except in the guest rooms at San Simeon.

Hearst was also against vivisection and capital punishment, both spiritual inheritances from his mother, and in these cases he was attacked by the realists as an arrant sentimentalist. But he also believed that Communists should not be permitted to teach in the public schools, and on this the sentimentalists attacked him as a fake realist.

Occasionally he took foursquare stands like Calvin Coolidge's minister who was agin sin, and no one of any reputation could denounce him. His papers fought long and hard against narcotics, for example, a good many years before the rest of the press interested itself in the traffic. In 1934 he came out against decadence, and speaking with the voice of authority, he asserted: "We have aged too fast. We have become rotten even before we became rich. We achieved sudden wealth, and the luxury which followed in its path, instead of developing naturally in the direction of culture and refinement, curdled overnight into licentiousness and depravity."

It must be noted, however, that in viewing with alarm the depravity that had overtaken art, letters and drama in America, Hearst was careful to exempt the silver screen, on which, he declared blandly, the "era of cheap indecency is over."

Long before the Kefauver committee, in December 1934, Hearst was saying, almost in the words of the Senator from Tennessee: "We should begin now making constant and vigorous editorial campaigns for extensive Federal secret service organization to combat crime in the United States. We cannot depend at all on incompetent and corrupt local agencies. . . . Underworld criminal activity, underworld corruption of police machinery, is nation-wide. The fight to save the country from crime and corruption must be nation-wide. . . ."

Here the master spoke authoritatively, since no papers in the United States had printed more news of crime and corruption than his, and at least in some cities the Hearst newspapers had not struggled to save the souls of the police department.

In the fight against Communism, which brought Hearst the most attention during the course of his last years, it is the boast of the Hearst newspapers that they have been "guided BY FACTS and have never been influenced BY DELUSIONS."

The facts are that Hearst followed much the same path that many an honest liberal pursued in the twenties and thirties—first, believing that a new democratic era had dawned in Russia, then progressive disillusionment, and finally a full awakening to the bear outside the door. It must be said that Hearst's disillusion came earlier than that of most liberals, but then the threat of Communism to the interests of a man like Hearst was much plainer, much sooner, than its terrible threat to the existence of men of good will everywhere.

In the effort to prove that he had never been deluded for a moment, Hearst had to resort to some interesting revisions of history. The czars, he said, had been overthrown by a "Social Democratic" revolution during the first World War, and toward these good revolutionists the Hearst papers had expressed "a benevolent attitude." But then some wicked revolutionists, a Bolshevik minority, had usurped power "with the connivance of the German militarists." Even then the Hearst papers had upheld the right of the Russians to choose their own government "without outside interference," particularly during the period of the initial Five-Year Plan, when American engineers were helping to industrialize the country. The Hearst papers even "published a notable series of authoritative articles in commendation of the Russian efforts."

Somehow a Bolshevik snake got into Paradise, however, and the Kremlin betrayed not only the Russian people, which was bad enough, but then "the BOLSHEVIKS THEMSELVES made it the duty of the Hearst Newspapers to oppose Communism IN THE UNITED STATES," and later they "compelled the Hearst Newspapers to produce and to publish THE

TRUTH about the Communism IN RUSSIA." In brief, they made the mistake of betraying Hearst.

The betrayal was real enough. On March 1, 1918, Hearst called the Bolsheviki "the representatives of the most democratic Government in Europe," and he argued: "We recognized the IMPERIAL Government of Russia, but when Russia secures a DEMOCRATIC Government we have so far not recognized it. Does not this seem to discredit our professions of a war for democracy?"

A year later he addressed an editorial letter to the Hon. James A. Reed, a member of the Senate Foreign Relations Committee, in which he warned that Bolshevism would spread like a prairie fire in America unless corrective legislation was enacted. A blow for conservatism? Not at all, because he respectfully suggested that "Congress and the Administration should use their great powers to obviate or eliminate THE CONDITIONS WHICH CREATE BOLSHEVISM." And what were those conditions? Why, "the result of a certain lawlessness and violence and brutal disregard for the rights of others which characterize the only autocracy we have in this country—the autocracy of wealth and privilege. . . ."

It took Hearst quite a few years to wake up to what the Communist conspiracy was all about. It was, in fact, 1934 before he could report sadly: "We recognized Russia. Now it is just as well to recognize what we recognized. It is the same old Russia as under the Czars. It is the same old tyranny under a different name. . . ."

When he became aware of what the Kremlin intended to do with the world, it is likely that Hearst was profoundly shocked and frightened. If there was one thing in the world he honestly and wholeheartedly believed in, it was love of country. His was not a spurious patriotism, but an absolute devotion, an intense nationalism. This led him to the most violent of all his crusades, a violence in which the good became inextricably intermixed with the bad.

His enemies said he was "soft" about Fascism, but that was not because he admired the ultimate barbarities and negations of the Fascist regimes; he considered them bulwarks against the Communism he feared most, and because he wanted to believe it so much, he believed that the free world could do business with Hitler and Mussolini. He would even, by his own admission, not have turned his back on Fascism in America if it were necessary to fight Communism. In 1934 he predicted that "Fascism will only come into existence in the United States when such a movement becomes really necessary for the prevention of Communism." He was not awake to the menace of Fascism until it knocked on the door of Pearl Harbor.

The excesses to which Hearst's anti-Communist zeal led him, and continued to lead him until he died, need not be rehearsed here. No doubt if anyone had questioned him on the point, he would have given a Communist answer: "The end justifies the means." To cite one example, it may have been a salutary thing to flush out whatever Reds were teaching in the colleges, but the Hearst method in the end tarred as Red every teacher who failed to embrace Hearst's philosophy. In this he was the forerunner and the bellwether of the political cult that has flowered in the last decade, the totalitarianism of the right. With Hearst, as with others, it had its roots in the reaction to Roosevelt, and came to full bloom in the divisive split in American life between nationalism and internationalism.

When one surveys the whole range of Hearst's crusading, a day-by-day affair beginning in 1887, several facts emerge. One is the nearly total absence of victory on large issues. Another is the surprising number of successes on small ones. A third is the gradual swing from Democratic to Republican principles, even including the hated high tariff, which Hearst finally admitted in 1934 was a good thing if it included the farmers as well as the industrialists.

Those who scoff at Hearst's lack of principle in these crusades would do well to remember how unpopular some of them were. Supporting Bryan in 1896 cost the *Journal* $100,000 a month in advertising and circulation. Hearst was considered a traitor to his class, and no other paper of any consequence in the East came out for Bryan. In this case, relief came from the Bryan voters in the outlying precincts of New England, New York State and Pennsylvania, who belatedly discovered that their champion had a champion.

"The country needs a rest," Hearst said in an editorial when the election was over. Certainly *he* did. He sent flowers to Bryan.

The crusade against McKinley would have cost him his life if he had showed his face to the mob. It was a crusade as bitter as that against Franklin D. Roosevelt, and no doubt there were some New Dealers who harbored the homicidal thoughts about him that fleeted through the minds of McKinley men.

The crusades against the trusts may have been faked in some instances, as has been charged, with the idea of trading silence for advertising, but this could not possibly have been true in more than a few cases, because of the sheer number of combinations Hearst took on, and because he actually did lose advertising constantly.

Former Hearst executives who no longer have to put the best face on things say that the advertising departments on the papers always met with more than ordinary resistance, and it increased through the first three decades of the century as the result of Hearst's constant pressure against big business, which generated a hatred and distrust of Hearst newspapers among businessmen generally.

A major crusade, which won him denunciation as a Socialist, was on behalf of municipal ownership of public utilities. He battled the gas trust, the power trust, the traction trust and the whole complex of interlocking trusts which fixed rates and services for millions of people in a "public be damned" spirit until state and federal governments regulated them. It was not popular to be against these trusts.

The platforms of Hearst newspapers in the early days were usually built around woman suffrage, the direct vote for United States senators, a graduated income tax, municipal ownership and operation of traction companies, the initiative and referendum, a workmen's compensation law and the improvement of schools. Hearst was consistently for all these reforms until, one by one, they were accomplished. In his later years he soured on the whole idea of municipal ownership through what he considered its failure in San Francisco.

Clarence W. Shearn, one of Hearst's oldest associates and for years his chief legal counsel in these countless crusades, says that he once asked Hearst why he devoted a good part of his time, money and energy to crusading. The answer he says Hearst gave him sounds somewhat as though it was intended to be reprinted in an official biography, as in fact it was.

"While I was in college," Hearst is supposed to have said, "I saw about me two classes struggling. On one side were capitalists, to whom I supposed I naturally belonged. On the other side were masses of inarticulate people. Big business was always represented by clever and able lawyers. The other side was virtually unrepresented. I made up my mind to try to help the weaker side. I never changed. I shall keep right on."

Although this statement appears ridiculous to people who have observed at first hand how particular crusades were carried out by the Hearst newspapers, there is good reason to think Hearst believed that it truly represented his feelings. And in the years of trust-busting, from about 1900 to the first World War, the fight of the Hearst newspapers was truly for the people, whatever personal defections or circulation gains may have been involved. They were a strident, demanding voice which, if nothing else, helped to keep the issues alive in the public mind until legislative correction was compelled.

But trusts were no longer a live controversy by the time the war was over, and Hearst had to turn elsewhere. He had a ready-made issue, one in which he believed: the battle against the League of Nations. As an isolationist before the war, it was natural that he should be the voice of the League-wreckers. The implacable opposition of President Wilson, the only politician who ever consistently shunned him, was an added reason for the importance he attached to this campaign. It was, he said later, the most important of his life. He told Mrs. Older:

"Other editors might have carried on my other campaigns, but there was no one else with so many newspapers actively interested in defeating the League of Nations. I am a pacifist in the sense that I always try to keep the United States out of war. If it had not been for my papers, this country might, through the League of Nations, have become involved in war."

This opinion was echoed by Senator Hiram Johnson. "Without the campaign made by Hearst, the United States would probably have been in the League of Nations," declared the Senator, who had by that time forgotten the unpleasant things he had said about Hearst in San Francisco a few years before.

On the whole question of war and peace, nationalism against internationalism, Hearst was consistently attacked by both sides. Before each of the two World Wars he was isolationist—"pacifist," as he would have termed it—and consequently under fire from those who would take arms in defense of democratic ideals. Yet his militant patriotism, which called for a big Army and Navy and a big air force in time of peace, was assailed with equal fervor by some of the same people who applauded his isolationism.

Thus the eternal Hearst paradox. Small wonder that the only person who remained unconfused was Hearst, to whom it was all very logical.

Logical and, one might add, a part of the Hearst personality. He loved the theater but he was too shy to indulge in personal theatrics, so Jane Addams may well be believed when she describes how his voice broke with emotion as he attacked capital punishment in 1927 before the American Crime Study Commission.

There was no doubt, either, of his indignation in 1932 when President Hoover ordered the routing of the bonus marchers in Washington, which was performed to the accompaniment of tear gas and bloodshed by his able Chief of Staff, General Douglas MacArthur. The word from the White House was that these veterans were Reds and agitators. Hearst took their part. He had had recent experience of such charges. Strange as it may seem now, in 1928 he had been violently attacked by Samuel Insull during the Chicago utilities baron's effort to prove that everybody who opposed private ownership of utilities was a Communist, or at least a pink theorist. That made Hearst as deep-dyed a Red as Stalin, since no one had opposed private ownership so vociferously or for so long a time.

Hearst's indignation over the bonus-march incident may be judged by the telegram he sent to E. D. Coblentz, then editor of the New York *American:* "I do not care if every paper in the United States comments favorably on Hoover's action. I think it was the most outrageous piece of stupidity, if nothing worse, that has ever been perpetrated by the Government. If the idea is to develop Bolshevism in this country, there is no better way of doing it. Certainly the action of the Government cannot be excused or explained, if it had any other purpose in mind. . . . If you think turning the rules is too hysterical, do not do it. But I feel like mourning not only the death of the veterans, but mourning the passing of American sentiment and democratic principles. . . ."

This was a private telegram, not intended for publication.

Wherever there were Hearst newspapers, there were Hearst crusades: In Washington, pure milk and a standard weight for bread. In Boston and New England, lower coal prices and a protective tariff on women's shoes. In Seattle, municipal lighting, airports and exploitation of Alaskan reindeer herds. In Oakland, public ownership of water. In Detroit, telephone and gas rates. In Baltimore, the price of sugar. In Rochester, scholarships for children. In Albany, civic improvement. In San Antonio and Atlanta, new school buildings.

It was in the translation of a crusade, from Hearst to the particular newspaper, that unreality set in. To Hearst it was the large issue, whatever it might be, that was important. His instructions were explicit, but without much regard for the grass-roots reality of a situation. To the men in the newspaper shop, taking these orders from on high, it was a matter of producing what would appear to be results. Failure was not tolerated.

Thus to Hearst the giving of orders and the subsequent results as they appeared in the columns of his newspapers were part of a well-worn cause-and-effect pattern. In the earlier days of his papers, the effect, if any, proceeded directly from the cause and Hearst was on hand to see it in operation. But in the later years, he simply assumed that the pattern persisted, and it never occurred to him to question the validity of what one of his papers printed.

To cite a specific example, there was the business of the "Paul Revere" trains, an idea which Hearst promoted in 1938 while he was fighting President Roosevelt's bill designed to reorganize the executive and departmental structure of the Federal government, a bill which presumably Senator James F. Byrnes, who sponsored it, now shudders to recall.

The anti-Roosevelt press was up in arms over this measure. Someone in the Hearst organization suggested that it would be a good idea to run "Paul Revere trains" to Washington, loaded with protesting citizens—a more luxurious version of the bonus march. The idea elicited an instant communiqué to all editors from San Simeon:

"Paul Revere trains to Washington are splendid idea for all our Eastern papers and should be undertaken immediately. We might be able to get trains not only from our main cities in which we publish but from cities within our reach. These trains may exert tremendous influence. Doubtless the expense can be partly defrayed by patriotic citizens journeying on the train and partly by the papers. . . ."

A few hours later came this second thought from San Simeon: "Chief says Paul Revere trains must be financed entirely by occupants. Please investigate local sentiment and wire this office if sure trains can be arranged immediately. Likely bill will come to vote Monday afternoon."

One of the reporters who was on the executing end of this crusade recalls that "we were busy all day calling people to urge

them to organize a trainload and go to the capital as Paul
Reveres. The whole office was busy on the train story while
the day's news was pretty much ignored. It seemed to us that
we, as reporters, spent more time promoting campaigns and
drives on orders from San Simeon than we did covering the
news—and yet Hearst was always preaching that the function
of a newspaper was primarily news."

What happened in Chicago to the Paul Revere train offers
a splendid example of the unreality of the Hearst method, and
of the difference between the world as seen from San Simeon
and as seen from the sordid vantage point of the working press.

The Chicago *Herald and Examiner* reported as follows on
April 6, 1938: "Mobilized spontaneously, a great cross-section
of Chicago and Illinois was preparing last night to depart for
Washington in personal protest against President Roosevelt's
government reorganization bill.

". . . Even as thousands of protest messages continued to
cramp local telegraph facilities, postal clerks and carriers affili-
ated with the Civil Service Boosters League organized a delegation to join the Paul Revere movement to Washington.

"Delegations from the Association of Commerce and the
Junior Association are already in Washington, waging a relentless fight against the dictator bill, and will join the Paul Reveres
upon their arrival."

When the Paul Reveres embarked for Washington next day,
the opposition newspapers made an effort to count the heads of
those "mobilized spontaneously," a nice contradiction in itself.
The Chicago *Daily News* estimated that 350 persons heeded the
call. The *Daily Times*, a pro-Roosevelt paper, was much less
optimistic and caught the *Herald and Examiner* with its crusade
down. The *Times* reported:

"A *Times* reporter, checking through the 'special Paul
Revere' car—in fact the whole train—was unable to find any
Paul Reveres. Later, checking a list of half a dozen Paul Reveres
listed in the morning paper story, the *Times* was able to find one
who had gone to Washington.

"His name is Morris Stein. He sells fruits and vegetables.

"The morning paper in an early edition told of departure of one Paul Revere as follows: 'Swinging onto the train as it pulled out of the station was Fred Brandstrader, representing a group of Evanston business men. Lacking baggage or tickets, he shouted: 'Weather made it impossible for me to get home for my bag and I had to dash out of a conference and run for the train, but the defeat of this vicious bill should come first with every American.'

"Mr. Brandstrader got off the train at Englewood station. He denied shouting anything except the name Brandstrader. Mr. Brandstrader returned from the Englewood station to the *Times* office. He is a *Times* reporter. His real name is Karin Walsh.

"He had been told to go along to Washington, if he could find any Paul Reveres. But, being a conscientious reporter, Mr. Walsh came home. Mr. Brandstrader disappeared from later editions of the morning paper. Why, no one knows."

This episode followed by a little less than a year Hearst's telephoned instructions to Coblentz on May 28, 1937, that he wanted no more criticism of President Roosevelt or the Administration. He said that they were popular and were doing what the public wanted, and concluded: "We are of course still against burdensome taxes and the extravagances of bureaucracy."

Another case history, following closely upon the Paul Revere incident, shows graphically how Hearst could seize upon a small development in the day's news and blow it up to the proportions of a major crusade within twenty-four hours.

The occasion this time was a letter written by Eleanor "Cissy" Patterson, Hearst's old friend and publisher of the Washington *Times-Herald*, outlet in the capital for the fanaticism of the McCormick-Patterson newspaper axis. With her customary reticence, Cissy had caused to be printed on the front page of the *Times-Herald* an "open letter" to President Roosevelt, informing him that the United States lay paralyzed in the grip of a great fear. Industry and progress were stricken, she said in substance, by this fear, and the whole nation was trembling on the brink of disaster—as it had been trembling in the pages of these papers for nearly five years and would continue to tremble on into the unforeseeable Democratic future.

"This fear," said Cissy to the President, "is fear of you." She urged him to drop his reform measures, keep silent, and permit the opposition to run the country.

Hearst read this extraordinary pronouncement with approval, and shortly from San Simeon emanated a wire to the editors of Hearst papers: "CHIEF INSTRUCTS PAPERS TO PRINT THE ELEANOR PATTERSON LETTER. LOS ANGELES EXAMINER IS USING. UNDER TWO COL HEAD AS NEWS STORY ON AN INSIDE PAGE."

Next day he started the ball rolling in earnest: "Surely reprint conspicuously Eleanor Patterson's open letter to President Roosevelt. I sent instructions last night to all papers to print it—I now repeat the message." This was signed Hearst, and the tone of it was unmistakable.

A little later that day Hearst had dispatched a telegram of his own to Mrs. Patterson, cheering her on, and following it came an instruction from Coblentz in New York: "Chief has released his telegram to Mrs. Patterson and instructs that it be run on page one all Hearst morning papers and afternoons where no mornings in issues of tomorrow, Thursday, April 7, usual typography and position of page one editorials."

An addenda to that message came a few hours later, a note to editors: "Please run at end of Chief's telegram to Mrs. Patterson, set two-column measure FFLC [a type designation], the following: Quote this newspaper invites its readers to write to the editor their suggestions as to what the President should do to dissipate the fear that is paralyzing industry and progress and imperilling the welfare of the nation."

Specific instructions, marked RUSH RUSH, followed from the editor of the Los Angeles *Examiner:* "Chief directs that the following head be used over his letter to Mrs. Eleanor Patterson, release and position of which are subject to instructions to be sent by Mr. Coblentz." The dictated head, written by Hearst, ran:

## HOW TO FREE THE
## NATION FROM FEAR

(bank)    A Letter Supporting Mrs.
Patterson's Plea
(smaller type)    by W. R. Hearst

Shortly came another flash from Los Angeles: "Just talked with Chief. Chief directs his letter to Mrs. Patterson be printed on page 2 (two)."

Los Angeles got a worried query from Chicago in reply: "Editors here asking, if, in view Chief's letter being ordered page two, the 'By W. R. Hearst' line under head is still okay."

Reassurance from Los Angeles: "Yes, the 'By W. R. Hearst' line is part of the bank."

And so it went, on that and many other occasions. Somehow the Republic survived.

The orders from San Simeon, of course, were not always concerned with such cosmic affairs, although they were specific enough even in small matters, especially when Miss Davies was involved. Here is a direct order from Hearst:

"Managing editors all papers and radio editors all papers: Please kill too much reference to Laurette Taylor and make clear that Miss Davies on the radio is delivering her own version of Peg which she played in talking pictures, the only screen talking version which has been produced."

This was a relayed instruction from the Los Angeles *Examiner:* "At the direction of Mr. Hearst the enclosed seven pictures of Miss Marion Davies are being sent you for publication according to a recent Universal Service message from Col. Willicombe." The instructions accompanying the pictures said: "Ask all papers to run the attached pictures of Miss Davies, and run them big—4 cols. or so."

The eye of Hearst was everywhere. Here is a message from San Simeon in January 1935: "Some of our papers have been giving publicity to a newsreel called 'The March of Time.' As we have a newsreel of our own to promote, Chief instructs no publicity whatever shall be given to 'The March of Time' news-reel, either in the news columns or on radio pages, or anywhere else in the paper."

One can only imagine the sensations of a Hearst editor upon getting such an order as this, coming from Coblentz in 1937: "Supplementing his instructions to be on the alert for exclusive news beats, the Chief further instructs as follows: 'We do not want special stories—we want Big NEWS stories. An ITEM may indicate a big news story, just as a small outcropping of ore may lead to a big mine. Good editors should not only handle the news which comes into the office, but watch for and get the big news which lies hidden under small outercroppings."

No editor had any illusions about what kind of "news" ore the Chief had in mind. They were reminded from day to day by such messages as this one of March 9, 1938, from Willicombe: "Chief instructs all papers follow strongly the election in Seattle and call it 'The Revolution Against Revolution.' Chief says to get big story not only for tomorrow, Thursday, but to follow it up in any way possible."

On that same day, Hearst ordered his editors to play up strongly, in news interviews, opposition to the British trade treaty. In Chicago, however, where there was a large Czechoslo-vakian population, he permitted his editors to withhold an edi-torial attacking the Czechoslovakian trade treaty. The editorial ran in other cities where the Czechs were not an influence in cir-culation figures.

Thus the endless flow of instruction, crusading and maneuver-ing from San Simeon, Wyntoon, Los Angeles, New York and elsewhere as Hearst preached his beliefs from the columns of his newspapers, with an utter disregard for whether the columns were news or editorial. Sometimes it was hard to distinguish one from the other.

But the crusading and maneuvering, the shouting and the exposé, led relatively nowhere in the end. In 1936, when the Hearst papers had been particularly blatant in their attack on

the Administration, and again in 1939 and 1940, when they renewed the isolationist policies of *circa* 1916, there were boycotts
here and there of Hearst papers, or of his newsreel, which faithfully followed the propaganda line. These were shadowy rein-
carnations of the public rage Hearst had once generated with his
policies.

Oswald Garrison Villard noted wryly in the *Nation:* "It is
amazing . . . to hear Wall Street men now praising Hearst
when they themselves, or their fathers, in 1898 and again at the
outbreak of World War I were violently denouncing Hearst and
having his newspapers thrown out of clubs and libraries."

It was difficult, in fact, to generate any large-scale antipathy
to Hearst; not many would have agreed with Villard that there
were "few menaces as great in American life. . . ."

The constant reiteration of Hearst policies in his papers for
nearly a half century had produced a kind of acceptance. He
had become something of an institution, as safe and reliable as
the Republican Party. Those who opposed him were no longer
particularly afraid of him. Those who agreed with him found
him a dependable reassurance in troubled times. In New York,
where once the *Journal* had at least stirred up the masses, if it had
not changed their voting convictions, the same masses were reading Captain Patterson's comic strips surrounded by a newspaper.

And the *Journal*, merged with the *American*—what had happened to that eloquent champion of the people? It was the favorite reading of the homeward-bound businessman as he retreated
at eventide to his suburban comforts in Westchester County on
the New York Central, or to the plusher precincts of Connecti-
cut on the New York, New Haven and Hartford. In these later
years, Hearst presented in the evening pages of the *Journal-
American* the largest menagerie of extreme right-wing writers
ever gathered under one journalistic tent, and these were the
chief solace of a great many of the people Hearst had spent most
of his life attacking.

As the militant kind of Americanism that Hearst had always
championed achieved a new popularity in the late forties, the

politicians of both parties were eager to pay him homage. He
was at last, near death, a thoroughly respectable figure. More
than half a million people gathered on the Sheep Meadow in
Central Park on May 22, 1950, to hear Bernard Baruch, Hearst's
ancient enemy in the New York transit wars, and Mayor William O'Dwyer, representing that Tammany which had been
Hearst's implacable foe for decades, cite the Mahatma of San
Simeon for his initiative in founding and sponsoring "I Am An
American Day." Mr. Baruch offered the thesis that the *Journal-
American* was following Hearst's precepts "in bringing to Americans the benefits, opportunities and advantages we all have in
living under our Flag, an emblem of freedom and liberty."
Mayor O'Dwyer was somewhat more conservative. He ob-
served that the day would be "a memorable occasion for all."

A year later, on July 22, 1951, Navy Secretary Francis P.
Mathews, representing a President and an Administration which
Hearst had frequently depicted as hardly fit to inhabit the earth,
let alone to govern the American people, announced that a gold
medal would be presented to the publisher, to accompany the
Distinguished Public Service Award, the Navy's highest civilian
honor, which had been given him in March 1948. At that time,
he was cited for his "outstanding personal contribution to the
Navy's successful prosecution of World War II," and the then
Navy Secretary, John L. Sullivan, had hailed him as "the nation's
leader in the fight for an armed force second to none in the
world."

The master paper salesman had come a very long way.

# CHAPTER SIX

## THE MAN WHO WOULD BE PRESIDENT

THE STORY of William Randolph Hearst's sixty-odd years in American politics is about as sordid a tale as could be related. It is not a partisan story, nor simply the narrative of a rich man who thought he could buy the White House and suffered frustration because the voters put another kind of price on it.

It is a sad story, because it illuminates the worst characteristics of our two-party system, leaving precious few of its virtues on display. No one comes off well in the telling of it with the exception of the voters themselves, who, in spite of the venality, cynicism and inconstancy of the politicians, seem always to have known, with that instinct for which Lincoln so much admired them, who was truly in their interest.

Hearst's role in this drama is, as usual, a part no one else could have played. The only suitable understudy for him would have been Horace Greeley, the guiding light of that Great Moral Organ, the New York *Tribune*, who performed in the Republican political drama the same part of always-the-best-man-but-never-the-bridegroom that Hearst enacted in the Democratic Party.

Both men hungered for political office with an appetite that surpasses understanding. Greeley never attained it, and Hearst had to be satisfied with a term in Congress. Their hearts were set ardently on the presidency, and in this ambition they were rudely thwarted for opposite reasons. The Republicans thought Greeley too moral; Hearst was not moral enough for the Democrats.

The word "morality" is used here in its campaign, vote-getting sense. Its true meaning had nothing to do with the case. Greeley and Hearst were shunted aside time and again by the professional politicians of their parties for reasons which had to do with their attractiveness as candidates. The professionals understood that these men were not vote-getters. Time and the ballot box proved them correct.

Greeley tried to gain the presidency by sheer persuasion; he was clumsy and ineffectual at practical politics. Hearst enjoyed the game and played hard at it, played it with his driving energy and ever-flowing bank roll, but unfortunately with a minimum of talent and a positive genius for not understanding the mood of the voters.

His active career in politics, which extended in a personal sense to 1922, and in a behind-the-scenes manner until the convention of 1932, was concentrated entirely in the Democratic Party, where his money was always welcome but not his talents. His first overtures to the party are recorded as early as 1876, when Phebe took him to the formal brick house on Gramercy Square to meet Governor Samuel J. Tilden, a hero in whose honor he had named his dog. Tilden, in the gracious manner of a candidate who was indebted to the boy's father for financial and other varieties of support, patted him on the head and advised him to be a good boy and as good a Democrat as his father. Willie rewarded this well-intended advice by pointing to an Italian sculpture of "Flora" and remarking in his childish treble, "Mr. Tilden, you've got a 'Flora' just like ours at home!"

In that period, Hearst was more interested in art than he was in politics, a balance immediately reversed when he became a newspaper publisher. From the earliest days of the *Examiner*, he was in the political puddle up to his neck.

For a time his chief contribution was financial, since that was the main thing he had to give the party, but with the establishment of the *Journal* in New York, and its sensational circulation rise, he became a potentially important mouthpiece.

It was the Spanish-American War, however, that elevated Hearst to national prominence and gave him a not entirely deserved reputation as a man who could make wars as easily as he could create newspapers. Apparently Hearst believed this himself, as may be adduced not only from his much-quoted wire to the artist Frederic Remington in Cuba, "You furnish the pictures, I'll furnish the war"—a communication which he frequently and fruitlessly denied later—but from numerous other references. Some of Hearst's men believed it too. James Creelman, the correspondent who captured the Spanish flag in the battle of El Caney, wrote in the *Review of Reviews* for November 1898 that he wanted the flag for the *Journal* because "the *Journal* had provoked the war, and it was only fair that the *Journal* should have the first flag captured in the greatest land battle of the war."

The viewpoint of the professional historian contradicts the standard thesis that Hearst started the war. In modern histories of the United States, he is credited only with being the leading voice in the journalistic chorus that rose from coast to coast, demanding war with Spain. It is doubtful that even this raucous urging could have provoked the McKinley Administration into an adventure that was obviously against its own best interests, had it not been for the jingoes in Congress and such other stentorian calls to action as Colonel Roosevelt emitted from time to time. The voices of reason, like Godkin's in the *Evening Post*, were lost in the tidal surge of super-patriotism, and eventually McKinley had to yield to a public ground swell that had grown to the proportions of a tidal wave, sufficient to have boosted him from the White House if he had remained adamant.

In all this clamor, Hearst's voice was not the first, although it was the loudest. Pulitzer was first to exploit the cause of revolution in Cuba, but Hearst quickly surpassed him. Dana and Bennett in New York, Joseph Medill and his *Tribune* in Chicago, and leading newspapers in other American cities joined the pack.

There was a significant difference in the Pulitzer-Hearst drum-beating and that of a good many other newspapers. The issue between the two publishers was circulation. Pulitzer made the first pass at Cuba; it was successful on the newsstands. Hearst took up the challenge, and that led to the most publicized circulation war in journalistic history, with the result that the *World* and the *Journal* got far more credit for starting the war than they deserved.

A good percentage of the other newspapers in the country clamored for war because they reflected the state of mind of their readers. As the Washington *Post* put it, "The taste of Empire is in the mouth of the people. . . ." It had been there, as far as the Caribbean was concerned, since 1825.

Hearst and Pulitzer sounded the emotional keynote on which the war was fought—the liberation of Cuba. Both probably knew that the real reason was the serious disruption of America's hundred-million-dollar trade with Cuba, caused by the collapse of the country's sugar economy. Though the revolution had caused this collapse, at the root of the revolution was the tariff policy of the United States as well as Spain, which eventually ruined the sugar market and created the despair that flamed into revolution. It was true that Spain's political and economic strangle hold on Cuba was also a root cause, but to Hearst and his fellow jingoist editors and the effervescent patriots in Congress, Spain the cruel, Spain the exploiter, was the sole cause of it all.

The Cubans, it must be remembered, had been fighting the insurrection by themselves for three years before the United States came to their aid. But during that time their agents in New York and Washington were obtaining much valuable help.

An important part of it came from Hearst, who seized this heaven-sent opportunity to rivet down the *Journal's* precarious position, and, at least from his own standpoint, took over the war at an early date. There was a constant stream of high-priced talent en route from the *Journal* during the preliminary stages. Creelman went to Madrid as an ambassador without any portfolio except Hearst's instructions to make the Spanish Government see the light. Charlie Michelson was sent to Cuba and promptly got himself arrested and clapped into Morro Castle. A reporter named Grover Flint took down a jeweled sword, a small token of affection from Hearst to the insurgent General Maceo.

For a while the *Journal* had to depend for its news on Cuban propagandists in New York—hardly a handicap, because the rewrite men simply dressed up the latest rumors as dispatches, the copy desk put Havana datelines on them, and the trouble of on-the-spot reporting was saved.

But to a man of Hearst's imagination this was only an expedient, and as soon as possible he sent Richard Harding Davis to report the revolution and Frederic Remington, the artist, to cover it pictorially. They made a distinguished combination, although one would not have thought it to see them the night they sailed for Cuba. Their departure was in keeping with the cloak-and-dagger manner in which Hearst conducted what he grandly referred to as "our pet war." While a chartered steamer waited for them at some dark and secret pier, and a curtained hack lurked in a side street to whisk them to it, the two intrepid journalists killed time in Sam Chamberlain's office.

Davis killed it by playing himself—the strong, silent correspondent. Remington, to whom the prospect before him was unknown and perilous, paced up and down and intermittently dashed out to fortify himself against the ordeal at a nearby saloon. He embarked in a haze of joyous anticipation.

To get the news from Cuba to the nearest American telegraph office, Hearst sent his own yacht, the *Vamoose*—127 feet, cost $80,000—which had succeeded his 50-foot Herreshoff speedboat. The *Vamoose* was a present from Phebe after she had got herself wet in the smaller *Aquila*, but Hearst had scarcely used it because it proved impossible to transport from New York to the West Coast. The only path lay across the Isthmus of Panama, on the lines of the Panama Railway Company, whose president was unfortunately the father of the novelist Amelie Rives; her novel, *The Quick or The Dead*, had been indelicately torn apart in the *Examiner*. Colonel Rives was as sensitive about his daughter's literary output as President Truman came to be about *his* daughter's singing, and he flatly refused to let his railroad accept the yacht as freight. It had to be sent back to New York.

With Davis and Remington and others to get the news, and the *Vamoose* to bring it to the cable stations, Hearst began the needling of McKinley that made him a hero to the Democrats and a scourge to the Republicans. Every provocative act he committed was seized upon by the pro-war, anti-McKinley element in Congress, which included some influential members of the President's own party.

There was, for example, Remington's famous picture, reproduced five columns wide in the *Journal*, showing three young Cuban girls being searched before they were allowed to proceed to the United States. One of the girls, her buttocks turned bashfully toward the artist, was nude. Both Davis and the girls later denied that anything of the kind had taken place, but several senators rose in Congress to take a stand against the State Department, Spain, the procurement of female slaves in Havana, and sin in general.

Hearst had of course bitterly opposed McKinley in the election of 1896, joining in the newspaper chorus against him which was on the lowest journalistic level since the days of Lincoln. It ceased on Hearst's part briefly one April day in 1897 when the President was a guest of the City of New York while General Grant was laid at rest in his new Riverside Drive tomb. McKinley was crowded off the *Journal's* front page by a giant bewhiskered image of Grant, wrapped in a flag, spread over nearly the entire page.

Then McKinley went back to Washington, and the private war against him was resumed. To Hearst he represented the capitalistic Republicanism which was anathema to Democrats, and particularly to Democratic publishers whose papers had built their circulations by opposing everything McKinley was for. It was McKinley and Wall Street against Hearst and the people.

From McKinley the people got logic and reason, as far as the Cuban revolution was concerned. Hearst gave them romance, salted down with old-fashioned sex. He gave them that most incredible story in that most unlikely of wars, the story of Evangelina Cisneros. Latter-day critics of Hearst have attempted to water it down, but even if their strictures were accepted wholesale, the tale of Evangelina's imprisonment and escape is still the chewy stuff of which bad but best-selling novels are made.

Consider the principal ingredients: a beautiful girl of eighteen, reared gently in an excellent family; a bloody revolution; imprisonment in a dingy jail; rescue by a daring gentleman of Old Virginia, the correspondent for a famous American newspaper; and at last, the adulation of the entire United States, including its reluctant President.

The fact that Evangelina did not entirely deserve such attention failed to detract from what unexpectedly befell her when George Eugene Bryson, a Hearst correspondent, heard of her story in August 1897 and filed a dispatch about it to New York. Bryson played it for all it was worth, describing how she had refused the advances of an amorous colonel, an aide of the Spanish general Weyler, called "The Butcher" in Hearst's papers. In return for her virtue, said Bryson, the Spaniards had wrenched her from her father's arms, sent him to the Spanish island prison of Ceuta, off Gibraltar, and incarcerated her in the Rocojidas, which Bryson described as a sort of prison cage in Havana where women criminals of all sorts were herded together and subjected to the taunts and evil suggestions of the men who gathered outside it.

The facts of the case may have been somewhat different, if one believes the *World's* sleuths whom Pulitzer set on the trail as soon as he saw what a circulation-getting *cause célèbre* Hearst was making of the affair.

According to the *World*, which prodded Fitzhugh Lee, American consul-general in Havana, into making an investigation, Miss Cisneros herself admitted that her father was an underground leader of the revolution, whom the government had banished, along with his daughter, to a penal colony on the Isle of

Pines. There, said the alleged confession, she used her girlish charms to entice the colony's commander to her father's house, where revolutionary sympathizers among the prisoners attempted to cut his throat.

The investigation also cast doubt on the character of Rocojidas Prison and the condition of its celebrated inmate. The Rocojidas, said Mr. Lee, was an old jail but not a primitive iron cage. Miss Cisneros had a suite of rooms at her disposal, and her jailers placed as few restraints as possible on her movements.

Nevertheless, the indubitable fact remained that she was in jail and had been there a year, that she was refined and beautiful, though not above being an accessory to assassination. Besides, no one wanted to believe the *World's* facts, if they were facts. In its present state of mind, the country wanted to believe Hearst's story, which got better as it went along.

Unquestionably Hearst sensed the full circulation value of Evangelina's plight, but from the vantage point of a half century or so, it appears that he believed Bryson's story himself. It aroused in him the indignation always near the surface whenever a woman was mistreated—no doubt seeing the image of his mother in every abused female. He cabled forthwith to Bryson: "Rescue Evangelina Cisneros from the Rocojidas, no matter what it costs."

In view of subsequent events, Evangelina had need of that dagger which, Bryson romantically disclosed, her father had given her at their parting, and was even more in need of the advice he gave her to go with it: "Courage is king. Be brave, my beloved." For Hearst was quite willing to make an international incident out of the girl's plight, and rescue her even if she had to be carried feet first from the Rocojidas.

James Creelman, who was adept at propaganda stories, was assigned by Hearst to whip up American sentiment for Evangelina's release, one of the first results of which was a petition to the Spanish government, signed by hundreds of thousands of women, including such eminent females as Mrs. Jefferson Davis, Mrs. Mark Hanna and Frances Hodgson Burnett. The Catholic clergy and laity sent their petitions to Pope Leo XIII, who told the Queen Regent of Spain that it would be an act of Christian charity to show clemency toward Evangelina.

The commotion brought an end to the patience of the Spanish government in Cuba. Bryson was ejected from the country, and Evangelina for a while was put in solitary, where she had time to contemplate her picture (printed daily) and spell out the words of her tragedy in the stack of *Journals* Bryson had left her.

But her savior was already on the way. Hearst had called in Karl Decker from the Washington bureau and instructed him to replace Bryson. It was a good choice. Decker was resourceful and daring, he had spent three months in Cuba with the insurgents earlier in the revolution, and best of all, he was a gallant Virginian, something he had in common with Fitzhugh Lee.

The hearts of these two Southerners beat as one when they thought of Evangelina languishing in the Rocojidas. The fact that there were Negro women along with the prostitutes who were her companions seems also to have figured in their indignation. At any rate, Lee acted in a manner that should have worried the State Department, and secretly supplied Decker with aides, who swore a solemn oath never to recognize each other or Decker in public.

The plot, already thick, became thicker. From his room in the Inglaterra Hotel not far from the American consulate, Decker spread his net. He met his fellow conspirators late at night in a bare little room on the waterfront, and after a few weeks of getting nowhere, he talked to the fair Evangelina herself and slipped a note to her. In the note he inquired if she had any plans for escaping.

Miss Cisneros appears to have been ready with a plan right out of the dime novels, though one has only the word of the *Journal's* dashing correspondent for it. She asked for opium concealed in candy to knock out her roommates; for acid to cut away the bars on her cell; for a rope to descend to the roof of the jail, from which she could escape to an adjoining house. The rescuers, she said, must stand guard below and let her know if the way was clear, one if by land and two if by sea—that is, the wave of a lit cigar if danger were present, the toss of a white handkerchief if it were safe. She thoughtfully enclosed a plan of the jail with this reply.

Hearst would have been proud of the way Decker responded to Evangelina's message. He rented a house adjacent to the jail, and under the pretext that it needed whitewashing, sent a Negro to do the job, by which means he contrived to smuggle twelve feet of ladder into the house. Unfortunately he could find no opium—perhaps Hearst's anti-narcotics campaign had depressed the market—and so Evangelina was compelled to the prosaic deceit of pleading a toothache, for which the prison doctor innocently gave her enough laudanum to knock out the entire cell block if it had been necessary. A soupçon of the drug in her roommates' coffee was enough to dispose of *them*. To make it appear that she had joined them in a night's sleep, she draped a sheet about her slim person in the shape of a nightgown.

An hour and a half after midnight she was ready, but at this point Decker and his little helpers demonstrated that they were really only amateurs at international jail-breaking. They bungled the whole business. They got their ladder across the space between the roof of the house and the prison roof; one man climbed across to hold it, and in the process knocked off a chunk of cornice which resounded cheerfully below in the still Cuban night. Decker pulled back the ladder, leaving his man stranded, while the warden stepped outside, made a sleepy, perfunctory examination, and went back in. Decker threw out his ladder again and made the passage himself this time, armed with a saw —not as romantic as Evangelina's acid idea, but more practical. He found the prisoner waiting at the bars, where she had been for the last two and a half hours while her rescuers fumbled about in the darkness.

Decker began hacking away at the bars with his saw, but they rattled enough to wake the dead, let alone the laudanum-drugged ladies inside. Evangelina must have uttered a few pungent observations in Spanish, but the semi-official biographer swears that all she said in English was a frightened "Go! Come back tomorrow night!"

Nothing if not resourceful, Decker was on hand the following midnight, equipped this time with a couple of Stillson wrenches and a handy carriage poised in the side streets. As an added precaution, he sent an aide with a bottle to get the warden drunk, a mission easily accomplished. Again the ladder, again the agile Decker, and this time, taking advantage of the dent he had made in the main bar the night before, he wrenched it apart with his wrenches, Evangelina slipped out, leaving her twice-drugged friends behind, and tripped across the ladder to safety.

After a night in hiding, she spent the following day getting her hair trimmed like a man's, slicking it tight with pomade, and fitting her girlish figure into a sailor's uniform. On the third day, the crisis came. She strolled out of the hideaway in disguise as Juan Sola, 18, a sailor registered on the steamer *Seguranca*, lying in the harbor and bound for New York that evening. It was then 5 P.M.

Down the streets of Havana toward the waterfront swaggered Evangelina. Behind her, at a discreet distance, walked Decker and his men, hands in their bulging pockets, foreshadowing unconsciously a whole era of Grade-B movies. They sighed in quick release of tension as Juan Sola walked up the ship's gangplank. Then they repaired to a sidewalk café, and from a table looking out over the harbor they saw the *Seguranca* steam off toward freedom. When it was safely out of reach of the shore batteries, the captain, who was party to the plot, ordered nine short blasts of the whistle. By that token, Decker knew he had succeeded. He went home to write his story.

While the Spaniards rushed about arresting the wrong people —sixty of them altogether—Decker's story went one way, to Key West by the purser of a friendly ship, and he went another— into the hills and the welcome of the rebels.

It was a story in keeping with the spirit of the episode. Decker signed it "Charles Duval," and it began in part:

"Evangelina Cosio y Cisneros is at last at liberty, and the *Journal* can place to its credit the greatest journalistic coup of this age. It is an illustration of the methods of the new journalism, and it will find an indorsement in the heart of every woman who has read of the horrible sufferings of the poor girl who had been confined for fifteen long months in Rocojidas Prison. . . . I have broken the bars of Rocojidas and have set free the beautiful captive of monster Weyler. . . . Weyler could blind the Queen to the real character of Evangelina, but he could not build a jail that would hold against *Journal* enterprise when properly set to work. . . ."

The headline Hearst wrote for the story was also in keeping: "An American Newspaper Accomplishes at a Single Stroke What the Best Efforts of Diplomacy Failed Utterly to Bring About in Many Months."

Meanwhile, the object of *Journal* enterprise was brought out of hiding on the *Seguranca* and feted by the passengers. Those who thought to find her a regal young beauty discovered that she was only a frightened little Cuban girl, bewildered by the whole affair and uncertain what would happen next.

She could not possibly have imagined what actually happened. A huge crowd was at the pier in New York to welcome her; she had a triumphal procession up Broadway, was whisked into a Waldorf suite paid for by Hearst, and began a round of entertainments and general charivaris.

Decker, the hero, was close upon her heels, arriving via the Spanish steamer *Panama* on a forged visa in response to Hearst's cable, "Good work. Return immediately." He took her to a reception at Delmonico's, where a crowd of 120,000 people surrounded the packed restaurant, gaping at the fireworks set off from Madison Square, singing what they fondly imagined were Cuban songs, and cheering impromptu patriotic speeches. Inside, while Hearst skulked shyly amid the potted palms, Evangelina, dressed in virginal white, made a small speech in broken English which nobody heard, and brushed at her eyes with a handkerchief while the ladies present had a good cry with her.

It is said that Miss Cisneros kissed Hearst's hand when she met him, and in fact this sort of gratitude and enthusiasm overwhelmed a large number of emotional patriots about the country. Governor Sadler, of the sovereign state of Missouri, suggested in a ringing declaration of faith that Cuba could be freed if only Hearst would send five hundred of his reporters as an expeditionary force.

There was no answering call to arms from the men of the *Journal* office. They had gone on to nobler efforts. While their readers were sopping up the details of Evangelina's rescue in a long fictional version of the story, running serially in the *Sunday Journal* and hardly to be distinguished from Decker's own dispatches in the daily, Hearst was setting a booby-trap for Dupuy de Lome, the harassed Spanish Ambassador to the United States.

The Ambassador had already denounced Hearst and his paper and protested the affair to the President, but McKinley was helpless. With the whole country singing paeans to Evangelina, he could do nothing but give her an official greeting, while de Lome sulked.

A few weeks later, early in February 1898, Hearst exploded his bomb beneath the Ambassador. It was a personal letter from de Lome to a Cuban friend, obtained in the Havana post office by means not unfamiliar to the Hearst method, and held for nearly a year and a half, again consonant with the method, until the right moment. On the heels of his Cisneros triumph, Hearst published it under the blaring headline: THE WORST INSULT TO THE UNITED STATES IN ITS HISTORY.

It was hardly that, but it *was* an indiscreet discussion of McKinley's character, which de Lome naturally supposed no one but his friend would ever see. The Ambassador wrote that he did not admire the political climate in Washington and he regarded the President as a weakling, a "low politician, catering to the rabble."

That did it. De Lome resigned at once, and the United States moved a step nearer to war.

It was only a few days after this incident that de Lome,

Evangelina and every other preliminary agitation were forgotten in the disaster of the *Maine* explosion. The *Journal* exploded, too, in a skyrocket blaze of colored flags on the front page on the following morning of February 16, 1898. The paper offered a $50,000 reward for detection of the perpetrators, and Hearst himself started the fund for the Maine Memorial at Columbus Circle with a thousand-dollar contribution. And for the first time, the editorial page carried that historic slogan, "Remember the Maine!"

Hearst intended that no one within hearing of the *Journal* should forget the tragic ship. On the morning of the seventeenth, a *Journal* extra announced: "The War Ship Maine Was Split in Two by an Enemy's Secret Infernal Machine!" One of Goddard's famous cross sections was spread over page one, showing exactly how it was done, with a torpedo under the ship detonated from shore. Some Hearst critics have contended that Hearst agents perpetrated the deed, or that at least he was an accessory before the fact, but this can hardly be taken seriously. Hearst may have been a warmonger, an activity he shared at the time with Teddy Roosevelt and other distinguished names, but he would as soon have blown up the *Journal* office as an American battleship and its men.

If any small morsel of good came from the event, it fell to McKinley, who was rewarded with the only kind words the *Journal* ever had to say about him, in an editorial written by Hearst himself. "McKinley, the man of diplomacy, was a cinder in the eye of the American people," Hearst said in this backward compliment. "But McKinley, the man of action, begins well. He has signed the war resolution of Congress and sent his ultimatum to Spain."

By an odd chance, the first shot fired by Spain when the war began fell upon the *Journal's* dispatch boat, the yacht *Vamoose*, renamed the *Buccaneer*, as she lay near Morro Castle. The iron flung from one of the castle's mortars bounced harmlessly off the ship and fell into the water, while the crew sent up a derisive shout. The last laugh was on the Spaniards; they seized the boat when they saw they were not likely to sink her.

Hearst sent a small navy to replace the lost ship. By the time American forces were in action, he had set up a regular ferry system between Cuba and Kingston, Jamaica, where there was a cable station. By rail and carrier pigeon, copy came from Richard Harding Davis, Stephen Crane and the dozen or so other correspondents on the scene, to be transported to Kingston on one of a half-dozen steam vessels, a yacht, a Red Cross boat, an ocean-going tug or a Brazilian cattle boat.

*Journal* circulation began to reach incredible heights. Dewey's victory at Manila, reported on a Sunday, sold 1,408,000 papers. Like everyone else, Hearst claimed a news beat on the story by an hour, but history gives the award to the Chicago *Tribune*. The *Journal's* complete report of the battle a week later sold 60,000 more papers than the previous high mark and established a world circulation record.

Shortly after Dewey's victory, Hearst committed his most outrageous act as a publisher. He heard by way of the Madrid grapevine that the Spaniards intended to sail a fleet through the Suez Canal to effect the recapture of Manila. He cabled Creelman, who was then in London, to go out and buy an English steamer, hire a crew to man her, and take the ship down to "some part of the Suez Canal where we can sink her and obstruct the passage of the Spanish warships."

That would have been a logical and effective way to head off the Spanish fleet, if there had been any fleet to send to Manila, but it was also an act in total defiance of the United States and British governments, not to mention international law, and might well have precipitated war between the two countries. Fortunately, Creelman was unable, or said he was unable, to buy a steamer.

There was a rush of public figures to the Cuban front. Unlike any other war in our history, the men most interested in starting it were the most eager to be in the front lines. Hearst's first inclination was to organize a regiment of cowboys—it would give him an opportunity to demonstrate his equestrian talents—but Roosevelt, his personal enemy, anticipated him. Balked on land, he turned to the sea. The Navy Department, always his friend because he constantly beat the drums for a larger fleet, gave him an ensign's commission. Scouring the docks about Manhattan, he found a tramp steamer, the *Silvia*, which he chartered and sailed for Cuba.

Besides Hearst, the *Silvia's* passenger list included James Creelman; W.R.'s old California friend Jack Follansbee; J. C. Hemmant, a photographer who had packed in his luggage the first motion-picture equipment that ever went to a war; and an assortment of *Journal* reporters, artists and other functionaries. In the ship's hold Hearst had installed a small printing press, and he had brought along a mechanical crew able to turn out a daily paper on it.

Once at the front, Hearst worked as hard as he had in New York, but on the upper echelons of reporting, interviewing military leaders, American and Cuban, including the commander of the insurgents, General Calixto Garcia, receiver of the legendary message. Garcia, in a white uniform, tears reportedly falling on his cheeks, presented Hearst with the flag of the eastern department of Cuba, "in commemoration of the services of your paper for liberty. . . . This flag is the best thing the Cuban Republic can offer its best friend."

For the first time the *Journal* printed news stories carrying the byline, "W. R. Hearst," written in the heroic style of the day. One of them began:

"From the top of the ridge where I write I see the monstrous form of Sampson's fleet lying in semicircle in front of the entrance of Santiago harbor, while here at our feet masses of American soldiers pour from the beach into the scorching valley. Vultures wheel lazily above the thorny, poisonous jungles. They have already fed on corpses of slain Spaniards. Santiago and the flower of the Spanish fleet are ours, although hundreds of men may have to die before we take possession of them."

The largest battle Hearst covered was El Caney, into which he stumbled almost by accident. His dispatch, datelined "With the Army in Front of Santiago, July 1, midnight, via Kingston, Jamaica," did no more than mention the battle at the beginning. He wrote of the aftermath, and then, with a professional interest, of how it was fought.

"I have been at the artillery positions all day," he said, "to see what our guns could do. There is no question of the skill and courage of American gunmen. Their work is as near perfect as gunnery gets to be, but there was no artillery to speak of. The War Department furnished the necessary heavy guns, but they remained in the rear because of the difficulty of transportation from the coast."

That morning—Hearst disclosed in a rather leisurely way as his lengthy story went on—he and Honoré Laine, a Cuban Army colonel on leave as a *Journal* correspondent, had started out on their horses, at the rear of the general American advance toward Santiago. For eight miles they rode over rough terrain, shot at occasionally by rear-guard Spanish troops. Their destination was a house where they expected to meet some officers for lunch, but instead they rode smack into the bloody struggle for the little village of El Caney.

After a vivid description of the battle, Hearst's story went on:

"Laine and I hurried up to the stone fort and found that James Creelman, the *Journal* correspondent with the infantry column, had been seriously wounded and was lying in the Twelfth Infantry Hospital. Our men were still firing an occasional shot. From the block-house and isolated trenches from which the Spaniards could not safely retreat, flags of truce were waved. Guns and side-arms were being taken away from such Spaniards as had outlived the pitiless fire, and their dead were being dumped without ceremony into the trenches after Spanish fashion.

"When I left the fort to hunt for Creelman I found him bloody and bandaged, lying on his back on a blanket on the ground, but shown all care that a kindly skillful surgeon could give him. He was pretty well dazed and said, 'I'm afraid I can't write much of a story. If you will write it for me, I will describe it the best I can.' "

It was Creelman's account of this affair that got into the history books, by way of his autobiography, *On the Great Highway*, published in 1901. In it he wrote:

"Someone knelt in the grass beside me and put his hand on my fevered head. Opening my eyes, I saw Mr. Hearst, the proprietor of the New York *Journal*, a straw hat with a bright ribbon on his head, a revolver at his belt, and a pencil and notebook in his hand. The man who had provoked the war had come to see the result with his own eyes, and, finding one of his correspondents prostrate, was doing the work himself. Slowly he took down my story of the fight. Again and again the tinging of Mauser bullets interrupted. But he seemed unmoved. That battle had to be reported somehow.

" 'I'm sorry you're hurt, but'—and his face was radiant with enthusiasm—'wasn't it a splendid fight? We must beat every paper in the world.' "

As he had wandered into the battle of El Caney, Hearst also by chance got into the major naval contest at Santiago. It came about because Hemmant, the photographer, had been voicing the immemorial complaint of photographers, "No action pictures," meaning especially of the Navy. The complaint was justified for a good reason. The American fleet was lying off Santiago Harbor, where it had effectively blockaded the Spanish ships. There had been no action, only waiting.

Hearst, as the world's most picture-conscious editor, was anxious to satisfy his photographer. It occurred to him that on the Fourth of July the fleet would be firing several patriotic salvos, and pictures of these could be offered the *Journal's* readers as war photos without fear of detection.

Thus, at dawn on the Fourth of July, 1898, the old tramp ship *Silvia* ambled up to the American position in time to see the finale of the brief struggle in which Admiral Schley demolished

Cervera's fleet. Its remnants were beached and burning in every direction. Hearst boarded the still burning warship *Vizcaya*, accompanied by a reporter and a photographer, and they walked the hot decks on their heels. Then, after a brief adventure in the heavy surf with the *Silvia*, they headed her toward Cervera's flagship, the *Infanta Maria Teresa*, lying crippled on the beach.

On the way they sighted a covey of Spanish sailors on the beach. Hearst hailed these miserable survivors, and Mrs. Older adds that "some of the reporters made demonstrations with fire-arms." She says that Hearst swam ashore and captured them, after making them bury their dead, then took his prisoners to Admiral Sampson, who instructed him to take them to the *St. Louis*, where he got a receipt for them.

Forty years later, Damon Runyon described this episode with the modesty of retrospect in an interview with Hearst on his seventy-fifth birthday. "The Americans drove the Spanish ships ashore and Mr. Hearst landed and captured 27 prisoners, though he said it was not an heroic feat because they wanted to be taken. Then he said he had quite a time turning them over to the American forces. He tried to deliver them aboard the battleship *Texas*, but the commanding officer ordered him off in great irritation, saying: 'We don't want any yellow fever on this ship.' Finally Mr. Hearst induced the commanding officer of the converted liner, *Harvard*, to accept his prisoners and give him a receipt. 'Ah, well, we were young. It was adventure,' he commented."

Ah, yes—those gay times would never come again, when Hemmant could take pictures of the prisoners kissing the American flag and raising three cheers for their conquerors, and when Hearst himself could sit on one of the *Vizcaya's* dismounted guns and write about the scenes of carnage and bloodshed about him. Such a war was not to be had every day.

The *Journal* was in at the diplomatic death. By exercising its customary methods of getting the news first—in this case, it was said, by bribing a Spanish diplomatic secretary—Hearst's paper was the first in the world to print terms of the peace treaty, and crowed editorially over the feat that it was "a journalistic achievement believed to be entirely without precedent. Such enterprise makes Senatorial secrecy an absurdity."

Thus the war ended, with the Spaniards and McKinley confounded, the United States a world power, and Hearst a hero to the Democrats and the Cubans. The island's first president, Tomás Estrada Palma, assured him: "I do not believe that we would have secured our independence without the aid which you rendered." As late as 1949, the Cubans were still expressing their gratitude, awarding him their highest decoration, the Grand Cross of the Order of Carlos Manuel de Céspedes, at a ceremony in the Cuban Embassy at Washington, witnessed by two hundred and fifty diplomats, government officials, military leaders and Spanish-American War veterans. Hearst's son, W.R., Jr., accepted the decoration on behalf of his ailing father.

By that time the old man had forgiven and all but forgotten the Spanish government which he had once described as the most monstrous on earth. A pair of cannon from Morro Castle reposed on a terrace at San Simeon, and scattered about the grounds were pieces of Spanish architecture transported bodily from Spain in spite of protests that he was looting the country. He and Millicent had even been received by King Alfonso. The unpleasantness of 1898 was doubtless not discussed between them.

As for Evangelina Cisneros, that innocent young heroine had proved to be an ungrateful foreigner. Out of her gratitude, and at Hearst's particular urging, she had become a United States citizen, enabled to skip several of the annoying requirements by the benevolence of the government. But she insisted, perverse girl, on marrying a Cuban gentleman and going to live in Havana for the rest of her days.

At least she had the grace to be married in a proper place. The ceremony took place on Fitzhugh Lee's farm in Virginia.

II

Hearst stood at the peak of his prestige when the war ended. It was not until later that his part in it came to be fiercely debated. Those who opposed him at the time consisted of a few conservative editors and some of McKinley's friends.

Riding on the crest of a popular esteem he would never know again, Hearst did not hesitate to lay down the law to the Democratic Party. His editorial of November 1898, "The Democratic National Policy," did not suggest what that policy should be, it demanded—expansion to Hawaii, the West Indies and Philippines; construction of the Panama Canal; the erection of "great national universities" at West Point and Annapolis; the finest Navy in the world; the "total separation of the Army and Navy from politics."

"The Democrats in Congress cannot do better than adopt this, the *Journal's* National Policy, as their National Policy," Hearst declared forthrightly. "It is popular, it is Democratic, and it is right. . . . The Democracy has the great fight to continue against the forces of special privilege and corruption and greed. It cannot afford to weaken its influence and diminish its power for good by adopting attitudes in opposition to national progress and development, which are unpopular, undemocratic and essentially wrong."

He was still riding high in 1900, when, as president of a national association that included several thousand Democratic clubs, he controlled a substantial bloc of political power. It was good experience for him: he had to appear for the first time as a public speaker before the national convention of this association in Indianapolis, and conquered the stage fright that had hampered him on previous occasions.

In this election year, Hearst renewed the attack on McKinley, the trusts—and Mark Hanna, the representative of both—with an arrogance and savagery which stirred up much of the pre-war bitterness against him. With Davenport's cartoons, and editorials by Brisbane, McEwen and himself, he laid about with a fervor that would have been biblical had it partaken more of principle. As Thomas Beer described it:

"Marcus Alonzo Hanna [was] revealed in all the newspapers owned by William Randolph Hearst as an amalgam of all sins.

He was foulness compact. He was the red boss of Cleveland's city politics. The town council trembled when he sent minions to address it. He had stolen a theatre from poor John Ellsler, foreclosing a cruel mortgage and rejecting the man's plea for time. He ruled Cleveland from his office, terrorizing unions and ruining rival street railways. He sent poor sailors, forced on his ships by bestial labor masters, out to sea on the wintry lakes, cold and starving, unpaid and mutinous."

McKinley, of course, was depicted as twice a monster, until even Hearst was abashed at an editorial (probably McEwen's) which suggested that if shooting were the only way to get rid of bad men, then shooting might be justified.

By one of American history's oddest coincidences, it was on the heels of this editorial that William McKinley, the business-man's idol, was felled by an anarchist's bullet, and Hearst, hearing the news in the Chicago *American* office, remarked softly and accurately, "Things are going to be very bad."

He could not have stated the case more conservatively. A wave of hatred for anarchists swept the country, and Hearst, who was accused of inspiring the assassination by generating hatred of McKinley among the masses, was called "a teacher of anarchists." He was hanged in effigy, while his papers were tossed out of clubs, libraries and newsstands. A gun lay always on his desk; the mail was frisked for bombs.

It was an opportunity not to be missed by the rival newspapers. The reporters sent to Buffalo to cover the assassination hammered away at Leon Czolgosz, the assassin, trying to get him to admit he had been inspired by reading Hearst papers. Czolgosz said he had never seen a Hearst paper. The rival publishers were not discouraged; they wrote that a copy of the *Journal* was found stuffed in the assassin's coat pocket.

The damning editorial was recalled, and also an item that damned still further, an Ambrose Bierce quatrain that has earned a spurious immortality. Of this quatrain and its consequences Bierce, certainly no admirer of Hearst, wrote in a reasonable vein:

"Soon after the assassination of Goebel of Kentucky—which seemed to me a particularly perilous 'precedent' if unpunished— I wrote for one of Mr. Hearst's New York newspapers the following prophetic lines:

> *The bullet that pierced Goebel's breast*
> *Can not be found in all the West;*
> *Good reason: it is speeding here*
> *To stretch McKinley on the bier.*

"The lines took no attention, naturally, but twenty months afterward the President was shot. . . . Everyone remembers what happened then to Mr. Hearst and his newspapers. His political enemies and business competitors were alert to their opportunity. The verses, variously garbled but mostly made into an editorial, or a news dispatch with a Washington date-line but usually no date, were published all over the country as evidence of Mr. Hearst's complicity in the crime. As such they adorned the editorial columns of the New York Sun and glazed upon a billboard in front of Tammany Hall. . . . There was even an attempt made to induce Czolgosz to testify that he had been incited to his crime by reading them [the Hearst papers]—ten thousand dollars for his family to be his reward; but this cheerful scheme was blocked by the trial judge who had been informed of it. During all this carnival of sin I lay ill in Washington, unaware of it; and my name, although appended to all that I wrote, including the verses, was not, I am told, once mentioned. As to Mr. Hearst, I dare say he first saw the lines when all this hullabaloo directed his attention to them."

Bierce could not resist tempering this generous estimate with the thought that Hearst's newspapers had "always been so unjust that no injustice could be done to them, and had been incredibly rancorous toward McKinley, but no doubt it was my luckless prophecy that cost him tens of thousands of dollars and a growing political prestige."

It was not the money that worried Hearst; he knew how quickly people forgot, and indeed the *Journal* came out of its disgrace with its net paid circulation still the largest in the world. But he realized it was necessary to fight back. In doing so he took the bold approach, pointing out with justice that his was not the first newspaper in New York or elsewhere to call a President names. The *Sun*, he recalled, had gone on vituperating against Grant and Garfield after they were dead and buried. The *Post*, which had taken a lofty view of Hearst from the beginning, had itself referred to McKinley as "a liar, a renegade, a traitor," and during the Cleveland Administration had charged that the President was the father of an illegitimate child which he kept secreted in a Buffalo almshouse.

In one of his own editorials, Hearst struck back at his enemies in kind—unregenerate, unashamed, admitting nothing, denying everything.

"From coast to coast this newspaper has been attacked and is being attacked with savage ferocity by the incompetent, the failures of journalism, by the kept organs of plutocracy heading the mob," he asserted. "The Hearst papers are American papers for Americans. They are conservative papers, for the truest conservatism is that radicalism which would uproot revolution-breeding abuses. . . . All the enemies of the people, of the democratic people conscious and unconscious—all who reap where others have sown, all the rascals and their organs, and many fools caught by the malignant uproar, are yelling at the Journal. LET THEM YELL."

With this barbaric yawp, he let them, for the most part, and confined himself to attacking individuals, particularly the new President, Mr. Roosevelt, who told Congress in his first message that Czolgosz had been inflamed "by the reckless utterances of those who, on the stump and in the public press, appeal to the dark and evil spirits of malice and greed, envy and sullen hatred." The Republican senators knew well enough who was meant. So did Hearst.

In a way, it was fortunate for Hearst that Roosevelt had succeeded McKinley. In the excitement of his reign, and the new quarrels stirred up, the public forgot to be angry at Hearst for the old reasons. Many thought up new ones, but these were more safely in the field of party politics.

For Hearst concluded in 1902 that the time had come for him to start on his way to the White House. He had been doubtful about it because of the McKinley episode's effect on the voters, so doubtful that he permitted Brisbane, who was ambitious on his own account, to entertain dreams of Congress. He had even assured his friend Artie that he would get him the nomination from the Eleventh District, a Southern kind of territory in which the Democratic nomination was equivalent to election. At the last minute Hearst conferred with the Tammany chieftains and decided to risk it. Brisbane was brushed aside with cruel practicality and Hearst got the nomination.

He waged a gaudy and completely unnecessary campaign, inasmuch as he could not have lost the election except by running naked around Times Square at high noon. But it brought him to the attention of the voters, and that was what he desired. No voter could have missed the final rally at Madison Square Garden, which was filled inside and out. Those outside, milling around in the square, inside cordons formed by 850 policemen, saw the best show. They witnessed campaign cartoons spelled out in colored lights, fire balloons red against the night sky, and skyrockets in such a profusion as had not been seen since the *Journal* celebrated the declaration of war against Spain.

Inside, Hearst made political history by speaking only ten minutes. The speech clung to a familiar theme: the Republicans were the captives of the interests and therefore not to be trusted in public office. Other speakers on the bill were more effulgent. They included two former governors, David B. Hill of New York and James H. Budd of California, and Grover Cleveland's Vice-President, Adlai Stevenson.

To no one's surprise, Hearst was elected, by the largest margin ever recorded in the district. After a holiday in Europe, he was ready for Congress.

Congress, it appeared, was not ready for him. The members regarded his appearance in the club with ill-concealed suspicion, suspecting that his mission was to promote his personal program, which he had insisted was not only Democratic but "right." Hearst did nothing to dispel this suspicion. He gave the appearance of a congressman, dressing in the customary frock coat and congressional black hat with broad brim, and making no effort to conceal his growing stoutness, appropriate to a man of forty. But beyond that, he showed no least inclination to be a congressman.

He rarely attended sessions—only nine times in one six-month period—and when he came, he pursued a lone course, antagonizing the leaders of both parties. The Democratic leader of the House did not even speak to him after an early, violent quarrel over Hearst's program. He was distrusted and disliked, except by a few cronies like Champ Clark of Missouri, who came from the Hearst country in that sovereign state and appeared to feel a familial as well as political affinity with Hearst.

It was quite clear why Hearst was in Congress. He had his eye on the presidency, and he used the House as a sounding board for his policies by introducing progressive reform measures, publicizing them widely in his papers, and then letting them die in committee. He was, in effect, conducting a political campaign for one job while ostensibly serving in another, and he was happily relieved of assuming any responsibility for the enactment and enforcement of his measures.

In these tactics lay the key to Hearst's utter failure as a politician. He imagined that he did not need the professional politicians to advance his cause, that money and his newspapers were enough. If he had been a master tactician, he might have proved himself correct, or if he had enjoyed the overwhelming personal appeal of a man like Eisenhower, to cite a modern instance. But he was no tactician—the professionals regularly made a monkey of him—and he was simply not a vote-getter. As time went on, he developed the illusion that he was a vote-getter by reason of the huge crowds that flocked to hear him, but it seemed people came largely out of curiosity, to examine at first hand the fabulous side show of journalism they had heard so much about. They came to the tent, looked upon the two-headed calf, and went home to vote for the other candidate.

While Hearst's career in Congress may have been a failure as far as his constituents were concerned, it had its practical, if temporary, successes. In spite of the general antipathy between him and his colleagues, he emerged with the loyal support and personal friendship of several men who would be helpful to him—men like Champ Clark, and Jack Garner of Texas, Lamar of Florida, and Shackleford of Missouri. The bills he sponsored, while they were not appealing to the professionals, attracted to Hearst for a time at least the attention and political support of a few high-minded, honest and able reformers who gave his ambitions a surface coating of complete respectability.

It was difficult for a Democrat, a liberal, or a plain reformer to be against the ten major bills Hearst proposed in Congress. They included measures to provide for direct election of senators, an eight-hour day for mechanics and workmen employed on government contracts, Federal aid to supplement state funds for building good roads, detailed appropriations estimates from Federal departments, curbing of the Standard Oil monopoly, more Federal control over trusts, strengthening of the power and jurisdiction of the Interstate Commerce Commission, Federal ownership of a complete telegraph and cable system, increased salaries for the Supreme Court, and establishment of the parcel-post system.

Here was a progressive platform which represented the stand Hearst advocated in his papers, and in general the stand of the Democratic Party. Its opponents were, quite naturally, the railroad, oil and utilities interests, along with the entrenched conservative leadership in the Federal government. The individual measures, with some exceptions, represented the kind of reform which could not be delayed too long, and at least half of them were enacted into law pretty much as Hearst proposed them, although under different sponsorship and at later dates.

From Hearst's standpoint, he had laid out in his first year in Washington, regardless of the actual time he spent there, a pro-

gram he considered sufficiently appealing to permit his name
to be presented to the Democratic convention of 1904 in St.
Louis. This was accomplished by a Western orator named
D. M. Delmas, who told the assembled Democrats: "For the
first time in history, California presents as a candidate for the
great office of Chief Executive of the Republic, one born and
reared on her soil, William Randolph Hearst," a man who, he
went on, could be compared only with Jefferson in his devotion
to the plain people.

A man who, the eloquent, rich voice of Mr. Delmas proclaimed in a rousing peroration, was "the unconquered antagonist of all schemes by which man, trampling right and justice
underfoot, builds his fortune upon oppression and wrong, the
foremost living advocate of the equality of man . . . the champion of the rights of toil, the foe of privilege and monopoly, the
friend of all who labor and are heavy laden . . . William Randolph Hearst."

Clarence Darrow jumped to his feet and seconded the nomination, amid cries of acclamation from the California delegation.
Then came the balloting. The unconquered antagonist, champion and friend got 200 votes. Judge Alton Brooks Parker, a
duller but somewhat more respectable candidate, got the nomination.

Back in New York again, Hearst became the rallying point
for Democrats unable to stomach the Tammany leadership,
and for the "clean government" reformers who saw in him a
possibly potent independent candidate, able to get control of
the transit lines, the gas and light interests, and other sources
of corruption away from the Tammany boss, Charles F. Murphy,
and the Wall Street entrepreneurs who supported him. This
somewhat unnatural alliance was the result of a mutual protective association that had developed between the men who
financed New York expansion and those who controlled its politics. Murphy used the names of the financiers—men like Thomas
Fortune Ryan—to cast a holier light on Tammany, and the

financiers used Murphy's entrenched power to accomplish the finagling necessary to their vast schemes.

Out of this situation rose the Municipal Ownership League, formed on December 22, 1904, with Hearst as chairman and names like Samuel Seabury and Senator John Ford on its committee list.

The League's first public endeavor was to oust the Tammany mayor, George B. McClellan, from office in the election of 1905. Seabury and Ford virtually pleaded with Hearst to run for the mayoralty, and Hearst, with the proper show of reluctance, consented in October, declaring that in such grave times a man had "no right to consider himself, least of all his personal affairs." His personal affairs had to wait, in any event, until 1908, the next presidential year. Meanwhile, the mayoralty loomed as a possible steppingstone.

By this time Hearst had a better understanding of what a politician had to do to get into office, and with his customary furious energy, he left nothing undone in his campaign for City Hall. He spoke a dozen times a day, mostly to the workingmen who had to be swung away from Tammany to the Municipal Ownership League ticket if his election was to be possible. They appeared to receive his advances gladly. He made a triumphal procession through the Bowery one night, and on up to the Grand Street Opera House, pausing along the way for short sermons on the evils of trusts and boss rule. On the Sunday night before election, he addressed in Madison Square Garden the largest gathering ever seen until that time at a political meeting in New York City, 100,000 outside and 40,000 inside, including a 120-piece orchestra. The crowd gave the candidate an ovation lasting seventeen minutes when he appeared.

On the day before election, Hearst made a final appeal to the voters in a manner which elicited the admiration and apprehension of Tammany. The Irish, he urged, should vote as Robert Emmet would wish them to, the Jews as Maimonides would counsel, the Poles as Kosciusko would do it, the Italians as

Garibaldi, the Hungarians as Kossuth, and the splendid un-hyphenated Americans should take their guidance from Jefferson and Lincoln, who was not really a Republican.

Tammany had foreseen the strength of Hearst's appeal to the voters and had taken the proper means to forestall it. The fearless antagonist got his first painful lesson in the inefficacy of third parties and the need for professional organization. As the semi-official biographer puts it, "dark work was done," a handsome understatement of the case. Tammany simply stole the election by the crudest means available to machine politics. They bought some votes and discouraged others with blackjacks and fists. Floaters and repeaters arrived in droves from as far away as Philadelphia, Troy, Newark and Hartford. Even cats and dogs voted on that epic day. To make sure that these efforts did not go unrewarded, a quantity of ballots was tossed off Brooklyn Bridge into the equally dirty East River. McClellan won by 1800 votes.

The results of the fraud were widespread. Its perpetrators went largely unpunished, in spite of the legal actions which followed; a few patsys went to Sing Sing, their employers lived to vote again. But the ripples it spread persisted to the farthest edges of the shore.

From the long-range standpoint, Hearst perceived that he had one more chance, the gubernatorial election in 1906, to consolidate his strength and gain New York for himself in 1908, an acquisition he had foreseen in the campaign of 1904 would be essential if he were to be nominated and elected to the presidency. Bryan, into whose reformist shoes Hearst had eased himself, had made this mistake of neglecting East for West; Hearst had no intention of repeating it. Everything now depended on getting the governorship.

To attain the hill in Albany, he saw too, as a result of the mayoralty election, it would not do to antagonize Charles F. Murphy any further. As it was, he had almost gone too far. During the McClellan campaign, they had traded the usual political insults, Hearst comparing the boss with previous Tam-

many criminals and finding no one worse in the whole inglorious register except Tweed, while Murphy devoted himself to
Hearst's private life, describing him as a "debauchee of a peculiarly depraved type." This led to a brief cleanup of the *Journal's* scandalous pages and the prosecution of poor Bennett for
his dirty little ads.

These had been the amenities of the campaign, but where
Hearst had gone too far was in his indignation over the fraudu-
lent balloting. The *Journal* had caricatured Murphy as a convict
in a striped suit, accompanied by an editorial diatribe beginning,
"Every honest voter in New York WANTS TO SEE YOU IN
THIS COSTUME."

Murphy was hurt. As a practical politician he paid little attention to what was said during a campaign except as it might
affect votes, but the campaign was over and the ground rules
called for ceasing and desisting. He never forgave Hearst for
the cartoon.

But on the other hand he was not so insulted that he refused
to do business with W.R. when the publisher came, early in 1906,
loaded down with olive branches and propositions. The idea had
been originally to frighten Murphy with a show of strength.
The William Randolph Hearst Municipal Ownership League,
which had accomplished nothing nationally and lost an important
election in New York City, had been changed to the Independence League, which as a third party was intended to entice
voters who had avoided the Hearst name and the idea of municipal ownership. Unfortunately, the Independence League had
insisted on nominating a full slate of candidates, besides naming
Hearst for the governorship, a move not calculated to soothe
the Tammany breast. Consequently Hearst came to Murphy
with the necessity of getting the boss's co-operation in securing
enough delegates for the nomination at the convention in Buffalo. In return, he could promise his Independence League following and the respect it commanded among non-machine
voters. Thus united, the Democrats could hardly fail to win the
election.

Murphy consented to the deal and secured it by the usual unfailing methods. He instructed State Senator Thomas F. Grady, as chairman of the convention's membership committee, to see that Hearst-committed delegates were seated and anti-Hearst men thrown out wherever it was possible. "It was the dirtiest day's work I ever did in my life," the Senator remarked later with justifiable pride.

It was, indeed, a redolent affair, considered whole. Neither Murphy nor Hearst had wanted each other, but Hearst realized he needed machine support and Murphy was willing because his power had been impaired by a break with McClellan and the increased strength of the Independence League. A wit of the day observed of Hearst's part in this affair:

*So I lashed him and I thrashed him in my hot reforming zeal,*
*Then I clasped him to my bosom in a most artistic deal.*

The unholy alliance of Tammany with so notorious a journalistic figure as Hearst—for despite his failures in politics he was probably the country's most discussed man, aside from Theodore Roosevelt—produced alarm in the Republican camp. It was necessary to nominate a man of the most impeccable virtue, who would be in startling contrast before the voters. No other man qualified so well on these counts as Charles Evans Hughes. His vote-getting powers were questionable because of his aloof and dignified manner, but he had already shown himself an able enemy of the trusts, thus cutting some of the ground from beneath the Democrats' feet, and in addition, President Roosevelt had promised him the full support of the Administration. Mr. Hughes listened, and he too heard the call.

When the campaign began, Hearst pulled out all the stops. As he traveled about upper New York State on a special train, he made innumerable back-platform speeches, exhibited his wife and two-year-old son George, shook hands with the firemen and engineers, stopped off at county fairs, and talked to the voters wherever they would have him—streets, tents, halls, open automobiles, sidewalks. When babies were named for him, their devoted parents were rewarded with silver cups. Two hundred young ladies from Elmira College gathered at the station to hug the candidate's wife, kiss his son, and yell with athletic fervor: "Rah! Rah! Rah! El-mi-ra! Elmira College! Boom! Rah! Hearst!"

Hearst's speeches took the familiar tone. Hughes was a lawyer who had defended the trusts, and his friends were friends of the trusts. He coined the phrase "animated feather duster" to characterize Hughes's mustached appearance, a phrase he reiterated in the immemorial manner of the hustings.

The Republican candidate refused to reply in kind. He pursued his dignified course, and those who had a chance to see him and hear him discovered that he was not icy and remote but a human being after all. When it was suggested that he ought to emulate Hearst and follow tradition by kissing babies, he replied with a twinkle, "No, I will not make any appeal to the passions of the populace."

There was some doubt as to how this kind of campaigning might be influencing votes. Roosevelt sent his secretary, Elihu Root, into New York to do some stumping for his friend. In a speech at Utica, Root spoke of Hearst in a way reminiscent today of Hearst editorials about Franklin D. Roosevelt thirty years later. If one substitutes F.D.R.'s name for Hearst's, the resemblance is startling.

"Day by day and year by year," Root said, "Hearst has been sowing the seeds of dissension, of strife and hatred throughout our land. He would array labor against capital, and capital against labor; poverty against wealth, and wealth against poverty. . . . He would destroy that respect for law, that love of order, that confidence in our free institutions which is the basis of true freedom and true justice. . . . He spreads the spirit, he follows the methods, and he is guided by the selfish motives of a revolutionist. . . ."

It was a lofty speech, but in it Root did not hesitate to resurrect Bierce's ill-fated verses about Governor Goebel and the subsequent assassination of McKinley. Of this, Bierce made his own acid comment:

"When Mr. Hearst was making his grotesque canvass for the governorship of New York, the Roosevelt Administration sent Secretary Root into the state to beat him. This high-minded gentleman incorporated one of the garbled prose versions of my prophecy into his speeches with notable effect and great satisfaction to his conscience. Still, I am steadfast in the conviction that God sees him; and if any one thinks that Mr. Root will not go to the devil, it must be the devil himself, in whom, doubtless, the wish is father to the thought."

Merlo J. Pusey, Hughes's biographer, records that Hearst replied to Root's attack before it was given, since the speech had been released in advance. As Root and Hughes rode from the railroad station to the hall, newsboys tossed them the *Journal*, which boasted a front-page cartoon depicting "Root the Rat" gnawing at the common people's defenses. Utica Republicans were busy tearing up copies of this edition and throwing them about the streets.

In the hall itself, an impassioned colloquy took place. Tammany hecklers yelled down from the balcony, "It's a lie," when Root made a charge against Hearst.

"Throw him out!" yelled the pro-Hughes crowd.

"No, let him stay and learn," Root replied, stilling the tempest with a dramatic upraised hand.

Some historians contend that it was this single speech of Root's which cost Hearst the election.

Whatever Hughes's own quiet campaigning lacked in virulence was more than compensated for by the non-Hearst press. Every other paper in New York supported Hughes. The *Herald* and the *World*, quite naturally, were the most savage attackers of Hearst, but the *Sun*, the *Times* and *Evening Post* were restrained only by comparison. Pulitzer wrote to Frank Cobb that he was "simply crazy about Hughes." This passion, expressed editorially, moved Hearst to reply with personal attacks on Pulitzer during his campaigning.

Thus the battle roared on to its conclusion. For Hearst, the end was the usual rally at the Garden. It was stage-managed with his eye for the theatrical. The place was swathed in flags, including twenty-four Irish emblems. Millie and little George sat in a box, from which George rose and waved a small American flag at the crowd, who gave him three cheers and a demonstration. The noise from cowbells, whistles and human throats was deafening as the candidate strode down the aisle to the stage, where he received an eleven-minute ovation. Mrs. Older believes it was "probably the most dramatic moment in Hearst's life."

A *World* reporter has obligingly provided a brief portrait of Hearst as he appeared at that moment. He presented, said the reporter, "a striking figure, the predominant notes of which were the clear, pink-tinted complexion of his face, a white Ascot tie knotted under a high, turned-down soiled white collar in which nestled a little brown pin that looked as if it might have cost as much as forty-five cents. His light tawny hair was sleek and brushed over his forehead, a stray lock reaching almost to the brow of his left eye. His tall straight figure was encased in a long Prince Albert coat that was shiny at the elbows and was long at the sides. His trousers of dark gray stripe had not been recently creased. Mr. Hearst's first act upon reaching the platform was to rub the back of his left hand over his mouth. Then he picked up a beer glass and poured into it a drink of water from a cracked white pitcher that stood on the reading stand.

"He turned to Henry A. Powell, who had called the meeting together, made a remark, and the corners of his mouth turned up in a broad smile of almost childish pleasure. Then he faced the audience, gripping the rail in front of him with both hands, drumming upon it with his fingers. His right foot tapped in unison with the crash of the band of one hundred and fifty pieces behind him. He bowed as each succeeding wave of cheers bellowed at him from the front."

Again, as in the previous year, he seemed at last on the brink of success. Yet, on election night, the returns showed that Hughes had been elected governor by nearly 60,000 votes. In his anxiety to be nominated by any means, Hearst had fatally offended Pat McCarren, the Brooklyn Democratic boss, whose anti-Hearst delegates had been among those flattened by the efficient Grady steamroller. McCarren retaliated by sending out the word: his followers were to scratch their ballots. This defection in the Democratic camp was enough to account for most if not all of Hughes's plurality, though it is possible that Root's speech may have stampeded some independent voters.

Ironically, the Murphy-Hearst strategy worked perfectly in every other respect. All the Democratic candidates except Hearst were elected. The repudiation was even more striking when it was considered that the campaign had cost Hearst $500,000, while Hughes had spent only $619.

Hearst's comment on the election reflected his bitterness. "I congratulate the bosses on their foresight in defeating me," he said, "for my first act as Governor would have been to lift the dishonest officials by the hair of their unworthy heads."

He would not admit it for a time, but Hearst understood in that dreary November aftermath of the election that his dream of the White House had all but disappeared in this humiliating defeat. He had been personally discredited and rejected by the voters, in spite of the fact that he had left nothing undone that money and influence and professional politicking could accomplish.

Disconsolate, he took Millicent and George and set out for the familiar surroundings and perennial solace of California. On the way he stopped off in St. Louis, and as he walked through the city room of the *Post-Dispatch* to the office of the Associated Press, he was stopped by Joseph Pulitzer's 21-year-old son and namesake. Joseph, Jr., had been sent to the paper, his father's original property, to learn the business the hard way, as Senior had learned it. He had been reading Hearst's campaign speeches as they came in on the wire, and he had not liked what he read.

Reminding Hearst of the insults to his father, he inquired: "Did you utter them deliberately and meaning they should be believed, or did you say them recklessly in the heat of the campaign?"

Hearst was in no mood to temporize. "I usually mean what I say," he answered curtly. Young Joe's lips tightened and he swung a haymaking right into Hearst's stomach. Millicent, who was with her husband, seized his arm before he could retaliate, and *Post-Dispatch* men hurried up to end the fight, which had been historic but inconclusive.

After a season of relaxation in the calming atmosphere of his mother's ranch, Hearst returned to take up the struggle. He had not quite given up, but he was in a different mood. A good deal of the campaign's rancor had been forgotten. He chanced to be in Albany, and remarked, "I think I'll walk up the hill and see Featherduster. I wonder if he'll be glad to see me."

The "friend of the corporations" and the "dissolute demagogue" met in the new Governor's private office, where they exchanged civilized pleasantries for a half-hour.

"The Governor is a pretty human sort of fellow," Hearst told a friend afterward.

# CHAPTER SEVEN

## THE MAN WHO WASN'T PRESIDENT

IF HE COULD NOT be President, Hearst decided in 1907, he would be a maker of Presidents, and perhaps get in by the back door. Although money was not a factor in his decision, he had already spent a million and a half dollars on his ambitions without result and perhaps he concluded that further expenditures and effort could be more profitably applied elsewhere.

The political realities still called for another try at an independent ticket in 1908. The Republicans had nominated William Howard Taft, a man as safe and sane as Hughes, while the Democrats had named the ubiquitous Bryan, whom Hearst considered as discredited as himself. Thus at the July 1908 convention of the Independence League in Chicago, Hearst told the sweating delegates that they would be well advised to steer away from both sanity and previously defeated candidates. The League adopted a platform, read by Hearst's lawyer, Clarence Shearn, which was a stewpot of every reform, trust-busting, government-owning, voter-saving measure Hearst had been advocating for the past decade. It had a built-in California plank calling for the exclusion of cheap Asiatic labor, and some of its other provisions, like government ownership of railroads and telegraph lines, would be considered radical even today.

As an opponent to such celebrated figures as Taft and Bryan, the party mistakenly chose a complete unknown for its candidate. Thomas L. Hisgen, of Massachusetts, the man the lightning struck, was qualified for the job primarily because the Standard Oil Company had allegedly tried to put him and his four brothers out of the axle-grease business, whereupon they had gone into oil and fought Standard for the next twenty years. As a companion piece to this stalwart, the convention nominated a Southerner, John Temple Graves, of Georgia, later a Hearst columnist, for Vice-President.

It would have been a campaign unrivaled in dullness except for the bombshell Hearst threw into it without warning on September 15, 1908, with the reading and publication of the famous Foraker letters.

Debate, some of it rather peculiar, still exists about this correspondence, which tended to prove that the Standard Oil Company had been influencing legislation in Congress with bribes to both Republican and Democratic senators, particularly to the Honorable Joseph B. Foraker, the distinguished Republican from Ohio. The most damning documents were letters concerning payments which had passed between John D. Archbold, Standard's remote and arrogant president, and Foraker.

How Hearst came by these letters, and when, depends on who is telling the story. Mrs. Older says that John Eddy, "a stranger to Hearst, called at his hotel and submitted" the letters. Eddy may well have been a stranger, but he was also a New York *American* reporter. She further says flatly that how Eddy acquired these letters "is unknown."

The truth, as disclosed by less partial biographers, appears to be that Hearst had begun to acquire them three years before as the result of a conspiracy on the part of the stepson of Archbold's trusted butler, who was employed at the company's offices, 26 Broadway, and another office employee. These gentlemen progressively rifled Archbold's files and sold the letters to Hearst, who accumulated the evidence over a period of years and waited for the most strategic moment to disclose it.

That moment came in Columbus, Ohio, while Hearst was stumping for Hisgen. Foraker's home state and capital had been selected as the logical place.

Jack Lait, present editor of the New York *Daily Mirror*, in a columnar obeisance at the bier of the Chief, recalls dramatically but incorrectly that "the whole nation knew that he was to read the first of the damning letters," a reading Lait places five years before it occurred. However, if one is to believe the semi-official biographer, a thrilling conversation took place in the Columbus hotel room that day after Hearst had read the letters which Eddy had just brought to him so fortuitously.

"These letters are treason. The world must know. I'll read some to the audience tonight!" Hearst is said to have exclaimed.

"It can't be done." This from a companion, who may have been Lait himself, since he was a self-confessed first aide on the tour, as a young reporter.

"George Washington intercepted a letter that cost Major André his life," Hearst is said to have reproved the doubter. "Washington would have hanged Benedict Arnold if he could have caught the traitor."

It may well be doubted whether these immortal words were ever spoken.

In any event, and at the expense of Mr. Lait's memory, the audience in Columbus was anything but hostile, silent and tense, as he recalls, "awaiting the actual text of the deadly letter." Instead, they appear to have been so bored and apathetic that they missed the point entirely as Hearst read the evidence in a quiet voice, and it was not until the speech was published that the reporters descended on him en masse in St. Louis next day.

But Mr. Lait's intention was kindly. His reminiscence was meant to relate a story illustrating Hearst's generosity. He reports that as Hearst got to the page which should have contained the letter in the typescript made up for him from his longhand notes by the hotel stenographer, he paused, shuffled the pages, then announced in the dramatic silence, "It seems that the stenographer, in putting together the pages, left one out— the one with the letter." Whereupon, Mr. Lait says, he rushed from the wings with the missing page and the Chief read it.

"But he had been deeply embarrassed," says Mr. Lait. "The hesitation, the pause, my walking out on the stage, had broken the tension; some laughed; many whispered. The stenographer's blunder had intruded as the world waited."

As they were about to leave for the train, he remembers, Hearst pulled a fifty-dollar bill from his pocket and gave it to Lait, who was still "boiling angry" over the incident. "Put this in an envelope," said the kindly man who had just shredded a fellow politician's fortunes by means of stolen letters which were later discovered to have been altered to produce a greater effect, "and leave it for the hotel stenographer. When she hears what happened, she will feel terrible."

Mr. Lait adds, understandably, that this is an anecdote he had never before written.

The disclosure of the letters, in any case, was a dreadful shock to the Republicans. A wave of sheer political horror traveled right up Pennsylvania Avenue to the White House, where President Roosevelt, another fearless enemy of the trusts, thought it expedient to swallow his pride and summon Hearst to the White House, in an attempt to find out just how extensive the prospective damage would be.

When the two old enemies faced each other, the President with difficulty commended Hearst for his exposure of corruption in high Republican places, and then, deciding that he might as well know the worst, inquired suddenly, "Do any of the letters contain anything about me?" Hearst reassured him: "Nothing that will harm you."

It was not a comforting reassurance. As the Brooklyn *Eagle* put it, Hearst "ran a live wire through the leaders of both Houses," and unfortunately the President, who seems to have been personally blameless, was present at the electrocution of some valued henchmen.

Hearst went about the country, reading more letters, and concluding as usual in Madison Square Garden, where further communications disclosed that Standard had succeeded in corrupting some members of the press, and that ambitious plans had been laid to buy off the Associated Press, no matter what the cost.

There were attempts at rebuttal. Senator Boies Penrose of Pennsylvania issued an open defiance. Roosevelt pointed out that it was he who had succeeded in getting Standard indicted twenty-nine times in Illinois and New York and then had the trust sued under the Sherman Act, with a resulting decree of dissolution.

The letters created a great stir in political circles. Foraker and two other members of Congress retired from public life. Yet, once again, the election came and with it the second complete repudiation of Hearst: Taft's Republican victory was overwhelming, and Hisgen ran last in the field of five. He polled only 83,628 votes. In his own state, John Temple Graves got exactly 77 votes.

The Independence League's slogan had been, "Vote for Hisgen, Graves and principle." The comment of an unlettered but able Democratic boss had been: "People don't want no principle, they want to be on the winning side."

It was difficult, almost impossible, for Hearst to believe that he carried no weight politically. With him it was not a question of principle at all. In the case of the Hisgen campaign, he had carefully prepared a bombshell, exploded it, and then watched the voters disregard it. He had, he thought, played according to the rules of politics, but the result was never what he hoped or expected.

He smarted from his wounds, and might have given up politics altogether, except that the irresistible temptations presented by another controversy in New York City politics compelled him to try once more. It was a disastrous decision in every respect. He took on an opponent far more formidable than he seemed at the outset, and the character of the campaign added neither credit nor circulation to the Hearst newspapers.

The leading candidate for mayor of New York in 1909 was William J. Gaynor, a tough and irascible Justice of the Supreme Court, a man as willfully independent as Hearst, and far less inclined to make deals. Pulitzer and the *World* had long supported him as a man of courage and integrity. Boss Murphy considered him a good candidate in spite of his independence, because that factor alone would enable Tammany to offset the threat of possible fusion candidates backed by Hearst, who in spite of his defeats was still the only rallying point in municipal politics for the reform element.

It was remarkable but true that even the most astute and honest of the reformers still considered that Hearst best represented the unbossed, clean-government faction in the voting population. He had even drawn the local Republicans into his orbit, since a fusion ticket seemed to be the only method by which they could get a candidate into office.

Oddly enough, Gaynor believed at first that Hearst was on his side, and the publisher had gone so far as to assure him of it personally. Yet in the September maneuverings before the city conventions took place, the Republican-Fusion-Hearst forces refused to commit themselves. Hearst implied that if Gaynor ran on behalf of Murphy's Tammany Democracy, his virtue was in serious doubt. The Judge retorted tartly, according to his biographer, Mortimer Smith, that to question his principles was "like asking St. Paul if he were a Christian."

Murphy had no doubts about Gaynor, and such confidence won the Judge's heart. He was duly nominated with a Tammany slate. The Republicans put up a colorless banker, Otto T. Bannard. That left Hearst in his customary unassailable moral position. The Democratic candidate was a representative of Murphyism. The Republican aspirant was a servant of the trusts. There was nothing for it but to run for the office himself.

He made a few alterations in the familiar pattern. The Independence League had acquired a bad reputation for losing candidates, so it was renamed the Civic Alliance. Otherwise the mixture was as before. Except that this time it is possible Hearst did not really expect to win, and only hoped to embarrass Tammany by splitting the ticket hopelessly so that if Gaynor won he would find himself without support in the Board of Estimate.

The chief result of his nomination, however, was the outbreak of an appallingly savage feud with the Judge, who could not understand why Hearst, who had always supported him editorially in the past, should now withdraw his aid. He recalled Hearst's personal assurance of help. Hearst denied it. "He came humbly up to my house once, twice, thrice, hat in hand, of his own accord and in his own interest," Hearst said of his one-time ally. "Judge Gaynor is not a life-long friend, or a deeply loved brother to whom a blind devotion is due. He has been to me merely a representative of certain ideas, an exponent of certain principles. While he was supporting those principles I supported him."

Gaynor accepted this repudiation with deceptive melancholy. "I am going through an experience of breach of faith and plighted word that I did not deem possible in this world," he lamented. A few days later he turned both vituperative barrels on Hearst and the war was begun.

The Judge had been in politics a long time. He knew Hearst's weakest points, one of them being that as an incipient congress-man the publisher had accepted Murphy's Tammany support with open arms. "And oh dear me," said the Judge, "how long since he was on the Tammany ticket! How dainty and how nice, and how delicate is the conscience of this man about the Tammany ticket just at present!"

There was much more in the same vein, and as the election neared, Gaynor descended to new depths of scurrility. On the public platform he declared that Hearst's face was one "which almost makes me puke," and sometimes he shrieked at his detrac-tors, "Shut up, you slanderers, you blackguards!" As his biog-rapher notes, it was difficult to believe that this man "held a studious and intelligent social and political philosophy."

It was equally difficult to believe that Hearst did not retort but insisted on discussing the issues. He left the low blows to one of his political henchmen, a master at it but still no match for Gaynor, who declared to an astounded audience that Hearst was "filled up into the weasand, yes, into the goozle, with promises."

Gaynor won the election easily, with Hearst a poor third, but it was an inconclusive victory because W.R.'s strategy, designed for defeat, had worked this time, and Murphy found himself with a new Board of Estimate on which Tammany was not represented.

But the victory was as hollow for Hearst as it was for Murphy. He saw this last, forlorn chance at public office slip from his fingers, and as he contemplated a bleak political future, he turned the full force of his vindictiveness on the new mayor.

It was as though the campaign were still being fought. Before Gaynor had been in City Hall a month, the *Journal* was publishing post-election letters between Gaynor and Murphy, indicating that the fine hand of Tammany was in control. There was an indignant demand to know where Hearst got the letters. A plausible theory was that one of the publisher's far-flung operatives, probably sent up from Chicago, had bribed a chambermaid to retrieve whatever went into Murphy's waste-basket in the hotel room at Mount Clemens, Michigan, where he was taking the baths and relaxing after the campaign.

Brisbane, called upon to make a speech about this time at a dinner of the Genesee Society, brought the whole affair into the open with his usual tactlessness by declaring that if the letters "were stolen, as some say, was it not a plain duty to steal these records of that medley of corruption, Tammany Hall, and of those rascals with the red faces and thick necks who compose it?"

The guests sitting in the plush splendor of the old Waldorf-Astoria banquet room winced, inasmuch as the tables were thick with representatives of Tammany Hall, both highly placed sachems and common warriors of the wards.

State Senator Grady, who had loaded the Buffalo convention with Hearst delegates at Murphy's orders, rose to reply "as one of the gang of red-faced thick-necked grafters" and made the open charge about bribery of the chambermaid, "a much more dignified" proceeding than "simple theft," he remarked dryly.

Three months later the battle of the banquets was resumed in the same room, when Mayor Gaynor himself rose at the annual dinner of the Associated Press and American Newspaper

Publishers Association and dissected Hearst before the shocked gaze of his fellow publishers and Woodrow Wilson. It was a deliberate, bitter speech. "A newspaper proprietor who is simply bent on cutting throats is an awful spectacle," the Mayor said. "In no nook or cranny of his head or heart is there the slightest sense of truth or justice. We may pity him, but we cannot in the interests of public morality and decency remain silent about him." He then accused Hearst of "forgery and falsification of a public document," referring to another *Journal* exposé attempting to prove that his election had been bought.

"It is high time," Gaynor concluded solemnly, "that these forgers and libellers were in state's prison, and the time is not far distant when some of them will be there. And just think of a man who is capable of doing things like this being possessed of the notion that he is fit to hold any office, from Mayor to President of the United States. Morally speaking, his mind must be a howling wilderness. . . ."

The deep silence that followed this speech was broken by enthusiastic applause and what the *Tribune* aptly called "the hottest row that has been seen in a dining room in the memory of regular diners in this city." Thomas T. Williams, Hearst's New York business manager, tried to speak, but the publishers would not listen, and the toastmaster refused to let him have the floor. Red-faced and shouting, Williams thrust a fist under Gaynor's nose and cried, "Are you afraid, Mr. Mayor?"

Through it all, Gaynor stood cold and aloof, while cooler heads like Adolph Ochs tried to restore order and the crowd yelled its disapproval, winding up with "three cheers for our honest Mayor." It took the combined efforts of Oscar, the Waldorf's maître d', a covey of detectives, and a few of Williams' friends to get their man out of the dining room so that the banquet might proceed.

By a grisly coincidence, this public feuding, which reminded a good many people of the McKinley days, was followed only four months after the dinner riot by the near-assassination of the Mayor, who was shot as he stood on the deck of the *Kaiser*

*Wilhelm der Grosse,* about to sail for Europe. The would-be assassin was a disgruntled employee of the Docks Department who had been fired from his job and blamed Gaynor for it.

The non-Hearst papers were enchanted by the news. They recalled Czolgosz and McKinley, and at first glance it appeared that this repetition of history would certainly be enough to hang Hearst. The *World* sent a young reporter named Herbert Bayard Swope down to interview James J. Gallagher, who had done the shooting, with the hope of confirming the rumor which had instantly swept the city, that a *Journal* editorial attacking the Mayor had been found in his pocket. If that had been true, Hearst might have had a hard time escaping public wrath. To the acute disappointment of the opposition, Gallagher told Swope that the only paper he read was the New York *Times.*

Gaynor was more than willing to believe that Hearst had inspired the act, and said as much in a letter to his sister, who repeated the charge to Hearst. He replied with unrelenting coldness which offended many citizens, since Gaynor was still dangerously ill: "I am exceedingly sorry that Mayor Gaynor was shot, and if Mayor Gaynor has said what you tell me, I can only add that I am exceedingly sorry that his injuries have affected his mind. . . . His experience did not abate his evil temper nor his lying tongue."

The feud continued until Gaynor died in 1913. The two met once in public, a little more than three months before the Mayor's death, when the Maine Monument Committee, of which Hearst was a member, was received in the Mayor's office. Gaynor and Hearst regarded each other grimly. Hearst's long, equine face was cold and passive; Gaynor seemed on the point of launching into a tirade. Instead they shook hands perfunctorily and the day's activities, to celebrate the dedication of the Maine Memorial in Columbus Circle, began without incident. George Hearst, by that time nine years old, held out an innocent kind of olive branch later in the day by joining Gaynor's little daughter, Marion, at the dedication ceremonies. The Mayor and the publisher showed no inclination to go any further, however, and in fact did not meet again. This meeting occurred on May 29; Gaynor died in September.

By the time these events occurred, Hearst's role in politics had changed as the result of two more setbacks. In 1910 he had made a halfhearted attempt to revive the Independence League and organize a ticket on which he would have run as lieutenant governor, but there was so little enthusiasm for either him or the League that he backed down from the hustings in dismay before election, to spare himself the humiliation of another defeat. Then, in 1912, he had been repudiated in a well-planned attempt to dictate the choice of a candidate at the Democratic Convention in Baltimore.

His aides in this unhappy venture were a rather oddly assorted crew: two representatives of Wall Street, August Belmont and Thomas Fortune Ryan, and the familiar dignified, paunchy figure of Charles F. Murphy, who always looked more like a banker than a Brooklyn bartender who had made good with the worst political machine since Tweed's. All of these men had opposed each other at one time or another, with biting words and intricate maneuvers designed to destroy. Now they sat peacefully together in the hectic, sweltering bear pit of the nominating convention. Peacefully, that is, as far as the nature of the occasion permitted, for their fellow delegates regarded them with an apprehension which had been chilling their veins since the Jackson Day dinner in Washington on January 8, when Hearst, John Temple Graves and Boss Murphy had appeared together, a triumvirate which cast a doubtful shadow on the plans of Woodrow Wilson's managers.

Hearst had made a little speech in honor of Jackson, whom he admired. He told his fellow Democrats that they had the best opportunity since Grover Cleveland to "restore democracy," that is, get a man in the White House. They applauded that, but then they were appalled when they learned that the candidate Hearst considered best able to take advantage of the opportunity was his old friend, Champ Clark.

The reasons for his choice were entirely personal. Hearst

despised Wilson because the Princeton professor represented everything he was against—higher education, internationalism, free competition and the open shop. Wilson had fallen even deeper into mortal error by lending his support to Gaynor in 1910, when he was Governor of New Jersey. In sum, there was not a square foot of common ground on which Wilson and Hearst could stand.

Besides Wilson and Clark, the other possible nominee was Bryan, who insisted he was for Wilson, but whose fatal affinity for the White House was so well known that it was considered he stood ready to step nobly into the breach if the convention became deadlocked.

Hearst had no intention that it should be deadlocked. That was why he had made his peace with Murphy and cast his lot with the Tammany-Wall Street machine. Previous experience had seemed to indicate that this was the best way to influence delegates and win elections.

But again, as in the past, Hearst made a mistake. He underestimated Bryan—his toughness and determination, the strength of his intention not to be destroyed—and it was Bryan and his delegates who held the fate of the convention as ballot after ballot went by and Clark, under the two-thirds rule, could not quite make the necessary total, though he led Wilson at one point by 556½ to 350½.

Parting the haze of his smoke-filled room with a large and eloquent hand, Hearst pleaded with Bryan, his old friend and present liability, to be reasonable. He recalled, with emotion in his high voice, how much money he had lavished on Bryan in 1896 and 1900, trying to get the hero of the Platte elected. Champ Clark's daughter recalled how her father had walked, possibly barefoot, about the hills and valleys of Missouri, borrowing money to throw into the Bryan war chest. But it was no use. Bryan refused to change his mind.

As Frank I. Cobb remarked editorially in the New York *World:* "Compromise was possible until it became apparent to every intelligent man that the Ryan-Murphy-Belmont-Hearst coalition had set out to strangle progressive Democracy, destroy Mr. Bryan politically, and prevent the nomination of Woodrow Wilson at any cost."

This was true, but it was also true that the Wilson backers were well aware that in the 1912 mood of the nation, still rocking from the scandals of the past six years, it would be suicidal to permit a machine-dictated, machine-controlled candidate to run. It was essential to oppose Taft's incumbent standpatism and Roosevelt's insurgent progressivism with something better than a hardy perennial like Bryan or the wheel-horse emptiness of Champ Clark, who also carried the stigma of Hearst and his questionable friends. The more farsighted party chiefs saw in Wilson an idealistic, ultra-respectable standard-bearer, a man who must have been sent by Heaven to the Democrats in their hour of need.

He was nominated on the forty-sixth ballot. Bryan had broken the dam by getting a resolution passed which pledged the convention not to back anyone supported by the New York delegation—a direct slap at Hearst. Wilson then needed only the support of the machine politicians to get the nomination, and eventually they came to him, including Murphy and the Tammany men, who saw which way the wind was blowing and sought the leeward.

In the three-cornered campaign of 1912, Hearst had nowhere to go. Roosevelt's platform advocated most of what he preached, but he could not bring himself to support a man who had snubbed him socially and politically. (The White House doors had always been open for Phebe on her infrequent trips to Washington, but never for her son.) Nor could he support Taft Republicanism; that would have been unthinkable, and disastrous to circulation. There was nothing he could do but back Wilson, whose principles and person he hated, and who had even rejected his support with these cutting words: "I want the Democratic presidential nomination and I am going to do everything I can, legitimately, to get it, but if I am to grovel at Hearst's feet, I will never have it."

Nevertheless, the Hearst papers, if not Hearst himself, advocated a Democrat for the presidency, even if it had to be Wilson. W.R. reserved his personal comments about the candidate until after he was safely elected. A month after Wilson took the oath a letter in the Washington *Post*, signed W. R. Hearst, reproached him for such varied faults as appearing personally to deliver his first message to Congress and for reading the London *Times*, a subversive foreign publication. Hearst also appeared shocked that Wilson had come out for that Democratic staple, a low tariff.

The fact that he took space in a Washington newspaper to say so was in itself indicative of his new political role. With the Baltimore convention he had been discredited as a maker of Presidents, as in 1906 he had lost his own chance for the White House. The professionals in the party wanted no more to do with him, since his touch was fatal to a candidate. For his part, Hearst wanted no more of *them*, at least as their relations had been in the past. He turned his back on the active political stage.

But he was far from through with politics. The growth of his chain and the consequent spread of his interests cast him, at least in his own mind, as a lonely fighter for high principles. He would move behind the scenes where he could, and he was still devoted to the broad interests of the party, but now he was not Hearst the candidate, nor Hearst the kingmaker, but Hearst the empire builder whose many and far-flung businesses commanded a respect his inconsiderable vote-getting talents could not.

It was hardly a new role. He had developed it during the Spanish-American War, before he had allowed himself to get into the pitiless savagery of the political arena. Now, with considerably more power if not influence at his disposal, he was prepared to devote it to no man's interest save his own.

The swing away from domestic to foreign politics in 1914, and the divisive public emotions it inspired, gave him the stage he required, and from the first he was a leading player on it, cheered and hissed in more or less equal measure until in the end he was nearly thrown off into the wings.

Hearst began by viewing the first World War from a Californian standpoint. His first signed editorial on the subject, "The Cost of Kings," was an argument advancing the novel thesis that the struggle on the Continent was a civil war between rival factions of the occidental nations, which could result only in weakening them and would correspondingly lend strength to "Oriental aims, ideals and ambitions."

"One nation," Hearst noted with horror, "allied with Orientals is actually importing Orientals onto the scene of this conflict to show them how they may meet and possibly defeat Occidentals in modern warfare—a lesson which will be readily learned and ever remembered."

As for the actual conflict, he added disdainfully, it was "a war of kings," born of a "medieval misconception of the importance of royalty . . . a war of inherited medieval traditions, of imperial greed and glory."

A week later he made an appeal for peace—not to the governments involved, but to the press of England, specifically to Lord Northcliffe, publisher of the *Times* of London, and Lord Nurnham, publisher of the London *Daily Telegraph*, both of which were co-operating with him in the gathering of war news. He asserted flatly: "I believe that if the appeal is made now to the press of all nations, and by the press of all nations, the war can be stopped and will be stopped."

If it were not, he predicted darkly, "there may be war and worse than war. There may be riot and revolution and red anarchy in the centers of government and the relentless revenge of the outraged masses, resentful at their endless and needless sacrifice."

Here was implied the isolationism which shortly cost Hearst the good will of the British press, government and people. In fact, it was soon apparent that Hearst was not on the side of the Allies. He spoke editorially of whether "the luminous German thought should be victorious or not in Europe," and he made it plain that he considered the United States had no business in preventing the victory.

The logic of hindsight has made Hearst's pre-1917 role more villainous than it was in reality. The mood of the public in that tense period was pro-German, if it was anything, and the mood of the press so markedly reflected it that there was difficulty for a time in getting correspondents accredited to the Allied side. The Germans welcomed American newsmen.

The slogan of Wilson's 1916 campaign, "He kept us out of war," represented the only time he ever saw eye to eye with Hearst, who for the moment had to support him again, although he had been rebuffed once more in 1916. This rebuff had its origin in the character of Hearst's opposition to the war. Like all his crusades, it was violent and extreme, fed by his natural Anglophobia, his inordinate love for the Irish, and his sensitivity to the circulation elements implicit in both attitudes.

His bitter attacks on Wilson's every step away from strict neutrality had made his papers so hated in Canada, where he was unloved anyway because of his often expressed yearning to annex the Dominion, that it became a crime to have possession of a Hearst newspaper. In England, the British stood it as long as they could, then they closed the lid on Hearst's brazen practice of editing the cable news in New York so that it sometimes bore little relation to what had been passed by the censors. The British Government demanded the news reported be printed as approved, and asked that the offenders be discharged.

Hearst had seldom been more indignant. The empire builder had been shouting a monologue on the stage, and some flunky in the wings had rudely shouted, "Pipe down." He wrote a burning editorial in October 1916, beginning, "I will apologize for nothing, retract nothing, alter nothing," and ending with the promise that he would "take a personal pleasure in giving our readers and clients the most complete information of the utmost truth and value, and in getting it from more trustworthy sources than the biased and bigoted English censorship affords."

The British were in no mood to argue. They prohibited their

cables and mails to the Hearst newspapers and kicked out his correspondents. It was decided to make an appeal to the President, but Hearst himself could not make it. Earlier in the war, he had made an attempt to build a private bridge to the White House, convinced that perhaps the President and he could make an alliance based on their desire to avoid war. The attempt had been made through an intermediary, Grenville S. MacFarland, who was instructed to keep the whole matter confidential if it turned out that Wilson did not want to see Hearst, who specifically requested a meeting.

Wilson was quite blunt about it. "It is out of the question for me to see Mr. Hearst," he told Joseph Tumulty, "on any business of any kind and I would be very much obliged to you if you would convey that intimation to Mr. MacFarland so that this suggestion might be as if it had never been made."

As a result of this snub, Brisbane was elected to complain about the British Government's treatment of the Chief. He was almost plaintive in his letter. Theodore Roosevelt, who had come out for intervention and was a well-known Anglophile, could communicate freely in Britain, said Artie, but Hearst was cut off from the British public entirely.

Wilson permitted himself a dry touch of academic humor. "I very much appreciate this letter of Mr. Brisbane's," he instructed Tumulty, "and hope that you will tell him so. I hope you will tell him at the same time that I really think the best way to treat Mr. Roosevelt is to take no notice of him. That breaks his heart and is the best punishment that can be administered. . . ."

The same thing could be said of Hearst. As the great debate flared higher in American life and he was more deeply embroiled in it, there is no question that he was having the time of his life. Undoubtedly he had not enjoyed himself so much since 1898. Mrs. Older says that in these days he "lived at his highest."

One of the highest of the high points was the giant peace meeting he organized at the Sixty-ninth Regiment Armory in New York, one of many such meetings he ordered his papers to spon-

sor. At this affair, the chairman was no other than Judge Elbert
Gary, head of the Steel Trust. Judge Gary must be credited
with remarkable insight. He never once took Hearst's trust-busting, his pronouncements on the eight-hour day, or his ostensibly
pro-labor attitudes seriously, and remained W.R.'s faithful friend
through all his vicissitudes. Sometimes he grew "almost humid"
in praise of his fellow capitalist, one biographer recalls.

On the stage of the armory, Hearst was in good company.
Besides Judge Gary, there was Vice-President Marshall, who
said he was against war, and Speaker Champ Clark, who was
against war too and always had been, though the Democrats had
shown precious little appreciation of it in 1912. Madame Schu-
mann-Heink, already feeling the pressure of superpatriotism,
sang "Let Us Have Peace," specially composed by Ernest Ball.

The occasion was replete with remarkable oratory, but none
more astounding than the pronouncement of Governor Glynn
of California that "Woodrow Wilson and William Randolph
Hearst stand shoulder to shoulder for the peace of the world."

If they did, it was the strangest alliance on record. At the 1916
Republican convention in Chicago, the delegates were astounded
to see the fearless champion of the Democrats among them,
earnestly soliciting them to nominate a Progressive capable of
beating Wilson. In his anxiety Hearst even approached Theodore Roosevelt, languishing in the Republican doghouse for his
unblessed excursion of 1912, and pleaded with him to come home
to Chicago and be forgiven. Roosevelt was not above making a
deal, and was in fact anticipating one that would bring him safely
back to the party fold, but he knew better than to do it on
Hearst's invitation.

No other Democrat but Hearst would have had the gall to try
to name the candidate of the other party, and a still unforgiven
renegade at that. But then, Hearst had no more illusions about
Roosevelt than about himself. In spite of the virulence of their
enmity, he had attempted to get Roosevelt on his payroll as soon
as T.R. was out of the White House. Morrill Goddard had been
sent first to sign him up, but the quarry was cagey. Hearst then

delegated the pursuit to Moses Koenigsberg, who tracked Teddy from the *Outlook* office, where he had been a contributing editor for a short time, to his Oyster Bay lair, offering him propositions in both places. Nor had Hearst misjudged his man. Roosevelt expressed no moral indignation whatsoever about being asked to write for Hearst. He considered the offers carefully, no doubt weighing money against the outcry which would certainly arise if he thus repudiated in effect everything he had said before. In the end he accepted a rival offer from *Metropolitan* magazine, lower-paid but safer.

Roosevelt was not to be had at Chicago, however, and the assembled Republicans, with an arrant disregard for Hearst's feelings, nominated his opponent of ten years ago, Charles Evans Hughes. Time had not enhanced W.R.'s appreciation of "Old Featherduster," though he was willing to admit that Hughes was "exceedingly honest, extremely moral," but not, he lamented, "the least progressive." The new candidate had, Hearst said as he sorrowfully quit Chicago, "the political advantage of being thought to be a progressive by the confiding masses, and being known to be reactionary by the privileged classes. He is therefore likely to get the votes of the one and the contributions of the other, and thus may be triumphantly elected."

The statement kept his record for political prophecy intact.

There was nothing to do once more but support Wilson, although the President showed no more inclination to welcome it than he had before.

As the nation reached the brink of war and patriotic fervor swept the country, Hearst's position grew daily more tenuous. But the more tenuous it became, the more stubbornly outrageous was his behavior, until he stood very nearly alone among Americans in public life, except for the voice of neutrality raised by La Follette in the Senate, the steadfast pacifism of Bryan, and the hate cries of a few eminent Anglophobes.

He opposed every measure intended to help the Allies, from the first loan to France down to the shipment of ammunitions to Britain. He was against arming American merchant vessels, though he urged the United States to arm itself to the teeth. "Armed neutrality" was the phrase that ran through his editorials, speeches and other writings. He was even willing to make an attempt to find extenuating circumstances in the sinking of the *Lusitania*, and did so, to the horror of his editors and business managers, who went so far as to send him a petition beseeching him to listen to the public before it was too late. He ignored them.

France followed England's example and barred Hearst newspapers and correspondents from the country. When this news arrived at the New York *American* one midnight, nobody knew what to do about it except Joe Willicombe, who remembered his own dictum, "Never wake up the Chief for good news; it's the bad news that requires immediate attention." He called Hearst, who came instantly awake, as he always did, dictated an editorial on the spot, followed it with a lead for the page-one story on the event, and returned to his bed.

With his papers banned in both England and France, Hearst continued to get pieces about the war from the best writers in both countries, and Italy in the bargain. Kipling, Doyle, Shaw, Hall Caine, Israel Zangwill and others contributed from England; Rostand and Maeterlinck from France; d'Annunzio and Ferrero from Italy.

On the eve of war, with evidence to the contrary on every side, Hearst still believed—as always, because he wanted to believe—that he spoke for the people, and the people did not want war. When a Berlin newspaper cabled him for a statement on the subject, he replied: "I believe that the majority of the people in the United States are entirely undesirous of war with Germany. I believe also that the people of Germany are equally undesirous of war with the United States."

That statement was made only a month before war was declared. Hearst saw nothing but doom when the declaration came. He warned the country that it had better prepare to suffer "the furious and terrible onslaught of a victorious Germany."

With America committed, it might have been supposed that

Hearst, whose main preachment was patriotism, would have backed the government unequivocally. It was not so. By his peculiar reasoning, his duty lay in two directions, diametrically opposite. America must win and so the war had to be supported, but he had no more belief in it than he had before. Thus he placed himself in the peculiar position of fighting it with one hand and opposing it with the other.

As far as the public was concerned, he had taken the most untenable position of all, and resentment against him mounted. His essential theme, held today in isolationist quarters, was that the war was being fought for the benefit and profits of Wall Street and the trusts. Hearst's idea of fighting it was to build an air and submarine fleet to attack Germany if necessary, but meanwhile to stay as neutral as possible and, if it could be done, make a separate peace with Germany.

On the other hand, he draped his papers in American flags, called for armaments far beyond what was asked, petitioned for universal military service, shouted a verbal "Hurrah" for the draft, erected enlistment stations wherever he had papers, gave three thousand columns to the promotion of Liberty Loans, put on a six-week Red Cross drive in two colors on his editorial pages, subscribed with his staffs for nearly a million and a half dollars' worth of bonds, and even while he criticized these and other measures, and the war itself, promoted them as though they were his personal ideas.

It was not enough. Nor could it be, when only six months after America's entry the Hearst morning papers declared that the German Government was "a benevolent despotism inaugurating many of the popular benefits which our government and other democratic and semi-democratic governments have since adopted. . . . Germany, deprived of its autocratic government and delivered over to the democratic rule of its people, would be just as little a menace to the peace and progress of the world as Russia is, since it has been democratized, and just as effective a force for progress and for the promotion and protection of the white man's civilization as any other nation."

This editorial and others like it were written by a man named Francis, whose real name, it turned out long after the event, was apparently Diefendorf. Those who worked with him recall that Francis-Diefendorf was exceedingly unpopular with other Hearst men, both personally and politically. Most of the Hearst employees, including many of his top executives, opposed the Chief's views on the war, and they shuddered whenever a new and more violent Francis editorial appeared.

The one quoted above caused a tremor to pass through the whole Hearst organization, as a result of which Carvalho resigned in protest. Koenigsberg, who recalls the incident, speculates as to what would have happened to the Hearst papers if it had been discovered that the strongest pro-German editorials appearing anywhere in the United States were written by a man whose real name was said to be Diefendorf.

What did happen to them was reminiscent of the McKinley days, except that this time the government was as aroused as the public. In November 1917, Hearst was denounced as an evil and a menace before a packed audience in Carnegie Hall by James M. Beck, former Solicitor General of the United States. The boycott against his papers, already in force in five Allied nations, began to spread through the United States.

The government began to interest itself in the Hearst papers and in the Chicago *Tribune*, which was following the same party line. A staff of lawyers, working under Attorney General Thomas W. Gregory, was busy combing these papers, looking for seditious utterances. Hearst himself was not at all disturbed. As he once remarked in another connection, he enjoyed being investigated. But his editors and other executives sweated under the microscope and some quit, unable to stand the strain. Poor Brisbane was called to Washington by a Senate investigating committee and compelled to admit that $500,000 of the money used to buy the Washington *Times* from Frank Munsey had come from a coalition of German-American brewers—after the declaration of war.

Hearst was perfectly aware that he was the darling of the

Irish and German nationalist elements in New York, and it was like him to make capital of the situation. Ironically, his popularity with these voters gave him a political status in New York City that he had not enjoyed before. Tammany leaders came to him in 1917 and besought him to lead them to victory in the mayoralty fight, but Hearst, who now thought of himself as a world figure, would not consider risking even the chance of a local humiliation. He would, however, consent to hand-pick the candidate.

The man upon whom the Hearstian hand fell was John F. Hylan, an ex-day laborer and elevated motorman whom the New York *Times* has described charitably in retrospect as a "grave and ponderous-minded Brooklyn politician." His most striking attributes were a profound reverence for everything Hearst said and did, and a monumental incapacity for his high office which was so ludicrous that New Yorkers were continuously entertained during his eight years in City Hall.

A strange attachment grew up between Hylan and Hearst. They had nothing whatever in common, yet they appeared to enjoy each other's company socially. One supposes that Hearst was human enough to welcome his friend's unquestioning and undeviating adulation, while Hylan considered himself privileged beyond other mortals to be accepted on an equal footing by the great man. Honest tears came to his eyes on occasion when he spoke of Hearst.

Once the two were eating in the dining room of the Waldorf when they saw a down-and-outer peering at them wistfully through the glass. Both were so overcome that they invited him into the dining room to share Oscar's goodies.

This idyll was marred by the attempts of Hearst's enemies and the Federal government itself to find out whether W.R. was, in fact, an agent of the German Government, as he sometimes appeared to be, if he were judged by what he wrote. These efforts can be forgiven on the basis of wartime hysteria, but it is more difficult to understand the opinions of later investigators who appear to be convinced that Hearst reporters were in reality

German spies and that the publisher was engaged in high-level intrigue with von Bernstorff, the German Ambassador, and others.

The proof, then as now, depends largely upon the guilt-by-association process. There is little question that von Bernstorff attempted to make use of Hearst's well-known German sympathies, but it can scarcely be proved that he succeeded. Hearst's isolationism and Anglophobia led him to favor Germany over England, but it is totally inconsistent with his character to imagine that he would conspire against his own country.

What began as a Republican campaign slogan—"A vote for Hylan is a vote for Germany"—wound up as a serious charge growing out of carefully circulated rumors. These rumors asserted that Hearst had been a guest at a secret dinner in Sherry's given by a man known as Bolo Pasha, a Parisian newspaper publisher who later turned out to be a German spy, and that this exotic character, along with von Bernstorff and von Papen, was closeted with Hearst in a sinister conference at the Clarendon, which they left by means of a secret exit.

Unfortunately for romance, the dinner had been duly reported in the papers, since it had taken place in a public dining room and had been attended by various well-known personages. As for the Clarendon conference, the official version is that Bolo Pasha visited Hearst in an effort to get paper for his Paris publication. It is not impossible that other matters were discussed, since the devious Pasha succeeded in planting more than a million dollars about America in places where it would do the most good, this money having been handled by the J. P. Morgan Company and the Royal Bank of Canada, but it is as unlikely that Hearst was involved in any conspiracy as it would be to implicate these sober institutions. Only the amateur historians who are passionately convinced that the war was brought about by the financiers, aided by such publicists as Hearst, continue to believe that the Clarendon apartments were the breeding place of treason.

The secret passage was also non-existent, in the same category as the report of the zealous spy-hunters who declared that mys-

terious colored lights were flashing signals from Hearst's apartment in the Clarendon, presumably to accomplices of the Kaiser
nearby, or even to submarines anchored in the Hudson. Upon
investigation these proved to be interior lights, turned on and
off, reflecting through Hearst's superb collection of stained-
glass windows, the best in the world.

Hearst's attitude toward the public animosity against him was
one of polite contempt. When a woman in a New York restaurant hissed the word "*Boche!*" at him, he is said to have taken
off his hat, bowed to her, and murmured, "You're right, madam.
It is all bosh."

He was increasingly conscious of the clamor against him, however, and for the sake of his papers, if nothing else, made a serious effort to look more respectable. He organized a movement
to rebuild France's ruined villages, luring to the committee such
people as Cardinal Gibbons, Sarah Bernhardt and James W.
Gerard. On July 14, 1918, he caused the San Francisco *Examiner*
to publish a large and gaudy edition commemorating the fall of
the Bastille, with Divine Sarah, making her last appearance in
the city, posed in color on the front page holding the tricolor
dramatically over her head. Mrs. Hearst was busy in New York
with emergency relief and civic projects, including the establishment of her Free Milk Fund for Babies.

It was no use. Hearst discovered that one of his butlers was a
Secret Service agent, on the search for incriminating papers. The
Clarendon was watched day and night, first for the colored lights
and then to keep tabs on Hearst's visitors.

No matter how mistaken he might be, it was galling to a man
of Hearst's intense patriotism to think that his own government
did not trust him. It was one thing to have a President or a senator denounce him. That was politics. But it was quite another
matter to be tailed like a suspected criminal and to be charged
almost daily with treason by somebody. It never occurred to
him to modify his stand. He was convinced as usual that everybody else was out of step. But his usual robust health began to

show the effects of strain, and the doctor sent him to Mount Clemens, Michigan, for a rest.

While he was there, the most damaging blow anyone had struck against him came from the pen of Theodore Roosevelt, whose old enmity for Hearst had been highly intensified by the events of the war, in which T.R.'s had been nearly the first and certainly the loudest of the voices to be raised in defense of democracy. He had spent a good part of the war baiting Wilson, attacking him in public, in private, and at a dollar a word in the pages of *Metropolitan* magazine, the successful bidder for his services against Hearst's *Cosmopolitan*.

Now he wrote a letter to a friend in the Senate, ten thousand words long, virtually frothing at the mouth. In it he made unlikely intimates out of Hearst and Wilson, using the one to attack the other. Wilson was a tyrant who had suppressed free speech and the press, he declared, and besides was incompetent, a player of politics, and worst of all, a moral coward who had not closed up the Hearst newspapers before the war began, which of course would not have been suppression but a patriotic measure.

The letter, printed in the Congressional Record and then distributed in pamphlet form everywhere in the country, caused the animosity toward Hearst to boil over.

It was a repetition of 1901. Citizens burned Hearst papers in the streets and tore them off newsstands when they found a dealer foolish enough to sell them. They were banned once more from clubs and libraries, and friendships were strained by callers who departed any house wherein they found the offending paper.

From the bucolic solitudes of Mount Clemens, Hearst returned a characteristic answer to Roosevelt, calling him an opportunist who had written the letter "for pay . . . to aid and advertise those magazines and newspapers which pay and support him, and to reflect upon those magazines and newspapers which do not hire or admire him." The personal attack had not bothered him, he said, but he considered it shocking that Roosevelt should so constantly attack the United States Government during wartime, a practice he apparently believed should be confined to such honest critics as himself who were free of T.R.'s "partisan hostility." Hearst even contrived to get in a dig at his ancient foe, the oil trust, pointing out that *Metropolitan* magazine was allied by ownership to Standard Oil.

It was clear that it would take more than words to save Hearst and his papers from serious damage. Not even when they were such words as Mayor Hylan's, uttered with considerable feeling to reporters in Florida: "I want the people to know Mr. Hearst as I know him. I had an entirely different impression of him until I knew him. We were on the beach yesterday and a jellyfish had closed about a little toad. Mr. Hearst flicked it away with the end of his cane and said: 'Why let the poor little thing suffer?' I think that typifies what I like in Hearst."

But Hearst's kindness to jellyfish did not impress the irate citizenry, caught in the blood and anguish of war, much less President Wilson, who was so upset by the manner in which the Hearst papers had handled his speech making Memorial Day 1918 a day of prayer—they had edited it to suit the Chief's purposes —that he asked the Attorney General whether something couldn't be done about it legally. The address had been "altered and, nevertheless, published with my signature," Wilson complained. "This constituted, I should suppose, something very like forgery, and I would very much like to know whether there is not some legal process which we could institute to bring this habitual offender to terms."

Fortunately for Hearst, the Armistice ended the critical threat to his interests. A glimpse into his mind, showing how differently he thought of the events between 1914 and 1918, was provided by an editorial letter published in the Hearst newspapers on December 13, 1918. Brazen it might be, but cynical and insincere it was not. Those in a position to know him best testify that the attitudes he expressed in this "policy" editorial were those he actually felt. Judged by what had gone before, however, an ordinary citizen perusing the editorial could have been excused for scratching his head and muttering, "Who's crazy now?" The statement of "Hearst policies" went as follows:

"Before America entered into this war I was, as I have frequently said in my instructions to the editors of my papers, neither pro-English nor pro-German. My attitude was that of Mercutio—'A plague o' both your houses.'

"I could see nothing but an attempt on the part of both England and Germany to involve the United States in the war, and to use the United States as a catspaw to pull their chestnuts out of the fire.

"Under those circumstances, my policy of America FIRST and ONLY and ALL THE TIME led me to strive to keep America out of the war on the side of either belligerent, and to endeavor to bring about a league of neutral nations to protect the interests of neutrals against the aggressions of both of the belligerent groups.

"In the pursuance of this policy I sometimes wrote against the aggressions of England against American interests and sometimes against the depredations and outrages of Germany.

"Since the entrance of America into the war I have unquestioningly acquiesced in the wisdom of the decision of our Government to make war on the side of the Allies, and I have given the Allies almost utter and unreserved support as I have given our own country.

"This I have done because that course during wartime has seemed to me the best course—and in fact, the only course to be pursued in the interests of our United States of America.

"Having once embarked on war, it was absolutely necessary that the war should be won and that all dissension or division of opinion should be suppressed until after the war was won.

"When peace is finally declared, I resume my rights to opinion and to expression of opinion independent of the wish or advantage of any foreign country and subservient only to the interests of my own people and my own country."

What this astounding declaration appeared to mean two years later was that Hearst, for the first time in his life, supported the

Republican candidate for the presidency, Warren Harding, and in New York State opposed the Democratic nominee for governor, Al Smith. This time he was on the winning side in both cases, an overwhelming reversal of form. The reasons were again personal. He regarded Harding as a man opposed to Wilsonian internationalism, now carried on by his successors, and he was against Smith because Al was against Hylan, though Smith had come "hat in hand" to the Clarendon, according to Hearst, and pleaded for support.

The result of the Harding landslide, which swept away Smith's bid for re-election, was that Hearst had entree to the White House for the first time since Grover Cleveland's day, and Smith was more than ever his implacable enemy. He viewed Harding's victory as a triumph over Wilson, and consequently one for him. "Mr. Wilson wanted a referendum on the League of Nations, and he has had it," he wrote from Los Angeles. "This overwhelmingly Republican election is not a victory for the Republican Party, although the Republican Party will make the mistake of thinking that it is. Nor is it a defeat for the Democratic Party. . . . Bryan was right when he said, 'At the end of Wilson's term of office there will be no Democratic Party. There may be a Wilson party, but there will be no Democratic Party.' "

Momentarily Hearst had visions of the presidency once more. He had a grip on the New York machine through Hylan, and on the potent Chicago machine through Mayor William "Big Bill" Thompson, his only near rival in Anglophobia, who owed his position to Hearst and his Chicago papers. Hearst's power in California was enormous, even frightening. But the good opinion he had of his chances was somewhat dampened in 1922, when an incipient and inspired presidential "boom" for him was received without enthusiasm by the rulers of both major parties.

He still clung to the third-party idea, partly out of stubbornness and partly because there was nowhere else to go. With the idea of eliminating Boss Murphy in New York and thus proclaiming himself once more as the champion of reform, he fought

Tammany's candidates for the judiciary in the election of 1923, but to his chagrin, Murphy succeeded in recording one of the largest victories in the Hall's sordid history. In a triumphant post-election statement, Murphy proclaimed Hearst "politically dead."

But he had already been written off the year before when his Presidential boomlet had simmered down to opposing Al Smith for the Democratic nomination for governor, and Murphy, in a temporary alliance with Hearst, had planned to make him governor and Smith a United States senator.

It was then that Smith had delivered himself of his historic verdict, "No matter how long I live, you will never find my name on the ticket with that bastard."

Smith's disaffection had a curious origin. He had endured with equanimity everything Hearst said about him in his first campaign for the governorship, but just as Murphy could never quite forgive Hearst for portraying him in prison stripes, Smith never forgave Hearst for accusing him of being in league with the Milk Trust and permitting New York's milk to become contaminated. In a bitter diatribe at Carnegie Hall, Smith was not simply indulging in campaign oratory when he recalled that his mother, lying ill in 1919, had cried out in her delirium, "He didn't do it. He loves children."

Politically, the decade of the twenties was largely for Hearst a running fight against Smith and a gradual desertion of the insurgent forces he had so long supported. He was no more successful than he had ever been at playing the game, but he could not give it up, though by now he was spending most of his time in the creation of San Simeon. When the Brooklyn *Eagle* called him there in 1922 to inquire after his prospects as a candidate, he told the paper, "I am a rancher enjoying life on the high hills overlooking the broad Pacific. If you want to talk about Herefords I will talk with you, but not about politics."

The *Eagle* did not believe him, and of course it was only a passing piece of rhetoric, as the events of the following years proved.

The warfare with Smith was savage. In 1924, Hearst was able to exert enough pressure on the Democratic Convention in New York to prevent Smith's nomination, and the following year Smith retaliated by making Jimmy Walker mayor in opposition to Hylan's bid for a third term. No deals were necessary for or against Boss Murphy this time. He died in 1924, the only way he could ever have put himself above politics.

Smith tried to hang the shroud of the Ku Klux Klan about Hylan's neck, a ludicrous idea in itself, and Hearst had to express himself on the Klan issue—a tightrope he had no taste for walking, since it put him in danger of offending one or the other of his two largest segments of readership in New York, the Irish Catholics and the German-Americans. He expressed himself plainly on the issue—"My personal opinion is that the Ku Klux Klan should be repudiated as an undemocratic and un-American institution threatening the peace and unity of our country"—but he did it no oftener than absolutely necessary, until the issue had died down.

So anxious was Hearst to unhorse Smith that he went to the unprecedented length in 1926 of supporting a child of the trusts, Ogden Mills, trustee of a New York bank and director in at least four great corporations. Smith was delighted by the endorsement. He predicted that his own victory was certain because Mills had been given the kiss of death. He proved to be correct, and hopefully taking Smith at his word on this point, Hearst endorsed Al for the Democratic presidential nomination in 1928.

If Smith feared that Hearst would support him and thus certainly bring about his defeat, he need not have worried. The darling of W.R.'s heart was Andrew Mellon, a capitalist he would have scorned in earlier days, whom he now supported for the Republican nomination.

To understand how Hearst felt at this stage, it is only necessary to recall what had been happening to him for the past quarter century. He had appealed to the people time after time, and they had rejected him at the polls. He had repudiated, or at least appeared to repudiate, his own class, but gradually their interests had become more and more his own. And finally, his original cynicism had become corrosive as he observed that the leaders of both parties, with the exception of Wilson, could be dealt with in one way or another.

With Harding he had found a sympathetic understanding and a role in national politics denied to him on the local level. By an odd paradox, he was far more welcome in the councils of the Republican Party than in his own. He might be the "kiss of death" to the powerful Democratic leaders of New York State and City, but in Washington he was made welcome at the White House under the Republican administrations of both Harding and Coolidge. He lunched there frequently with Harding, and the President would have visited him at San Simeon if death had not cut short his Western trip.

With Coolidge the alliance was closer. It was a friendship which even at this late date defies satisfactory explanation. The two men enjoyed each other's company at the White House, on the presidential yacht, and at San Simeon. Utterly unlike in every way, they found themselves in almost celestial harmony. Observers at the time could make nothing of it. T.R.B., the *New Republic's* famed and astute Washington correspondent, called it "one of the most significant and remarkable political phenomena of the period. That Mr. Hearst, whose journalistic talons have been deeply sunk in the back of every national administration, regardless of party, since he became a figure in the publishing world, should turn his twenty-odd newspapers into almost pro-Administration organs, and have the brilliant Brisbane regularly and frequently anoint and glorify the President, instead of assailing him with his customary ferocity, is an interesting and amazing thing."

The friendship persisted despite the fact that Hearst embarrassed the Administration in 1927 with the sensational publication of "documents" purporting to show that certain interests in

Mexico were plotting against the United States, and that four senators had been paid $1,115,000 for the purpose of advancing this conspiracy in the Senate.

Not only was the State Department placed in an uncomfortable position which the President shared, but the uproar in the Senate was considerable when it was discovered that the four senators, whose names were deleted from the published documents, were Borah, Heflin, Norris and La Follette—the kind of insurgent fighters customarily supported by Hearst and his papers.

In the subsequent congressional investigation, Hearst provided his own handwriting experts to help prove his guilt, since the documents were rather easily proved to be forgeries from beginning to end. Once more, it appeared, he had been offered a story he wanted to believe was true and made no effort to find out whether it might be false. Hearst's excuse is still cited as a masterpiece of evasion:

"If the handwriting experts should all agree that the documents we have produced bear evidence of having been fabricated, I will not dispute that decision further than to maintain persistently and I believe patriotically, that the logic of events gives every evidence that the essential facts contained in the documents were not fabricated, and that the facts—the political facts, the international facts—are the things which are of vital importance to the American people and to the loyal representatives of the interests of the American people."

The statement has always been one of the whips used by Hearst's critics to scourge him, but the advantage of a quarter century provides a somewhat different view. What were these "international facts" which Hearst insisted must be right even though the documents were forgeries? Two of the most important of them were that Japan was plotting against the United States and that strong Communistic elements existed in Mexican politics.

In the public outcry against Hearst which followed this incident, Coolidge maintained a discreet and customary silence.

Their friendship was not disturbed. In return, Hearst stood by his silent partner when the President alienated most of the rest of the nation's press by a speech he made in 1928, dedicating the National Press Club Building. Coolidge deplored the "constant criticism of all things that have to do with our country . . . and the attempt to foment class distinction and jealousies," which he said tended to "weaken and disintegrate the necessary spirit of patriotism. There is always need for criticism, but there is likewise need for discrimination. . . . Life is made up of the successful and the worthy. In any candid representation of current conditions they have the first claim to attention. In the effort of the press to destroy vice, it ought not to neglect virtue. . . ."

This foursquare stand against sin offended most publishers, but the Hearst papers interpreted his remarks as meaning that the President was impressed with "the fact that the foreign correspondents of certain American newspapers are more interested in furthering the interests of foreign governments than in furthering the interests of the United States. . . . The President wants to stop this business of foreign governments influencing American governmental policies by subtle control of the American press."

If the Coolidge-Hearst alliance was not enough to confuse those who attempted to follow W.R.'s thought processes, his relations with Hoover were even more mystifying.

Hoover appears to have been aware early in 1928 that the support of Hearst would be helpful to him in the campaign, considering the publisher's virtual control of the delegations from California, Illinois, and—through his long-time friend, Honest John Garner—the Texas delegates. He considered it important enough, at least, to drive down to Los Angeles from Palo Alto and lay before Hearst a delightful prospect of what could be expected to occur if he were elected. It was a magnificent vista that he disclosed—highways, waterways, dams, flood control, conservation, all on a nationwide scale, and sponsored by the government. These were projects Hearst had been advocating for years, most of which were destined to be carried out by

Franklin D. Roosevelt, fought by Hearst every step of the way.

At the Republican convention, all was not sweetness and light because Hearst still toyed with the hope that his friend Andrew Mellon, another member in good standing of the trusts, could be nominated and elected, and then Mr. Mellon's long efforts to do away with the income tax, which had now become number one on Hearst's list of needed reforms, might be accomplished. It was obvious, however, that the banker was not the man of the hour, and that Hoover, reaching the climax of a long, carefully planned campaign that had been going on for nearly ten years, was going to be nominated and probably elected. And Hearst, who by this time made no pretense of supporting Democratic presidential nominees, having concluded that the party had died in 1920, threw his strength and his delegates behind Hoover.

The resulting victory seems to have done little to cheer him. His editorials after the event have a somber tone and include several gloomy and generally accurate prophecies, like the one he made only a few weeks after the election: "The next great war in which England is engaged, no matter whether she emerges victorious or not, will mean . . . the complete Socialization of the British Isles and the British Empire."

An uneasy truce existed between Hearst and Hoover until the full effect of the Great Adjustment began to be felt in 1930. Hearst did not blame the President for the Crash, as some were inclined to do, but he did think that in the crisis Hoover should adopt the Hearst Plan for saving America, since he seemed to have none of his own. The plan was pure New Dealism—a five-billion-dollar "peace loan" to the unemployed, government control of the liquor industry, and a six-hour day.

Hoover, of course, would have nothing to do with such radical schemes, but Hearst kept firing away, and for a time he sounded like the sterling champion of old. "Leaders must be reminded that business exists for the service of men," he declared on the radio in 1931. "The maladjustment in industry, glutted markets on one hand and undernourished people on the other, constitutes a serious indictment of management in the large."

Meanwhile, he had opened up his heaviest guns against the Administration. One can only imagine Mr. Hoover's bewilderment, to be attacked in terms reserved usually for Democrats. "There is too much bureaucracy, too much autocracy creeping into our Federal Government," Hearst complained in October 1930. "There is too much disposition on the part of government to prescribe what we shall think and what we shall say and what we shall do and what we shall eat and what we shall drink."

By March 1932 he had concluded that the White House was an annex of the Kremlin. Here is an editorial written on March 26, 1932. It is difficult to believe that Hearst wrote it about Hoover, not F.D.R.

> Clever chaps those disciples of Lenin and Stalin in the Government at Washington!
>
> They are going to tax the country into prosperity.
>
> They are going to make the country wealthy by stopping the spending of money.
>
> They are going to improve business by decreasing business.
>
> They are going to relieve unemployment by relieving those that are now employed of their jobs.
>
> They are going to give all the money to the Government, so that the only people who will have any jobs will be Government employees.

Mr. Hoover was never one to take kindly to criticism in any event, and since this must have seemed to him something right out of *Alice in Wonderland*, it is no wonder that two months after the above editorial appeared he refused flatly to see Hearst, as Wilson had done before him. Again the approach was made through an intermediary, Louis B. Mayer, the motion-picture executive, who was a power in West Coast Republican circles.

Hearst wanted to know what the President's plans were for the election year. Rebuffed so coldly, he concluded that the Republicans were temporarily bankrupt of leadership, and rather than try to break Mr. Hoover at the convention, he chose to try the Democrats one more time, with results far more fateful than he realized, else he would have embraced Hoover like a prodigal son.

It is a sad commentary on the nature of politics that he was still on good terms with Democratic leaders in spite of his romances with Harding and Coolidge. When he returned to America in 1930, after the French Government had expelled him from the country, he was met by a reception committee which included not simply Democrats, but some of the most respected liberal leaders of the party. One biographer records that Hearst's eyes "filled with tears at seeing so many politicians gathered to greet him." They included Senator Robert F. Wagner and Representatives Sol Bloom, Emanuel Celler, Samuel Dickstein and Fiorello LaGuardia, among others.

He was not exactly without friends, therefore, among the Democrats who gathered at the Chicago convention of 1932. Hearst himself remained at San Simeon, leaving the management of affairs to James Farley, who was then in company he would now hate to contemplate. Mr. Farley was acutely conscious of which side his political bread was buttered. The California, Texas and Illinois delegations were more or less under Hearst's thumb. By agreement between Mayor Anton Cermak and Hearst, Illinois and California were to vote together, and as Illinois went, so would go Indiana. A formidable power bloc indeed.

Hearst was ostensibly committed to his friend Garner, having come out for him publicly, but he had indicated that he would not be averse to Roosevelt, a fact Farley was counting upon if the pinch came. Earlier in the year, Farley had carefully steered his man over dangerous waters when Hearst had tried to smoke him out on his views about internationalism.

The pinch came after the third ballot, when Roosevelt held a commanding lead but faced defeat by the two-thirds rule if there was another ballot. In this crisis, Farley called San Francisco and got John Francis Neylan, the tall, aggressive Irish attorney who had undertaken to unscramble Hearst's affairs a few years before and by this time was second-in-command.

Farley told Neylan that Roosevelt would have to have California and Texas at once, and Illinois too. He offered a cleverly threatening alternative: Newton D. Baker might get the nomination if Roosevelt did not. When Neylan had conveyed this information to Hearst by telephone, the publisher was aghast. Baker was for the League of Nations and a corporation lawyer in the bargain. He sent out the word at once. Garner gave up Texas, Cermak surrendered Illinois, California and Indiana followed, and Franklin D. Roosevelt owed his nomination to Hearst.

During the campaign, Hearst heard himself for the last time classed with the radicals. In Madison Square Garden, the scene of so many Hearst preludes to defeat, Hoover called down the wrath of conservatism on Roosevelt and Hearst. In St. Louis he continued the theme: "The people deserve to know whether he [Roosevelt] will support or repudiate Messrs. Wheeler, Norris, Huey Long, W. R. Hearst and others in their long continued efforts to put government into large business undertakings. . . . They deserve to know if he joins with the same William R. Hearst in his opposition to the disarmament conference now in progress. Does he join with Mr. Hearst in his opposition to the promotion of peace by the Kellogg Pact?"

The campaign ended, and Mr. Roosevelt was in the White House, placed there by the efforts of a man who only five years before had spoken feelingly of the need to restrict Chief Executives to two terms. A new era appeared about to dawn. Hearst instructed his editors and managing editors on November 28, 1932: ". . . We should now print our political news drastically condensed, and above all it should be printed without the slightest bias." The "now" delicately suggests that it had not been so printed before. "Our advocacies will of course be confined to the editorial columns," he went on blandly. "Furthermore, if any editorial is received which seems to be too partisan or to be out of harmony with the progressive thought of your section, that editorial can be held up and the advisability of printing it further discussed. . . . Be genial, be helpful, and above all be fair. Stop printing a political broadside and make a newspaper that will be read by the whole community."

A few months later the National Recovery Administration had ended the honeymoon, and Hearst was the sworn enemy of the Blue Eagle. According to Emile Gauvreau, then editor of the New York *Mirror*, the Chief wanted to toss out all the NRA labels bearing the offending bird. As Brisbane reported it, "When Mr. Hearst looks at that Eagle, he has to postpone his dinner. I've told him it would be too obvious to throw it out all at once. Roosevelt has got the people with him by promising them everything, and it has got so that you can't take a crack at him without bringing our own readers down on us. The thing to do is to gradually reduce the size of the Blue Eagle in our engravings until it croaks from anemic shrinkage."

The compromise was ingenious but difficult. There were two birds in the *Mirror*, one in the left front page "ear," or box in the upper corner carrying the weather report, and one over the editorials, which was eliminated at once. The front-page Eagle was reduced day by day in a slow process of strangulation which left both Brisbane and Hearst unappeased.

"I can still recognize him," Brisbane muttered. "He's beginning to look more and more like a moth-eaten Soviet duck. But he's still visible."

Much as they might have disagreed, there is abundant evidence that Hearst and F.D.R. were not personal enemies, that in fact they had a curious kind of respect for each other as adversaries. Their acquaintance had begun years before Roosevelt entered the White House.

Gauvreau recalls the story of the three old naval prints Hearst had once bought from a Lexington Avenue art shop, not knowing that they were prizes the young politician ardently desired to add to his collection. While Roosevelt was still in Albany as Governor, Hearst sought his endorsement for some pet project and promised him anything he could provide in return for the favor.

"Fair enough," said the Governor. "How about selling me those naval prints of yours?"

Their identity had to be described more fully before Hearst could recall them from his mass of art treasures, but when he remembered them, he declared it was a favor he could not grant. "Why, my warehouses are full of things I've never seen," he concluded. "It would be impossible to find those prints."

Roosevelt grinned. "That's the kind of static wealth I want to break up," he said.

In a White House interview, the President later talked freely to Gauvreau about Hearst's attitude, accepting it calmly and with good humor as the inevitable result of public life. "Hearst is making his usual noise," Roosevelt remarked. "A number of others are yelling fairly loudly. I suppose Hearst is already planning deafening broadsides for the next campaign!" Of Brisbane, the President added, "Somehow I feel he isn't as bad as the others."

Emissaries from Hearst appeared at the White House from time to time, and often they were greeted by the President's jovial roar, "Well, how's dear old W.R.? What's he up to now?"

There is some evidence that Roosevelt made gestures toward discharging his political debt to Hearst in the early days of the New Deal by granting him various small favors, and for a few months Hearst sounded like a convinced New Dealer in his editorials.

The NRA was the beginning of open warfare. It was followed by Hearst's opposition to unemployment relief payments, farm subsidies (he had never been particularly sympathetic to the farmers and their problems), and all the social security measures proposed by the New Deal. Hearst was opposed to such measures simply because they meant income tax increases, and since its institution he had been denouncing the income tax as a "monstrous racket." His idea of a tax was the pet project of the conservative right-wingers—a sales tax.

It was guerrilla warfare for a time—at least well into 1934, when Hearst made his momentous summer pilgrimage to Germany. Before he departed, he had lunch with the President at the White House and told reporters afterward that he was "entirely in sympathy" with Mr. Roosevelt and with what he was doing. No one took this declaration very seriously.

In Germany that summer he developed another kind of sympathy which not only deepened the gulf between him and the Administration, but, like the unfolding of an old newsreel, recalled the hectic, nearly disastrous events of 1914–18.

Hearst's love affair with National Socialism has often been denounced by his critics as proof that he was really a kind of native fascist, a bringing up to date of the idea that he was an agent of the Wilhelmstrasse. It was said, too, that he approved of Hitler's anti-Semitism. Those views were held not only by distinguished liberals, but by Stalin, who referred to him in *Pravda* as a "gangster journalist" and a friend of Hitler's.

Apparently Hitler, at least, knew better. Taking note of the fact that a good share of Hearst's ablest executives and writers were Jewish, the chancellor asserted in one speech: "A gigantic organization of press lies was built up, and again it was a Jewish concern, the Hearst press, which laid down the tone of the agitation against Germany."

Anyone who knew Hearst well knew that he was no anti-Semite. On the other hand, his myopic political views led him into the company of anti-Semites and American fascists. Hearst never thought it necessary to repudiate the nightshirt crowd which applauded him, though he considered it President Roosevelt's duty to disavow publicly the Communists who gave him their unsought support.

The root of Hearst's affinity for National Socialism was easy to discover. It stemmed directly from his Anglophobia and Francophobia and from his blind isolationism. Thus in August 1934 he was quoted in the New York *Times* as declaring that Germany was "battling for her liberation from the mischievous provisions of the Treaty of Versailles. . . . This battle, in fact, can only be viewed as a struggle which all liberty-loving peoples are bound to follow with understanding and sympathy."

From Germany he cabled his famous editorial, "The Creed of a Progressive," which appeared in the Hearst papers on August 15. In it he declared himself as "definitely Progressive, but a practical Progressive like dear old Theodore"—who must have rotated in his grave at the reference.

Going on in a reminiscent vein, Hearst recalled that he had advocated the remonetization of silver, the election of senators by the people, the direct primary, woman's suffrage, and indeed, "every sound progressive man and measure before the American people" in the past fifty years.

Toward the end, in describing what he was against, the real purpose of the editorial emerged: "I stand solidly for proved American practices and policies and principles. I am opposed to revolutionary theorists. I am averse to inexperienced surgical experiments on the vital parts of our industrial anatomy. I am equally averse to ill-considered architectural experiments on the foundations of our American house and home."

It was a fair, if perplexing, statement of his beliefs. Hearst believed in whatever he thought was right for the country, and whatever he thought was right, was right. There had been no change whatever in his state of mind since the 1890s, when he informed the Democrats that his program for them was "right" and therefore must be adopted. It accounted for the remarkable number of people and opinions he considered correct, though they might be at odd variance with each other.

Before he came home that summer of 1934, Hearst interviewed Hitler on September 16. Apparently he was impressed by the Fuehrer's fanatic power, and visualized him as a bulwark against Communism in Europe, a view not uncommon then in some influential quarters in America, and even commoner now. In any event, Hearst came home with a lucrative news contract in his pocket and a conviction that Hitler was on the right track. He had seen nothing of the black side in Germany, of course, and although he must certainly have known about it, as usual he believed what he wanted to believe.

Hearst's political naïveté was never more evident in the campaign he waged for Hitler after his return to America. The appearance in the Hearst papers of syndicated articles by Hermann Goering, and of pseudo-news stories describing the "amazing economic recovery" brought about by the Hitler regime, and fervent praise of Germany's desire for peace and struggle against Communism could not have failed to put both Hearst and his papers under the same shadow of doubt that cloaked them in 1914 and thereafter.

Yet Hearst stubbornly refused to believe that anyone but a Communist could fail to agree with him, until the overwhelming evidence of persecution of Jews and Catholics and the rising protest against his pro-Hitler articles convinced him at last that he would have to give up the campaign. He still thought he was right. One editorial excused the excesses of the regime on the ground that Hitler's ministers had got out of hand and were acting without orders. But he denounced anti-Semitism specifically, and although he had no sympathy for a war on Germany, on the other hand he made no further flagrant attempts to defend Hitler's actions, since they were now clearly indefensible.

On the home front, however, easier game lurked in the bushes. It was Hearst's earnest conviction that institutions of higher learning, which he had always disdained, were full of dangerous characters. Professors were men who, by and large, believed in internationalism, in the New Deal, in the income tax and in all the other things he considered most dangerous, and therefore they were probably Communists or fellow travelers. In 1934 he declared all-out war against them.

It is conceivable, looking back on that fantastic crusade with a calmer eye, that a far wiser editor than Hearst could have done a real public service by filtering out by shrewder means the few professors who actually were involved in the Communist conspiracy. But to have separated these men from the thousands of honest liberals who unwittingly supported the Communist line simply because the Communists professed to be in favor of their ideals would have taken a knowledge and discrimination Hearst did not possess. It is difficult to say who would have possessed it, though many since have offered themselves as ideal candidates.

In the resulting commotion of the war against the campuses, Hearst did manage to flush out a few genuine extreme radicals, but in the process of carrying out his customary shotgun kind of operation, he ruthlessly slashed the careers and reputations of a good many other men who were guiltless, and his betters from any standpoint.

There was no discrimination whatever in Hearst's attack. That soul of conservatism, Nicholas Murray Butler, was pilloried because he had been president of the Carnegie Endowment for International Peace, which Hearst said was "the most SEDITIOUS proposition ever laid before the American public."

At New York University he centered his attack on such noteworthy liberals as Sidney Hook and James Burnham. At Columbia he indicted virtually all of the Teachers College faculty. At the University of Wisconsin, where there was in reality a relatively effective Communist infiltration of the student body, Hearst disclosed his profound ignorance of what Communism was all about by accusing the professors of sex orgies. At Wisconsin and at the universities of Chicago and Illinois, Hearst's commotion brought solemn inquiries by the legislatures, which produced nothing.

Before the campaign simmered down, it turned out that the Communists had taken over the churches, the Y.M.C.A. and the Y.W.C.A. The New Deal, of course, was composed almost entirely of Communists, a view popular today in some unreconstructed quarters.

These excursions into cloudland were a prelude to the 1936 presidential campaign. By that time those amusing ironies which the twistings and turnings of the Communist line have always produced had placed Hearst and the Kremlin together in an uncomfortable Greek chorus. Both denounced the New Deal as the Raw Deal, the NRA as the "National Run Around," and so on, through a dismal catalogue.

Before the campaign began, Hearst had come to an open rupture with the President because of Roosevelt's advocacy of

American entrance into the World Court, and the veto of the Patman bonus bill completed the schism. Now, in the opening months of 1936, Hearst's was the loudest voice amid all the clamorings that rose from the conservative press, proclaiming the end of democracy unless Alf Landon were sent to Washington by an aroused citizenry.

They were an ill-matched pair, Landon and Hearst, but then it was an ill-matched campaign. It was no more startling to see pictures of Hearst and Landon, arm in arm amid the homey environs of Kansas, than to see H. L. Mencken, the scourge of the booboisie, campaigning in the Landon entourage with an enormous sunflower button in his lapel.

It was a year of strange and unnatural alliances, but to some the strangest, and saddest, was the spectacle of Al Smith, who had fought Hearst at every turn from 1919 onward, endorsing Hearst in public because they had both broken with Roosevelt. It was not a sight calculated to arouse enthusiasm among the voters.

Nor was Hearst's frontal attack on the Administration of much use in attracting other than deep-dyed Republican ballots, and Roosevelt, with his keen political insight, knew it. When Hearst day after day tried to pin the Communist tail on the Democratic donkey, the President let the campaign reach its most unconscionable lengths, then he issued a statement through Press Secretary Stephen Early, attacking the "planned attempts of a certain notorious newspaper owner to make it appear that the President passively accepts the support of alien organizations hostile to the American form of government."

This statement was timed shrewdly to counteract the climax of a series of articles in the Hearst papers designed to show that a vote for Roosevelt was a vote for Stalin. It also caught Hearst out of the country, in Amsterdam, from where he cabled a reply that possessed the enchantment of distance and little else.

The campaign uproar was augmented by an indiscreet message from Hearst to his Washington editorial writer, James T. Williams, Jr., marked "Confidential" but unfortunately not kept that way. In it he asked for a series of editorials calling for the impeachment of Representative John J. McSwain, a short-tempered South Carolina Democrat who was then chairman of the House Military Affairs Committee. McSwain had figured in the attempt of the Senate Lobby Committee, using the Federal Communications Commission as a lever, to compel Western Union to turn over Hearst's wired orders to his Washington staff. Hearst had begun a suit for an injunction against the committee.

As the *Herald Tribune* reported the effect of the memo to Williams, "Rep. McSwain . . . was not a little hurt to learn that Mr. Hearst considered him, and wished him to be publicly portrayed, as 'a communist in spirit and a traitor in effect,' as well as 'the enemy within the gates of Congress, the nation's citadel.' He replied in an oration so impassioned that, at its close, after he was done accusing Mr. Hearst of 'turning on the spigot of venom and of falsehood and of traduction of character,' he had to hurry from the wildly cheering House for medical treatment."

Less than two weeks later Senator Lewis B. Schwellenbach rose on the floor of the Senate to denounce W.R. as "a degrader of the American press, a potential Fascist, a user of stolen documents, an operator of sweatshops," and enough other invective to make his speech "the most violent exercise in invective at this session," which was already distinguished for the clarity and purple tone of its language.

Later the courts decided that the Lobby Committee had indeed violated the Fourth Amendment and sinned against Hearst, but as Arthur Krock observed in the New York *Times*, "the Senate replied, 'Hearst is a bad boy.' And cheered itself."

The campaign reached an ultimate point in absurdity when both parties disowned Hearst, the Democrats pointing out that he was Landon's friend and supporter, the Republicans recalling that it was Hearst who had brought Roosevelt to power.

Landon did not dare to disavow Hearst personally, since it was painfully true that he had been a political unknown until Hearst built him up to presidential campaign stature. Damon Runyon had been ordered to start the ball rolling as early as

November 1935, with an article for *Cosmopolitan*, titled "Horse and Buggy Governor," and Merryle S. Rukeyser, Hearst's eminent financial writer, had been sent to Kansas to inspect Landon as a potential candidate. The ball rolled still farther in December 1935, when Hearst's private railway car paused in Kansas en route to San Simeon, and its passengers, who besides Hearst included Brisbane, the newspaper publisher Paul Block, and Cissy Patterson, had lunch with the peerless candidate and remained to praise him for the benefit of the afternoon papers. Hearst: "I am favorably impressed, to put it very mildly." Block: "He is an even bigger man than I had previously thought." Cissy: "He is just the solid, common type of man we need in the White House."

After that the campaign roared along to the mournful conclusion foreseen by everybody but those who, like Hearst, believed only what they wanted to believe and heard nothing down at the club but Landon. Hearst returned from a quick trip to Europe early in November 1936, freely predicting that Landon would win easily and that war was not imminent.

He had the grace to admit a few days later that he had been stunned by the result, but as an old hand, having been in politics for nearly fifty years by that time, he knew exactly what to say.

His old friend, the President, could be compared only with Andrew Jackson in his popular appeal. In fact, said W.R., "If Andrew Jackson's policies were essentially democratic, why is it not reasonable to concede that Mr. Roosevelt's policies may be equally so—dictatorial in manner and method but democratic in essence? When I was a great admirer of Mr. Roosevelt . . . I gave him a picture of Andrew Jackson and a letter of that great American. . . . I thought then that Mr. Roosevelt resembled Jackson. Perhaps I was more nearly right then than later."

Having delivered this dubious compliment, he relapsed into brief silence until it was time to take up the blackjacks again. There was the "court-packing" bill to fight, and the bill to reorganize the executive branch, and then, superseding everything that had happened since 1917, the great struggle once more to make isolationism prevail.

Hearst fought against the second World War on the same grounds and in much the same way as he had fought against the first one. His admiration for Hitler's Germany had been of briefer duration than his affection for the Kaiser's, and he was not involved in cloak-and-dagger affairs, nor did he encounter the widespread public condemnation of him and his works that he had suffered before.

The fact of the matter was that Hearst had begun to be an old story. For those with long memories, it was like witnessing an old movie seen before. For others it was something like arguing with an institution.

Grandiloquent gestures were made. In February 1939, Hearst instructed George Rothwell Brown, his Washington correspondent, to submit a "questionnaire" to the members of Congress, so that their views might be presented in his papers. Never was a questionnaire so loaded.

"Should the President be at liberty to precipitate war regardless of the wishes of Congress or of the people?" it began forthrightly and went on to inquire whether the American people should or should not be led "either by the President or by the Congress into a war to protect the foreign lands and alien principles of Socialist France, Communist Russia or Imperialist England? Are not the basic causes creating war, not only in Europe but in Asia, the fundamental conflict between the autocratic rule of Fascism and the class despotism of Communism? Should America take sides in this conflict?"

Obviously Hearst thought it should not. He did not change his mind when war actually began, instructing his editors to "Be neutral. Be American. Keep the United States out of war. Keep us out of alien conflicts and foreign entanglements."

Two months after this instruction, President Roosevelt remarked to his press conference that most of the accusations against the Administration's foreign policy had come from the

Soviet press, the Nazi press, the Republican National Committee and the Hearst newspapers.

Asked by the Associated Press to defend himself, Hearst rose to the bait. "The Hearst papers are never quite sure that they can support or oppose the President's policies, because those policies change so much on their way from expression to execution. But we are quite sure that we oppose Russian Communism, German Nazism, and English and French imperialism. We support American liberty and democracy, American freedom of the press and freedom of speech, including freedom of the President to take a few fireside shots occasionally."

Roosevelt is said to have chuckled when he read this statement, perhaps reflecting that it carried more of Hearst humor than of Hearst sting. It may have been that W.R. was somewhat resigned to the inevitable, a possibility raised in public a few months later, in July 1940, when in his new column, "In the News," he asserted flatly that entry of the United States into the war was not only more than a probability but "may be set down as a certainty." The prediction was received with enthusiasm in a place where Hearst was certain to appreciate it least. The headline in the London *Daily Mail*, over a news story about the prophecy, was "U. S. Swings to the Empire—'In War Within a Year.' " The British press interpreted Hearst's remarks as meaning that the American press and politicians were becoming more sympathetic toward Britain.

It is worth noting that Hearst added another prophecy to which less attention was paid at the time. The eventual victor in the war, he said, would be not Germany or Britain, but Russia.

When the United States entered the struggle at last, Hearst was able to give it more enthusiastic co-operation than in 1917 because the immediate foe was the Japan he had warned against for nearly three decades. Here was something a Californian could sink his teeth into, and Hearst sank his with a zealousness that sometimes gave the impression the war had narrowed down to a contest between the Hearst empire and the Japanese empire.

In other respects, nothing had been changed. The war seemed

to bring Hearst alive again, after the financial troubles of the thirties, and during the war years he was as active in his own peculiar methods of prosecuting it as he had been in 1918. When he appeared at a policy meeting with his editors in March 1942, *Time* magazine noted that he was "springy of step" and looked "fitter than he had in years. . . ."

The only person who appeared not to be pleased by the renascence was Miss Davies, who protested, "Gosh, I'm getting so fed up, with Pop spending the whole time talking politics."

Besides talking, he criticized Roosevelt's conduct of the war in the same unsparing way he had Wilson's, and with a virulence which the intervening decades had not diminished. Great was the surprise in Hearst offices all over the country, therefore, when the President died and the obituary that came over the wires to Hearst papers was one Hearst wrote himself. Editors and readers who were accustomed to the daily diatribe which had prevailed since 1934 were astounded to read what Hearst said about his adversary. It was a sober, gracious piece of prose, generous and completely without any last barb.

Reading it, one could begin to assess at last how much old-fashioned politics was involved in the struggle between these men and how much of it was actually meant. There had been personal animosity between Hearst and Theodore Roosevelt, Hearst and Wilson, Hearst and Al Smith. But between the publisher and F.D.R. there was something very nearly like respect, and a liking that transcended political issues. These two old campaigners understood each other, even though they could never agree on what they understood.

The distance between what Hearst papers said and what the Chief really felt on some issues was aptly expressed by Miss Davies after Hearst's death, when in a reminiscent mood she recalled the case of Westbrook Pegler, and although she was quoted only in part, the shock must have been severe to the faithful. The full quotation follows:

"Both W.R. and I always had great respect for Eleanor Roosevelt. She is a great woman. Anna Roosevelt is also a friend of mine and a fine person. When Pegler started hacking at Mrs. Roosevelt day after day it got boring and annoying. Now, old W.R. was not one to hide behind a woman's skirts but he didn't like the way Peg attacked Mrs. Roosevelt. He didn't think it was right to pick on a woman that way. I didn't like it either, not a bit. W.R. wired Pegler many times to cut it out. Each time Pegler laid it on thicker. So we decided to move him off page three and put him back where he belongs. I never read his stuff any more."

After the war, as Hearst's failing health led him slowly away from the public stage and down the long hill to oblivion, he acquired almost a respectability. In 1947, on the sixtieth anniversary of his beginnings as a publisher, Senator Arthur Capper eulogized him in the Senate, finding in his career "a human factor that especially marks him. Nothing engages his sympathy so quickly as the helpless on earth; nothing inflames his anger so much as wrong to those helpless." In the House, Representative Edith Nourse Rogers, the Massachusetts female Republican, asserted that Hearst's "goodness and greatness" would make him rank with America's leading statesmen. "Whenever the term of public servant requires a synonym, I believe it will be Hearst."

There was one more crusade left in the old man, and that was for General Douglas MacArthur, the last of the long list of white hopes who had decorated Hearst's political career. It was a lengthy and, for the most part, eminently unsuccessful list. MacArthur did not part from tradition.

The genesis and character of this last gesture were revealed with surprising frankness by William Randolph Hearst, Jr., three months before his father died. Art Buchwald, columnist of the Paris *Herald Tribune*, discovered Bill Jr. sipping tomato juice in the Ritz bar on a warm May afternoon and quoted him as follows:

"We've supported Mac for a long time, long before any of the other papers jumped on the bandwagon. This policy was based primarily on Pop's judgment. Pop doesn't know anything about the Far East and depends on Mac's judgment. He and the old man are very close. Surprisingly enough they even look alike and their noses slant the same way. They also think alike. It was Pop's idea to run MacArthur for president in 1948. He did it without Mac's permission. Being in the East and getting the feel of things, I knew the campaign was doomed to failure. Pop's secluded out there on the West Coast and every once in a while he gets out of touch with things. But he was right about Mac-Arthur and his popular appeal. Pop has a sixth sense about things like that.

"Our editorial policy [on the Far East] will be guided by Mac's thinking. There was only one thing over which we weren't in agreement with Mac: he advocated staying in Korea while Pop has been for pulling out. I wanted to fly out to Tokyo when Mac was there and get a briefing on what was going on but Pop didn't want me to go. It would have helped clarify a lot of things.

"There's no such thing as an isolationist any more. But Pop's policy is to think primarily in the interests of the American people. We have pointed out the dangers of alliances with other nations and we want them to show us evidences of their good faith before we stick our necks out. With our pacts now we'd be obliged to go to war over anything. Persia, for example, or for some other picayune reason. We think allies can be dangerous to the American people and we're pointing it out in our editorials."

(Young Hearst later wrote a letter to the Paris *Herald*, after Buchwald's column carried the interview, denying he had said that Pop didn't know anything about the Far East. What he meant, he said, was that Pop hadn't been out in the Far East and so depended on Mac's judgment.)

Thus, in some respects, it seemed that times and Hearsts had not changed very much. In a more practical way, however, the senior Hearst in his last months could tell sadly that times had changed more than he cared to think. Until his death, he did

266 WILLIAM RANDOLPH HEARST

not consider MacArthur as a losing dark horse, any more than
he had the countless other losing candidates he had supported.
His policy, as ever, was right and should be adopted.

But as the weeks slipped away toward death, the man who
had sought the presidency, had tried to make Presidents on his
own account, and did make the most controversial one since
Lincoln, and had once been able to command powerful political
machines in New York, Chicago and San Francisco—this man
who had for years been virtually the law in California found
himself in the end with only a feeble remnant of his remarkable
political career.

He had difficulty reducing a drunk-driving charge against
a young actress who was a friend of the Beverly Hills family.
He had even more trouble making an assault charge stick against
a singer who was not in favor at the Beverly Hills court.

These fretful troubles took place in 1948. Twenty years before, William Randolph Hearst could have accomplished easily
such simple acts, and others much more difficult. He could
have done it with a single telephone call.

# CHAPTER EIGHT

## WORLD'S GREATEST COLLECTOR: ART, REAL ESTATE, MOVIES, TREES, ANIMALS AND MEN

EVERY YEAR for fifty years William Randolph Hearst spent a million dollars on his art collection. At the end of a half century he had accumulated about twenty thousand different items, worth in the aggregate somewhat more than fifty million dollars, since there were a few years when his collecting bill was nearer two million. In these flush periods his acquisitions represented a quarter of the entire sales of objects of art in the world.

That side of his collecting alone made him the greatest collector of modern times, perhaps of any other time, but it was only one side. In Hearst the acquisitive instinct was developed to the point of artistic nymphomania. It overflowed into such divergent fields as real estate, motion pictures, trees, animals and human beings.

In each of these tributary fields his collection was impressive, but the scope of his major interest was downright incredible. It was spread halfway around the world, from St. Donat's in Wales to Bronx warehouses spread over city blocks, to four other warehouses in California, besides what was more or less permanently on display at San Simeon and Wyntoon. When half of it was sold at Gimbel's in 1941, the astounding pile of goods covered three and a half acres in the store. Nobody but nobody had ever held such a sale.

The sheer weight of Hearst art led to the widely held view among the laity that it was all quantity and no quality. Art experts, however, knew that of the 504 separate categories in the collection twenty were outstandingly good, and five were the best to be found among private collections. The five were silver, Gothic tapestries, armor, English furniture and Hispano-Moresque pottery.

He was least interested in rugs and painting, though he neglected neither. At one time he had the finest Navajo rug collection in the West, and the oriental rugs in his various palaces were of the finest. Yet dealers used to see him tiptoeing about the boundaries of an exquisite oriental, strangely reluctant to tread on it or to do more than admire it subjectively. As for painting, only the most representational art interested him. "He liked what was three-dimensional, what could be touched, what made its point immediately and succinctly," according to a New York *Times* art critic, Aline B. Louchheim. "Painting is an art of illusion. It held less appeal for him than did the four stereopticon lanterns which stood amid the magnificence of the Great Hall [at San Simeon]—for the views they offered of himself in Europe with his wife or Miss Davies had a three-dimensional 'reality' he did not find in painting."

In every other category, however, his taste was excellent and his knowledge extensive. As Mrs. Louchheim puts it, "He knew too much to be fooled." There were few acknowledged masterpieces in his collections, but on the other hand, the percentage of junk was low and proportionately no higher than in small collections.

Besides the knowledge and love of art objects that his mother bequeathed to him, she started him off in a practical way with the items she had accumulated since 1885, including most notably a set of tapestries from the Barberini Palace, which was the basis of Hearst's great collection in the field.

Hearst bought for himself when he was only ten years old, touring Europe with his mother. The Egyptian carvings he acquired on that trip were augmented slowly at first, but about 1893 he began to follow the art sales of the world and was soon known to dealers everywhere as a young man with an insatiable appetite and a private mint to satisfy it.

Once he had tasted the joys of serious collecting, he was a

lifelong addict. It is doubtful whether anything he ever did gave him so much continuous satisfaction. Collecting took precedence over any other activity. Business, publishing—whatever it was had to wait while he prowled the galleries and auction rooms. He scribbled editorials on the covers and margins of auction catalogues while he waited for what he had come to buy to be offered.

Often a conference would be interrupted while W.R. talked to one of his agents, who would be posted in an auction room somewhere. These agents constituted the best spy system in the business. They were everywhere, sending back to the Chief a constant flow of reports and catalogues. The catalogues alone comprised a formidable part of the San Simeon library.

Whatever might be for sale went up sharply in price as soon as it became known that the Mahatma of San Simeon had his eye upon it. To alleviate the load thus placed upon the traffic, Hearst employed various devices. A frequent visitor to San Simeon recalls putting on her oldest clothes and going up to San Francisco on shopping expeditions for the Chief.

In the auction rooms Hearst used pseudonyms—W. R. Woods was one—and he had fifteen or twenty of them, divided among types of auctions; that is, whether furniture, books, silver, or whatever else was on sale. In Berlin, he was one of four customers who patronized an armorer's shop; two of the others were Henry Ford and Andrew Mellon.

Those who called Hearst a gigantic spendthrift charged that he "bought and forgot," that he was only interested in buying. But in fact he had an elephant's proverbial memory, and to make sure he would never forget entirely, he had each acquisition photographed and documented, and the results mounted in enormous inventory albums. He called them "still lifes." He pored over these volumes by the hour. From them he could order out of his stores anything he desired to see or enjoy.

Even with the aid of this documentation, he sometimes underestimated the size of particular categories. He once called in an expert to catalogue the silver on his yacht, estimating it would take an afternoon. Ten days and ten late nights afterward, the expert was still at it, hopeless of finishing until he had enough time to make a thorough search of the galley and ship's pantry.

The salient feature of Hearst's art collecting was his relentless will to acquire whatever he wanted, regardless of obstacles. Unlike newspaper crusades and politics, here was a field in which he could really exert his power. There are numerous stories extant about how he exerted it, and few that record his frustrations. The frustration stories have become classics by reason of their rarity.

One of the best known, which deserves retelling, concerns the sale of the great Spitzer collection in Paris, an occasion so notable that national museums everywhere in the world sent their directors, top-heavy with all the available cash that could be provided, to gather treasures for their galleries. This occurred early in Hearst's career, while he was still occupied in San Francisco with the *Examiner*, but he contrived to tear himself away and go to Paris, where he inspected the fabulous array of items. While he was there, the date of the sale was postponed three months so that the British Museum (of all institutions, the one most likely to irritate Hearst) could get more money for its proposed purchases. Not daring to leave the struggling *Examiner* for so long, he commissioned a French agent to act for him. The agent was instructed as to how much he could offer for what Hearst wanted: a collection of Tanagras, terra-cotta statuettes which the Greeks had used as grave decorations for their most beloved dead.

On the way home, in mid-Atlantic, W.R. got to worrying about the ability of his agent to carry out orders; he was naturally suspicious of any Frenchman or Englishman. He wrote out his wishes in detail and at the end added, "Of course, I don't want any of the darned old things which will run up to fabulous prices."

When news of the sale came over the wires three months later, he read with dismay that his Tanagras had been sold to another buyer at a lower price than he had authorized. "Why did you not buy the Tanagras?" he cabled. The answer came by way of a formal little letter from the French agent.

"In your letter of instructions written from the steamer you said, 'I don't want any of the darned old things which will run up to fabulous prices.'" the commissioner recalled. "I did not comprehend the meaning of 'darned,' but I looked it up in the dictionary and found that it meant repaired. All the Tanagras had been repaired or restored. They date from the third century B.C."

Such stories belong to Hearst's early collecting period. By the time he was in full stride, he left nothing so important to chance. One of his art aphorisms was, "It's easy to get money, but hard to get the work of art you want. You must buy it when you can."

He meant it literally. Early one morning at San Simeon he was perusing his New York papers when his eye chanced upon a Wanamaker advertisement offering an antique 20-foot-long refectory table for $7500. His trained eye recognized it at once as the missing piece in a set of five from a Bolognese monastery. He had paid French & Co. $5000 for the first three, and another dealer $3500 for the fourth table when it appeared on the market. The fifth seemed to have disappeared until the ad smote his eye. It was 5 A.M. in the California morning, three hours later in New York, but Hearst called his agent in Manhattan and told him what to buy. The agent was on hand when Wanamaker's opened.

These five tables are the ones to which guests sat down in the Great Hall at San Simeon.

The most famous story of his well-lubricated persistence concerns the Spanish monastery at Sacramenia, which he wanted so badly that he provided the town with a new church, since the monastery had been its only place of worship, then had a road built down the mountainside and a railway spur constructed so that he could bring the building down piece by piece, pack it, and send it to America. The entire operation cost him $400,000.

It was not enough for Hearst to own one transplanted monastery, a feat unique in the history of collecting. He had two. The Sacramenia acquisition was a well-publicized part of the

Gimbel sale and was sold to an undisclosed buyer. The other, known as the Monastery of Santa Maria de Ovila, dating in its oldest parts from the twelfth century, was plucked from the banks of the river Tagus, eighty miles northeast of Madrid, and found its way in a mountainous pile of packing cases to the alien meadows of Golden Gate Park in San Francisco, where it lay for some time awaiting unpacking to be presented to the city's municipal museum.

It was no inconsiderable gift. The monastery had a church with two side chapels and a gallery, a monks' dormitory, a refectory with walls more than five feet thick, a chapter house, a kitchen, a Gothic sacristy, several workshop rooms, and a cloister one hundred feet square.

There it lay in the park, waiting to be assembled nearby, the stones partitioned off in marked boxes; all that was needed were the money and labor to put them together according to a master diagram. While the city was trying to raise the money, fire swept the boxes and destroyed most of them, leaving the stones intact but the monastery itself hopelessly scrambled, "the greatest jigsaw puzzle of all time," as one observer put it.

Large purchases like the monasteries were gargantuan whims, though they represented the kind of art that pleased Hearst most—medieval and religious. This taste was a direct reflection of his mother's influence and his attitude toward her, which pervaded his every activity. One would not need to be a psychiatrist to be able to see the significance in Hearst's favorite art subjects, youth and maternity, and in the fact that the faces of the Madonna and her Child gazed out at San Simeon's visitors everywhere one looked, from tapestries, needlework, marble, terra cotta, glass, pottery and oils.

Aside from whatever inner psychological urge Hearst may have satisfied with his art collecting, it was his primary recreation, the only one that entertained him continuously. He was a habitué of Fifth Avenue and of Fifty-seventh Street in New York, often as an idling window shopper, his eyes searching the windows for art objects that pleased him. He spent long afternoons in auction rooms, a telephone near at hand into which from time to time he murmured his editorial orders even as he concentrated on the bidding.

His New York *Mirror* editor, Emile Gauvreau, tells of spending an afternoon with the Chief in one of the Fifty-seventh Street emporia, looking over hundreds of photographs depicting choice Scottish castles, medieval fireplaces, paneled interiors and old masters for sale. From these pictures on that one afternoon, Gauvreau reports, Hearst bought the rooms in a seventeenth-century French cloister and a sixteenth-century fireplace.

Gauvreau saw one photograph he admired. It was a painting of a blonde young woman lying in provocative luxury on a divan. Hearst laughed and rejected it.

"Blondes come high, old masters last longer," he said.

Inevitably Hearst fell into the hands of Joseph Duveen, the suave and subtle master dealer who provided some of America's richest men with the most expensive art educations in history. In this relationship Hearst was a child among the other noted children in Mr. Duveen's seminar. The episode is discussed with considerable charm by S. N. Behrman in his fine biography, *Duveen*. Mrs. Hearst described Willie to Behrman with affection as "a stingy feller" and spoke of Duveen as "a gentleman salesman in a cutaway." As Behrman says, his "connoisseurship was so respected by her husband and his friends that only with fear and trembling did they show him the possessions they had garnered before they came under his guidance."

Millicent recalled that Hearst finally dared to bring Duveen to the Clarendon, where, according to her recollection, which seems shaky on this point, the principal adornment among the treasures was a pair of bas-reliefs of angels, supposedly executed by Rosellino. The ensuing scene is described thus by Behrman:

"Duveen moved through the clutter of antiques, tapestries, and statuary with the air of a man who has plenty of thoughts but is too well bred to voice them. Finally, the increasingly despondent host stood him before the two angels. Duveen made a barely audible remark that cast doubt on their legitimacy, then left, presumably to comfort himself with the contemplation, at his own place, of some genuine Duveens. There was a sad interval after his departure; Hearst was like a college boy who, after cramming hard for an exam, has the terrible feeling that he's flunked it. He was suddenly seized by a devastating doubt about everything he had. He shouted despairingly to Mrs. Hearst, 'If those angels aren't right, then nothing is right!' "

From Behrman's biography it is clear that Duveen misjudged Hearst in one respect. He thought of him as an accumulator, not as a collector. To qualify as a collector of the Duveen school, it appears, one should not have had the numerous collateral interests that engaged Hearst, interests which, though it may be an indelicate suggestion, subtracted from the cash that might otherwise have gone to Duveen. Of the fifty million Hearst spent on art, only about five million of it went into the Duveen coffers, consequently the master dealer placed Hearst among the small fry.

This disdain did not prevent Sir Joseph from exercising his extraordinary talents upon Hearst whenever the occasion offered. One such occasion occurred on an afternoon when W.R. had been having a trivial quarrel with his wife and appeared at the Duveen galleries seeking solace, as he so often sought it, in the pleasure of buying something. As it happened, Duveen was just leaving with a Van Dyck portrait, "Queen Henrietta Maria with Jeffrey Hudson and a Monkey." He was taking it home to his wife, he explained, because he himself was living in a rather cool atmosphere at the moment, originating from his habit of selling the furnishings from beneath Lady Duveen's unappreciative nose.

Duveen seemed to be in a hurry, but of course he would take the time to permit Hearst to see the Van Dyck, and of course it was exactly what Hearst wanted. They engaged in a characteristic Duveen duel, the dealer insisting plaintively that the picture was promised to his wife and he could not part with it under any circumstances, Hearst polite but insistent that he must have it. As Mrs. Hearst so aptly described the master's technique: "Duveen didn't want to sell his stuff, but they always badgered the poor feller till he gave in."

In this instance he gave in when the figure reached $375,000, which Duveen intimated that Hearst was a fool to consider. It was not until after the deal was concluded and he had departed in triumph that Hearst, the heat of battle dying down, began to agree with Duveen. By the time he got home, he was feeling sheepish about the whole incident.

"I've done a terrible thing," he told his wife. "I've gone over to Joe Duveen's and bought a picture. I paid $375,000 for it."

Only Mrs. Hearst could have replied to such a confession with equanimity. "When *I'm* upset," she observed mildly, "I just go out and buy a hat."

Fortunately she liked the Van Dyck, and Hearst began to feel better about it too. After all, he *had* the picture.

He had other fine and satisfying possessions. There were his tapestries, hanging everywhere in his empire, on the walls of the Clarendon, San Simeon, Wyntoon, Beverly Hills, St. Donat's, and more packed away in storerooms—the best private tapestry collection in the world, equaled only by the Spanish royal tapestries. One of the prizes in this collection was a series of six said to have been inspired by Cardinal Wolsey. Another had been one of the treasures of the Vatican.

Then there were his early Grecian and Egyptian potteries, important archaeologically; and the Gothic mantels, an unexcelled collection; and a similarly unsurpassed inventory of old silver, some of which had belonged to Queen Elizabeth, whose private room he removed from England piece by piece—the very room, he was assured, where William Shakespeare read to the Queen from his manuscripts. And there were the rare possessions in marble, including an exquisite Hermes from the Island of Samos, and the paintings by old masters—English, French, Dutch, Italian—enough to stock a small museum.

These were the connoisseurs' pieces. Nearly as precious to

Hearst were those less valuable items which reflected his inner life, like the silver-mounted Mexican saddles, ever-present reminders of his sunny childhood.

This sentimental facet of his acquisitiveness was evident in his library. The books at San Simeon were housed in a room nearly a hundred feet long and thirty feet wide, roofed by a ceiling taken from an Italian palace. There were plenty of first editions and other rare books in it—more when his New York library was moved to the Coast—but it contained also his mother's volumes and those he read for his own pleasure: Dickens, Thackeray, Frazer's *Golden Bough*.

The book he treasured most was *The Life of Mrs. Phebe Hearst*, a superb example of the bookmaking art of John Henry Nash. It was printed from specially cast type on a specially made paper and was bound in Germany in white vellum. Hearst and Nash had a brief tussle about the book. The publisher wanted it done his way, and in a hurry; Nash insisted on doing it his own way, and at his own leisurely pace. Nash won, and Hearst liked the book so much when he saw it that he exclaimed, "John, you'll always be welcome at the ranch, whether I'm there or not —and bring your friends."

Nash's work on the book had a curious by-product. It suggested to him the format for an edition of Dante which later became famous in antiquarian circles and was placed in the Royal Library at Windsor Castle.

The liquidation of Hearst's immense collection was almost as spectacular, in its way, as the acquisition of it. His decision to dispose of anywhere from a half to two thirds of his holdings was made in 1937, at a critical point in his fortunes, with the idea of avoiding inheritance taxes and building up cash reserves, which he badly needed at the time. Not only was he selling, it must be remembered, but for the first time in fifty years he stopped buying.

With a good part of the collection exposed for sale and catalogued, and its fluidity dammed up at last, it was possible to make some appraisal of its worth. A few experts placed it as low as fifteen million, but most were in agreement on the fifty-million figure, or near it. In any event it was more valuable than the collections of other rich men, such as Mellon's, worth nineteen million, or Widener's, worth about the same figure.

The sales which followed the decision of 1937 created a sensation, not only among the curious mobs which thronged Gimbels in February 1941—100,000 persons in the first week, who came away with a half million dollars' worth of art—but among collectors and dealers, who gathered in the auction rooms of New York and London to bid for the real prizes.

Thus the world's greatest collector became through his possessions what he had hoped to be in his newspapers—all things to all people. Armor sold from $4.50 into five figures; Egyptian statuettes went for as little as thirty-five cents at Gimbels. Benjamin Franklin's spectacles brought $325, and a marble statue of Aphrodite fetched $9875. John D. Rockefeller, Jr., Marshall Field and other rich collectors acquired some of the rarer pieces as gifts for museums.

Times had changed since the collecting began. In November 1937, shortly after the great decision, Hearst's splendid collection of old English silver was sold at Sotheby's in London. The prices it brought were only fractions of what had been paid originally.

Hearst's love of silver was so great that once he tried to buy the same piece twice. Reading his own art publication, *International Studio*, he had seen a certain treasure from Lord Londonderry's collection described, and ordered his agent to buy it at once. The agent reported it had been sold. Find it then, Hearst commanded, and he named the substantial figure he was willing to pay to get it. He was not embarrassed, only relieved, when it was discovered he had bought the piece himself, five years before, for about half of what he was now prepared to pay.

In the liquidation process, it was the Gimbel sale which naturally attracted the most attention. Besides the commotion at the store, which went on for months, the sale inspired magazine articles by Jack Alexander in the *Saturday Evening Post*, by

Geoffrey Hellman in *The New Yorker*, and a cartoon by Peter Arno in the same magazine.

The cartoon depicted a testy gentleman and his mink-coated wife in the unfamiliar precincts of Gimbels, the lady bending joyfully over some obscure prize, the husband exclaiming at her elbow: "If you're so hell-bent on buying something that belongs to Mr. Hearst, you can get a *Journal-American* for five cents."

Mr. Alexander wrote that the store's campaign was a "masterpiece of showmanship. At the beginning, special backdrops were painted to put the antiques in suitable settings and a Hollywood expert was brought East to create dramatic lighting effects." He had asked Hearst why he ordered the sale, Alexander reported, and W.R. had told him: "I am not disposing of all my art collection, only about half of it. The remainder I propose giving to museums. You know I am not merely an art collector, but a dealer in art and antique objects. I shall reserve some things for my children, things which they can use advantageously. But the children naturally would prefer for the most part inheritances which would bring them an income. Taxes have a restraining influence on bequests, of course, but I make donations to public institutions with some frequency."

That typical Hearstian statement expressed in as refined a way as possible the idea that the old man needed money.

About fifty thousand persons turned out for an invitation preview of the sale, held on three consecutive evenings after store hours. There were charge-account patrons, Union Leaguers, clubwomen, curators, antiquarians, people with money and no other distinction, and conservative critics like the late Edward Alden Jewell of the New York *Times,* who wrote with hardly concealed astonishment: "Only an experience-toughened specialist wearing blinders could, we cannot but decide, fail to be staggered by the sheer inclusive heterogeneity of this vast congeries of art objects of all periods and from all parts of the world. The impact is amazing."

It amazed even Mrs. Hearst. Hellman disclosed in *The New Yorker* that she had appeared in the big Bronx warehouse before the sale began, looking about to see if any of her own possessions had become involved with the "vast congeries." Standing rather helplessly in the midst of it all, she had remarked wonderingly to an attendant, "How could one man buy all these things?"

"Well, if you don't know, who does?" the attendant had responded gallantly.

Millicent spoke out of her thoughts. "I think he went out and bought things whenever he was worried," she said.

A dealer who knew him well added a more telling postscript after Hearst died: "He bought as if he thought he would live forever."

Death brought a renewal of selling late in 1951, a series of auctions at the Parke-Bernet Galleries in New York. To the noted firm's spacious new home on upper Madison Avenue came a steady flow of buyers and the merely curious, but a far different crowd from the 1941 turnout at Gimbels. These were people from the upper strata, for the most part, come to see what had been in the Beverly Hills house, or hopeful of picking up something relatively cheap so they could say they had a small piece of Hearst's immortality. They gossiped and whispered through the big, brightly lit rooms, gesturing with canes, adjusting eyeglasses, consulting the catalogues, and eventually sitting with the professionals in the auction room.

First to go were about 250 lots from the New York warehouses, worth about $200,000. Among the rarities were a Greco-Roman Parian-marble statue of Apollo, out of the Hamilton Palace collection; the Von Hohenstein cup, dating to 1526; and a stained and painted glass lancet window from the Cathedral of Sens.

At the same time, Miss Davies offered a batch of the treasures from the Beverly Hills house, including Paul Manship's bronze group of "Diana with Hound," a wrought gold snuffbox from the Paris of 1760, and old masters from the sixteenth and seventeenth centuries. The paintings, sold first, brought $62,910. The sculpture, furniture, silver, rugs and other knickknacks realized $72,585. What they had cost Hearst could only be imagined.

When the Hearst warehouse treasures were brought into the auction room, they produced two days of spirited bidding and a total take of $170,455, only slightly less than their estimated worth.

A few spectators with a knowledge of Hearst history watched the bidding for one item with fascination. It was the prize of the sale, the Cellini cup, considered one of the rarest English silver items in the world. Made in London in 1623, this silver-mounted ostrich-egg cup had brought nearly $30,000 at an auction in 1924. It was said Hearst had paid more for it. The Earl of Warwick had once owned it, and so had J. P. Morgan.

There it sat on the stage, lustrous and beautiful, while the signals flew around the auction room and the smooth voice of the auctioneer purred persuasively into the microphone. A stocky genial gentleman appeared to want the cup more than anyone present, and after a time the others gave up.

The Cellini cup's new owner was Clendenin Ryan, the grandson of Thomas Fortune Ryan, Hearst's Wall Street ally in the old political wars of New York. The price he paid for the remembrance, if it *was* a remembrance, was $10,500.

Art, as well as politics, had entered a new era.

II

When it came to collecting real estate, Hearst suffered from the same frustration that haunted his political career. It was a matter of large dreams and small successes, but small only by comparison with his outsize dreams.

The large dream he had about real estate was to create where Columbus Circle and the Maine Memorial now stand a collection of holdings which would result in renaming the Circle for himself, and eventually developing a kind of Hearst Boulevard out of Fifty-seventh Street, from the Circle to the East River. That, in a symbolic way, would have linked politics to art.

In a practical way, if it had been carried out, it would have created for Hearst a realty empire rivaling his newspaper chain.

For a time in the booming twenties it appeared that he was well on the way to creating it. Before the depression stopped him, he and his associates owned or controlled from thirty to forty million dollars' worth of New York properties, not including his newspaper plants. By the time he died, these holdings had been reduced by the depression and thirteen years of reorganization and liquidation to a few parcels, hard to pick out from the protective camouflage of dummy corporations. All that remained of empire were newspaper properties, ranches, mines and timber acreage.

The first purchase Hearst made, aside from his homes, was the sentimental acquisition of Abraham Lincoln's farm homestead in August 1906. These sixty-two acres of Illinois prairie, a priceless historical site, he gave to the State Chautauqua Association.

His first serious dabbling in real estate came in the early years of Mayor Hylan's administration, when it was possible to get the lowest possible tax assessments and helpful zoning interpretations. It was in this first flush that he dreamed of renaming the Circle Hearst Plaza, and running two golden threads from it along Fifty-seventh and Fifty-ninth streets.

His steps in this direction were inspired and guided by Arthur Brisbane, who felt about real estate as Hearst did about medieval art. Brisbane derived as much inner satisfaction from contemplation of a splendid skyscraper fully rented as Hearst did from his monks' praying stalls. In Hearst he found the ideal partner— a man with enthusiasm, ready cash and very little knowledge of real estate.

They formed Hearst-Brisbane Properties, Inc., with Hearst holding the principal interest. Brisbane was also involved as vice-president in the operations of the Balm Realty Corporation in New York, and he was a major entrepreneur in the Florida land boom of the twenties—to such an extent that the excessive amount of Florida praise in the Hearst papers caused pain to the publisher's California friends, until W.R. began loyally chopping it out.

Brisbane's way with Hearst was simple and effective. He planned and sponsored buildings, then persuaded the Chief to invest in them. The plan rested on a shaky foundation, however. As Lee Cooper, real estate editor of the New York *Times*, wrote after Hearst's death: "The joint ventures . . . were subject to heavy carrying charges and high mortgages based on inflated valuations; and in time the heavy burden caused Mr. Hearst apparently to grow cool toward further investments of this type."

Before he cooled, Hearst and Brisbane had collected a half dozen large midtown hotels, several theaters, some skyscrapers and an assortment of smaller buildings. The pride of the collection—at least from the standpoint of Brisbane, who lived there for years—was the 41-story Ritz Tower, a luxurious apartment hotel on the northeast corner of Park Avenue and Fifty-seventh Street.

The real end of Hearst's property dreams came on the sad day in 1938 when the bondholders took over control of this building, under a plan which saved the Continental Bank and Trust Company from having to foreclose.

The passing of the Ritz Tower from his control was one of the first steps in the program of gradual liquidation of Hearst investments outside of publishing. The dissolution, in its New York real estate phase, was handled by the brokers and agents, Huberth and Huberth, whose president, Martin Huberth, Sr., was an old Hearst friend and associate. He was chairman of the board of the Hearst Corporation at the time of Hearst's death.

Some of W.R.'s Fifty-seventh Street properties had passed to Miss Davies along the way, and these were placed after his death in the hands of Herbert Charles & Company, a realty sales and management firm, for sale or improvement.

While the empire never materialized, at least something could be salvaged from the real estate collection, and until the depression cut back its earnings to a dangerous point, it was profitable, on the whole. The same could not be said for his motion-picture collection. That particular extension of his acquisitiveness cost him more than two million dollars before he was through. True, it gave him Marion and so could be considered well worth anything it cost, but on its own merits, the Hearst motion-picture phase was a failure.

He began collecting in March 1913, when the head of his newspaper photographic departments, Edgar B. Hatrick, suggested making motion pictures of Woodrow Wilson's inauguration. Thus, innocently, Hearst's political enemy started him on the road to cinematic ruin. The inauguration was shown at a Broadway theater on March 5, prints of it were rushed to other Hearst cities, and the first newsreel was born.

With a newsreel company organized to make weekly releases, the Hearst-Selig Weekly, Hearst was in the motion-picture business, and almost immediately in trouble. A cameraman, Ansel Wallace, had the enterprise to make a shot of President Huerta, of Mexico, sipping brandy in his palace garden, an invasion of his privacy which so irritated the President that he had Wallace tossed into jail and sentenced to be shot. Hearst had to call up his old friend Bryan, then Secretary of State in Wilson's cabinet, and get him to intervene.

While these alarums were occurring, Hearst was branching out in the direction of popular romance, in keeping with his newspaper formula. There he achieved, without realizing it, his only claim to cinematic immortality by associating with Pathé in the making of *The Perils of Pauline*, starring Pearl White, of fond memory to older citizens. What is not so well known is that Hearst and Pathé, drunk with successful peril, followed up Pauline's cliff-hanging exploits, the forerunner of modern soap opera, with such quickly forgotten classics as *The Exploits of Elaine* and *The Mysteries of Myra*, and undoubtedly would have gone farther if they had not run out of alliteration.

It was only a step from these to full-length silent features. Hearst and Millicent were both fascinated with the art by this time. They made amateur pictures at San Simeon in the summertime, and W.R. often dragooned house parties into performing epics which he wrote and directed himself.

The first Hearst motion-picture company, the International Film Service, built its own studio in 1919 at 127th Street and Second Avenue, in the upper reaches of Manhattan, and in these primitive studios Alma Rubens and Ramon Novarro starred in Fannie Hurst's *Humoresque,* and Marion appeared in *When Knighthood Was in Flower* and *Little Old New York.*

M. R. Werner, who was present during these historic scenes, has recalled in a *New Yorker* article that Miss Davies was "very goodlooking, modest and genial, but unfortunately she had not yet learned to act. The most expensive people were hired to give her lessons and the product was being released by Paramount and netting a steady loss to Mr. Hearst. Nobody had discovered that Marion Davies was a natural comedienne and not a romantic heroine, although we had directors whose salaries varied between $1,000 and $2,000 a week. Mr. Hearst loved to see Miss Davies dressed in beautiful clothes and so most of her pictures had to have a fairy-tale interlude. We arbitrarily put Sleeping Beauty into one scenario of a Hearst magazine story that had not even mentioned Sleeping Beauty and several other nursery tales were interjected into other highly routine nonsense. The scenario department was always busy with Hans Christian Andersen and the Brothers Grimm."

Hearst came up to the studio occasionally for conferences, Werner recalls, but if serious argument developed he would choke it off in his high-pitched drawl: "After all, I own this company."

Somebody once asked Hearst whether there was any money in motion pictures. "There are several millions of my money in it," he replied with his characteristic irony.

Before he removed his production facilities to Hollywood and the upper Manhattan fairy-tale era ended, Miss Davies endeared herself to the people of that dreary neighborhood. Old residents, who loved her, remember how she gave impromptu parties for them at Christmas and presented toys to the children, many of whom would not otherwise have had any. One Christmas it took thirty policemen to handle the crowd.

Famous Players-Lasky distributed the pictures first made in New York. In the succeeding Hollywood phase, Hearst made his most successful pictures in association with Metro-Goldwyn-Mayer. Some of them were *White Shadows in the South Seas, The Floradora Girl* (with Miss Davies), *The Big House, Blondie of the Follies* and *Peg o' My Heart* (both with Marion), *Gabriel Over the White House* and *Operator Thirteen*. It was Hearst who produced *Broadway Melody*, the first musical in sound.

Hearst and M-G-M parted company in 1934, allegedly over a refusal to let Marion play Elizabeth in *The Barretts of Wimpole Street*. In any case, Warner Brothers succeeded M-G-M as distributors and Miss Davies' contract holders. They made *Page Miss Glory, Shipmates Forever* and *Special Agent*, but Hearst's producing career was nearly over. The depression had begun to hit him heavily, and making pictures was an expensive luxury.

The reason for Hearst's failure as a movie mogul was his customary lavishness, in this case without anything like an adequate return for it. Ilka Chase recalls that the best part she ever had in Hollywood was in *The Floradora Girl*. Everyone considered a Davies picture a plum, she said, because "time meant nothing, and your salary was apt to continue for weeks and weeks."

*The Floradora Girl* deserved preservation for one scene, in which Miss Chase advised Marion on how to get and hold a rich man.

Hearst took an extremely moral attitude toward motion pictures. He was forever chiding Hollywood for its bad reputation and its sexy pictures. He remarked editorially in October 1927, "Suggestive films and ultra-sex films have become altogether too numerous of late. Their effect on the community is bad and their reaction on the industry is bad." Then the man who had made yellow journalism a part of the language went on, "The explanation of this flood of sex films is simple. That is the cheapest and easiest way of attracting the attention of a certain prurient element of the public."

In making movies, however, Hearst practiced what he preached. His pictures were totally unlike his newspapers, and he considered himself as having played a major part in preventing the medium from falling into the sinful state which he believed had engulfed the stage and literature. He honestly thought, as he wrote in 1933, that the screen was "much more of an educational factor than either literature or the stage drama."

Even after his own producing activities had dwindled away, he thought of himself as a guardian of the screen's morals, and when he could combine righteousness with an attack on someone not currently in favor, he threw his weight around with conviction. In a private memo to his editors on February 23, 1936, he advised:

"The Mae West picture, *Klondike Annie*, is a filthy picture. I think we should have editorials roasting the picture and Mae West and the Paramount Company for producing such a picture —the producer and director and everybody concerned.

"We should say it is an affront to the decency of the public and to the intelligence of the motion-picture profession.

"Will Hays must be asleep to allow such a thing to come out, but it is to be hoped that the churches of the country are awake to the necessity of boycotting such a picture and denouncing its producers. After you have had a couple of good editorials ROASTING the indecency of this picture, then DO NOT MENTION MAE WEST IN OUR PAPERS AGAIN WHILE SHE IS ON THE SCREEN. AND DO NOT ACCEPT ANY ADVERTISING OF THIS PICTURE. . . ."

As a collector of motion pictures, Hearst ultimately experienced far more joy from seeing movies than making them. The nightly rite of the cinema, begun in the earliest days of San Simeon, continued nearly until the end of his life, although in the last year or so the schedule was cut to one or two a week, and then monthly as the end neared.

Of the thousands of pictures he saw, Hearst had no special favorites but he had a secret weakness. Once he ordered a mediocre film run night after night, to the puzzlement of his guests, except those close enough to him to know that the long minstrel-show sequence in it was what enchanted him. He seldom intimated the fact for some reason, but he loved minstrels and would endure repeatedly anything else in a picture for the sake of them.

His favorite stars varied down the years. Marion, of course, was his perennial favorite, and her old pictures were screened for his enjoyment (and hers) time after time, long after they had ceased to fascinate other people. Lawrence Tibbett was a favorite, and then Gene Tierney. Probably the last star for whom he expressed a decided preference was Shirley Temple, who was a friend of the family, like Miss Tierney.

If he happened to be away from his home haunts, Hearst would go to a local movie house, and it was in one of these, in San Francisco, that he and Marion sat one night and watched the unfolding of a life remarkably like his own in Orson Welles' *Citizen Kane*. They slipped in and out of the theater so unobtrusively that no one saw them, thereby cutting off the manager from the most lucrative kind of publicity. When a friend asked him later how he had liked it, he looked away thoughtfully and replied, "We thought it was a little too long."

Contrary to legend, Hearst rather enjoyed seeing himself portrayed on the screen, and naturally did not believe Orson Welles, its writer, director, producer and star, when he denied that the story was based on the publisher's or anyone else's life. Among those who were not amused, however, was the Hollywood gossip columnist, Louella Parsons, one of Hearst's most devoted and partisan friends. She saw the picture at a special preview, in company with two Hearst lawyers, and came out with a considerably elevated temperature.

There followed an ill-considered attempt to suppress the picture, but RKO, with some $800,000 invested in it, was defiant. Though W.R.'s power was notably diminished by that time

(1941), he might at least have seriously embarrassed the company if he had been personally enraged. As it was, he sat back and let Miss Parsons and his lawyers carry the assault, with the result that *Citizen Kane* was a success, in spite of the fact that the Hearst papers boycotted Orson Welles, apparently for life, and for a time would not mention RKO productions either. On the day Miss Parsons saw *Citizen Kane*, her review of a new RKO picture, *Kitty Foyle*, was dropped from the Los Angeles *Examiner* after the early editions, a typical method of Hearstian attack.

But it must not be imagined that Hearst, the collector, devoted all his time to managing the motion-picture industry, engaging in huge property deals and cornering rare silver. He collected assiduously in such exotic fields as trees, flowers and animals. No one knows exactly why he loved animals, aside from dogs, but trees and flowers were an expression of his passionate love for beauty, which his mother had imparted to him and carefully cultivated in his childhood.

He was especially partial to trees. He told a San Simeon visitor one day: "I used to come up here with my father as a boy. In those days we had a little cabin just about where we are now sitting. He used to be very fond of that tree"—he pointed to a huge oak—"and so am I. That's why, when I found it interfered with the view from one of my windows, I had it shifted so carefully that it never knew it was being moved. I never destroy a tree."

Someone once told Hearst that the City of Los Angeles planned to cut down all the palms on a certain boulevard leading out of Hollywood. In great concern, he made plans to buy the palms and have them all taken out to San Simeon. The rumor proved to be untrue.

He permitted nothing to stand between him and the acquisition of a tree. Experts once told him it would cost $150,000 to import some trees he wanted for the grounds at San Simeon. Confronted with this figure, Hearst merely shrugged and lifted his shaggy eyebrows. The trees arrived soon after.

On another occasion he ordered his landscape men to move a 100-year-old oak thirty feet to one side. They told him it could not be done; the tree would have to be cut. According to legend, Hearst called in his own experts—several editors of his papers—and ordered, "Get it done." The move was accomplished by the construction of a concrete flowerpot, out of reach of the roots, and the tree was then jacked along a trench, inch by inch, into the pot. The job cost nearly $40,000.

Hearst thought nothing of spending thousands of dollars to move a tree four feet, so that a path might have the proper curve, but he refused absolutely to cut one, unless he was faced with some immutable fact of nature.

The magnificent cypresses which surround the terraces at San Simeon were snatched from death by Hearst, who saw them standing in a row at Paso Robles, thirty feet high, and learned they were to be destroyed. Appalled, he bought them and built a box around each one to protect them for a year. The following year he had crews watering and taking care of the trees, establishing them in the boxes, and the year after that they were ready to be transported to San Simeon in their artificial bases.

Hearst loved all kinds of trees, but he was particularly fond of blossoming trees: eucalypti, red-berried pyracanthas, oleanders, orange, lemon and grapefruit trees, and a dozen other delicious flavors. Every kind of fruit and nut tree that was capable of thriving in California grew on the acres of San Simeon, along with giant oaks, pines and redwoods, so that the grounds were a luxuriant flowering wilderness, like nothing else in the world.

The garden at the ranch was equally glorious. It was a virtual transplanting, in spirit and partly in actuality, of Phebe's beloved garden at her ranch. Red, white and yellow roses were transplanted from there and allowed to climb up in riotous profusion along the lofty trunks of the palm trees on the Enchanted Hill, as the lavender lantana and pink ivy geraniums covered the stone walls of the terraces. And there were zinnias, gladioli, dahlias, camellias, hibiscus, jasmine, daphne and hybrid heathers until hell and a ladies' garden club wouldn't have it.

Mrs. Older has provided us with a revealing view of the master at work in his garden. In his planting, she wrote, he produced "swift, dramatic effects as in his newspapers. Overnight gorgeous beds of multi-colored tuberous begonias are created by transplanting blooming plants from hothouses. One of his garden surprises with a touch of mystical magic came on an Easter morning when the guests at San Simeon awoke to find the ground under the oaks covered with tall, white Madonna lilies. All night by electric light a large corps of men had worked to prepare for the celebration of Easter at dawn."

The mystically magic touch was less apparent in the handling of the animals at San Simeon, but they were displayed with the same fine collector's touch. Visitors were aware of their presence at once when they drove up the mountainside, as they were confronted by large signs admonishing them to "Beware of Wild Animals," warning that "Reckless Driving Will Not Be Tolerated," and advising that "Animals Have the Right of Way."

The zoo and game preserve, the largest private collection in the world, was established on two thousand San Simeon acres, protected from the guests by an eight-foot-high woven wire fence ten miles long. In this enormous enclosure roamed sixty species of grazing animals and thirty kinds of jungle animals.

As an animal collector, Hearst began modestly with spotted deer from India. Then, patriotically, he added Montana black buffalo, but he had to go afield again to buy yaks from Tibet, Australian emus, musk oxen, elk, antelope, kangaroos, a camel and two giraffes. The latter were bought by Jane Head, his London agent, who was not in the least disturbed to find a cable from her boss one day advising her to leave at once for Africa and buy a pair of giraffes.

For a time there were lions in a huge pit, a collection begun with a present of two baby lions to Hearst from Joseph M.

Schenck, the movie mogul. Eventually there were four lions, but in time they were replaced with polar bears. The tigers were also eliminated. Hearst got bored with them; they were too tame.

There was hardly anything in the Bronx Zoo, or the other great American collections, that could not have been found in Hearst's at its peak. There were cheetahs, a spotted leopard and a black panther, cockatoo and eagles, several kinds of monkeys and chimpanzees, orangutans and gorillas, elephants and mountain lions, bison and zebras, llamas and cassowaries, and a variety of bears. By way of contrast, a flock of prize Wyandottes clucked around a chicken ranch, Holsteins and Jerseys grazed on a complete dairy farm, and elaborate stables housed the fine Arabian horses Hearst bred.

At San Simeon the great collector had everything on one place: the best of his art and his real estate; anything he desired to see in his private movie theater, including his own triumphs and failures; his most beloved trees and flowers; enough animals to fill a small ark.

The only part of his incredible collection that could be summoned to but not anchored at San Simeon were human beings. Hearst collected men, picking them with such care that the inner circle survived year after year of jealousy, backstage politics, and the master's changing states of mind. While there were many who left his employ, many who condemned him on and off his payroll, there were these others, intensely loyal until they or he died. Those who survived him were loyal after death.

Was it a fear-inspired faithfulness? Probably in a few cases. Was it a cynical willingness to hang onto a good thing at any cost? Again possibly, for a few. But it cannot be denied that a hard core of the men Hearst collected and at least two women outside his romantic life were personally devoted to him. Considered together, the stories of the men around Hearst, both the inner circle and those on the periphery, make a fascinating footnote to the Yellow Kid's life.

## III

The man closest to Hearst was the one least publicized. Colonel Joseph Willicombe knew the Chief at the very beginning, as a reporter on the San Francisco *Examiner*. As his private secretary for more than three active decades, he knew Hearst better than anyone else. Although he went into semi-retirement several years before his death in 1948, Willicombe remained closer to his boss than nearly anyone else except Miss Davies. Hearst respected Willicombe's ability and, when they grew older, became increasingly fond of him as a person, as he tended to be toward men of his own era.

For his part, Willicombe performed what must have been the most trying secretarial job in the world with awesome skill. He became crotchety toward the end, flying into a rage if someone disturbed the mail on his desk in the office he occupied on the second floor of the Examiner Building. But most of the time he was equable and always appallingly efficient.

His power was enormous. In the days of San Simeon and Wyntoon, he was the single link between Hearst men and their Chief. He was the final judge as to whom Hearst would see. Even after his supposed retirement, he came up twice a week to his San Francisco office from his home in Carmel Valley, and there he kept a knowledgeable finger on the pulse of the whole San Francisco area. Through his experienced hands flowed the crank letters and the exclusive stories that visitors were continually desirous of presenting in person to Mr. Hearst.

How Willicombe worked with the Chief has been described elsewhere, but the daily clipsheet routine and the framing of "Chief says" memos were only part of his job, although it was certainly the most important part.

Another chore that he probably performed with less relish was that of satisfying Hearst's sudden whims and otherwise unexplained orders. The real burden in this respect, however, was carried by the editors and reporters of the Hearst papers in Los Angeles, since most of the odd items W.R. felt a sudden need for were procured by them. The items ranged from fancy lingerie to exotic laxatives. Salesmen in Los Angeles department stores became accustomed in time to placing boxes containing thousands of dollars' worth of goods in the arms of eighteen-dollar-a-week copy boys.

A difficult order, not the result of a whim, was one occasioned by a fire at Wyntoon in 1943, in which the kitchen and dining room burned down. The fire started when Walter Howey, a visiting editor, tripped over the wires of a new photo transmission machine he was demonstrating for Hearst's benefit. After the fire, Willicombe sent out the word to get a temporary kitchen for immediate installation, before the inhabitants perished of starvation amid luxury.

The Hearst men in Los Angeles and San Francisco who fanned out over the countryside hunting kitchens were frantic. It was wartime, and not even Hearst could command the building materials and labor to put up anything permanent. Willicombe had intimated that even a tent would do, but this was not to be had at once. Then someone thought of buying a carnival commissary, or "grease joint," in carny argot. One was found, but the owner, who was doing a highly profitable business, showed no eagerness to drop everything and hurry to the fastnesses of Northern California. He thought to stall the proceedings by demanding gas-ration coupons, but these were produced. Then he remembered a rodeo in Mojave that he had agreed to play, and he issued a flat declaration: Mr. Hearst would have to wait two days.

On this issue negotiations broke down. The commissary went to Mojave; the Hearst carnival packed up and came down to the Santa Monica beach house.

This was one of Willicombe's few failures. He thought nothing of ordering a vaporizer flown out from Cleveland, to be met at the airport by reporters at 4 A.M. in the morning and rushed to Hearst. Harder but not impossible was the search conducted in 1947 for Deer Park cookies, a confection the Chief remembered from his youth and got a sudden yearning to experience again. It took an intensive search, since finding these old-fashioned cookies was much like locating an out-of-print book, but two boxes were produced.

Probably the last memo Willicombe sent down was the one immediately after V-J Day, in which the Chief commended his papers for their pyrotechnical handling of the Japanese surrender. Hearst moved to San Simeon shortly after this event, and Willicombe went into semi-retirement. His stocky figure, surmounted by a light Western hat like a sheriff's, was seen only in San Francisco. He was described officially as "inactive."

His place was taken by E. O. ("Bill") Hunter, a man much like Willicombe in temperament, who had been secretary to the publisher of the Los Angeles *Examiner*. He and Ella ("Bill") Williams, Hearst's housekeeper and confidential secretary, handled details at the Beverly Hills house until the Chief's death.

When Willicombe died in 1948, so little was known about him even on Hearst papers that they were compelled to carry an INS obituary, written in New York and datelined Monterey. That was partly because he was so close to Hearst and so important in the organization, and partly because it was recognized that few occurrences upset the Chief more than the passing of someone from his own era. Consequently his editors never knew whether to play up or down such a death and made few preparations for it.

Irascible as Willicombe could be on occasion, editors would rather hear his voice on the wire than the Chief's. They were terrified when Hearst chose to relay his requests in person because he seldom repeated himself. It was necessary to get what he said the first time in his high, squeaky voice, or you were lost.

The night editor of the San Francisco *Call-Bulletin* once picked up his telephone to hear the unmistakable voice asking peremptorily for what sounded to him like Berkshire pigs. So aghast was he by this request, unusual even for the Chief, that he mustered the courage to ask for a repetition. Hearst was in a rage, but he repeated in a tense, cold voice several times, and at last it dawned on the editor: Smyrna figs.

It took all night to get them, but they were found and for once no head-lopping took place.

The lot of a Hearst editor, especially the top ones, was never a happy one. Consider his position. His newsprint was bought for him by remote authority, his national advertising sold in the same way, his circulation methods handed down from on high, his lead editorials written by unseen and all-powerful hands. As publisher of a Hearst paper, he did not even have the right to fire his own managing editor, unless by specific order. He was expected to do only two things: make his paper popular and profitable, and thus satisfy Hearst.

Whether a man could take this kind of life, permitting his personality to be suspended in the vast web of Hearstian politics and methods, depended on his temperament. Sometimes it seemed that the most spectacular talents were those least able to stand the strain. At least two of Hearst's best men committed suicide.

One was Victor Watson, the hard-bitten circulation expert and "crusade" specialist who built the Chicago papers and engaged in numerous other activities, including supersleuthing. Born near Tammany Hall, the product of a Jewish mother and an Irish father, Watson became known as the "bad boy" of the organization. The most telling story about him concerns the headline he wrote on the story of Hitler's ascension to the chancellorship: COMMUNISTS RULE GERMANY. When protest was made, Watson yelled, "He's against the government, isn't he? So he must be a communist." The headline was not printed.

Watson's life ended in a plunge from a New York hotel room. The other suicide was that of Ray Long, the brilliant editor of Hearst's *Cosmopolitan*, who shot himself.

Earlier Hearst men were inclined to less drastic means of leaving the service. Homer Davenport, the cartoonist, toured the country after he left Hearst, delivering speeches to luncheon clubs in which he told lurid tales of his ex-boss's alleged sex life. Arthur McEwen did much the same thing by starting a rival

San Francisco paper, in which he unsuccessfully attempted to use his extensive knowledge of Hearst method to beat the master at his own game.

Against these meteoric temperaments could be balanced such conservative, steady men as Edmond David ("Cobbie") Coblentz, who at this writing can boast of more than fifty years in Hearst service, surviving the Chief to edit his recently published "self-portrait." As supervising editor of the morning papers for many years, Coblentz was the funnel through which the Chief poured a great many of his policies and ideas.

The more vocal of Hearst's mouthpieces, and so much a personality in his own right that he sometimes overshadowed his boss, was the redoubtable Arthur Brisbane. Emile Gauvreau, in what is probably the best portrait of the Great Thinker ever drawn, describes him as "like some chopped-off trunk of oak, his profile almost a straight line, extending into a double forehead. He had a face which might have been of flint, a firmly mortised jaw manipulated from thin, unsmiling lips. His steady eyes had the metallic blue of steel. . . ."

Brisbane had three strong prejudices—stronger, that is, than the innumerable others he cherished. He shared Hearst's phobia against taxes, particularly high real estate taxes; he hated dogs as much as Hearst loved them; and he was convinced that the only men in history who had ever amounted to anything had blue eyes.

After an early education in France, where he was profoundly influenced by the French liberals and his Socialist father, he began his career at eighteen as a cub on Dana's *Sun,* where he distinguished himself by covering one of John L. Sullivan's fights on an instant's notice when the sporting editor was taken drunk. Thereafter he was sent to London, and although he covered Parliament and the political news of the day, he again attracted attention by the tear-jerking feature he wrote on Charley Mitchell's attempt to fell that same John L. Sullivan for the benefit of his "dear little kids at home."

By this time it was apparent to Dana that he had in his employ a man who knew how to talk to the masses. He brought Brisbane home, made him managing editor of the *Sun*, and so gave him a whole newspaper to speak with. He spoke so well that Pulitzer hired him as chief editorial writer, and there he emerged in his full glory, until Hearst hired him and transported him to heights never attained by any other of his executives.

As a Hearst man, Brisbane exercised to the fullest his single extraordinary talent—an ability to popularize, talking politics and philosophy, as Will Irwin put it, "in the language of truckmen." He had mastered the art, another writer remarked, "of stating a part so that it will seem a whole." He drew on his classical education in France, on his command of a dozen languages, on his incredible memory, to direct an endless flow of simplified knowledge toward his readers, who numbered in the millions. They got it colored by Brisbane's pragmatic, businessman's philosophy, what Irwin called his "insincere sincerities," and by an oversimplification which was often just this side of absurdity.

An example of Brisbanian logic and popularizing wrapped in one glorious package is his defense of yellow journalism, delivered as part of a speech he was making around the country in 1909, at a time when the Hearst papers were smarting under attack. Brisbane would stand before his audience, wherever it might be, thrust his high-domed head forward and declaim in his rasping, aggressive voice:

"The whole human race, according to the highest authority, has been exterminated once already because it wasn't going right and only the rainbow protects it from a repetition. They say that the Hearst papers are yellow. Remember that the sun is yellow and we need a little sunshine. Think of the colors of the rainbow!"

Hearst recognized in Brisbane a man who would be absolutely loyal to him and who could do much toward making his papers the successful mass medium he wanted them to be. Later he saw in Brisbane's schemes to make money and his insatiable appetite for real estate a valuable adjunct to his collecting ideas. In neither

case did "Artie" disappoint him, but there remained between the
two men, in spite of their close mutual association for nearly
forty years, an inexplicable distrust. It may have been that Brisbane, a man of monumental ego, perceived that Hearst really had
a kind of tolerant, half-amused contempt for him.

There sat Brisbane, grinding out millions of words into his
dictaphones, dogmatic, harsh, obsessed with money and his own
ideas, while over him sat Hearst, serene and remote, manipulat-
ing him with a power he could never possess, even as the world's
highest-paid editor. Presumably it was galling.

Brisbane was aware of a widely circulated remark Hearst once
made about him: "Arthur comes to me all the time with some
wonderful plan to make money, but when I examine into it, I
find the profits are to be divided 90 per cent for Arthur, 10 per
cent for me." The very tone of the remark made their relationship to each other clear.

One can imagine the gloating satisfaction in Brisbane's voice
when he told Gauvreau one day, a few years before his death:
"I don't own the Ritz Tower. I knew the crash was coming
two years after I had put that building up and I advised Mr.
Hearst by letters and telegrams to dispose of his properties
before the catastrophe. He would wire back: 'Arthur, don't
frighten me, Arthur, don't scare me! Things will never be as
bad as that. Real estate is the best thing to own.' So I went to see
Mr. Hearst and I said, 'If you think real estate is so good, I'll sell
you the Ritz Tower,' and by God, he bought, and you know
what happened after that! He had to keep that thing going for a
time at a loss of damned near $125,000 a month."

With some conviction it may be said that the two men had no
illusions about each other. On Brisbane's side one can cite the
story Heywood Broun delighted to tell about the day when
Hearst, anxious to lend an aura of liberalism to his papers, tried
to hire Broun to write for him, using Brisbane as his intermediary.
It was not the first time such an attempt had been made. With
Kobler as the go-between, Hearst had previously attempted to
snare Walter Lippmann, then the brilliant young editor of the

New York *World*. Lippmann had listened politely and refused, almost with amusement. Now it was Broun's turn.

The big, shambling man, looking somewhat out of place in Brisbane's formally luxurious Fifth Avenue home, heard the editor offer him a contract at three times the income he was making. He refused. Brisbane appeared disappointed but not surprised. Before he departed, Broun stood admiring the portrait of Brisbane's father which hung above the fireplace.

"What a marvelous face your father had," he remarked. "It reflects the calm outlook of a man who is right with himself."

"Yes," Brisbane agreed, his voice gloomy. "He looked that way because he never had to work for Hearst."

The story gives Brisbane more credit than he deserves. He never *had* to work for Hearst. He swallowed his pride and whatever principle may have been involved simply because no one would ever have paid him so much for what he did, and no other organization was so constructed as to give him the liberty of expression he enjoyed.

Hearst seemed to realize how completely in his power Brisbane's particular temperament had placed the man, and he appeared to take a delight in needling Arthur as he did no other executive in his employ. For years he had few opportunities because Brisbane carried out every assignment given him with his customary thoroughness and profitable result.

Eventually there came the inevitable day, however, when he began to slip. As publisher of the New York *Daily Mirror* in the early thirties, he had the all but impossible task of catching the paper's chief rival, the skyrocketing *Daily News*. When his impending failure began to be evident, Hearst sent him a series of sarcastic notes and telegrams, phrased with the sardonic humor which passed for wit with him. One, for example, read: "Dear Arthur, you are now getting out the worst newspaper in the United States."

Doggedly, hurt and stung by Hearst's attitude, Brisbane kept driving himself and his men until he died in 1936. Before death came he suffered the final humiliation, if the story is true, of arriving at the San Simeon gatehouse past which he had rolled in triumph so many times, come to plead his case in person. And because Hearst knew he was coming and could never bring himself to argue a man's shortcomings with him in person, especially an old friend like Brisbane, he sent down to the gatehouse that message from which there was no appeal: "Mr. Brisbane is not expected."

Nevertheless, a strange and perverse affection existed between them, and in spite of everything that had happened, there was at least some truth in the eloquent tribute Hearst wrote for his friend on December 26, 1936, though in the light of previous events much of it seems like mockery.

"I know that Arthur Brisbane was the greatest journalist of his day," Hearst wrote in part. ". . . The pen that wrote the columns which millions read for their enlightenment and encouragement is stilled. I grieve for that and realize the loss; but I grieve as deeply, and more truthfully, that that pen will no longer write the intimate letters of friendship, full of pleasant wit and quiet wisdom, and sincere and sound advice. I grieve inconsolably that the long, long friendship, uninterrupted by a single quarrel or definite difference of any kind, is ended—that I will no longer know his enjoyable and helpful companionship, and that the world in which I must spend my few remaining years will hold for me a blank space, which had been so unforgettably filled by my more than friend and more than brother, Arthur Brisbane."

Of a different stripe than Brisbane was Solomon Sells Carvalho, but quite as unusual a personality in his own way. Where Arthur was the man of the people, Carvalho was the ascetic, the remote figure behind large operations. He loved to sit in his dim, uncomfortable office in the Rhinelander Building in New York and attempt to intimidate his visitors by arranging for them to sit in a strong shaft of light from the windows while he stayed in the shadows.

Koenigsberg recalls visiting him one day and seeing this man whose portrait, he thought, might well be entitled "Reason,

Triumphant," take a pair of twelve-inch scissors from his desk and trim his precise little goatee. This may be a matter of heredity among Hearst executives. A top man who survived the Chief sometimes discomfits his subordinates by clipping the hair in his nostrils while they confer with him.

Whatever his personal faults, Carvalho was nearly indispensable as general manager of the Hearst publications. The Chief admired and respected his ability as he did that of few other men, though their personal relationship was occasionally stormy. Twice Carvalho quit in protest over Hearst policy, and both times there was a consequent abrupt downturn in the Hearst business index, so that he had to be rehired. Carvalho took the hard problems of management off Hearst's shoulders, solved the insoluble dilemmas, dealt coolly and efficiently with the stable of executive temperaments under his command, and Hearst was grateful for his abilities. Hale and cheerful at eighty-four, though in nominal retirement, Carvalho was stomping around the office stiffly on his artificial leg and giving advice to Hearst editors.

In considering the relationship of Hearst to these men who were close to him, whom he collected along the way, the dominant note time and again is propinquity. Always Hearst was the center of the constellation; the stars had to realize it in one way or another.

There was, for example, the celebrated case of Fremont Older, who died in California in 1935 a year before death took Brisbane and Kobler from Hearst's employ. Older and Hearst had met as early as the late eighties, when Older had become one of the *Examiner's* first reporters, brought off a remarkable scoop, and been warmly congratulated by the young publisher, who promised him a glowing future on the paper.

But responsibility frightened Older, who had fallen in love with the carefree ways of the newspaper business in that golden era, and he departed the *Examiner*. They met again in 1903, when the Olders, on their way to Europe, encountered the newlywed Hearsts honeymooning across the Atlantic. Then for years afterward Older knew what it meant to run a struggling sheet in the same town with Hearst, discovered the pleasures of attempting to compete without money against a Hearst paper which could afford to do anything.

In 1918, when Older was managing editor of the San Francisco *Bulletin*, he was ordered to drop his battle for Tom Mooney, and Hearst sent his famous wire: "Come to the *Call*. Bring the Mooney case with you." Thus, after fighting Hearst in print for years, Older came to him for the rest of his working life and found that they had more in common than he thought. They had both fought the Southern Pacific, and both were isolationists. It was Older who first saw Hearst's sentimental poem, *The River*, and printed it.

The reverse of this relationship was Hearst's sudden parting with Moses Koenigsberg, one of his most trusted executives for a decade. Koenigsberg had rendered the Chief exceptional service by rescuing INS from an inglorious death and rejuvenating it, and he had managed Hearst's various feature and syndicate services with skill and profit. Yet he was fired summarily, by the most unusual method the Chief ever used.

Koenigsberg had been awarded the Cross of the Legion of Honor of France early in 1928. Shortly after the announcement was made, an editorial appeared in the Hearst papers denouncing Americans who accepted foreign favors. Along with it was printed a letter from W.R. suggesting that a Hearst man who accepted such a favor would be expected to resign. One paragraph of the letter declared flatly: "I am distinctly and definitely opposed to any representative of our newspapers or news services receiving any decorations or honorariums from a foreign government, except for patriotic service rendered America's allies in the time of war."

There was nothing for Koenigsberg to do but resign, though, as Gauvreau pointed out later, it was no secret that Miss Davies had accepted with gratitude the Award of Merit from the French Dramatic Academy, and it was not returned even after Hearst had added cause to disdain the French when they ejected him from their country a few years later.

It could be said, therefore, that neither long service with him nor long opposition to him was a deciding factor in Hearst's decision to collect or uncollect a man. He was also given to brief love affairs with men who were momentarily of the highest usefulness to him.

One such man was Philip Francis, the Francis whose real name was said to be Diefendorf and who wrote the lead editorials in Hearst's morning papers from 1914 to 1921. Francis was anything but a lovable character. Koenigsberg describes him as "short and squat, with a swarthy complexion, protuberant eyes and saltant gait. . . . Meeting him stirred self-reproach for keeping in mind the picture of a giant toad."

Francis was closer to Hearst, however, than nearly any other man in the organization during those seven war and postwar years. They shared a crusading zeal to keep America out of the war, to encourage Germany and discourage the Allies. Hearst was content to be the champion of America first, but Francis set himself up as the champion of all "oppressed" countries, and his office was likely to be filled with revolutionists from Ireland, Russia, Latin America, the Levant and the Balkans.

During the years of the war, Francis enjoyed the Chief's complete confidence and, more than that, a personal friendship which everyone else found inexplicable. Koenigsberg, who despised Francis, got into an argument with him at the Clarendon one day while both were waiting to see Hearst. Francis went into the presence first, and a little later Hearst sent out a servant to cancel his appointment with Koenigsberg.

The affair went on until the war ended. Then Hearst had no further use for Francis, and he disappeared from the inner circle, retiring in the blaze of a testimonial banquet. Until his death in 1924, he continued to write for the Hearst papers and attained notoriety in other publications by the revelation of a questionable stock-promotion deal he undertook in Mexico.

Always there was one guarantee that could ensure a man's staying collected. If he produced and continued to produce circulation, he would have had to kill a dog or turn out to be a French spy before Hearst would uncollect him.

A case in point is Walter Winchell. As St. Clair McKelway said of the gossiper in his *New Yorker* profile, when Winchell came to the *Mirror* in 1929, he "sent a quiver of vigor through the aging Hearst organization. . . . If he had been an upstart on the *Graphic*, he was an upstart who, with the assistance of Hearst, stayed up."

Winchell was probably the most exotic item the publisher ever collected, and although there was no close personal relationship between them, they remained mutual admirers until the controversial incident of 1939, when the columnist's battle for the interventionists clashed head on with Hearst's isolationism.

Winchell has denied specifically, as recently as December 20, 1951, that Hearst censored his column, then or ever. But there remains the memo from the Chief to all Hearst editors, dated March 28, 1938: "Please edit Winchell very carefully and leave out any dangerous or disagreeable paragraphs. Indeed, leave out the whole column without hesitation, as I think he has gotten so careless that he is no longer of any particular value."

This was not the first time he had warned his editors about Winchell; it was the last and unmistakable command after a series of "recommendations" and "suggestions." The result was the immediate deletion from Winchell's column of all comment on events beyond the limits of Broadway.

On the date the memo was received, the column contained three long paragraphs blasting dictatorships. Six days before, the column had measured twenty-two inches of type in one Hearst paper, seven of them devoted to a condemnation of Hitlerism.

On the day following the order, four inches of anti-Fascist material were chopped from the original wired copy, and in the first four days only two references to the tabooed subject got into Winchell's home paper, the New York *Daily Mirror*, and these were deleted from the wire copy sent by the Hearst syndicate to 125 papers in the United States.

The action bears out Winchell's expressed belief that there were some things Hearst believed in so strongly that he would risk offending his best circulation-getter to defend them. At that time, circulation experts estimated that Winchell accounted for 200,000 of the *Mirror's* 700,000 circulation.

There was little danger of losing Winchell. For one thing, he was tied fast to Hearst by a contract that would have been difficult to break, and highly undesirable to do so because the figures it mentioned were not easily obtainable elsewhere.

In a state of epic frustration, Winchell turned to the most unlikely of alternates, the despised (by Hearst especially) pages of *PM*, Marshall Field's New York tabloid. For *PM* Winchell wrote secretly a column devoted almost entirely to advancing the cause of intervention. The byline he used was Paul Revere II, and the style he employed was sufficiently disguised so that ostensibly the Hearst executives never suspected. Former *PM* editors tell of long telephone conversations with Winchell, in which he bewailed his ties to Hearst and expressed a hitherto concealed passion for joining the forces of good represented by *PM*.

But he did not leave, to no one's surprise, and two years later, on the publisher's seventy-seventh birthday, Hearst devoted part of his column, "In the News," to praise of his wandering gossiper. His great difficulty with columnists, said Hearst, was that they knew too much, and it was hard to confine them "to the work they are engaged to do, or supposed to do." He had argued with Winchell many times on this point, he said, but they were "friendly arguments, of course, because of my admiration for the man and his genius."

As a collector of men, Hearst had his ruthless aspects, but in collecting women, his reverence for the sex made him a far different hobbyist. It was difficult for women to understand the fear in which most men held him, because to them he was always courteous and considerate. In them, undoubtedly, he forever saw the gentle figure of his mother.

Of the women who worked for Hearst and became his friends,

two stand out as examples of his collecting in this field. One is Louella Parsons, the movie-gossip columnist, and the other is Winifred Black Bonfils.

Louella's life was twice nearly ruined inadvertently by Hearst before he made her rich and an intimate. She arrived in Chicago after the first World War, widowed and with a baby to support, and began to work for the *Tribune*. Later, after a brief try at writing scripts for Essanay, she worked for the Chicago *Herald*, and it was there she began turning out a movie-gossip column at forty-five dollars a week. Hers was the first such column in journalism.

The column was a victim when Hearst's *Examiner* killed the *Herald* and left it for dead. Louella went on to New York and sold her idea to the *Telegraph*, where it was immensely successful until Hearst competition killed that paper too. Before its demise, however, Louella saw *When Knighthood Was in Flower*, and reported honestly that she considered Marion Davies a real star. That did it. Through Miss Davies she met Hearst, and soon she was working for him at $250 a week.

Sebastian Flyte, otherwise Speed Lamkin, has disclosed in an eloquent profile of Louella, in the Los Angeles *Examiner* on April 1, 1951, that when the columnist was felled by serious illness, Hearst called her on the telephone and said: "You're discharged, Louella, on full salary, of course, until you're completely well." He insisted on sending her to California until she had recuperated, and when she was ready to come back to New York, he instructed her to stay there. When she protested, "What about my column?" Hearst replied succinctly, "We'll syndicate it."

That was the kind of treatment which commanded in Louella the fierce loyalty demonstrated in the *Citizen Kane* incident. It was the treatment he extended to all women, and to a very few men.

Winifred Bonfils, who began with Hearst and stayed with him until her death, knew what it was to have been collected by him. It filled her with profound gratitude, but also with the knowledge that she had given her life and everything in it to his service.

When she was dying, Hearst's solicitude toward her was like that of a brother. Every hour he sent her warm, encouraging messages designed to cheer her and make her feel his presence though he could not be with her at the moment.

A caller found her in tears, reading one of these messages. They talked for a time of her work on the Hearst papers, of the happy times she had spent at San Simeon with the Chief. As death approached, her mind was full of this man who had so dominated her life, and as the visitor prepared to leave, the woman whom millions had known as Annie Laurie waved with a peculiarly despairing gesture toward her house and what it contained.

"It's all—all Hearst," she murmured.

# CHAPTER NINE

## HOW HE SPENT HIS MONEY

PLENTY OF American millionaires had more money than Hearst, and most of them handled what they had with more wisdom, but none enjoyed his wealth as much. That was because of Hearst's attitude toward money. He did not regard it as invested capital or as an industrial resource. He thought of it with charming simplicity as something to spend.

John Francis Neylan, Hearst's former chief counsel and the man Hearst could thank for preserving a substantial portion of his wealth, took the stand in a stockholders' suit brought against the publisher in 1940 and explained with a clarity that startled the courtroom exactly how his client felt about finances.

"Money as such bores him," Mr. Neylan declared candidly. "His idea of money is that it is something to do something with. He is a builder. He wants to build buildings. He wants to build magazines. He wants to develop ranches. He builds hotels in New York. His idea is to build, build, build all the time. I have said it repeatedly that in his make-up there is just almost a blank space in relation to money."

It was this attitude and the fluidity of his fortune that made Hearst the most extraordinary capitalist of our time. Where men like Ford looked upon capital as something that worked for them, Hearst thought of it as a means of buying things. And where other newspaper entrepreneurs bought newspapers as investments, making careful investigations of their financial health before purchase, he acquired newspapers simply because he wanted them. If they were in a precarious position, he poured in money to make them profitable if he could. If he could not, he carried them at a loss until circumstances compelled him to sell. As *Fortune* phrased it in the famous analysis of 1935, "The core of the Hearst empire is accumulation. . . ." Hearst was not a speculator or a gambler, but neither did he invest.

How much of a beating can a great fortune take under such circumstances? An incredible amount, if it is given a clear start in a pre-income-tax era, and if a giant structure is not subjected to a major depression.

In the early years of the *Examiner* and the *Journal*, Hearst's struggle to establish himself in the newspaper business cost him $1,000,000 a year—of his father's money. As Phebe remarked, at that rate he could have lasted only thirty years. By the turn of the century, he had contrived to rid himself of $8,000,000 in one way or another. His attitude toward money was then no different than it would be in 1940. He owed bills all over New York, and art dealers knew him in those days and later as exasperatingly slow pay. Collectors were forever at his heels.

One of them recalls pursuing him to the railroad station, where Hearst was leaving on a journey. As the collector ran down the long platform toward the departing train, he observed the young publisher standing on the back platform, watching his sprint with evident enjoyment. He raced alongside the slowly moving car and W.R., with a grin, obligingly reached over to take the summons. Whether he had the cash or not, he enjoyed the game.

Harry Coleman, the former Hearst picture executive, recalls how adroitly his employer played this game in the early *Journal* days. "It was nearly always I who was called early in the morning to duck out on Park Row and get the best-equipped cabbie for the Chief when W.R. was ready for his bed in the Hoffman House," Coleman writes. "Sometimes it was necessary for me to get two hacks. I never paid much attention to the first hack because I knew it was intended only as a decoy to hoodwink the herd of insidious individuals who were usually lurking in every doorway along Nassau Street, waiting for an opportunity to pin a summons on the elusive Mr. Hearst. When I arrived in front of the Tribune Building with the first vehicle, a figure in a long coat, wearing a broad-brimmed buckaroo hat, would hurry down the steps and hop in. At that instant, a mob of ambushed process and subpoena servers would dive from their hide-outs and shove their scrolls into the ready paws of 'Hearst,' who was actually Harry Lewis, an artist, or whoever else happened to be handiest in the *Journal* office with a Hearstlike stature. W.R. himself drove off later in peace and safety."

His ventures began to turn the corner about 1904, and for nearly twenty years he made a substantial fortune on his own account. This was considerably augmented in 1919 when Phebe's twenty-two-page will bequeathed him a net estate of about $8,000,000.

By 1922 he was at the peak of his fortunes, with twenty newspapers, Universal Service and INS, King Features, the *American Weekly*, a string of magazines, a newsreel, a motion-picture company, many mines, and an operating capital estimated in the millions.

It was at this stage that he made his nearly fatal mistake. If he had left well enough alone, he might never have been in trouble, but in the San Simeon era of the twenties he spent $35,000,000 on his art collection and bought six more newspaper properties he didn't need. The result was his first financial crisis, in 1924, a crisis which continued in various stages until 1943. It took until that date to pay off in full the $65,000,000 worth of bonds which Hearst had begun to float in 1924 as the means of providing himself with working capital. In a year he had raised $15,000,000 in this manner, and by 1930 the banks, led by Chase National, had floated $60,000,000 in bonds, personally guaranteed by Hearst.

The man who saw to it that Hearst could keep his guarantee, who guided him through the hard times, and who became second-in-command of the empire, was John Francis Neylan, a young Irishman out of Seton Hall College in South Orange, New Jersey, who had departed for the Coast after his graduation, stopped in Arizona for a short time to make a little ready cash as a teamster, and, arriving in San Francisco, got a job from

Fremont Older on the *Bulletin*, where he became a political reporter.

At the state capital, he fell in with Hiram Johnson, who saw in him a man marked for better things, and plucked him from the newspaper business to be chairman of the State Board of Control. As an officeholder, Neylan was a novelty. He was against corruption and didn't care who knew it. A big, aggressive, completely fearless man, he blew through the graft-laden offices of Sacramento like a strong wind, leaving in his wake a debris of jailed, and some unjailed but jobless, public thieves. Before Neylan was through, Johnson was aghast at the powerful force he had unwittingly turned loose, but the state's finances added up correctly for the first time in years.

With this solid background, Neylan came up to San Francisco and turned his talents to the law. He met Hearst in 1919 when, as legal counsel, he arranged W.R.'s purchase of the San Francisco *Call*. The two men liked each other at once. As an Irishman, Neylan began with an advantage, but he also shared Hearst's intense and sometimes unreasoning patriotism; he had no use for foreign entanglements, less use for England, and in domestic policies they saw eye to eye. Both had, at that time, a reputation for being friends of labor, and they were at least nominally Democrats.

Neylan became Hearst's personal lawyer and general counsel for all Hearst enterprises in 1925. It was a significant step. Hearst placed in his friend a trust he had never given to any other man, listened to his advice, even accepted meekly when Neylan said no to something he wished to do—a privilege no one had ever been granted before.

The problem Neylan had with his client was to persuade him to sell something. His holdings had embraced so many unprofitable enterprises that it was costing him more to maintain his properties than they brought in. The situation caused him the kind of pain he felt most—a lack of ready cash.

In such a dilemma, the only satisfactory long-range solution was to permit the public to help carry Hearst's burden, and it was this type of arrangement Neylan made in 1927. To form Hearst Magazines, Inc., he broke off five magazines—*Good Housekeeping, Cosmopolitan, Harper's Bazaar, Motor* and *Motor Boating*—from Hearst Publications, Inc. They were then earning a combined total of $3,500,000 annually. A $10,000,-000 issue of 6 per cent debentures was underwritten by Halsey, Stuart & Co. on the basis of the new company, and Hearst was off to the races once more.

The plan was so successful that in 1930 Neylan was inspired with another scheme, which appeared sound on the surface but created endless trouble later. He planned and carried out the creation of Hearst Consolidated Publications, Inc., which combined W.R.'s six West Coast newspapers with the *American Weekly*, four Eastern newspapers and the American Newsprint Corporation. This in itself was a tacit admission of financial strain, because it meant the public would be invited openly to hold stock in his possessions.

Hearst Consolidated's first move was to give the Star Holding Company, the original Hearst organization, a $50,000,000 note plus all its common stock, amounting to 2,000,000 shares, and then arranged to pay it back by selling 2,000,000 shares of Class A 7 per cent preferred stock at $25 a share. The sale was accomplished by a mighty campaign in the Hearst papers, accompanied by an editorial crusade against phony stock deals.

The Class A stock was non-voting, and perhaps Hearst thought that was sufficient protection from outside meddling, but a clause was included stating that if four successive dividends were passed by the company the board of directors could be voted out by the stockholders and replaced.

To Hearst's and Neylan's credit it must be said that Consolidated paid its dividends at least once a year from 1930 to 1937 and averaged a fat 7 per cent. It can be said further that in the darkness of the depression years Hearst did not default bonds, mortgages, notes or dividends, and although he cut $7,000,000 off his payroll in 1932, by 1935 he had restored it to a level higher than before.

On the other hand, conditions were far from satisfactory in the affairs of Hearst Consolidated. For one thing, there was more water in its structure than it could bear satisfactorily. For another, that hitherto useful device, the Star Holding Corporation, had begun to be a nuisance. Star had been weakened by the creation of Hearst Magazines, since removal of these five money-making properties had broken up the old Hearst Publications, Inc., owned by Star, and when Hearst Consolidated was born, it appeared on the surface that the Star Holding Corporation had been eliminated, since there was nothing left for it to hold. What saved it was the 2,000,000 shares of Consolidated common given to Hearst. This meant that Star really controlled Consolidated, since the common was the only voting stock.

Unfortunately, as a personal holding corporation, Star was highly taxable, and in spite of Hearst's earnest endeavors, the New Deal continued to raise personal income taxes, so that in 1934 it became apparent that a way would have to be found to circumvent them. This was done by converting Star to an organization called American Newspapers, Inc., with Consolidated directly under its control. American Newspapers owned an immediate subsidiary, Hearst Enterprises, Inc., a private clearing house. Through it the ninety Hearst corporations cleared their debts. In 1935, this amounted to about $440,000 every day.

The structure at this point had the appearance of something created by Hearst's old enemy, Samuel Insull. Hearst owned the 10,000 shares of American Newspapers, Inc., which owned all 840,000 shares of the Hearst Corporation, which in turn owned all 2,000,000 shares of Hearst Consolidated common stock as well as Hearst Magazines, Inc. Hearst Enterprises, Inc., acted for all of them as a kind of vast accounting house. The Crocker First National Bank in San Francisco was the financial center of the whole operation, charged with the colossal job of keeping the accounts straight.

American Newspapers was the key to the structure. It was a giant holding corporation worth $197,000,000 in 1935, and about its affairs hung a cloak of mystery never fully penetrated. As Ferdinand Lundberg described it in his analysis, *Imperial Hearst*, it was "a secret chamber." This was so because it was not a public corporation like Hearst Consolidated and published no balance sheet or annual report. Its debits and credits were not indicated by the exhaustive balance sheet *Fortune* magazine drew up in 1935, nor did any of the standard financial reference books throw any light on its status. All that could be said about it with certainty was that it towered over the other eighty-nine Hearst corporations, big and little, some of which were also holding companies, but most of them not. American Newspapers continued to head the empire until December 1943, when its functions were wholly absorbed by the company directly beneath it, the Hearst Corporation.

Meanwhile, the weaknesses of Consolidated were disclosed in 1936 with the publication of a registration statement for $22,600,000 worth of debentures. The statement, required by law, disclosed that between 1924 and 1930 Consolidated had written up the value of tangible assets by nearly $5,000,000, and the intangibles by nearly $60,000,000.

The report disclosed other items likely to frighten stockholders. The reserve held for libel actions, for example, showed a balance of five dollars. At the time there were outstanding suits against the Hearst papers totaling about $6,000,000.

(It may be said in passing that the Hearst newspapers suffered no more than the usual libel actions, considering their number and distribution in large cities. A former Hearst legal expert with no ax to grind declares that the yearly grist of libel actions was normal in chain-newspaper operation.)

Although it was not known to the public at the time, there was cause to worry about Hearst's financial condition outside the affairs of Consolidated. An incident of 1933 showed plainly how far he would go to get ready money when the pinch was on.

In March of that year, he asked a Los Angeles bank for $600,000, offering to put up San Simeon, but the bank holiday intervened and blocked the loan. As it happened, Harry Chandler, publisher of the rival Los Angeles *Times*, was a large stockholder in the bank. He advanced the money and took the mortgage. Chandler's son Norman, who succeeded his father as publisher, granted Hearst several extensions on the loan, though the Hearst liquidators at one point encouraged him to take over the property.

The public found out about this mortgage when the Federal government investigated the bank to which the original loan application had been made. Until that time, Hearst himself had not known that his rival publisher held a mortgage on his property.

Later 165,000 acres of San Simeon property was sold to the United States Government for $2,000,000, leaving 75,000 acres.

There were other signs of imminent collapse in the Hearst empire of 1936 than Consolidated's report. Hearst was carrying far too many losing ventures along with such money-makers as *Good Housekeeping*, the Los Angeles *Examiner* and the *American Weekly*. These three publications showed a combined profit of $6,000,000 in 1934, but the profits of *all* his periodicals in that year were $5,000,000. Eighteen of his papers were known to be losing money in 1935. The New York *American*, which for years had been known as "the vanishing American," in 1935 had vanished to the extent of $1,000,000 for that year alone. Moreover, Hearst held more than 2,000,000 acres of real estate, an appallingly large percentage of which brought him nothing.

Burton Crane, in his analysis of the situation in the New York *Times* after Hearst's death, stated the case succinctly: "The attempt to hold on to everything for the sake of mere size proved unsuccessful." Obviously, the most drastic action was called for.

It was about this time, when the need for operating capital was desperate, that Miss Davies stepped forward and of her own volition offered to lend Hearst $1,000,000, which he accepted with the utmost gratitude.

According to one of her closest friends, Marion made the loan against everybody's advice. People reminded her, "If anything happens to Mr. Hearst where will you be?" Marion's answer was typical of her generous honesty.

"I didn't have anything when I first met him—what's the difference?" she said.

At the time the situation was so desperate that it appeared there would be no difference either way. Hearst seemed certain to go under, his empire tumbling about his ears, and with it would certainly go all of Marion's holdings.

Early in 1937 the climax came with a last-minute attempt to bail out by filing registration statements with the Securities and Exchange Commission for slightly more than $35,000,000 worth of debentures on behalf of Hearst Publications and Hearst Magazines. Under SEC regulations, the Hearst issues were required to be placed on exhibition for twenty days before sale. During this period, the SEC was deluged with protests.

The sharpest of these was filed by Paul Kern, Civil Service Commissioner of New York City, and Bernard Reis, an accountant. Their brief set forth the thesis that when a company sought to get fresh money from the public, stockholders could assume that, if obtained, it would be used to increase the profitable assets. The Hearst registration had been in two parts, one asking $13,000,000 for Hearst Magazines, the other seeking $22,500,000 for Hearst Publications. Kern and Reis charged that nearly all the first amount was to be used "for purposes foreign to the ostensible business of the company." Other parts of the proceeds, it was charged further, were to be used for St. Donat's Castle, and to buy a building from the New York *Journal* for $500,000 higher than its appraisal value so that Hearst Magazines would be relieved of a contract stipulating that it must pay the *Journal's* rent. The brief also asserted that Hearst Magazines' surplus had been seriously depleted by virtue of dividend payments to Hearst in excess of earnings.

Another brief was filed by the Labor Research Association, declaring that "the value of the present securities can be judged only after the financial condition of the parent [companies] has been disclosed." This, of course, was exactly what Hearst had no intention of disclosing.

Even the American Legion, Hearst's ally in chasing Communists, filed a thirty-five-page brief pointing out that a boycott of sorts existed against Hearst, which would limit his expansion, and it asked that the sale of the securities be delayed until the organizations conducting the boycott had been given an opportunity to testify at a public hearing. Other briefs argued that the publisher had suffered heavy losses in fighting strikes on his Seattle and Milwaukee papers and that these threatened the financial stability of the Hearst organization.

Presumably taken aback by the commotion he had stirred up, Hearst hesitated, deferred the effective date of the issues, and in June of 1937 went to New York and there sat down to consult with Clarence John Shearn, his friend and one of his lawyers since 1900. At that time he also represented the Chase National Bank.

What was said between Hearst and Shearn has never been told, but what followed with dramatic suddenness was the only complete surrender in Hearst's long career, and the seriousness of his plight may be measured by the totality of that surrender.

On June 23, the New York *American* folded and lost its identity in the *Journal*. On June 27, it was announced that Shearn had been made sole voting trustee for the next ten years of the 95 per cent of common stock Hearst owned in American Newspapers, Inc. Hearst retained the right to his earnings and to editorial control. The proposed debentures were withdrawn.

The startling move meant that Hearst had turned over the management of all his finances to Shearn, and indirectly to the Chase Bank. He was now to be an employee of his own publications. His salary was cut from $5,000,000 a year to $100,000 as head of Hearst Consolidated.

Shearn, the man who had so abruptly assumed such power, as well as one of the most complicated financial messes in history, was one of the few men in the world Hearst would have trusted with it. He had begun life as a newspaperman, a reporter for the New York *Times*, but almost the first story he wrote brought the paper a libel suit, and in helping to prepare the defense he fell in love with the law and became an attorney. He was the man who had helped Hearst in the legal maneuvers against the coal and food trusts of the nineties, who had written the measures he introduced in Congress, who had gone into politics with Hearst's aid and wound up on the state Supreme Court bench.

As lord high executioner, armed with virtually unlimited authority, Shearn did what Hearst could never do: he sold. The Rochester *Evening Journal* and *Sunday American* went first, on June 30. On July 21 the Washington *Times* was leased to Cissy Patterson, who added it to the *Herald*, which she had leased in April 1937; both were later sold to her. Universal Service was merged with International News Service on August 14; the Pittsburgh *Post-Gazette* was exchanged for the Milwaukee *Sentinel* and $2,750,000 on September 13 in a deal with Paul Block, Hearst's old friend; and on September 28, the Omaha *Bee-News* was sold for $750,000.

There Shearn paused, but only to consolidate his gains. In October he called in seven Hearst executives to aid him and formed them into a kind of supreme council, immediately nicknamed "the Young Turks" in financial circles. They were Thomas J. White, chief of the Hearst organization; Harry M. Bitner, general manager of Hearst newspapers; Richard E. Berlin, publisher of Hearst magazines; Joseph V. Connolly, head of the feature services, wire service and radio; Martin F. Huberth, Hearst's real estate adviser; F. E. Hagelberg, the general auditor; and William Randolph Hearst, Jr.

The announced purpose of the council was to follow a policy of "gradual liquidation as to some of the collateral and unrelated investments. . . ." Shearn had shown the way: the deals he had already made saved $5,000,000 a year. The committee followed his example by disposing of seven radio stations for $1,215,000.

Between 1937 and 1939, the liquidation crew accounted for six newspapers sold or scrapped, one news service and one maga-

zine (*Pictorial Review*) sold or scrapped, and radio stations cut
from ten to three.

But new troubles rose to plague the liquidators, and it was
clear that the end of selling was not yet in sight. Early in 1938
Hearst-Brisbane Properties, Inc., could not make the regular
monthly payments against principal on 6 per cent serial bonds.
The company intended to take advantage of the New York State
mortgage moratorium, it was announced.

As Mr. Crane describes the further misfortunes of the shrink-
ing Hearst empire: "Then Hearst Magazines began having trouble meeting the maturities on bonds, and Herman Place of the
Chase National Bank became virtually the dictator of that big
subsidiary. . . . Troubles piled up. The price of newsprint rose
from $42.50 to $50 a ton, costing the Hearst newspaper empire
five million a year. Advertising revenue dropped 25 per cent,
which meant ten million a year. Mr. Shearn put in . . . Connolly as general manager of all the Hearst papers. Mr. Connolly,
supported by the sole voting trustee, told Hearst publishers to do
their best and make their own decisions. Orders and directives
from 'the Chief' began to be ignored, if only occasionally. Hearst
was out of control of his own empire.

"In 1938 Consolidated managed to pay $1,600,000 against its
funded debt and $600,000 against back taxes, but it passed its
preferred dividend. This was an important matter, because the
Class A shareholders had the right to elect a majority of the
board of directors whenever four quarterly dividends were
passed. The 50,000 small shareholders might take over the best
Hearst newspaper properties if a fourth dividend were passed on
March 15, 1939. The dividends were $2,625,000 in arrears. The
$25 par value stock was selling at $6.25 a share. Somehow Mr.
Shearn found the money. The back dividends were paid. . . .
Despite stockholders' suits—at least one of which resulted in a
fat judgment—the empire weathered the crisis."

It was during this period of trial and tribulation that the Ritz
Tower was sold and soon after the great auctions of Hearst art
took place. Yet in 1939 Hearst still owned twenty daily news-

papers, fifteen Sunday newspapers, twelve magazines, some minor movie interests, three radio stations, King Features, the *American Weekly*, his mines and several assorted properties of varying value.

The stockholder's suit of 1940 provided the public with at least an inkling of what had been going on behind the scenes, and at the same time produced some interesting testimony about Hearst by Mr. Neylan.

Samuel Mann, a Consolidated stockholder since 1931, brought the suit and was joined later by four others. They demanded return of the 2,000,000 shares of Hearst Consolidated common and the $45,000,000 paid for properties taken over by Consolidated in 1930, rescinding of that transfer and the transfer in 1935 of three other properties, with return of the purchase price of more than $8,000,000, and, finally, an accounting and the appointment of a receiver.

When this case was heard in Superior Court, there were more attorneys in court than there were spectators—or at least so it seemed to those innocent bystanders who could qualify as spectators. That was because the assembled counsel represented the interests of no less than thirty-eight defendants—twenty-nine individuals and nine corporations.

A compromise was proposed in the battle, but it was fought by Neylan, whose deposition on the subject required a whole week to read in court. Neylan, who probably had more to do with the actions involved in the litigation than anyone else, asserted that he had devoted "more time and attention and more of my own funds to the protection of the rights of those stockholders than all the gentlemen in this room combined," an argument not many were inclined to dispute. "Forty thousand people put up $45,500,000," he declared further, "and I formed that corporation, and a large part of that stock was sold while I was in it, and I believed in the integrity of the corporation then and I believe in its integrity now. I am going to do my best to see that they get a fair run for their money."

Discussing the question of whether Hearst was worth the
$500,000 annual salary Consolidated paid him, Neylan waxed as
eloquent as was possible for a corporation lawyer. "The man
was at that time one of the greatest geniuses in the history of
journalism," he said. "I think history subsequently vindicated
my judgment because when you boys get up the line here and
find out what happened when they economized on Hearst's salary, you will probably figure that Hearst was cheap at $500,000
a year. It would have been vastly for the advantage of the Class
A stockholders if he had continued to draw his $500,000 a year."

In passing, Mr. Neylan paid his respects to Arthur Brisbane,
who was, he said, "to use the vernacular, all over the place. He
discussed everything, and Mr. Hearst had a great deal of respect
for Brisbane's opinion on journalistic matters. I don't think he
thought much of Brisbane as an analyst of investments or anything of that kind."

This may have been an oblique reference to Brisbane's opposition to Neylan's economy moves in the late twenties, when
Arthur had told Hearst he thought the new head man was an
Irish dreamer who must be insane to think of drawing back and
saving money against future contingencies when everyone knew
the world was moving into a new era so glorious it could hardly
be contemplated. Judging by his experience with the Ritz
Tower, Brisbane took a soberer second view of the new era in
time.

Neylan's version of the organization of Consolidated was that
he meant to give Hearst's ventures an element of "diversified
ownership. . . . When we had put out the original Hearst Publications bonds, and I remember particularly the refunding bonds,
in San Francisco the Anglo-California Trust Company handled
them, and on the day of the issue they asked me to go down there
to talk to their salesmen. And when I was outlining the issue,
the questions asked me by the men were related in the preponder-
ant majority of questions to the continuity of the institution in
the event of Mr. Hearst's death. They were pointing out that

there was sales resistance on account of one man being the directing head and so much of the institution being identified with him solely.

"Of course, Mr. Hearst in his journalistic career has always been an independent. He played the game by himself, and in his innovations he aroused great enmities. He has all the strength that went with a strong figure, and he has the enmities that went with a strong figure. And visualizing the future of that institution, I thought it would be of incalculable value to introduce into it an element of diversified ownership."

Later in his deposition, Mr. Neylan grew almost plaintive in describing the enormity of Hearst's problem. "I don't think any layman appreciates what an important thing to a newspaper enterprise it is to have it in the hands of the people who are thoroughly trained to the newspaper business. In other words, my original thought was to perpetuate the Hearst institution on the idea that it would always be carried on by the people trained in the newspaper business and so on, regardless of what happened."

In the end, however, the plaintiffs were awarded a judgment in a 222-page decision, handed down after fifteen months of trial. So complex were the transactions involved among the numerous corporations in the Hearst empire that even the lawyers were unable to estimate for a time what the award to the stockholders would amount to, but it was in the neighborhood of $1,000,000. Consolidated's stockholders were allowed a recovery against American Newspapers, Inc., while the Hearst Corporation and Hearst himself were allowed the difference between the court's valuation of certain newspaper properties sold and the price paid, with interest set at 7 per cent from time of payment.

Hearst won something of a moral victory, since the court held that none of the transactions of the last decade were to be rescinded. Hearst and everyone else connected with Consolidated, said the court, had acted in good faith and no fraud was involved.

By the time these events were concluded in October 1941, the

United States was on the brink of war. And it was American participation in this war, which Hearst had fought so ardently, that was a powerful factor in rejuvenating his battered interests. While it was on, newspapers had to be reduced in size as their circulations increased. The high taxes on corporations reduced the value of the advertising dollar, and consequently a good many companies invested their money in future good will. It was a highly profitable period, from a business standpoint, for all newspapers.

At the same time, two men were able to speed the rehabilitation process toward a triumphant conclusion. Joe Connolly, who was made president of King Features in 1939, understood perfectly the operation of Hearst journalism from the editorial side, and the help he gave to Shearn offset some of the negative side of the trustee's approach. Then the rehabilitators were fortunate in securing in 1940 the services of John W. Hanes, a Wall Street banker, former Undersecretary of the Treasury and SEC commissioner.

Hanes devoted himself to simplifying the tangled mass of Hearst corporations. His first act was to clear the furniture out of a room in his home and begin making little stacks of papers, one for each corporation. When he finished, he found that there were ninety-four separate corporations, each owing one another and any bank that would loan them money a total debt of $126,000,000.

By 1945, Hanes had reduced the ninety-four to about a dozen, and hoped to wind up with only four. More important, he had paid off all but $4,000,000 of the bank loans.

One morning in 1944, Hanes sent out a master telegram simultaneously to 43,000 stockholders, to prevent speculators from moving in, and was able, by offering the $25 par value instead of the $17 market price, to buy up 730,000 of those troublesome Class A shares in Consolidated.

All told, it was a famous victory. By 1944, Mr. Connolly was able to go back to directing the wire and feature services, Mr. Shearn was relieved of his long task, and a new committee was set up including Huberth, Hanes, and Richard E. Berlin. Hearst resumed control of his empire in most respects, and while he found it reduced, it was still the most substantial operation of its kind in the world, and from 1945 onward its separate parts all made money. The soundness of the structure was reflected in the wise purchase of four Canadian paper mills in 1946 and 1947, at a time when paper costs were threatening profitable newspaper operation everywhere, a threat which continues.

One indication of general prosperity was the fact that Hearst's salary was listed among the ten highest in the United States in the years just before his death. In 1946 it was $233,333, and in the following year it was $300,000.

If there is a moral in the story of Hearst's financial life, it may be this—that you can beat down a great fortune and reduce it to a quivering, apprehensive mass of tangled debts and liabilities, but it may nonetheless survive. The worst that could have happened if there had been no Neylan and Shearn, no management miracles, no rejuvenation, would have been a collapse, staggering to contemplate, that would have reduced a large number of people to comparative poverty—but one that would have left Hearst in such straitened circumstances he would have been compelled to subsist on a bare five or six million dollars.

While that might well have been fatal to a man of Hearst's temperament, it is not the kind of fate that would move other people to sorrow and meditation.

Only a man possessed of Hearst's peculiar attitude toward money, it must be said, could have lived through these vicissitudes with equanimity. It never occurred to him that he would have to live any other way than in the manner he had always lived. His heart disease was caused by old age and not by worry over his accounts. In the face of financial problems that would have driven any other man to an early grave, Hearst was not beset by ulcers or insomnia.

W.R. was a man who put money in its place. He even managed to take some of it with him: his casket was the best that money could buy.

# CHAPTER TEN

## A PORTRAIT OF HEARST
## AS A HUMAN BEING

WILLIAM RANDOLPH HEARST was the China of humanity. His continental mass was imposing, infinitely complex, and nearly impossible to describe. Like the modern Orient, he could be depicted in exactly opposite terms, depending on who did the depicting, and he was as full of paradoxes as a political history. Any kind of definitive summary of him would be likely to end up in a paraphrase of Noel Coward's memorable comment on China, "Very large, Hearst."

Very small, to continue the paraphrase, his effect on other human continents, when the final score was added. Wealth, newspapers, power—in the end their total effect on the rest of humanity was in inverse ratio to their magnitude.

Few people understood how to handle Hearst. It took a man of Winston Churchill's experience and stature to do it without his even realizing it. About 1932, Churchill visited at San Simeon, and after dinner the conversation centered on military strategy, on which Hearst, like Colonel McCormick, fancied himself an authority. Churchill exhibited the consummate tact for which he is famous by permitting himself to be outargued about the Gallipoli campaign. At the end of Hearst's exposition, proving conclusively how different the outcome would have been if Winnie had enjoyed the benefit of W.R.'s advice, Churchill removed his cigar and remarked, as only he could do it, "Mr. Hearst, I believe you're right."

W.R. never looked so gratified. A few days later, to the utter astonishment of veteran Hearst readers, an editorial appeared from the master's hand, arguing for a union of English-speaking peoples.

This story says that Hearst was human. In his lifetime that was difficult for a good many people to believe. Those who experienced his ruthlessness, the idealists who thought him the apotheosis of cynicism, the cynics who were irritated by his unprofitable clinging to strongly held beliefs, and the general public, who regarded him as remote, powerful and unpredictable —all these thought of Hearst as something removed from the race of man.

Yet he was a man like other men. It would be difficult to regard in any other light an individual who was described affectionately and accurately by a friend as looking, "when he walks away from you, like the hind end of an elephant with its pants falling off." He was a big, rather unkempt man, with sloping shoulders and a large head, whose air of controlled power and energy hid a natural shyness and a monumental inferiority complex. He lived all his life in the unreal world of the very rich, yet somehow he retained an engaging quality of folksiness that he displayed to his family and the intimates of the inner circle. He seemed to be afraid to display it anywhere else.

As a boy, he learned at the earliest possible moment how money could be used to smooth out hard pathways. His parents sent him to public school, the North Cosmopolitan Grammar School, with the idea of giving him a democratic education, and there the hard-boiled little savages from the lower classes resented him intensely because he had good clothes, good manners and the affection of his teacher. Willie wanted desperately to belong. In the dangerous, primitive world of children, he recognized himself as an outsider. The other boys intended to beat him up and told him of their intention frequently. Desperately Hearst besought his mother to stop sending the family carriage for him and pleaded with her to sew some patches on his clothes so he would be indistinguishable from the underprivileged. Still the beating impended.

By instinct, one surmises, Willie thought of the solution. He invited the head man of the gang to his house, and there fed him jelly, ice cream and cake, after which the young leader, perceiving he had come upon a good thing, called off his juvenile thugs. If this incident produced a budding cynicism in the active brain of Willie, it is understandable. He saw emotion defeated by the power of money. It was a long time before he was convinced that the coin had another side.

When the boys got to know him, they found the rich kid not as alien as they had supposed. He behaved as all red-blooded American boys are presumed to behave. He led an assault force of compatriots, armed with rocks, on Professor Lunt's Dancing Academy, thus successfully precluding an early entrance into the mysteries of its curriculum. At home he launched a mechanical mouse amid an afternoon gathering of his mother's friends, and occasionally a carefully husbanded specimen of California wild life would be found in his pocket.

The evidence indicates that Willie passed through this stage quickly; it may have been no more than protective coloration in the first place. He discovered literature at Lincoln Grammar School, where he acquired his lifelong fondness for Dickens, particularly *Dombey and Son* and the character of Captain Cuttle. Hearst was always delighted to find a Dickens man on one of his papers.

At about the same time, he discovered the theater, and as an adolescent devotee of San Francisco's thriving stage he saw Edwin Booth's *Hamlet*, Jefferson's *Rip Van Winkle* and Clara Norris in *Camille*, which made so profound an impression on him that the camellia was thereafter his favorite flower; the garden at San Simeon was resplendent with them.

The theater inspired him to return to Professor Lunt and learn dancing. He proved to be good at it, and enjoyed it so much that he was the beau of the ball in the gay New York days. Veteran musicians recall playing for private parties which would have ended long before daylight if Hearst had not kept on slipping large bills to the orchestra and twirling about the floor, often outlasting every other male.

From the standpoint of personality development, it can be seen that he was rather more normal at this stage than other rich boys, and at the same time he had developed a cultural appreciation lacking in most youngsters his age, rich or poor. In his brief year at St. Paul's, this pattern persisted. On the side of normalcy, he hated compulsory chapel, and he captained the baseball team. On the side of the unusual, he sent the following desperate, precocious telegram to his Eastern guardian, who had failed to reply promptly to a self-invitation for the holidays: "For God's sake, please ask me to New York."

Willie's complete departure from normalcy occurred when he went to Harvard. Of the many personalities Harvard has sheltered who failed to fit into the Cambridge mold, Hearst must have been near the top of the list.

One biographer, John Winkler, describes him in this period as "a slender shoot of a fellow whose sandy hair was parted in the middle and who wore a tie of Harvard crimson." His other ties foreshadowed the extremities of the surrealist school, and his clothes were of a dudish Piccadilly cut. It was the one time in his life that he paid much attention to what he wore; in later years only his valet saved him from disreputability. He would never have had his shoes shined if left to himself.

Phebe came with her son to Cambridge when he entered and saw to it that he was established in quarters befitting him. She surveyed his modest apartment in Matthews Hall with distaste and sent out immediately for the decorators to do it over. A library was built into the walls, and new mahogany tables were equipped with Harvard-red enameled smoking sets.

In these luxuriously remodeled precincts, Will Hearst entertained his friends. The proportion of entertainment to learning was not a tribute to scholarship. To supplement the ordinary diversions of student life, Will offered something of a road show in himself. He sang, plucked the banjo, tapped out a neat buck-and-wing, did imitations and comic dialect routines, and played practical jokes. He was much in demand for smokers, week ends in Boston and Hasty Pudding Club plays.

The stories told of W.R. at Harvard well illustrate the prime aspects of his unfolding personality. One concerns his rescue of the *Lampoon*, campus humor magazine, whose staff boasted such lights as Owen Wister and George Santayana. A distinguished but perennially unprofitable venture, the *Lampoon* was drifting toward extinction under the direction of Hearst's boyhood friend, Eugene Lent, when Will arrived at Harvard, and for the sake of Lent, or maybe just for the hell of it, took over as business manager.

For what happened next we have the word of two authorities who were never found in agreement again, Santayana and Hearst. The philosopher wrote in 1901: "The business editor alone took a serious, responsible view of the situation. The rest of us cultivated a philosophic disbelief in Space and Time." Hearst wrote in a report to his mother in 1885: "We took up the *Lampoon* when the subscription list numbered three hundred. Nine hundred dollars a year came from subscribers and three hundred a year from ads, making a grand total of twelve hundred. As it takes fourteen hundred to run the thing, we scoured the country for ads. We ransacked the college for subscriptions. In fact, we infused energy into the *Lampoon*, and now we stand on a firm basis with a subscription list of 450 with $900 in advertising, making a grand total of $2250 and leaving a profit of $650 after the debt is paid."

The way Hearst accomplished this miracle was a preliminary exercise in the uses of wealth applied to journalism. With his virtually unlimited allowance he roamed through the shops of Cambridge and Boston, buying clothes, haberdashery and porcelains for his collection, vastly pleasing the shopkeepers, who were then solicited for advertising while they were in a kindly mood. The important thing was to get advertisers, he believed, and it mattered little how much per head it cost to get them. But he went out after new business, too, with student solicitors, and applied in embryonic form the high-pressure tactics he used later.

Hearst contributed nothing editorially to the *Lampoon* except some anonymous comic poems and a few sketches. But he entertained lavishly in his rooms at midnight suppers, where guests had to be careful not to sit on his pet alligator; officiated as vice-president of the baseball team; and collected first editions. Once he wired hastily to his father for three thousand dollars to buy a choice copy of the *Federalist Papers*. His friends were fellow Californians, most of them rich men's sons, whose energies were devoted largely to drinking and hell-raising. Willie drank only an occasional beer, but otherwise he led the pack.

Scholastically, as Mrs. Older herself admits, he "majored in jokes, pranks and sociability." With one of the finest university faculties ever assembled available for his education, Hearst was always on the verge of flunking out. He excelled only in the history of fine arts, under Charles Eliot Norton, but that was natural, with the background Phebe had given him. He did fairly well also in German, English and geology, but in other fields he refused to use his brain. He could have stood near the top of his class, but he had been conditioned against learning and scholarship; consequently he dropped such subjects as philosophy, Latin and Greek, on the ground that they were not useful things to know—and this in an era when the classical education was considered essential to an educated man.

Nevertheless, he would probably have survived until graduation if it had not been for the celebrated practical joke that resulted in his banishment. His quarrel with the faculty had been a fairly constant one. They had not appreciated the indecorous cartoons of them appearing in the *Lampoon*. Nor had they been gratified by the frivolity Hearst arranged to celebrate Cleveland's election, which had tied up traffic with a parade and made the night sleepless with fireworks and revelry. For this he was rusticated, along with another ringleader, as noted elsewhere.

Not many months later came the incident which led to his expulsion, an elaborate hoax in which messengers delivered to a selected list of eminent faculty members a package containing a Christmas present for them—hand-painted chamber pots with their pictures pasted on the bottom inside. Hearst was not ordinarily given to scatological humor, but the implication was sufficiently plain to preclude his graduation. As Mrs. Older puts it with consummate delicacy, "But Harvard was no more for Will Hearst. . . . Before he took his degree he left Cambridge never to return. . . ."

When he took over the *Examiner* and became a publisher, he put the ways of youth behind him to a large extent, but the ways departed reluctantly and there were a good many loose ends dangling from his maturity.

Winkler, whose biography seems to display the human side of Hearst better than others, describes some of these loose ends as follows: "On one occasion he dragged one of his editors out to North Beach to see a monkey which would turn somersaults for peanuts. On another he fed an ostrich in Golden Gate Park a dozen oranges just to see how funny its neck looked with three or four oranges slowly following each other down its throat, plainly indicated by the bulges visible outside. The oranges being disposed of, he offered the bird the keys on his key-ring, one at a time. The ostrich swallowed the keys with relish and Hearst was in no whit disturbed by their loss."

Still another childhood trait that lasted most of his life was an inordinate fondness for fruit and candy. In the early *Examiner* days, he could be seen eating from a five-pound box of chocolates as he walked down the street, or with a pie in one hand and a jelly roll in the other, sampling each in alternation. At the theater he would dash out during intermission for a sack of candy as others would for a drink or a cigarette. These strolling-and-eating excursions customarily ended with Hearst presenting his unfinished candy or cake to the first group of children he happened to meet.

Winkler describes Hearst in his early twenties, as he began his career with the *Examiner*, as "tall, easy-moving, with pale blue eyes, of gentle, almost shy manner and pleasant smile." From that time until his marriage he was much the same kind of person.

He loved parties and good company; descending on New York in the giddy nineties, he found both. The *Journal* took most of his time, but not all of it. First-nighters saw him with fair regularity, and he appeared at Delmonico's, Jack's and the other haunts of society and theatrical folk. He also frequented the art galleries, and gave gay parties at the Hoffman House.

At the *Journal* he was still one of the boys, as he had been on the *Examiner*. He made up the first edition every night and consequently knew all the composing-room men by their given names. He spent the rest of the time in the city room and became as much a fixture there as the copy boys. In those days he was so approachable that those who worked with him constantly dared to call him simply "the Chief" to his face and "W.R." behind his back.

They were encouraged in such intimacy by the fact that Hearst not only worked along with them at their elbows, but when the last edition was put to bed, adjourned with them to the plant's restaurant, and there consumed one of his favorite foods, hot dogs well splattered with mustard. He had these sent up to the office frequently and sat quietly munching, editing with his free hand.

But as he plunged more deeply into politics and the creation of a newspaper empire, he began slowly and steadily to withdraw into the great role for which he had cast himself. The change could be seen in what he wore. He had discarded English clothes soon after Harvard, because further examination of the British scene on his whirlwind trips abroad had convinced him that he was being snubbed. His biographers, Carlson and Bates, record that "the whole country seemed to him a kind of Harvard on a large scale and with more rigorous laws. On one occasion he is said to have been arrested for some minor escapade [this is highly doubtful] and to have been much irritated by the London bobby's strange insensitiveness to offers that any New York policeman would have welcomed with alacrity."

Whatever happened to him in England, he hated the country and dropped its tailoring, its accent, which he had affected at Harvard, and some of the polite mannerisms that had been imported to San Francisco. In New York he emerged into a thoroughly American period, which went through varying phases but remained always 100 per cent American.

Around the turn of the century, Hearst customarily wore the straw hat and checked suit of the well-dressed sport, and the chromatic neckwear he had never wholly deserted. In his ties he often wore a pin made from the first twenty-dollar gold piece passed in trade over the counter of the *Examiner*—his version of, "I've got the first dollar I ever made framed on the wall right over there."

This sartorial phase was succeeded by the sober attire ushered in simultaneously with his election to Congress and his marriage. When he appeared in Washington, and when he was campaigning, he wore the conventional long frock coat, high collar, string tie and soft black hat of the congressman. More protective coloration, perhaps. In New York, with his wife, he discarded some of his louder effects, probably at Millicent's suggestion, and dressed the part of the conservative businessman. After 1912 that was his habitual dress, except for the casual clothes—loose jackets, open shirts and flannels—he lived in at San Simeon and the other California dream castles.

Marriage changed more than Hearst's clothes. As has happened to millions of other men, it sobered his tastes and brought out in him a rich vein of sentimentality that had been obscured before by his boyish pranks, his loud clothes, his gay life and his feverish devotion to getting his newspapers established.

Now, at Christmas 1903, it was possible to see W.R. for the first time in his famous impersonation of Santa Claus, a role he repeated until there were no more children to delight in it. The 1903 performance was for his wife's small cousins, but the following year his own first-born, George, named for the Senator, joined the throng marveling at how the good Saint could find his way to Lexington Avenue and Twenty-eighth Street and burst right into Chester Arthur's living room, sounding his bells like a convention of Swiss bell ringers.

Hearst viewed with a cold distaste those cynics who informed his children that there was no Santa Claus. As the first three boys grew up in the Clarendon, he tried to preserve their faith in the Saint as long as possible, and when reality set in, he gave them little moral lectures on the spirit of Christmas. Blessed with a father of Hearst's prodigality, it would not have been surprising if the boys had *never* stopped believing in Santa Claus.

Toward his family Hearst showed his simplest, least complicated side. With them he was so unlike the man he appeared to his editors and other associates that it must have been incomprehensible to Millicent and the boys when they read how he was regarded by those who feared or hated him, or who depended on him more than they wished was necessary. This is a common enough phenomenon, of course. American business and public life is full of those who are ruthless, hard and cynical in the office, but at night are transformed into gentle family men.

Hearst simply repeated history. Like the Senator, he was an indulgent father, and he deeply loved children, any children, especially his own. They made him frankly and unashamedly a man of sentiment.

Both he and Phebe had wanted a girl. Millicent's feelings in this matter are not recorded, but apparently she was content to have produced five sons. Before the twins were born in 1916, the last of the brood, Phebe had asked that the expected arrival be named for her, but Hearst had to wire: "Sorry, neither of the boys can be named Phebe."

Probably the last time the family was gathered at Christmas time in the old manner occurred in 1925, at the still uncompleted San Simeon. The Hearsts were more or less separated by that time, but for the sake of the children, appearances were maintained as far as possible. On this Christmas they made an occasion of it, because it was the first meal served in the new palace, in which electric lights had not yet been installed. Huge logs were placed in the carved sixteenth-century French fireplace, two Christmas trees were set up in honor of the twins, and the family gathered in the Great Hall for Christmas Eve dinner. Afterward, Hearst excused himself and soon Santa Claus did a reprise, more believable than any of the others because the enormous chimney could have accommodated eight reindeer without much trouble.

By this time the boys were in school, and the Hearsts, at opposite sides of the continent, exchanged notes about their progress, which never seemed to be satisfactory. They were chips off their father's scholastic block—indifferent if not actually antagonistic to learning, in and out of schools, until the family gave up. Millicent was concerned about this state of affairs, but Hearst was always indulgent, proud that they were so much like him.

An early letter in 1923 is typical of the period of sweetness and light. It begins affectionately, "Dear Millie," and goes on: "Aren't these two lovely letters from these two kids? [William Jr. and Randolph.] I almost cried over them. It is wonderful to think they have such high purposes and such good views. It shows they had a good mother anyway. W.R."

A few years later, the tone is quite different but the attitude is the same. Beginning more formally, "Dear Millicent," Hearst writes: "I have read the master's letter about Randolph, and I suppose David, too. There is nothing very surprising in this. These boys are simply behaving as the others did. We may not approve of their behavior, but it is characteristic of the clan.

"They do not take kindly to education. This is probably a defect, but Brisbane says, 'It takes a good mind to resist education.' Anyway, a certain kind of good mind does resist education. The boys seem to have active and independent mentalities, and perhaps are cut out to be good businessmen. I wish they would learn something, but apparently they will not. It is not the fault of the school. We used to think it was. We sent John and William to various schools. The lack of result was always the same. They [the twins] are simply more or less untamed and untamable."

Toward the boys themselves, Hearst was his most natural self, and they idolized him. In 1932, he sent David this wire in response to a birthday present: "Gosh! Those were swell ties. I can now burst into bloom, just like the flowers in the garden. How's everything? Love, Pop." A simultaneous wire to Randolph read: "Thanks a lot for the handkerchiefs. They are pippins. I am going to catch cold, so I can wave them around and show everybody. Love, Pop."

The boys grew up at San Simeon and Wyntoon, as much as anywhere, and consequently they were able to swim and play tennis and ride with their father, as rich boys whose fathers are largely preoccupied with business never have the opportunity to do. The close relationship, therefore, lasted into their maturity, and until Hearst's death they exchanged affectionate letters.

In 1942, for example, Hearst saw by accident a communication in which Bill Jr.'s secretary remarked that he, meaning W.R., "does not know me from Adam." The expression piqued his humor, and he wrote her a gently kidding letter beginning, "I do know you and I DO know Adam." It went on in a rambling, whimsical fashion, as the old man speculated on Adam's life in the Garden, and then went on to Noah, whom he termed the "greatest boat builder of his generation . . . the Henry J. Kaiser of his day," and it wound up like a Hearst editorial: "The peccadillos of our estimable ancestors should be overlooked, and we should consider the outstanding fact that if it were not for the advanced ideas and radical innovations of these progressive and open-minded ancestors of ours, not one of us would be here today, and the demand for Oregon apples and California wines would not be as widespread as it is. Iconoclastic descendants should realize these fundamental facts and desist from disparaging criticism."

He signed the letter, "Bill's Pop."

Sending a copy of it to his son, he added this thoroughly characteristic note, written exactly like one of his newspaper columns:

I wrote your secretary, Miss Ruman, a little letter kidding her about Adam.

She thought I did not know about him or about her.

But I DO.

Of course, I know a little more about Adam.

His life has been an "open book" as it were.

For a couple of million years he has had no more privacy than a goldfish—which must have been embarrassing before the fig leaf era.

His romance with Eve had been related at length in many volumes.

You have probably read something about it—I hope.

He and Eve left the Garden after they had been married and went out into the world to seek their fortunes.

They "lived happily ever after" no doubt, although their children gave them a good deal of trouble—most everybody's children do.

What else can you expect?

Yes, I think I may say that I knew Adam well.

He was about my age—at any rate it seems like that sometimes.

However, he is dead now, poor fellow.

I suppose you have heard about that, anyhow.

Or maybe you did not even know he was sick.

The rising degeneration does not seem to be greatly interested in us older folk.

It is discouraging.

I do not know exactly where to send the letter to Miss Ruman, so I am enclosing it to you.

Affectionately, Pop.

More than he believed in anything else, perhaps, Hearst believed in his sons. Not that he had any illusions about their widely varying abilities or their personal peccadilloes. He was as much a realist about these as he was about his own. But he believed in the bond between them, in the strong, continuous flow of "family" from the Senator and Phebe to him and to his sons. It was faith in the clan, in "our kind," as he expressed it more than once.

In the matter of religious faith, he felt as strongly as he did about the boys, but it was a subject he refused to discuss except on the rarest occasions. Those who saw the court life at San Simeon, or heard about it, or who knew Hearst only through his public life, refused to believe that he had any religion at all.

Others believed him a devout Catholic, and this was one of the many rumors widely circulated about Hearst which became an accepted part of the legend.

Neither idea had any validity. His excessive shyness prevented him from talking about so personal a matter, but he was religious in a fundamental sense, not a churchly one. He knew the Bible and biblical history well; a copy of the Book was always in his bedroom, according to his wife. He had a collection of Bibles —naturally, one of the best held by a private collector.

Mrs. Older relates that once, when Hearst was ill, a friend calling on him saw an embossed prayer on the table and re-marked, "No one should die without a prayer on his lips."

"No one should *live* without a prayer on his lips," Hearst is said to have answered.

The story that he was a Catholic had its origin in fact. He was brought up in his childhood as a Presbyterian, Phebe's faith, but his nurse, Eliza Pike, an ardent Catholic, was so anxious about the state of his soul that one day, when Phebe was away for the afternoon, she hustled Sonny to her parish priest and had him baptized in the Faith. When Phebe reminded her that the boy was still a Presbyterian, the nurse replied with dignity, "No matter, madam, the baby is a Christian!"

Unperturbed, Phebe sent him to the Presbyterian Sunday school, which he loved no more than other small boys. By the time he went to St. Paul's he had gravitated to the Episcopal Church, to which he belonged until his death.

When his son, Bill Jr., was only a year old, Hearst had an experience which nearly converted him to Christian Science. The infant had contracted pneumonia and was near death when Morrill Goddard's wife, a devoted Scientist, recommended the treatments of her faith. In time he recovered.

The grateful father was not quite converted by the experi-ence, but it made a deep impression on him, and his publications were always friendly to Christian Science. *McClure's* magazine attacked the church, and Hearst assigned Brisbane to write a series of articles in defense of Mary Baker Eddy, who was so pleased with the result that at her death Brisbane was the only one of her pallbearers not a Christian Scientist. Hearst himself, at this early period in his life, frequently accepted the aid of Science and declared it helped him.

However, the mysticism in Hearst responded most readily to Catholicism. He loved the pageantry and symbolic ritual of the Church, so much of which was represented in his art collection. Every Pope from Pius IX gave him the papal blessing, but his favorite of all the Popes was Leo XIII, who reminded him of an alabaster statue.

The Church was always grateful for his strong support of the Irish, his vigorous opposition to Communism and his interest in preserving Spanish cultural relics, but it is believed that because of his personal life it could give him no special favors beyond the papal blessing. A story circulated in 1949 that Pope Pius XII had conferred the Lateran Cross and the order of a Knight of St. Sylvester upon him, and the Vatican took special pains to deny it through a Secretariat of State broadcast over the Vatican radio. It was declared that the Moscow radio had spread the report, basing it on the presentation of a simple medal by the canons of the Basilica of St. John Lateran in Rome. The broadcast noted significantly: "Mr. Hearst has never received, and it is not foreseen that he can have, any papal honor."

Family and faith—these were the human sides of Hearst's character that were obscured by his highly debatable public life. They were the sides of this complex man that only those closest to him ever saw.

Another aspect in the same vein, but well publicized, was his love of animals. Dogs were by far his favorites, as his lifelong fight against vivisection testified, but he had a protective feeling for all animals, and in fact for anything, dog or human, that suffered persecution—unless it happened to be one of his own editors or someone who opposed him personally.

Charles Edward Russell was not exaggerating in that part of the highly biased tribute he paid his boss in *Harper's* for May 1904 when he wrote: "I once saw this even-poised, self-contained man thrash a Naples cabman for beating a horse, and once, with a dangerous glitter in his eyes, face down a crowd of Apulian peasants that he thought were maltreating an unfortunate man. Often I have seen him stop in the street and turn to watch out of sight a limping horse, a stray dog, or a man in trouble. . . ."

Cynics and non-dog lovers remained unmoved, but those who knew him best accepted it as one of Hearst's really sincere statements, and a revealing one, when he mourned publicly over the death of a dog in his column, "In The News," in the spring of 1942. Answering a letter of sympathy from his friend Frank Barham, of the Los Angeles *Herald-Express,* Hearst wrote in part:

"You know, Frank, a boy and his dog are no more inseparable companions than an old fellow and his dog. To his dog he is just as good as he ever was—maybe better because he is more appreciative of the dog's devotion. Anyhow, the dog and the old guy understand each other and get along 'just swell.' So I do miss Helen. I was very fond of her.

"She always slept in a big chair in my room and her solicitous gaze followed me to bed at night and was the first thing to greet me when I woke in the morning. Then when I arose she begged me for the special distinction of being put in my bed, and there she lay in luxurious enjoyment of the proud privilege until I was ready to leave. . . . Who could fail to be won by so much care and conscientious concern—so much attention and affection?

"Aldous Huxley says: 'Every dog thinks its master Napoleon, hence the popularity of dogs.' That is not the strict truth. Every dog adores its master notwithstanding the master's imperfections, of which it is probably acutely aware. And its master, unless he is lower in the animal scale than the dog, responds to such devotion. . . . So as your dog loves you, you come to love your dog. Not because it thinks you are Napoleon, not because YOU think you are Napoleon. Not because you WANT to be Napoleon. But because love creates love, devotion inspires devotion, unselfishness begets unselfishness and self-sacrifice, and that fact is more than a commendable quality in the animal kingdom. It is the eventual hope of humanity.

"Helen died in my bed and in my arms. I have buried her on the hillside overlooking the green lawn—where she used to run—and surrounded by the flowers. I will not need a monument to remember her. But I am placing over her little grave a stone with the inscription—'Here lies dearest Helen—my devoted friend.'"

Whatever a psychoanalyst might make of it, Hearst's love of animals was one of the few real constants in his life. Even in the hectic days of establishing the San Francisco *Examiner* he once sent his power launch, the *Aquila*, from his Sausalito Beach place at midnight to bring a veterinarian from the city so that a guinea pig's broken leg might be set, at a cost of five hundred dollars. In those days, too, Hearst would drop everything to attend circuses, which he loved. And there was no more frequent visitor at the zoo than W.R.

At San Simeon he made a pet of a spotted deer named Bessie, who had the run of the place. Mrs. Older recalls, too, the advent of Diana, the seal, who "waddled up to the warehouses and decided to adopt the ranch as her home," which pleased Hearst so much that he "abandoned national and international interests, and set his mind to work on Diana's future. By telephone he ordered a shelter to be made for her so that daily she might be fed fresh fish, and at the same time have a daily plunge in the Pacific. Soon Diana became so tame that she tried to live in the house of her keeper."

Walter Howey, the veteran Hearst editor, in the days when he was in his prime as editor of the Chicago *Herald and Examiner*, got a telegram from Hearst one day, dispatched at Dodge City, Kansas, where the train had paused briefly en route from New York to San Francisco, bearing W.R. and ten-year-old Bill Jr. As an old Hearst man, Howey was not astounded by the wire's contents: "In a box-car near a water tank about a mile west of Kansas City is a bawling, black and white spotted calf. Bill wants the darned thing."

Howey knew what to do. He instructed the paper's Kansas City man to buy the calf and send it to Phebe's ranch. Some doubt exists as to whether it was Senior or Junior who wanted the calf most. In any event, it lived at San Simeon until it died.

When it was a choice between animals and men, Hearst invariably put the animals first. At San Simeon he kept distinguished guests waiting at dinner for an hour while he sat with a dying dog. The death of a dog depressed him so much that he was unapproachable for days. On another occasion, at Wyntoon, a gathering of motion-picture, publishing and oil executives was kept waiting while Hearst cared personally for a new pet, a desert lizard named Clarence, who had just been bereft of a tail section.

Hearst, then, was a man who loved animals and children and revered his mother. What was hard for those who opposed him to understand was how a man with these sterling qualities could be, at the same time, so completely callous in other areas of human conduct. It is an ancient paradox. Without drawing invidious comparisons, it is safe to say that some of the greatest scoundrels in history loved their mothers and were kind to their dogs.

The Hearst described thus far is the same Hearst who inspired such dread of his despotism that executives on his papers feared every telegram that came from him, and feared most the wire that told them they were fired, the customary Hearstian method of dismissal. There is the wry story, perhaps apocryphal in fact but not in spirit, of the editor who returned from lunch and saw a telegram on his desk. Opening it in a cold trembling of anxiety, his glad cries of relief brought his secretary running. "It's all right, Miss Jones," the relieved one is said to have told her. "My father is dead!"

II

At San Simeon in the twenties, Hearst reached what might be called the full flowering of his personality. The personal political and journalistic struggles of the past were behind him;

the financial and physical troubles of the thirties and forties had not yet begun. He was at his peak.

Reporters traveling to San Simeon from the San Francisco and Los Angeles papers were sharply reminded of the truly stupendous difference between the world in which Hearst lived and the one his wage slaves inhabited. They stared at the curtained projection room, the maroon and gold-leaf swimming pool, and the baronial dining room with its long row of monks' praying stalls along the wall.

A reporter could think upon these things as he lay in an antique bed and contemplated a fabulously expensive gold-leaf ceiling. When he was permitted to stay overnight, and thus see the master at play, he hardly knew what to think. One reporter recalls a night—this in the later years—when Hearst, proceeding from the projection room after viewing a picture starring a favorite, Gene Tierney, paused at the billiard table and seized a cue. He aimed a half-serious shot and watched it slide away miserably. Embarrassed, he flung the cue down and moved off in melancholy to the elevator, and so to bed.

Visitors were constantly aware of his presence. He never appeared for breakfast, which he ate in his room, but his arrival for one o'clock lunch was heralded by a series of messages flashing through the establishment, made necessary because he liked to have his food ready for him precisely when he was ready for it. The girl at the palace switchboard maintained a liaison with the kitchen so that this co-ordination customarily functioned perfectly.

He was inclined to indulge sudden whims at the expense of guests. There was a period when Russian shirts were required for all male guests, not because of any sympathy for the Soviets but because Hearst was possessed of a sudden conviction that male clothing had become drab and offensive. Men arriving for the week end found themselves provided with three satin Cossack blouses—one red, one white, one black—designed to meet every occasion, both formal and informal. The blouses were not suggested; they were required.

A frequent visitor who knew Hearst well in the San Simeon days believes that this sense of power, in little as well as large matters, was the key factor in Hearst's personality. He knew about people en masse largely through the thousands of begging letters he got from them, as is the common experience of rich men. He may have sympathized with them in his cosmic yet personal way, but he felt himself removed from them. Consequently it was entirely logical that he should preach a public morality, yet think of himself as above the law, which applied to other, lesser mortals. Once a print shop in Oakland, about to print a biography of Hearst which he had reason to believe would be scurrilous, was visited by men who announced themselves as detectives and proceeded to take the shop apart, spilling the type out of the cases and ruining it. The printer had no recourse. It was well known in California that the entire judicial process in the state, from police courts to the upper benches, was highly sensitive to word from San Simeon.

This gulf between Hearst and other people could sometimes be observed by those who talked with him, finding him an excellent listener up to the point where he was no longer interested in what was being said. That point was usually reached when he had made up his mind on a subject. Then his pale blue-gray eyes became clouded and remote, and the visitor was uncomfortably aware that W.R. was not listening. Often he followed such a withdrawal by excusing himself briefly and leaving the room, after which a servant would appear and announce that Mr. Hearst had been called away by an urgent matter, asked the pardon of his guests, and hoped he would see them again soon. The latter phrase could be construed to mean years, or never.

His way of living at San Simeon and elsewhere reflected this trait of paying attention only to what interested him at the moment. His routine was haphazard. He wrote letters as he was moved to it, and he frequently failed to keep appointments. His day began ordinarily at ten or eleven in the morning and ended at two or three o'clock the next morning. The time in between might be occupied with eight hours or more of steady work, or he might let everything else go and pursue one of the several sports he enjoyed. For a man who could afford anything, these were surprisingly simple. There was, of course, a time when he spent a large share of his leisure moments on his 220-foot yacht, the *Oneida*, which had a large projection room on it for the inevitable evening movies. But mostly he liked to play tennis, ride, swim and walk. Golf never interested him, and driving, until he was old, was just a means of getting from one point to another. He was expert with a gun, either revolver or rifle. It amused him to surprise guests on the *Oneida* by knocking down a sea gull with a quick hip shot.

Another of his favorite diversions was window shopping, and he spent hours in New York prowling about bookstores, art galleries and antique shops.

At the San Simeon parties, Hearst was always somewhat aloof. Bridge bored him, but he liked to kibitz, a doubtful art at which he was adept. His guests were disconcerted enough to find him peering intently over their shoulders, but they were left in a state of exasperated awe when he remarked abruptly, "If I were you, I'd play that and that and that"—and prove to be absolutely right.

Those who were often in his presence say that he had an innate courtesy about him, even when he was angry. He never flew off in a yelling rage; his anger was cold and deadly. But he picked up every slightest remark. If someone he trusted remarked casually that a certain Hearst executive ought to do some particular thing about his publication, it was investigated at once.

He hated being thanked for anything he gave, but he loved to get small gifts, like candy, and opened the packages with all the delight of a child.

His behavior at social functions outside San Simeon, says Winkler, was not impressive. Apparently describing an actual occasion, he notes that Hearst "tosses his big, unfashionable ulster upon the floor of the entrance hall, remarking: 'Some one may find this useful to sit upon.' A dozen times or so in the next hour or two he jumps up to offer his place to an arrival, man or woman. He accepts a plate of salad and a glass of champagne. Few notice that he merely nibbles at the food and touches the wine not at all.

"People are brought up and introduced to the big man in the loose-hanging dress-suit. Hearst extends a flaccid hand in welcome, tucks in his long legs and does his best to produce some small talk. He doesn't succeed overly well, so he helps the waiters serve and threshes about making himself useful as assistant major-domo. A pudgy gentleman thanks him for the support the Hearst papers are affording in some matter of public moment and asks him to keep on the good work. Hearst emits his low, cold chuckle and replies: 'I am not so certain my support will prove an asset, Senator. You know there are a lot of people in this country who don't like me.' Later he retrieves his ulster and drifts through the doorway, leaving no consciousness of vacuity behind."

Those who viewed Hearst far from his native habitat were more likely to be impressed by his personality, and oddly, English writers provided some of his best notices. One of these came from Sir Hall Caine, who talked to him in 1922 on his last visit to England and the Continent with his wife. The three oldest boys and some Los Angeles friends went with them. The Hearsts were entertained at 10 Downing Street by Lloyd George and his daughter Megan, week-ended at Leatherhead, in the Surrey hills, with Lord Beaverbrook, and saw the sights.

The English reporters were shocked when told that he hadn't planned to attend the Derby because he cared nothing for the races. He recalled going to the Derby another year just to see the crowds and the spectacle itself. Departing before the big race of the day started, he left behind him gaping people on the sidewalks who had asked him eagerly who the winner was. They stared at his answer: "I didn't wait to find out."

Caine found him in a communicative mood. Prepared not to like the man who wrote so harshly of England, the British novelist wrote this description: "The personality of William Randolph

Hearst is a staggering surprise. Seen at close quarters across the width of a table, it gives the lie direct to nearly every preconceived idea that has been formed of his life.

"He is a tall, powerfully built man who must, one would say, have spent many of his early years in a health-giving life of open air. His face is large and strong. In repose, he is intensely serious. In conversation it is lit up by a smile of extraordinary winsomeness and even charm. His voice is soft and almost gentle. There is no excess of emphasis, no violence and no vehemence. His manner is pleasant and conciliatory. When strong opinions are expressed, they are put forward without any suggestion of infallibility of judgment. 'Well, yes, that is my opinion,' is a phrase frequently on his lips. . . . His speech and his movements are almost leisurely. There is nothing of the political fanatic about him, and nothing of the revolutionary. If his convictions are deep, they make no noise—in conversation at all events. If he has prejudices, he must reserve them for the press."

It would be hard to imagine what Caine would have considered a prejudice, because in return for this pleasant impression Hearst informed him that he considered England's policies misguided and accused the Empire of attempting to interfere in American affairs, citing the attempt to cancel war debts as a horrible example.

Whenever he was abroad, Hearst was inclined to dramatize himself, a tendency best illustrated by the case of his expulsion from France. This incident occurred in the summer of 1930, at the conclusion of a Hearstian gesture, in which he had simply gathered up a large party of friends and editors and taken them abroad for a holiday. The junketers stopped first in London, then Paris, and late in July entrained for Bad Nauheim in Germany, where Hearst intended to take the cure. This he did for a month, following with extreme care the prescription of baths and waters. When the doctors told him he should take an additional month of rest as an after-cure, he decided to return to Paris to the bucolic quiet of the Crillon. Hearst's idea of resting was to immure himself in a large foreign hotel.

On the way to Paris, he stopped at Frankfurt, where a reporter from the *Frankfurter Zeitung* interviewed him. He seized
the occasion to denounce the Versailles Treaty, which made him
more popular than ever in Germany. Apparently, however, it
called his presence to the attention of the French Government,
who waited only until the day of his arrival at the Crillon to send
around some officers from the Sûreté to tell him he was requested
to leave the country in no later than four days, and advise him
he was not to return unless given specific permission.

Hearst took the attitude that he was being expelled for the
Frankfurt interview, but he must have known that the reason
the French gave was the correct one. The government's version
was that two years before, Hearst's Paris correspondent, Harold J. T. Horan, had obtained by the customary Hearst means
a secret document detailing a naval agreement then being nego-
tiated between France and England, in contradiction of the
American Government's official position on naval disarmament.
Hearst looked upon this as exposure of foreign intrigue against
America. The French thought of it as none of his business. They
exiled Horan, and when the opportunity presented itself, they
banished Hearst.

Nothing could have pleased him more. He announced dramatically to Coblentz, Willicombe and Harry Crocker, who were
with him, that he would take the first train out of the country,
and presently they were all standing on a platform at the Gare
du Nord, while Hearst stalked up and down in high excitement,
eating peaches. In the compartment of the boat train, he wrote
in pencil his story of the whole affair, preserving dignity by
treating the French Government as an indulgent mother would
an erring child.

The expulsion created a considerable stir both in England
and in America, as Hearst knew it would. In London, crowds
welcomed him and he was treated to banquets. Back home, he
was met at the pier by politicians anxious to take a stand, delegations of war veterans, and a thousand or so curious onlookers.

He made a triumphal procession to California, stopping in Boston on the way as a guest of honor at the city's tercentennial celebration, and in Chicago, where he was banqueted once more. At home again, San Francisco, Oakland and Los Angeles turned out in his honor.

Speaking on the radio for the first time, on the National Broadcasting Company's network, he needled the Hoover Administration for not doing anything about the violation of his passport rights, and made an issue out of the acceptance by Americans of a foreign decoration—France's Legion of Honor.

He loved every minute of it, right down to the last hammy farewell to the affair on October 18, when he told an Oakland audience: "Now I am going to board a train and go down to my ranch and find my little hideaway on my little hilltop at San Simeon and look down on the blue sea, and up at the blue sky, and bask in the glorious sunshine of the greatest State of the greatest nation in the whole world. You know, my friends, it is about time I finished my Nauheim cure."

Drama in life appealed to Hearst even more than it entranced him on the stage, which may explain in part his perennial fascination with the flying machine. He flew as early as 1910 in a Blériot monoplane with Louis Paulhan, only a few years after the Wright Brothers' flight. That historic event had inspired him to have the *Examiner* sponsor a so-called "international aviation meet," to which Paulhan had contributed his services.

When the Frenchman offered to take him up, Hearst never hesitated. One of his attributes was an absolute lack of fear. He pulled on a heavy woolen cap, and the little monoplane took off toward the ocean from the Los Angeles field where the meet was held. When they returned, with Hearst half frozen from the cold upper air, he was so excited by the experience that he immediately offered a $50,000 prize for a coast-to-coast flight.

His interest was unflagging from that time onward. He was given various awards for his efforts in behalf of aviation, was elected an honorary member of the Aeronautic Society of New

York, and in 1929 was a heavy financial backer of the *Graf Zeppelin's* world tour. The big dirigible gave San Simeon a graceful aerial salute as it passed over.

Hearst never learned to fly, but he had the most intense admiration for those who did. His regard for Lindbergh led him to one of the frustrating episodes of his life, in which the man who cared less for money than any rich man found himself amazed by a disregard for money in someone else. He wanted "to do something substantial" for Lindy, like making him "independent for life." The rest of this illuminating story is told in W.R.'s own words, as related in a signed editorial on February 20, 1934:

"My moving picture company was associated with Metro-Goldwyn-Mayer at the time, and together these companies made a proposition to Mr. Lindbergh that he make on the screen the story of his interesting and inspiring young life. The compensation was to be $500,000 cash and a percentage of the profits of this picture.

"When Mr. Lindbergh came to my house in New York I brought out the contract, all signed and sealed and ready to deliver, except for his signature, and presented it to him.

"He smiled pleasantly as he read it, and then said: 'That is very fine and I appreciate it, but I cannot do it.'

"I naturally asked why, and he said: 'You know, I said I did not intend to go into moving pictures.'

"I tried to argue with him. I said: 'This is not a moving picture in the ordinary sense of the word. It is not a fiction story. It is the real story of your life, a thing that the President of the United States ought to be glad to have done for him. It is an historical record of a fine life and a great achievement to be preserved in pictures for others to see in years to come. Do not consider it as a benefit to yourself, but as an inspiration to others.'

"Young Mr. Lindbergh shook his head and said: 'I wish I could do it if it would please you, but I cannot, because I SAID I WOULD NOT GO INTO PICTURES.'

"I said: 'All right—but you tear up the contract; I have not the heart to do it.'

"And he stood there in front of the fireplace in my room and tore up half a million dollars and threw it into the fire."

Lindbergh was obviously a man after W.R.'s heart.

W.R., however, was not in his own person everybody's cup of tea. Ilka Chase, who saw him only briefly and had no reason to dislike him, found him "alarming." He scared her to death, she reports, "especially in the swimming pool, where he looked like an octopus. One day he dived in and came up quite near me, and the sight of his long head with the white hair plastered down over his brow by the water, and his strange light eyes gleaming on a level with my own, sent me thrashing to the far end of the pool."

Miss Chase remembers that one night after dinner she came upon Hearst and E. B. Hatrick, one of his executives, in a shadowy end of the dining room she had thought deserted. They were discussing a song Hearst wanted for a motion picture he was producing, and she overheard Hatrick saying, "I'm afraid, Mr. Hearst, we won't be able to get the rights," and Hearst answering in his high, thin voice, "Well, I'm afraid that will be regrettable."

Miss Chase adds: "I cannot describe the chill which went through me as I heard it. There was something so sinister in that light tone, and the pale, gleaming eyes. One thought involuntarily of the dark rumors which swirled about his name, of the ruthless qualities attributed to him. Woo! I scuttled back and gulped some champagne."

He seemed even more inexplicable to her when she brought her mother, Edna Woolman Chase, the distinguished editor of *Vogue*, to visit for the week end. Both women expected that Hearst would make some effort to lure Mrs. Chase to his rival *Harper's Bazaar*, since he had taken more than one editor from the Condé Nast staff and still had not succeeded in successfully rivaling *Vogue*.

They arrived in the afternoon, when there was no opportunity for conversation. Expecting to converse at dinner, they gathered in the Great Hall at the designated time with only four other persons besides Hearst and Marion. As the oldest woman present, and the guest of honor, Mrs. Chase moved toward Hearst's right, but discovered that Marion's hairdresser and another woman were placed at the host's right and left, leaving her somewhere down the table.

"What I'm dying to know," said Mrs. Chase, comparing notes after dinner, "is whether it was malice or just an original form of *Bazaar* etiquette."

They never found out. For three days they stayed at San Simeon, and Mrs. Chase never sat at her host's right and never talked with him about anything except California as she walked the terrace with him. The battle of the women's fashion magazines was not mentioned once.

In the later years at San Simeon, despite the financial problems that beset him, Hearst appeared to be given more than ever to sudden impulses and whimseys. Perhaps it was a sign of age. For example, he made the headlines in October 1935 with the announcement that he intended to close up San Simeon and live in New York, as a protest against high taxes. Louella Parsons predicted in her column that a good many Californians of wealth and prominence could be expected to follow him.

He was in New York a month, but no startling exodus of Californians occurred, the income tax laws remained unchanged, no further mention of his plight was made in the papers, and he returned to San Simeon in time for Christmas.

When he went to Wyntoon, Hearst was often moved to poetry. The beauty of the place, and his love for it, impelled him to make the attempt, though he was aware that poetry was not his genius. He wrote lyrical praises of nature, like *The Spell of the Woods*, which ran in his column in May 1940. It began:

> I am the forest of fir and pine,
> Shadow and silence and peace are mine.

Mine are the springs and the rills and brooks,
Which, rising in quiet hidden nooks,
Join hands with the river and joyously flow
To the widespread plains which lie below . . .

Occasionally the muse tickled him with an old piece of dog-
gerel and he tossed off something gay like *Ronda—A Spanish
Song*, columnized in December 1940. It went like this:

Did you ever have breakfast at Ronda
At the Fonda
De Cadiz?
Did you ever have coffee more creamy,
Hot and steamy,
Than that is?
You're a practiced and persistent eater—
Did you ever have ham that was sweeter,
Or bread that was whiter,
Or rolls that were lighter?

And seventeen more lines of culinary notes, interspersed with
memories "of the rapturous hours, 'Mid the scent-freighted
flowers, As the moonlight gleamed over the water, That I spent
with the innkeeper's daughter."

The best known of Hearst's poetical works was the one
widely reprinted after his death, called *The Song of the River*,
in which he appeared to look death in the face and discount it,
contrary to legend. The poem was written at Wyntoon and was
inspired by Hearst's contemplation of the turbulent stream rush-
ing by his lodge, forming the headwaters of the Sacramento
River. He handed the poem to his friend Fremont Older at dinner one night, with an awkward, shy gesture, and asked him
brusquely to read it and tell him whether he liked it.

Whatever Older's real opinion may have been—and there is
no reason to believe he *didn't* like it—he was enthusiastic about
the poem and printed it in the *Call-Bulletin*, where its appearance caused a small sensation, with its strange (for Hearst)
query:

> So why prize life,
> Or why fear death,
> Or dread what is to be?

And its almost defiant ending:

> So don't ask why we live or die,
> Or whither, or when, we go,
> Or wonder about the mysteries
> That only God may know.

A few years after these lines were written, the personality that was Hearst began to shrink, like his physical figure, into a shadow of the robust years before. The heart attack of 1947 ended his tennis. His walks were confined to short strolls in the garden of the Beverly Hills house. Motoring, which he had once disdained, was now a primary recreation, and once or twice a week he was bundled into one of his long black Buick sedans and taken for a drive into the country. He longed to get back to San Simeon, and even paid $85,000 for a herd of fifty Arabian horses he hoped personally to see installed at the "ranch." That hope was never gratified.

The man who had judged other men from an Olympian height was himself about to be judged.

# CHAPTER ELEVEN

## HOW IT ALL ENDED

"I DIDN'T KNOW for a minute he was dead," said the nurse who was with William Randolph Hearst when he died. "When I realized he was, I tried to ring or find a bell or something. I was new to the house and I couldn't find any way of letting people know downstairs."

In the room where death had come and gone so quietly, events began to move with bewildering speed. There was a brief period of confusion as the throat doctor arrived, too late to help, and then others: Richard E. Berlin, the top Hearst executive; Charles Lederer, Miss Davies' nephew; Bill Hearst Jr.; and Dr. Elliot Corday, Dr. Prinzmetal's assistant. Bill Jr. and his brother David had been in the guesthouse, presumably with Berlin. Lederer, who lived nearby, had been called immediately.

Berlin took charge. He was heard to say to the servants and the nurses, "You're all working for me now." Within ten minutes he began to carry out a plan which had been conceived in 1947, when Hearst had his first heart attack and the inevitable had to be faced. The plan had been perfected in the months before his death, so that now it operated with professional precision.

Pierce Brothers, undertakers in Beverly Hills, got the call for which they had long been waiting. Their hearse rolled up to the house through gates which were now suddenly unguarded, and going inside, they found Berlin, the doctors and the servants. They took Hearst's body away.

During the four hours needed to complete the embalming process, two of Hearst's servants guarded him even in death from anyone who might try to see him without an appointment. The mortician was instructed to proceed as fast as the law and his skill allowed. One of the firm complained afterward, "Nobody would tell me anything. I couldn't even find out whether they wanted flowers or anything. I had a hard time making out the death certificate."

When the embalming was finished, they placed the body, looking absurdly small and slight and not at all like the big, robust man who had inhabited it, into the finest copper casket money could buy, the kind that could easily cost as much as $20,000. Hearst was dressed in a suit of dark blue worsted. He wore a monogrammed shirt with cuff links. His blue tie carried a simple pink-and-blue design—the family coat of arms.

He had been dead only a little more than four hours when the casket, wrapped in a blanket, was loaded into a closed hearse and driven to Lockheed International Airport, where the long black car proceeded mysteriously into a private hangar, whose big doors were shut and locked behind it. Inside, the casket was carried to a plane belonging to a commercial pilot and loaded aboard. Four of the Hearst sons followed it, the hangar doors were opened again, and the plane taxied directly out to a runway, where it took off at once for San Francisco.

Back at the Beverly Hills house, it was nearly eleven o'clock, more than an hour after Hearst died, before Miss Davies could be roused from the deep sleep into which exhaustion and sedatives had dropped her. She put on a robe and came down to the bedroom where W.R. had died.

Of her emotions at that moment, she said later: "He was gone. I asked where he was and the nurse said he was dead. His body was gone, whoosh, like that. I didn't even know whether he was dead when they took him. Old W.R. was gone, the boys were gone. I was alone. They didn't even let me say good-by. Do you realize what they did? They stole a possession of mine. He belonged to me. I loved him for thirty-two years and now he was gone. Yes, I couldn't even say good-by."

That night, as Marion sat with her close friend, Constance

Talmadge, the telephone rang. It was Bill Jr. calling from San Francisco, the first word she had heard from the family. Marion described the conversation to Miss Talmadge and another friend: "I asked him when the services would be. I said, 'Look, you wouldn't let me say good-by to him. At least you can tell me when the services will be, so I can pray for him down here.' He said that the whole thing was up to his mother. I found out about the funeral by reading the paper the next morning."

She added: "I will never understand this if I live to be a thousand years. I couldn't believe they would do this to me," and she began to sing in a half whisper, "Little old lady in a big red room, little old lady in a big red room"—aimless words to a wandering tune no one recognized.

There was no lack of sympathy for her. Telegrams lay in huge piles, waiting for her to read them. Friends came hurrying to console her: Cobina Wright, carrying her poodle; Hedda Hopper, Eileen Ruby, Ann Shirley, Speed Lamkin, Rose Davies, Lederer and his wife; her niece Pat and Arthur "Dagwood" Lake, her niece's husband. The wires were from such personages as General and Mrs. Douglas MacArthur, Doris Duke, Joan Crawford, Herbert Bayard Swope and the Huntington Hartfords. There were more than three hundred in the first batch.

Although she had it in abundance, Marion did not ask for pity, nor did she indulge in recriminations or passionate dramatics. She behaved with a simple dignity that impressed and moved everyone who saw her. All that she felt was summed up in her wistful comment, "For thirty-two years I had him, and they leave me with his empty room."

In San Francisco, Mrs. Hearst had arrived by plane, and after some discussion it was decided to have a large, formal funeral. The undertakers in charge of it were N. Gray & Co., a century-old firm that had buried Phebe Hearst, besides a long list of notables, including Warren Harding and Hiram Johnson. Their men took Hearst's body to the dim recesses of the Chapel of Grace in Grace Episcopal Cathedral on Nob Hill, and there it lay for nearly two days in state.

W.R. had come to rest at last, only a few blocks from the house in which he was born. The first school he attended was nearby, and so was the office of the San Francisco *Examiner*. Roses covered the base of the casket, piled to cover the sides, and a glass window was provided for those who wanted to view him for the last time.

There were hundreds who wished to do so. They did not form long lines outside, as they might have for a movie star, but there was always a small crowd in the chapel—some friends, more acquaintances, and many of the merely curious who apparently wanted to look upon the man who had immured himself in splendor on a mountaintop in his lifetime and could be seen only by the privileged.

The curious appeared to be disappointed. One woman muttered, "Why, he looks just like anybody's grandfather." In the serene, waxen countenance that stared back at the viewers there was nothing to suggest the tremendous power of Hearst's living personality.

Meanwhile the flowers, more than three hundred pieces, overflowed the chapel. With a nice feeling for what the old man would have liked, the *Examiner* sent an American flag done in flowers, the stars made of forty-eight gardenias, the stripes fashioned of red and white carnations, and more gardenias forming a flagpole.

On the day of the funeral, fifteen hundred people filled the cathedral, five hundred stood through the ceremony, and a thousand more packed the street outside. The family, the honorary pallbearers and the press gathered. Among the mourners were veteran Hearst editors like Howey and Gortatowsky; veteran Hearst writers like Gene Fowler, Adela Rogers St. John, Cobina Wright, Sr., and Louella Parsons; dignitaries like Hugh Baillie, president of the United Press; Robert Gordon Sproul, president of the University of California; L. B. Mayer, the movie magnate; and L. M. Giannini, president of the Bank of America.

Governor Earl Warren, who had interrupted a Santa Monica vacation, led the honorary pallbearers, along with Mayor Elmer

E. Robinson of San Francisco. The list was as distinguished as though Hearst had been the President he wanted to be: Herbert Hoover, Bernard Baruch, Roy Howard, Colonel Robert R. McCormick, Mrs. Ogden Reid, Arthur Hays Sulzberger, Mrs. Older, General MacArthur, James W. Gerard, John N. Garner and others—most but not all of them friends to him and his philosophy when he was alive.

The service, from the Book of Common Prayer, lasted only thirty minutes, and there was neither eulogy nor sermon. The Right Reverend Karl Morgan Block, Episcopal Bishop of California, took for his lesson the fifteenth chapter of the First Epistle of St. Paul to the Corinthians, which tells of the resurrection of the dead and contains the verses, "O death, where is thy sting? O grave, where is thy victory?" The cathedral organist played Bach and César Franck, the men's chorus sang Malotte's setting of the Lord's Prayer, and the full chorus sang Dvořák's arrangement of the Twenty-third Psalm. In accordance with the liturgy, Hearst's name was not mentioned during the service.

When it was over, the police made a path for the mourners as they came out into the bright sunshine of California Street, and as a motorcycle escort of nineteen policemen led the way and at least one person fainted in the huge crowd, the cortege of twenty-two limousines started on its ten-mile journey to Cypress Lawn Cemetery in Colma.

The Hearst mausoleum is built like a Greek temple, atop a grassy knoll, surrounded by trees that W.R. loved—Japanese plums and Australian silk oaks. It is a fashionable part of a fashionable cemetery. Near it lie the Spreckleses, the Matsons and the pioneers of other old San Francisco families. Senator Hearst built the tomb in 1908, and conscious of recent disaster, he ordered it made earthquake-proof. The Senator lies at the bottom of a two-level space built to contain a dozen bodies. Phebe is on the next elevation. Her son was placed above her.

At the mausoleum, the committal service took only fifteen minutes. Bishop Block read the church's service, then Hearst's poem, *The Song of the River*.

While this was occurring, there was another funeral taking place in the cemetery. By a final curious irony, Hearst, the foe of capital punishment, was being buried simultaneously with a wife-murderer who had been electrocuted at San Quentin Prison that morning.

But W.R. was far beyond these earthly quarrels now. He did not even care that when the family and the pallbearers had paid their last respects and departed, the waiting crowd descended on the magnificent piles of flowers like a flock of birds and stripped the wreaths and decorations of their orchids and roses.

Far away, in Beverly Hills, Miss Davies had risen at ten-thirty after a restless night. A few minutes before the services were to begin, at 11 A.M., she took Hearst's little dachshund, Helena, and retired to her room. Before she went, she told a nurse: "I had thought I might go to church this morning, but I will just stay here alone. He knew how I felt about him and I know how he felt about me. There is no need for dramatics." And while the events of the funeral were taking place, she and Helena sat quietly together in the dimness of her room and thought of the past.

Thus, on a note of momentary anticlimax, the saga of William Randolph Hearst neared an end.

But it was only momentary. A few hours after he died, the 125 typewritten pages which constituted his will were filed for probate in Superior Court, done so hastily, the lawyers explained, that the empire might continue operating without interruption.

On the surface, the will contained no difficulties. It provided for the setting up of three trusts to divide an estate estimated unofficially at nearly $400,000,000. One, for his wife, was to contain $6,000,000 worth of Hearst Corporation preferred, the income from this sum to be hers, besides an outright bequest of $1,500,000 cash to pay the taxes that would be due on the stock. The second trust was to be for the benefit of his sons and contained enough additional preferred stock in the corporation to provide an annual $150,000 which the sons might add to their already high incomes as Hearst executives. Into this trust also went a hundred shares of Hearst Corporation common, probably a controlling interest.

The remainder, a residuary trust, was to be for the usual "charitable, scientific, educational and public purposes." In the will, Hearst directed that a memorial be built to his "beloved mother" which would contain at least part of his art treasures, "for the public enjoyment." He directed further that the beneficiaries of this trust should be the Los Angeles Museum, which had already been given more than $3,000,000 worth of art from his collection; the University of California, also a beneficiary while he was still alive; and the California Charities Foundation, a philanthropic organization he had set up previously. Into this foundation were to go the furniture, paintings, statuary and objects of art from Wyntoon, San Simeon and St. Donat's Castle.

The sons were named as trustees of all three trusts. As executors of the will, Hearst had selected Howey, Berlin, Huberth; William Baskervill, of his Baltimore *News-Post;* Harold Kern, of the Boston *Record and American;* Richard Carrington, Jr., of the Los Angeles *Examiner;* William Curley, of the New York *Journal-American;* and Henry S. MacKay, Jr., his personal lawyer.

There was a typical Hearst clause in the will. His acquisitive spirit lingered after death in these words: "I request my executors and trustees . . . not to part with the ownership or control of any newspaper, magazine, feature service, news service, photographic service or periodical, either directly or by sale, or by exchange of the capital stock . . . unless it shall, in their opinion, be necessary or prudent to do so."

By far the most important and interesting part of the will, however, was its nine codicils, running to sixty-eight pages of the manuscript. All but three were revoked in the final wording of the will, but their effect was, first of all, to change an original trust arrangement which would have provided a single family trust in which Mrs. Hearst and the five sons would have shared. The first codicil would have given Marion the Beverly Hills home, but it was canceled by one dated a year later, meaning simply that she had been given the home under another arrangement.

It was the provisions for Marion, not in the will or its codicils, which precipitated a legal quarrel that for a time threatened to turn the Hearst private life into a courtroom drama.

A trust fund dated November 5, 1950, had given her a lifetime income from 30,000 shares of Hearst Corporation preferred, the principal to revert to the sons upon her death. This was acceptable enough, but a few days after Hearst's death, attorneys presented to his executors a document which more than made up for Marion's omission from the will. It was a voting trust agreement, stipulating that Miss Davies was to have sole voting power in the Hearst Corporation. The agreement pooled her 30,000 shares of preferred with the 170,000 shares owned by Hearst.

There was an immediate and peremptory response from the executors: "This document was never executed and therefore might just as well have never existed."

On second thought, however, it was apparent that if a fight ensued the document might stand up in court. It had been the last of Hearst's shrewd acts and, as the estate's lawyers undoubtedly thought, the shrewdest.

The story of the voting trust agreement goes back to October 1950. It was then that Hearst began to be afraid Marion might be "pushed around," in the words of one close to him, after he died. To avoid that contingency, he instructed his attorneys to construct the agreement under the flexible laws of Delaware, where his interests had been originally incorporated. He meant it to enable Miss Davies to continue what would certainly have been a benevolent influence over his publishing empire.

While the agreement meant nothing more financially for Marion, it did give her firm control of his interests, which would endure for ten years or for life, whatever the Delaware courts might decide. Flights of lawyers descended on both sides, and it appeared that a long and possibly acrimonious legal battle might develop. "Do you know, in spite of all the years my father was a judge, I've never been in court," Marion remarked. "I don't like the idea of a fight. I'm not the fighting type. This is not very pleasant for me and I don't know what's going to happen, but I don't believe in disregarding W.R.'s wishes."

W.R. had certainly been clear enough on that momentous night of November 5, 1950, when he called one of his doctors and said, "I'd like you to come over and see me if you can. I want to discuss something with you."

Twenty minutes later the doctor was taken into Hearst's bedroom, where he found Lederer and the attorney, Gregson Bautzer. He witnessed the signing of the agreement which coupled the trust fund with the voting trust agreement. As Miss Davies recalled her part in the ceremony, "I was called to W.R.'s room. He said, 'I want you to sign this agreement.' We had talked it over many times and I knew what was in the agreement. I said, 'Do you want me to do this?' He said, 'I most definitely do.' So I signed it."

Explaining the purpose of the agreement later, she said: "He had a reason for having this agreement drawn up. I figure it this way: he thought I was the one who understood best what his policies and principles were and that I could see to it that his ideas were carried out. There was no money attached to it at all." And she added, "Gosh, I thought I'd have a peaceful time in my old age. Now, look at the spot I'm in."

The Hearst executors were in a worse spot. They could not attack the voting agreement with public dignity by charging W.R. with incompetency, nor by claiming undue influence. They could only hope to find a technical flaw. Obviously a compromise was called for.

Both sides had talking points. Mrs. Hearst's lawyers could, if they wished, file a community property suit. In the last codicil, Hearst had admitted in effect that he was without resources and had been saved by Marion's million-dollar loan in 1937. Since under California law a man cannot give away community property, anything he had accumulated since 1937 could be considered such property. What he had accumulated or inherited before and presumably dissipated was assumed to be his separate estate and not subject to community property laws.

On the other hand, Miss Davies' lawyers had consulted John Hanes, the New York corporation lawyer who had done so much to straighten out Hearst's tangled affairs, and Hanes had examined the voting trust agreement with trust specialists. He gave his opinion that the agreement was not testamentary in nature, and therefore was not covered by the laws concerning wills; it could not be attacked, he believed, except on grounds of incompetency. No one seriously believed that the executors would go so far as to discredit the Chief's good name.

While the outcome was awaited with anticipation in some quarters and dismay in others, the lawyers shuttled back and forth among the fifteen individuals and the representatives of two corporations who had to agree on a compromise. Describing these negotiations, Mr. Bautzer later remarked, "Whenever our discussions concerning this compromise got rough, I suggested one thing: remember the memory of the man by whose accomplishments you all gain. It turned out to be one of those compromises lawyers can sometimes bring off objectively."

It was finally effected, and a joint announcement designed to pour oil in every direction was issued. The statement blandly declared that, "despite the numerous stories that have been printed since the late Mr. Hearst's death indicating dissension between Miss Davies, the voting trustees now serving as such and the Hearst estate, there has in fact been no conflict between them and all questions as to their respective interests have been the subject of amicable discussion and have all been amicably resolved. . . .

"Miss Davies has relinquished all rights she may have to act as voting trustee for the stock of the Hearst Corporation for the reason, among others, that there is question as to when her right to act as voting trustee thereunder would commence. This question would have to be clarified by long court proceedings which all parties deemed unnecessary and undesirable.

"Miss Davies has every faith in the intentions and abilities of Mr. Hearst's sons and the other directors and executives of the Hearst enterprises to insure the continuity of Mr. Hearst's editorial policies, the furtherance of which would have been Miss Davies' only purpose in serving as a trustee.

"Although a great deal of Miss Davies' time is devoted to her private interests and her numerous activities in charitable enterprises, through which she has become well known and well loved, the most prominent of which is the Marion Davies Foundation's children's clinic which has served approximately 12,000 children a year for the last fifteen years, Miss Davies will continue to render services in her capacity as official consultant and adviser to the Hearst Corporation and the newspapers and magazines which it publishes. Such services will include advice on motion picture and other amusement activities."

Not introduced into this atmosphere of sweetness and light, but reliably reported to be a part of the compromise agreement, was the granting to the executors of full rights to Miss Davies' life story, in which case, Marion had said earlier, she would never write her autobiography at all. At least the executors could be sure it would never be written for the duration of the agreement, though if it had been, it could be nothing but a loving and respectful portrait of W.R.

On the Sunday night that the compromise was signed, Marion was entertaining a few friends in the green-walled powder room at Beverly Hills, sitting with informal state in a green easy chair. A portrait of her white poodle, Snowball, hung over the chair. She was wearing black lounging pajamas and a pink scarf. To some of those present she looked many years younger, relaxed and charming as always, her long blonde hair rippling down to her shoulders. Her image was reflected again and again in the mirrored doors of the powder room.

At her feet on the familiar white rug sat an old and good friend, Sonja Henie. They talked amiably while her future was being settled in the law offices. She had not met with any of W.R.'s sons or his executives, nor had she even heard from them personally. Momentarily she must have felt isolated. Even the Los Angeles Hearst papers, which had been delivered every day by messenger while the old man was alive, had stopped abruptly on the day he died.

Shortly before eleven o'clock the telephone rang. It was her nephew, Lederer, telling her the compromise agreement had been signed by everyone concerned. Marion began to cry softly. "Thank God it's all over," she said. "Thank you, Charlie, thank you. I'm so happy it's over, so happy."

Hanging up, she went back to the easy chair and sprawled out in it. "Well, I've sold my power for a dollar a year," she said. "Maybe I was wrong, but it's all over."

An hour later, as she stepped into the elevator next to the powder room, she said in farewell to a lingering guest, "Now I can take one last look at this house and go away."

Few people knew how far away she meant to go, in spirit as well as in person. On October 31, she married Captain Horace G. Brown, Jr., a Merchant Marine captain who had once been a cop in Richmond, Virginia. The ceremony took place at El Rancho Vegas, in Las Vegas, Nevada. His second wife, Grace Tibbett, had formerly been the wife of Hearst's great favorite, Lawrence Tibbett.

Marion and her captain had arrived by plane at 2:50 A.M., taken out a license at Las Vegas' ever-ready marriage bureau, which is open twenty-four hours a day, and been married in one of the ranch's bungalows shortly afterward. For the ceremony, Miss Davies wore a blue sweater, dark blue slacks, and blue suède leather slippers, dark glasses and a tan camel-hair coat. At the bureau, she had given her real name, Marion Cecilia Douras, and said she was forty-five, although her birth date in the World Almanac is listed, probably accurately, as 1897.

The newlyweds enjoyed a wedding breakfast of champagne, turkey sandwiches, coffeecake and beer, and departed for a Palm Springs honeymoon in a chartered plane. "I'm so proud of my wonderful family," said the new Mrs. Brown.

The bridegroom beamed. He bore a remarkable resemblance to Hearst, as W.R. looked in his younger days.

II

With these loose ends neatly tied up, the saga of William Randolph Hearst came to an oddly quiet conclusion as the Browns floated off toward the Pacific in a pinkish haze.

There remained only one question to be answered. What did it all mean? And some corollary questions: Would Hearst go down in history as a leader of the masses or their seducer? Was he one of the great figures of his time or a man magnified by money far beyond his true importance?

History had already returned a verdict as far as some professional historians were concerned. In 1936, Allan Nevins of Columbia, who can certainly be accounted among the best in the nation, wrote in the *Saturday Review of Literature* that he thought Hearst was one of the unhappiest figures in American journalism, and predicted he would be remembered "only as a curious and transient phenomenon." A few years later the equally distinguished Henry Steele Commager wrote in *The American Mind* that "Hearst and his chain represented all that was most sinister [in modern journalism]. . . . His debauchery of the public taste worked incalculable harm."

These judgments are confirmed by other professionals. A survey of modern histories of the United States shows that Hearst is not even cited in many of them, and in others is mentioned only for his part in precipitating the Spanish-American War and for giving the phrase "yellow journalism" to the language.

But if Hearst is worth no more than a few lines in the history books, there has been an entirely disproportionate amount of attention devoted to him since 1936, beginning with the three biographies published in that year.

That the viewpoint of those who have judged Hearst was almost entirely conditioned by the social and political outlook of the judgers is shown by the manner in which these biographies were reviewed. *Editor and Publisher*, the newspaper trade journal, which is never more than mildly critical of publishers, gave Mrs. Older's biography an enthusiastic send-off but was unkind to Ferdinand Lundberg's strongly anti-Hearst book and the Oliver Carlson-Earnest Bates collaboration, which was nearer to center. The left-wing magazines, *Nation* and *New Republic*, were on exactly the opposite side of the fence. The same division was discernible in the reviews given the books by metropolitan dailies. One of the few middle-grounders, Frank Luther Mott, dean of journalism teachers, asserted in a judicious appraisal of all the Hearst biographies, including John Winkler's earlier effort, that it was necessary to read all four to get a fair idea of the man.

The battle lines were sharply drawn in the forewords to the books themselves. Charles A. Beard's preface to the Lundberg biography was a bitter, partisan attack, hardly recognizable as coming from a scholarly historian. It may have been a response in part to the barrage directed against him for some time by the Hearst papers. A few years later, Hearst and Dr. Beard were allied in belief if not otherwise in their ardent advocacy of isolationism and the philosophy of the "revisionist" school of recent history.

Fremont Older's preface to his wife's biography, on the other hand, was wholly admiring. Thus, Dr. Beard's harsh estimate that Hearst would depart "loved by few and respected by none whose respect is worthy of respect" could be balanced with Older's belief that his Chief's activities would "constitute a history of the reform movement in America."

It should be remembered that in 1936 Hearst was a more controversial figure than at any time since 1918, more so than he would ever be again. He was highly popular with the Roosevelt-haters and the isolationists, savagely opposed by the liberals and internationalists who condemned his attacks on academic freedom, his hard-to-understand combination of pacifism and patriotism, and his open approval of the part Mussolini and Hitler were playing in Spain, not to mention his admiration for National Socialism.

Today, now that Hearst is removed from public controversy and his personality can be viewed whole from beginning to end, it is possible to appreciate the singular continuity of that personality, to see how it was always essentially the same and that the shifting tides of political events transformed friends to enemies and vice versa, until there was no man who could say he had always agreed or disagreed with Hearst.

Most men in public life who live as long as W.R. view people and events differently from decade to decade, in the light of their own evolving personalities. Not so Hearst. The beliefs he enunciated in his advice to the Democrats in 1898 were primarily the same beliefs he was advocating for the Republicans in 1951. Consequently a magazine like *Collier's* could rip him apart with vigor in the bad old days of 1911 and praise editorially "The Good That Hearst Did" in the good old days of 1939.

It was surprising, in fact, when Hearst died, the number of charitable words people found to say about him. Even the London press, which had never loved him except at brief intervals, was not unkind. In the *News-Chronicle*, Robert Waithman, the paper's Washington correspondent, observed indubitably that "It cannot be denied, he was a character." Lord Beaverbrook's *Daily Express* asserted that Hearst's anti-British reputation was highly exaggerated and called him "one of the great American figures of the age." Only the austere *Manchester Guardian* found itself able to assert with forthright candor: "William Randolph Hearst is dead and it is hard even now to think of him with charity. Perhaps no man ever did so much to debase the standards of journalism."

The Hearst papers themselves found it necessary to revise their appreciation of the Chief after they were able to organize a story that would compensate for the lack of preparation made for the event. Between editions, the Los Angeles *Herald and Express* found the voice which expressed the second, and amplified, sentiments of the whole chain. In the first edition, the paper said simply, "William Randolph Hearst, whose career as a publisher spanned more than half a century and ushered in the modern era of American journalism, died today." The second-edition story began: "William Randolph Hearst is dead. The greatest figure in American journalism, whose patriotism and wisdom had been a strongly guiding influence on the nation during a career that began more than a half century ago, died today."

As the news flashed around the nation on that August afternoon, the response was not what a good many of Hearst's enemies might have expected. Vice-President Alben Barkley, who was among those who had least reason to appreciate Hearst, paused before making a speech on Long Island and said, "Let us rise for a minute of silent prayer to honor a great American who has just died."

The New York *Times* and the *Herald Tribune*, of which the Hearst papers, through their chief columnists, had frequently spoken with contempt as sympathetic to the Reds and wreckers of American nationalism, were alike sympathetic, almost respectful.

The *Herald Tribune* concluded that "one cannot assess the final influence of that long and spectacular career. One can only say that he was a man of extraordinary talents, energies and insights, and that it will be long before his mark fades from our times."

The *Times* wrote editorially: ". . . No history of American journalism can ever be written without reckoning with him, and however critically he is appraised it will have to be said of him that he brought the printed word to many who had previously come close to ignoring it."

In the other New York papers, the estimates ran what could be considered a gamut. At one end was the *Journal-American's* editorial lead, "The world has lost a colossus," and the INS news story in the *Mirror*, which asserted that "The people stood in stunned silence in realization of their loss." At the other end was

the *Mirror's* successful competitor, the *Daily News*. Its obituary story avoided the word "colossus" entirely and concluded
with a quotation from Professor Nevins which appeared to be
a slight upward revision of the 1936 estimate: "His importance
has lain in the huge scale of his operations, and though he hardly
ranks as a great innovator—his sensationalism imitated Pulitzer's,
while E. W. Scripps preceded him in forming a newspaper chain
—the Hearst methods have profoundly influenced American
journalism."

A. J. Liebling, chronicler of the wayward press in *The New
Yorker*, in his summary of how Hearst had been treated by his
fellow professionals, offered an estimate of his own: "It occurs
to me that what is really important about Hearst is not whether
or not he was a great newspaperman, or a talented and cynical
amateur, or a great humanitarian, or a genius, or a liberal, or a
reactionary; he could have been any of these, but I believe that
as the years pass he will be remembered primarily as the man who
introduced the use of big money into the newspaper business."

As Mr. Liebling put it, the Hearst columnists "approached the
edge of the grave in print and threw a ceremonial fit," and the
*Journal-American's* cartoonist drew a picture which represented
the Statue of Liberty, a mourning band marked "William Randolph Hearst" wrapped around her marble arm. The front-page
promise of things to come inside the *Journal-American's* issue
of August 15 showed how the faithful stable had responded:

"Dorothy Kilgallen—Cites debt of gratitude for fascinating
and profitable career.

"Leslie Gould—Impact of his personality will never die.

"Merryle S. Rukeyser—American freedom more secure because of William Randolph Hearst's contribution.

"Cholly Knickerbocker—The underdog's corner was his
corner.

"Jack O'Brien—Study of radio and TV development reveals
detailed vision of W. R. Hearst.

"E. V. Durling—Best boss I ever had."

Westbrook Pegler was once more underprivileged, as he had been when President Roosevelt died. He was on vacation.

A day after this columnar mourning, Nick Kenny, the Hearst papers' poet laureate, apostrophized the boss in immortal lines which began:

> The Chief is gone, the man we all called Boss. . . .
> Colossus of an age that changed the world.
> The galleons of his genius knew their course,
> His fingertips around the cosmos curled.

One might turn from this surfeit of grief to the other side of the fence, where Max Lerner could be found musing in the New York *Post:* "For all his power and money, and the weight he could throw around and the men he could cow, and his castles filled with works of art, here surely was one of the most loveless and unloved figures in our history. In that lies the pity of it."

It was bewildering, but not at all unusual, to find Hearst as argued about in death as he had been in life, to see him praised and scorned, passing into history without any fixed place in it. One could foresee, stretching away into the future, a succession of future estimates which would always say in the end, "The definitive word waits to be written," or "Only history can be the final judge of Hearst's career."

One thing was at least fairly certain. William Randolph Hearst, Jr., was his father's successor, and Richard Emmett Berlin was the prime minister of the empire. Their ages at the time of ascension—Bill Jr. forty-three, Berlin fifty-seven—guaranteed that the new era would last a comparatively long time. The keynote of the new era appeared to be moderation. Extreme crusades would go, and a general note of restraint was already plain before six months had passed. It was equally clear that, whatever these new policies might bring, the stamp of his character that Hearst had put on his newspapers, whether good or bad, was bound to diminish no matter what was done or undone.

*Time's* pictorial counterpart, *Life,* in its obituary editorial, seemed in the minds of many observers of Hearst and the journalistic scene to have come very close to the heart of the matter. In a perceptive discussion of W.R.'s kind of journalism, the magazine noted that Hearst in his newspapers had managed during his career to "antagonize just about every existing segment of informed opinion."

That, perhaps, was the sum of his paradoxes. The individual paradoxes were more entertaining but not nearly as significant. The fact that his private life was an open scandal to the godly, but so moral in other respects he forbade risqué stories and profanity at his table and neither drank nor smoked; that he was so much against war he favored the largest possible army and navy; that he was the self-appointed leader of the reform element in politics, but opposed a real reform movement when it came— these and others meant simply that Hearst, like other men, was not black or white but gray, an ancient truism never better illustrated than in his career.

Hearst himself was ruefully aware of this, as he showed in his answer to the question of whether he had read one of the biographies. "If it doesn't tell the truth, it will make me mad, and if it tells the truth, it will make me sad," he replied.

In sum, Hearst was a powerful and paradoxical personality, the power and the paradoxes acting together as a catalyst to produce the whole unique man.

But it may well be that when the pundits and the historians and the biographers have all had their say and passed their judgments, the best evaluation of William Randolph Hearst will be the inadvertent one written in an old theater program of the Hasty Pudding Club at Harvard.

Shortly before he was ejected, Hearst made his farewell appearance on any stage except a political one, in a production of *Joan of Arc, or The Old Maid of New Orleans*. He played the part of Pretzel, the German valet of Philip of Burgundy, and the description of Hearst as Pretzel can hardly be improved upon:

"An interesting cuss, with a penchant for legerdemain."

The difficulties of assembling information about Mr. Hearst and his empire are too well known to rehearse here. These difficulties account for the extreme shortness of my list of acknowledgments, because all the people who were gracious enough to talk to me about Hearst, whether they were friends or enemies, requested that they not be thanked publicly.

I can only say, therefore, that I am exceedingly grateful to everyone who gave me information not obtainable elsewhere. I have tried to use this information, whether it came from friendly or hostile sources, in the fairest way possible. Aside from these contributions, I want to thank Mrs. Marion Henry, my researcher, for her excellent professional services, and Earle F. Walbridge for his careful reading of the manuscript.

Now, as to the standard sources:

Any Hearst biographer must necessarily begin with the mass of information in the four Hearst biographies written to date. Each has its particular value, which is assessed here for the benefit of bibliographers and future biographers.

John K. Winkler's "W. R. Hearst, An American Phenomenon" (New York, 1928) is generally favorable, and is rich in anecdotal material.

Mrs. Fremont Older's semi-official biography, "William Randolph Hearst, American," (New York, 1936) has often been scorned because of its completely uncritical tone, but it is nonetheless valuable for its wealth of family detail, which is absolutely reliable. Mrs. Older is the only one of Hearst's biographers who has had access to such information, and it is highly unlikely that any independent biographer will ever be given this opportunity. The material is highly selective, of course, but one may depend on that which relates directly to the family.

Neither Winkler nor Mrs. Older's books include bibliographies. In fact, the only Hearst bibliography extant of any real value is that compiled by Ferdinand Lundberg for his "Imperial Hearst" (New York, 1936). This best-known of books about Hearst is also the most biased, and Mr. Lundberg's viewpoint must always be taken into account. But it remains as the most thoroughly researched in relation to the means by which the Hearst empire was built and maintained. The excesses and pure opinions and points of view are readily apparent; the data about finances and similar matters is extensive and useful. The excellent bibliography is a fairly complete summary of printed material available on Hearst up to 1936.

"Hearst, Lord of San Simeon," by Oliver Carlson and Ernest Sutherland Bates," (New York, 1936) is the most unbiased of the biographies. It is both anecdotal and factual, and in most respects, reliable. The bibliography is relatively short but it is adequate.

The present work draws on all these sources, as any biographer must, but the facts are reassessed and presented in the light of events since 1936, in the modifications made possible by new information, and in the fresh perspective provided by Hearst's death. The new information is extensive, and as indicated previously, has come largely from private sources available to the author, and so cannot be listed here. The facts have been checked as carefully as is humanly possible; the Hearst organization refused any cooperation in this respect.

I have made no effort here to list the magazine and newspaper sources drawn upon; they were far too numerous, and are easily available to any researcher. The books issued since 1936, or not mentioned in previous bibliographies, which I found useful are listed by name and author in the text.

# INDEX